T3-BOY-219

THE DIPLOMATIC RECORD 1990-1991

Published in cooperation with the

INSTITUTE FOR THE STUDY OF DIPLOMACY

School of Foreign Service, Georgetown University

An integral part of the Georgetown University School of Foreign Service, the **Institute for the Study of Diplomacy** concentrates on the processes of diplomacy. Through its research and publication programs, the Institute seeks to improve diplomatic skills and broaden public understanding of diplomacy.

THE DIPLOMATIC RECORD 1990-1991

edited by
David D. Newsom
INSTITUTE FOR THE STUDY OF DIPLOMACY

WESTVIEW PRESS
Boulder • San Francisco • Oxford

The Diplomatic Record

Production of *The Diplomatic Record* is made possible by a grant from the Harriman Foundation.

Published in 1992 in the United States of America by Westview Press, Inc., 5500 Central Avenue, Boulder, Colorado 80301-2847, and in the United Kingdom by Westview Press, 36 Lonsdale Road, Summertown, Oxford OX2 7EW

Library of Congress ISSN: 1052-0309
ISBN: 0-8133-1386-4

Printed and bound in the United States of America

∞ The paper in this publication meets the requirements of the American National Standard for Permanence of Paper for Printed Library Materials Z39.48-1984.

10 9 8 7 6 5 4 3 2 1

Contents

DEPARTMENTS

Editor's Note

This second volume of *The Diplomatic Record*, covering events in 1990 and 1991, concentrates on three areas of the world where diplomacy was particularly active: the Middle East, Europe, and Africa. In addition, Chapter 10 addresses a global subject particularly relevant to the Middle East today: the Nuclear Non-Proliferation Treaty.

In Asia and Latin America, diplomats were also active, but potential chroniclers felt the time had not yet come to write meaningfully on such issues as Cambodia in Asia or negotiations on the future of El Salvador in Central America. Other key global issues such as the Uruguay Round of Multilateral Trade Negotiations and the preparations for the United Nations Conference on Development and Environment will reach definitive stages next year and are potential subjects for the 1991–1992 volume. *The Diplomatic Record* takes note of these and several other ongoing negotiations in "Looking Ahead."

The events that dominated the diplomatic circuits for most of the year were those related to Iraq's invasion of Kuwait: efforts either to prevent conflict or to create the coalition that would make military force effective. The initial essay addresses the effectiveness of diplomacy in this crisis. Then follow perspectives on the events from the standpoint of the United Nations, the Arab countries, the United States, the Soviet Union, and the Organization of Petroleum Exporting Countries.

Diplomatic activity in Europe was concentrated on the recasting of the security and political arrangements of that continent after the dramatic changes in Eastern Europe in 1989. Both to record recent events and to look at their future implications, we invited contributions from authors from Germany, the United States, and the Soviet Union. The result is a cluster of essays that chronicle the diplomacy surrounding the reunification of Germany and examine efforts to form new European structures from the perspectives of Washington and Moscow.

In this volume of *The Diplomatic Record* we have chosen to look at two areas in Africa where international efforts have been mounted to resolve disputes. One involves the actions of the Economic Commission of West African States to bring peace to a deeply divided Liberia; the other chronicles the progress of the United Nations toward establishing a referendum on the future of the Western Sahara. These are but two examples of active diplomatic moves to bring peace and stability to the continent; others continue in Angola, Mozambique, and, most recently, Ethiopia.

The year 1990 was also one of active multilateral diplomacy. The essays on the role of the United Nations in the Middle East and in the Sahara recognize this. So, also, does the essay by a knowledgeable participant in the negotiations on the Nuclear Non-Proliferation Treaty.

As in the first volume of *The Diplomatic Record*, the writers represent varied perspectives. They include diplomats, scholars, international civil servants, consultants, and journalists; in most cases, the authors have had direct involvement as participants in or observers of the events about which they write.

In "Recent Developments in Diplomatic Practice," we seek again to present important developments in the rules governing the practice of diplomacy—from the standpoint of the United States, Canada, and Hungary.

The chronology—through May 1991—lists milestones in diplomatic events from every continent as well as in specialized subjects such as trade and investment and the environment. The bibliography lists recent works on diplomacy published in the United States and Canada and benefits this year from a contribution from Brazil.

The appendixes include documents relating to the Gulf crisis—particularly the key resolutions of the United Nations Security Council.

As always, *The Diplomatic Record's* contents and the timeliness of its subject matter are limited by space and by the production schedule. Within these limitations, we have once again sought to present for the scholar, the journalist, and the student of international affairs the significant landmarks in the world of diplomacy.

David D. Newsom

About the Editor and Authors

John P. Banks, an associate at International Resources Group, is an economic and political analyst. He holds a Master of Science in Foreign Service degree, Georgetown University.

Charles Michael Brown is a graduate of the Master in Foreign Service program of the School of Foreign Service, Georgetown University, and a nominee to the Presidential Management Intern Program. He has served as a US Foreign Service intern in Africa.

George Bunn was one of the principal members of the negotiating team for the Non-Proliferation Treaty (NPT) in 1990, and he was general counsel for the Arms Control and Disarmament Agency, US Department of State, 1961-1969. He attended the NPT Review Conference as an observer for a nongovernmental organization. He is currently a member-in-residence at the Stanford Center for International Security and Arms Control, Stanford, CA.

Charles K. Ebinger, vice president of International Resources Group and director of the Kokomo Gas Corporation, is former director of the energy program at the Center for Strategic and International Studies, Washington, DC.

Carolyn McGiffert Ekedahl, a diplomatic associate with the Institute for the Study of Diplomacy, School of Foreign Service, Georgetown University, is coauthor, with W. Raymond Duncan, of *Moscow and the Third World Under Gorbachev* (Boulder, CO: Westview Press, 1990).

James E. Goodby is Distinguished Service Professor at Carnegie-Mellon University. During a thirty-five year career as a foreign service officer, he was head of the US delegation to the Stockholm Conference on Disarmament in

Europe, vice chairman of the US delegation to the Strategic Arms Reduction Talks (START), and ambassador to Finland.

David Hoffman is a diplomatic correspondent for the *Washington Post.*

Harold E. Horan was formerly US ambassador to Malawi, deputy assistant secretary of state for African affairs, and a staff member of the National Security Council. Most recently, he has been director of programs at the Institute for the Study of Diplomacy and now serves as a consultant to the United States Information Agency and the Department of State.

Ann Mosely Lesch teaches Middle East politics at Villanova University. She serves on the board of directors of the Middle East Studies Association, Middle East Watch, and the Middle East Research and Information Project's *Middle East Report.* She is coauthor, with Mark Tessler, of *Israel, Egypt, and the Palestinians: From Camp David to Intifada* (Bloomington: Indiana University Press, 1989).

David D. Newsom, former director of the Institute for the Study of Diplomacy, is currently the Hugh S. and Winifred B. Cumming Memorial Professor of International Affairs at the University of Virginia. He is a former ambassador and under secretary of state.

Berndt von Staden is former state secretary of the Federal Republic of Germany Foreign Office, 1981-1983, and former ambassador to the United States, 1973-1979.

Brian Urquhart is currently scholar-in-residence in the international affairs program at the Ford Foundation. He served in the United Nations Secretariat from 1945 until his retirement in 1986. From 1974 to 1986 he was under secretary-general for special political affairs. He is author of *A Life in Peace and War: Decolonization and World Peace* (New York: Harper & Row, 1987).

Abiodun Williams is assistant professor of international relations in the School of Foreign Service, Georgetown University.

Andrei V. Zagorski is vice director, Center of International Studies, Moscow Institute of International Relations, Ministry of Foreign Affairs of the USSR, and author of *Theory and Methodology of Analysis of International Negotiations* (in Russian).

THE DIPLOMATIC RECORD 1990-1991

Essays

Map 1.1 The Middle East

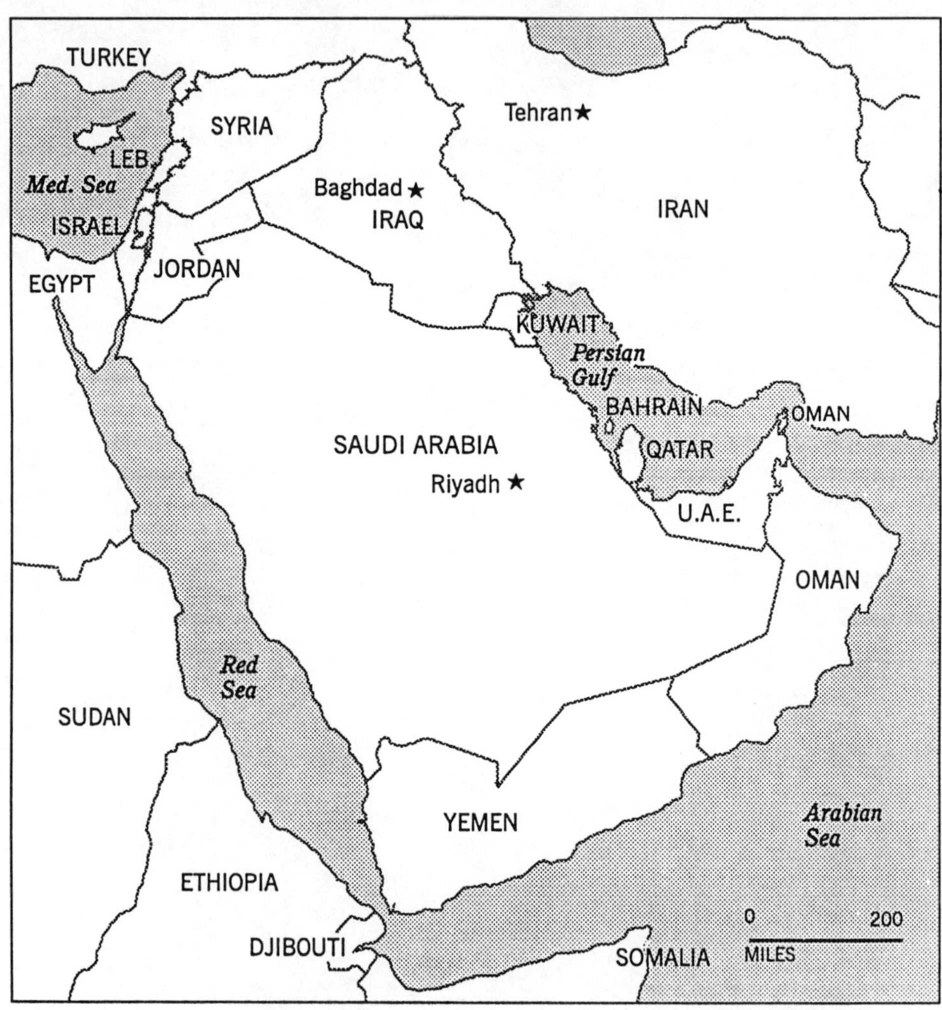

1

Diplomacy and the Gulf Crisis

David D. Newsom

Diplomacy is . . . the conduct of business between states by peaceful means.
—Ernest Satow

On August 3, 1991, Iraq invaded Kuwait and a few days later declared this previously independent country its nineteenth province. In the days immediately preceding the invasion, Arab governments had sought without success to prevent the aggression. Following Saddam Hussein's military action, diplomatic efforts to force Iraq's withdrawal widened to include non-Arab nations and the United Nations Security Council. Such efforts to find a peaceful resolution continued—even after a coalition of nations acting on the basis of UN Security Council Resolution 678 attacked Iraqi forces on January 16, 1991. Rigid positions on both sides precluded any compromise, and the world ultimately depended on military action to reverse the aggression.

Inevitably when war breaks out, the question is raised: Did diplomacy fail? The answer in the case of the Gulf War lies not only in the events immediately preceding the conflict but also in the history of the region and the perception each party had of the issues involved. The answer relates, also, to whether different policies or different signals might have prevented Iraq's invasion and whether, at the final hour, opportunities for conflict resolution existed.

The summary of Gulf War peace plans at the end of the chapter was prepared by Professor Allan E. Goodman of Georgetown University.

Diplomatic efforts were plainly not successful in preventing the war or in bringing about the peaceful withdrawal of Iraq from Kuwait. The roots of that failure lay in the nature of the issue, in the complexities of the region, and in the inability of the parties to read each others' intentions. Diplomacy did succeed, however, in the unprecedented creation of an international coalition allied against Iraq—first, in support of economic sanctions and later in the implementation of "all necessary means" including military action.

Creating the Coalition

Many factors made the success of this major collective security effort possible. European nations including the Soviet Union were prepared to follow the US lead, even if they did not totally agree with Washington's approaches. Undoubtedly, both France and Britain were motivated not only by economic and political considerations but also by recollections of their prior imperial responsibilities in the region. Germany, conscious of pressures from the United States, contributed financially and broke precedent by sending military aircraft to Turkey. Japan, after considerable debate in the Diet, contributed financially. The Soviet Union, giving priority to its relations with the United States and Europe, gave important diplomatic support but declined any military involvement outside its borders.

Saudi Arabia and the Gulf sheikhdoms, shaken by Iraq's aggression against a neighbor, after some hesitation requested American and allied help. President Hosni Mubarak of Egypt, angered by what he considered Saddam Hussein's betrayal and the challenge of Iraqi power, readily cooperated. In Damascus, Hafiz al-Asad calculated that the coalition's opposition to Iraq would further Syria's interests in the region. Turkey saw its interests in working with the West and at considerable financial sacrifice cut off trade with Iraq and permitted US air operations from bases on its territory.[1]

The effective creation of the coalition in this contest was aided by the success of the United States in obtaining the support of the UN Security Council and in establishing an allied military force in the Gulf region. At times, members of the coalition, including the Soviet Union and France, expressed the view that the United States, with its emphasis on removing Saddam Hussein and destroying Iraq's military potential, was exceeding the UN mandate. These expressions had little influence on US President

George Bush. Bush emphasized in his pursuit of both domestic and foreign cooperation that the UN resolutions demonstrated the strong support for US policies in the international community. To a degree not seen since the 1950s, Washington used the UN Security Council as an instrument of US foreign policy.

Iraq: Avoiding Isolation

Saddam Hussein's diplomatic efforts to prevent the isolation of Iraq before the war began were successful. The Arab world was deeply divided over issues relating to Israel, foreign alliances, and economic inequities, and substantial portions of populations in nations friendly to the coalition did not share the coalition's objective. By exploiting the Palestinian issue, the disparity between the wealth of the Gulf states and other poorer Arab states, and the historic aversion in the region to non-Arab intervention, Saddam Hussein was able to rally the Palestine Liberation Organization (PLO) to his side and gain mass support in Jordan, thus preventing a full consensus against him in the Arab League.[2] Through prior cultivation of ties with Yemen, Saddam was able to gain a voice in the Security Council. His tactics may also have inhibited Arab initiatives that might have been interpreted by Arab populations as efforts to acknowledge and justify Western involvement. In a dramatic diplomatic move toward Iran on August 16, 1990, Saddam acceded to Iran's position on the Shatt-al-Arab—an issue over which the two countries had fought an eight-year war. His move may have gained Iran's neutrality. If he hoped for active support against the Western forces from Tehran he was disappointed; Iran demonstrated its neutrality by impounding Iraqi aircraft that fled across the border during the war.

Differing Perspectives

Whatever Saddam Hussein's true motive in seizing Kuwait—whether to resolve his financial problems or to assert his wider role as an Arab leader—he sought to justify his invasion as a reaction to a vestigial colonial situation. His claim, for example, that Kuwait had been part of Iraq in Ottoman times and had been taken illegally by the British formed the basis for asserting that Kuwait was the nineteenth province of Iraq. In so doing he struck responsive chords among those who retained a fear of a reimposition of Western domination and among those who sought for a leader who would recover Palestinian rights from Israel. Inherent, also, in his position was an echo of the North-South economic split: the strong, industrial North imposing its will on less-developed nations. His position reflected the widespread view in the Arab world that a "double standard" existed in which the United States insisted on Iraq's withdrawal from Kuwait but not on Israel's from the occupied territories. The United States opposed the possession of weapons of mass destruction by Iraq but not by Israel.

For many in the Arab nations outside the Gulf the issue became not the aggression against Kuwait but Iraq's resistance to the perceived efforts of the United States to reimpose imperialism. The withdrawal of Iraqi troops from Kuwait became equated with the withdrawal of "foreign forces" from the Arabian peninsula.

President Bush created a different perspective—one based on his conditioning preceding and during World War II. The Iraqi invasion was unprovoked aggression—"Munich" in 1938; he did not want to be Neville Chamberlain. For Bush, the issue began with the invasion of Kuwait; what went before was not pertinent; to Saddam, it was everything. The security of access to oil and the potential threat to Israel gave President Bush further issues of major national and international concern to justify his actions. On these elements he built the concept of a moral war and the possibility of creating a "new world order." Saddam was endeavoring to preserve and extend his power; Bush was seeking to prevent the control of a vital area by a ruthless and unpredictable ruler. He was, also, without doubt motivated by a desire to avoid being labeled weak, as some had characterized President Jimmy Carter in his treatment of Iran, or duplicitous, as critics of President Ronald Reagan had labeled the Iran-contra negotiations. With the changes in Soviet policy, an American president was no longer deterred by the possibility of opposition from Moscow to the pursuit of US national interests in the Persian Gulf; the way was clearly open to a tough policy in defense of what he saw as those interests. The joint US-Soviet communiqué of August 2, 1990, calling for a Security Council meeting on the invasion of Kuwait, signaled this new diplomatic reality.

The US perspective was also shaped by the strong view of the United States' special role in the world, a view strengthened by the perceived victory of democracy over communism. To Americans—if not to Arabs—it seemed thoroughly appropriate that the United States, as the only nation with the power to do so, should respond for the international community to the Kuwait crisis. Principles of true collective security and the rule of law were at stake.

Presidential Leadership

Bush exhibited impressive skill in demonstrating the power of the presidency. The leadership in this crisis was strictly personal; George Bush made the decisions. By confining policymaking to a small group in the executive, he was able to retain remarkable control of policy. His delay in submitting the issue to Congress until the last few days before the UN deadline on withdrawal meant that many in the two bodies who might otherwise have opposed the use of force were reluctant to oppose the president at that critical moment. Throughout the crisis, the policy action was managed to minimize debate, either within or outside the executive. It seems clear that the president decided on his course of action early in August and did not wish to be deterred by listening seriously to contrary voices—including those with expertise in the region. Little evidence in fact exists that the president and his circle sought advice from any recognized area experts.

The Role of the Expert

The role of the regional expert is difficult in any administration. Tensions traditionally exist between the globalist, working in a worldwide strategic context, and the area specialist. This applies both within government, including the intelligence community, and outside. Among those who have lived, worked, and studied in the Middle East, the problem is further complicated because varying points of view emerge depending on the precise area of knowledge. The specialist who has spent years in the Gulf will have a perspective different from one who has been in Egypt, Algeria, or Israel. The scholar who has worked among peasants will observe a society that is quite different from the one experienced by an expert on urban issues; all will be subject to the pressures and biases of individual states and factions. When a president is personally conducting policy, challenges to his assumptions are seen as evidences of political bias or disloyalty. To suggest possible errors in the premises of policy is to risk being seen as an advocate rather than as an expert. To point out that citizens may have different views than their rulers and that US interests in the region have previously suffered because scant attention was given to such divisions is to court charges of undermining America's friends. Little room existed for the specialist with an understanding for the affected region, either in analyzing the prewar circumstances or in predicting what the region would require after the war.

So strongly did the president feel the correctness of his policy that other usual US foreign policy considerations became irrelevant; Syria's record on human rights and terrorism is one example. Jordan, a long-time friend of the United States, was at least temporarily cast aside because of what seemed to be King Hussein's equivocal stand on the Iraqi invasion. In the interest of maintaining the support of the Soviet Union, the administration took the domestic political risk of moderating its response to the Soviet actions against independence movements in the Baltic states. In many other areas, US policy seemed determined entirely by whether a country stood with Washington on this one issue. Long-term policy considerations—in the region and elsewhere—appeared to receive less attention.

No Room for Compromise

The two contrasting perspectives of Saddam Hussein and George Bush left virtually no room for diplomatic maneuvering or compromise. Strength on both sides was symbolized in the refusal to compromise. Any expressed Iraqi willingness to negotiate was conditioned on addressing the Palestinian issue and lacked any hint of a readiness to withdraw from Kuwait. For President Bush, any compromise—"rewards for aggression" or "saving face"—would be inconsistent with his firm position that the UN resolutions must be totally fulfilled before any discussion of other issues.

Presidential rhetoric served only to harden positions on each side. Washington's stress on the American role and the concept of a new world order—popular in the United States—undoubtedly confirmed suspicions in the region that Washington and its European allies were seeking to reimpose a form of imperialism in the Middle East. Saddam Hussein's insistence on the Palestine issue—popular in the Arab world—alarmed Israel and its supporters in the United States. To those supporting Bush's view, acknowledgement of Iraq's prewar grievances against Kuwait was unacceptable "mirror-imaging." To many Americans, to the coalition governments, and to most members of the UN Security Council, only one side was correct.

A series of miscalculations on both sides resulted from the mutual inflexibility. Saddam Hussein apparently calculated that the Arab states would not ask for US intercession, and even if they did, the United States would not in the end go to war; if the Americans were foolish enough to do so, they could not withstand the sacrifices of a long conflict. He seemed to believe that he had the power, through support in the Islamic world, to frustrate American designs by arousing Muslim populations and encouraging terrorism against US and other Western targets.

Warning Saddam

If President Bush had a formula for peace, it lay through impressing on the Iraqi leadership the consequences of a war; he appeared to believe that massive US and international deployments would give credibility to the threat to use force and lead to a decision by Saddam Hussein to withdraw. If Bush's frequent efforts to "get the message" to Saddam Hussein were calculated to intimidate the proud and ruthless Iraqi leader, they clearly failed; Bush seemed not to understand Saddam's determination to challenge the power of the coalition rather than suffer the humiliation of retreat.

A credible threat to use force can be effective in diplomacy, but only if conveyed in a manner that still leaves the other side some way out. American pressures on Iraq did not do this. The letter Bush sent to Saddam, which Iraqi Foreign Minister Tariq Aziz refused to accept,[3] appeared designed solely to inform the Iraqi president of the dire fate awaiting him if he refused to leave Kuwait. The text of the letter can be understood in diplomatic terms only if the US president anticipated—and, possibly, hoped—that it would not be accepted but that its language would be otherwise useful in demonstrating his "toughness" on the issue. It is doubtful that any government—including that of the United States—would accept a letter as threatening in tone. If one of Saddam's objectives in the crisis was to be respected as the leader of an important nation, the attitude of the US administration served only to deepen his resentment and increase his fear of humiliation. Although it can be persuasively argued that Saddam Hussein, because of his character, deserved no such recognition, the fact remains that the American tactics left little opening for a solution short of war. Doubling US troop strength in November and setting the deadline for withdrawal moved the situation inextricably toward armed conflict.

The divergence in perspectives extended also to the inability of each side to comprehend what was important to the other. Saddam Hussein appeared to find it difficult to understand that the United States would make so major an effort on the basis of principle or to secure oil or would be so strongly opposed to an "Arab solution" to an "Arab problem." In his thinking, an ulterior motive must exist—whether to destroy an Arab state that might threaten Israel or to reimpose Western domination in the region.

The United States, Islam, and the Arabs

Similarly, President Bush and his advisers found it difficult to understand that other Arab states would not be strongly affected by the takeover of one independent state by another. They found it hard to comprehend, also, that Palestinians would not strongly oppose the takeover of a state that had contributed so much financially to the Palestinian cause. They reacted negatively to Arab efforts to mediate and suspected that an "Arab solution" would not only delay forceful action but in the end would also permit Saddam Hussein some gain from his aggression. Americans were also disappointed by the lack of recognition in the Muslim world that forces from the Arab world (the Gulf states, Syria, and Egypt) and from other Muslim countries (Pakistan and Bangladesh) were part of the coalition forces.

US policymakers have always had a problem in acknowledging that close ties with the West can be damaging to the fortunes of Arab politicians and can make their regimes vulnerable to extreme elements. It is unacceptable in Washington to acknowledge that the United States is looked upon in the Middle East and in many other parts of the world as imperialist.

The crisis demonstrated again the serious difficulties in relations between the United States and the nations of Islam and, beyond those nations, the wider Third World. Nations such as India—with a Muslim minority—were uneasy about cooperation with the United States; the Indian government's agreement to permit the refueling of US aircraft en route to the Gulf created a governmental crisis in New Delhi. Even in the third generation after independence, myths and suspicions about Western powers persist.

Other Influences

In any confrontation of this sort, the information each side receives shapes perspectives. Saddam Hussein saw communication—primarily television—as a part of his diplomacy. Through it, he believed he could reach the populations of the coalition partners when their governments were not prepared to listen. With this in mind he broadcast pictures of himself with children of Western hostages, and he permitted the Cable News Network (CNN) correspondent, Peter Arnett, to remain in Baghdad. Through television and radio, also, he sought to appeal to Arabs who appeared more willing to hear his message than did many of their leaders. Possibly by watching the debates in Washington, also broadcast by CNN, Saddam seemed confident that public opinion in the United States would not support a sustained war.

The Iraqi president seemed also convinced that the Arab capacity to carry the war to the West through terrorism and to those Arab states in the coalition through "uprisings of the masses" would be further deterrents to attempts to recapture Kuwait or destroy Iraq. With Saddam's limited experience outside Iraq, he was probably susceptible to sycophants who portrayed the outside world in terms he wanted to believe. The proximity of Yasir Arafat added another element to Saddam's thinking. Whether Arafat took Iraq's side in the conflict because of the PLO leader's sense of the attitudes of his Palestinian followers or whether he truly saw this as an opportunity to recover Palestinian rights is not clear; what is clear is that he maintained pressure on Saddam Hussein to keep the Palestinian issue at the forefront of any discussions of a solution. Arab leaders friendly to Saddam such as Jordan's King Hussein apparently were unable to convince him of the dangers of his policy.

President Bush was undoubtedly also heavily influenced by the views of those he chose to consult. Former British Prime Minister Margaret Thatcher, who saw Bush only two days after the Iraqi invasion, may have recalled her Falkland experience; she certainly impressed upon him the need for a strong and determined response. The voices of the Saudi, Kuwaiti, and Egyptian leadership were, for him, the definitive views on the circumstances and reactions to policies in the Middle East. The Saudis, who felt seriously threatened by Iraq and willing to reverse their longstanding inhibitions against a foreign military presence on their soil, were probably the principal Arab voice shaping the conception of the issue by the US president. The Kuwaitis, with their dramatic reiteration of Iraqi atrocities, also had a major impact on the American president's thinking and actions. President Hosni Mubarak of Egypt, angered by what he considered Saddam Hussein's betrayal just before the invasion, was another strong voice influencing the president. The danger of reliance on like-minded voices, especially in an area as complex as the Middle East, is that many will tell the Americans what they believe they want to hear. Others will insist that they support US policy but cannot say so publicly; the nuances of differences between official and private expressions in the Middle East do not always get through to the outsider.

Search for International Support

Two quite different and inflexible views of the conflict thus confronted parties seeking to mediate. Whether the two sets of perceptions were genuine or contrived is beside the point. As obstacles to compromise, they were real. The Iraqi foreign minister clearly had little leeway in his discussions with foreign officials. US Secretary of State James A. Baker III seemed equally bound by the firm policy laid down and publicly stated by the president.

Conflict resolution in such cases hinges on whether either side wants a solution or whether steps toward negotiation are seen solely as a means of pursuing basic, uncompromising objectives. In Iraq's case, Saddam Hussein feared for his own future if he appeared weak. In the case of the United States, President Bush was concerned not only with continued support around the world but also with his own domestic political image. He clearly believed that any agreement to negotiate or any widening of the agenda of diplomacy beyond the Kuwait issue would be dangerous internationally and unacceptable politically. Pejorative and personalized rhetoric on both sides further increased the bitterness and lack of trust and inhibited genuine communication.

Strangely, diplomatic relations between Iraq and the United States were not suspended until February 6, 1991—even though the United States withdrew its mission before the war started and reduced the Iraqi staff in Washington. Other conventions of diplomacy were largely ignored or set aside in the Gulf crisis. Unofficial emissaries from the United States and many other countries had little success. Washington did not encourage mediation even by coalition partners such as France and the Soviet Union.

While Washington and Baghdad both sought to gain international support, others attempted to bring the crisis and hostilities to an end. Within days of the start of the military action, Operation Desert Storm, diplomats from Algeria, India, Iran, Pakistan, and the Soviet Union were seeking ways to end the war. Yugoslavia, as chair of the Non-Aligned Nations Movement (NAM), also tried, but the peaceful reversal of the Iraqi occupation of Kuwait faced more serious and, in the end, insurmountable obstacles. Diplomacy could not bridge the gap between two very different perceptions of the issue.

President Bush and his coalition partners did not share the outlook of the would-be peacemakers. The US, British, French, and Egyptian leadership steadfastly maintained that the future of the international system, and hope for a new order in the Middle East in particular, depended on punishing this instance of aggression and making it impossible for Saddam Hussein to make war on his neighbors again. Indeed, the more the war was prosecuted and the more bellicose Saddam Hussein's rhetoric became, the more US and allied leaders appeared convinced that the region and the world would be safe only if Iraq complied with all UN resolutions, including those calling for Saddam to be held accountable for committing war crimes. At several points during the period, President Bush also appealed to the people of Iraq to overthrow their president so that they and the region could be restored to peace.[4] At no point did the president appear to signal the least bit of interest in arranging a compromise with or for Saddam Hussein, and he focused all his personal diplomacy on maintaining the international coalition against Iraq.

Saddam Hussein wanted to talk only to those in other countries who were in power; his pride demanded it. Although he met unofficial envoys, his purpose seemed mainly to demonstrate that he was not isolated. Efforts of Arab and Muslim countries were equally ineffective. It was not until late in the prewar stage—in early January—that Arab nations such as Tunisia and Algeria, perhaps realizing that the situation had gone beyond the usual rhetoric, tried unsuccessfully to intervene and mediate.

Forms of international pressure short of military force were tried but abandoned. Saddam Hussein gave up his efforts to hold the citizens of coalition countries as "human shields" to prevent attacks; one can only assume that the benefits to him did not outweigh the negative image conveyed abroad. The economic sanctions imposed by the United Nations were tight but were given little chance to work. Although respected voices in the United States and elsewhere called for reliance on sanctions, the world will never know whether one of the most complete sets of sanctions against a single country in UN history might not ultimately have forced Iraq to withdraw from Kuwait.

The Return of Peace as an Option

The use of force and the threat to use force were pushed temporarily off the diplomatic stage in 1989 and 1990. Iraq's invasion brought back into play the intricate relationship between the military and the diplomatic arenas. The creation of the coalition by Secretary Baker illustrated the effective use of diplomacy without force. US diplomacy toward Iraq, however, was based almost exclusively on the threat to use force. When that failed, force remained the only option.

At this writing, many aspects of the diplomacy preceding the UN deadline remain unclear. Did Iraq ultimately intend to follow up its invasion of Kuwait with an attack on Saudi Arabia? Did Saudi Arabia reach the decision to request US help on its own, or was there overwhelming pressure from Washington? What concessions were made by Baker to members of the coalition—especially the Soviets and the Syrians? What led President Bush in October 1990 to conclude that economic sanctions would not work and that a further buildup of military force was necessary? Was the fear of a breakup of the coalition, of unrest during the month of fasting—Ramadan—coming in March, or that a prolonged support for sanctions without results would mean the issue would still be alive for the 1992 elections? Would attention to the voices of caution among Middle East experts have meant a partial victory for Saddam Hussein through negotiation or the prevention of a long-term, indeterminate US involvement in this volatile area? If answers are to be found at all, historians will record them.

Gulf War Peace Plans in Summary

1. Baker-Bessmertnykh plan, January 29, 1991

- Terms: The war could end if Iraq "would make an unequivocal commitment" to leave Kuwait and take "immediate concrete steps" to do so.
- Reaction: The plan was disavowed by the White House spokesperson shortly after it was released by the State Department in a commu-

niqué form. It is now considered to be the essence of the proposal made by President Mikhail Gorbachev in his meeting with Iraqi Foreign Minister Tariq Aziz in Moscow on February 18. (See 5 below.)

2. King Fahd plan, January 30-31, 1991

- Description: Iraq would announce its willingness to leave Kuwait coupled with an immediate cease-fire.
- Reaction: The idea arose in discussions between Fahd and President Hosni Mubarak (on January 30) and was followed by a meeting (on January 31) in Tehran of the diplomats from Algeria, France, Iran, Iraq (represented by the deputy prime minister), and Yemen. The meeting produced no announced results and the plan presumably died.

3. Rafsanjani plan, February 4, 1991

- Description: The Revolutionary Command Council proposed that Iraqi forces would withdraw from Kuwait if the allied forces pulled out of the Gulf region and Israel ended its occupation of the West Bank.
- Reaction: The White House immediately rejected this "offer," reiterating the demands that Iraq comply with all UN resolutions and that Iraqi military withdrawal from Kuwait be "complete and unconditional" and indicated by "concrete actions on the ground" (*Washington Post*, February 16, 1991, p. A-21).

Iraq's UN representative said (February 16) that the proposal did not contain "conditions" but "legitimate issues" to be addressed (*New York Times*, February 17, 1991, p. 20).

Soviet Foreign Ministry spokesman Vitaly Churkin noted (February 16) that the Iraqi proposal "is linked to many conditions which could render it meaningless" (*New York Times*, February 17, 1991, p. 1).

Saddam Hussein, in a radio address on February 18, rejected all demands that Iraqi forces withdraw from Kuwait unconditionally and declared that "our people and armed forces are determined to continue the struggle."

4. Saddam Hussein plan, February 15, 1991

- Description: an unpublished seven-point plan, including a pledge by Iran to "do everything in its power" to get the US and allied forces out of the region in return for Iraqi withdrawal from Kuwait and their replacement by "Islamic forces" (*New York Times*, February 10, citing Kuwaiti newspaper, *Sawt al-Kuwait*, p. 19).

- Reaction: The Iraqi deputy prime minister, Saddoun Hammadi, returning to Baghdad after a visit to Tehran on February 9-10, ruled out a withdrawal from Kuwait (as suggested by Iran) and indicated in a two-hour press conference that Iraq was determined to continue to fight. "We have told Iran that what is taking place is unrelated to Kuwait. The question now is American aggression." Hammadi advocated forming an Arab-Muslim united front against the allied coalition and severing diplomatic relations with the United States and other countries supporting the war in the gulf.

Rafsanjani, in a meeting with the visiting foreign minister of Burkina Faso, February 18, said that Iraq had in fact responded "positively" to the proposals and noted "the bright prospect visible with respect to the solution to the problem of the Persian Gulf region" (*New York Times*, February 19, 1990, p. A-6).

5. Gorbachev plan, February 4-23, 1991

- Description: Following a cease-fire, Iraq would "withdraw immediately and unconditionally all its forces from Kuwait" within a twenty-one-day period and under UN supervision. Once this withdrawal was complete, all UN resolutions sanctioning Iraq "will cease to operate." All prisoners of war would be repatriated within three days of the start of the cease-fire.
- Reaction: Communist Party of the Soviet Union (CPSU) "instruction" (on February 4) resulted in Gorbachev's appeal (February 9) to Saddam Hussein "to analyze again what is at stake for his country, to display realism which would make it possible to take the path of a reliable and just peaceful settlement." Gorbachev also expressed concern that the pace of war would create a "a threat of going beyond the mandate" of the UN resolutions or widen the war to an Arab-Israeli conflict (*New York Times*, February 10, 1991, p. 19).

In a February 12 meeting in Baghdad between Saddam Hussein and Soviet special envoy Yevgeniy Primakov, Saddam "affirmed . . . [that] Iraq has always called for tackling the situation in the region . . . through dialogue and political and peaceful means." Hussein also indicated that he would continue to resist US, Zionist, and other aggression (*New York Times*, February 13, 1991, p. A-14).

The Iraqi foreign minister met with the Soviet president on February 18 and carried terms of the proposal back to Baghdad.

In response to Soviet efforts, the White House spokesperson indicated on February 18 that the US position remained unchanged: Iraq must unconditionally withdraw from Kuwait. On February 19, President George Bush issued a statement that the Soviet plan "falls well short of what would be required" for the United States to stop the war and declared "there are no negotiations" (*New York Times*, February 20, 1991, p. A-1).

Iranian Foreign Minister Ali Akbar Velayati, at a February 19 press conference in Bonn, said that Tariq Aziz (who stopped in Tehran en route from Moscow) convinced him that Iraq is "ready to withdraw from Kuwait unconditionally" (*New York Times*, February 20, 1991, p. A-12).

On the evening of February 21, a spokesman for President Gorbachev announced that on the basis of meetings with Tariq Aziz, "the two parties came to the conclusion that it is possible to find a way out of the military conflict" (*New York Times*, February 22, 1991, p. A-6).

White House and other US officials, however, consistently maintained that the proposal imposed conditions that were unacceptable to the United States and the coalition partners and that "no negotiation [was] under way." President Bush personally rejected the Soviet plan as a basis for ending the conflict in a press conference on February 22 and gave Saddam Hussein until noon, February 23 to agree to withdraw unconditionally from Kuwait.

The Iraqi information minister responded to Bush later in the day by calling him "an enemy of God" and then rejecting what was termed "Bush's shameful ultimatum" (CNN Television broadcast, February 23, 1991).

President Gorbachev's special envoy and the foreign minister conducted additional negotiations with Tariq Aziz in Moscow aimed at "adjusting" the Soviet proposal to meet Washington's objections. A Gorbachev spokesperson later indicated in a statement issued late on February 22 that the agreement had been "toughened" and that a reply was not awaited from Baghdad. On February 23, Tariq Aziz issued a statement from Moscow saying that "the Iraqi Government fully endorses this plan and fully supports it." Washington did not support the plan.

The February 23 noon deadline passed without a breakthrough. The White House issued a statement of regret, indicating that "military action continues on schedule and according to plan." In a radio address Saddam Hussein expressed continued defiance and promised to turn Kuwait into a "crater of death."

6. Other initiatives

- China: The deputy foreign minister was dispatched to the Middle East on February 11. But Chinese diplomats found themselves unable to persuade either Baghdad or Washington to end the war by negotiations. The *New York Times* reported (February 20) that Deng Xiaoping regarded the war as an example of "big hegemonists beating up small hegemonists."
- Non-Aligned Nations Movement: Under Yugoslav chairmanship, NAM delegations approached (week of February 18) Iraq, the United States, and other coalition members to explore settlement possibilities. These efforts produced no results.
- Cuba-Yemen (with the support of India and China) proposed to the UN Security Council on February 14, 1991, a bombing halt coupled with the creation of a commission to investigate ways permanently to end the fighting. A US-UK veto was pledged if a resolution was drafted and put to a vote. No further action was taken.

Notes

1. For a more complete account of the US role in forming the coalition, see Chapter 4, "Coalition Diplomacy," by David Hoffman.

2. On August 3, the foreign ministers of the twenty members of the Arab League met in Cairo; fourteen voted to condemn the invasion. At a summit meeting on August 10, however, the majority condemning the invasion had dropped to twelve, with Algeria and Tunisia abstaining.

3. See letter from President George Bush to Iraqi President Saddam Hussein in Appendix A.

4. On February 15, 1991, speaking to the employees at the Raytheon Corporation, President Bush said: "And there's another way for the bloodshed to stop, and that is for the Iraqi military and Iraqi people to take matters into their own hands and force Saddam Hussein, the dictator, to step aside and then comply with the United Nations Resolutions and rejoin the family of peace loving nations" (*New York Times*, February 16, 1991, p. L-5).

2

United Nations Diplomacy in 1990

Brian Urquhart

IN JANUARY 1990 THE SWEEPING movement away from communism in Eastern Europe and the Soviet Union created a buoyant international mood and provided the basis for considerable optimism at the United Nations about both the political and economic future. The end of the Cold War had already allowed for striking improvement in the functioning of the United Nations, especially of the Security Council. In the field, a series of new and successful peacekeeping operations—in Namibia, Iran and Iraq, and Central America—reflected this improvement in the practical resolution of several long-standing conflicts. The five permanent members of the United Nations Security Council, divided for more than forty years by the Cold War, were taking the lead in trying to find a solution to the tragic plight of Cambodia, one of the most deeply afflicted martyr states of the Cold War.

In this promising international climate there was much talk of a renaissance of the United Nations and of a return to its original objectives as outlined in the UN charter. It seemed possible that the world organization, after the forty-year winter of the Cold War, could begin to play the role that had been written for it in 1945, a role shaped by the bitter lessons of World War II and the events that led up to it, including the failure of the League of Nations.

As the year moved on, this positive and forward-looking mood was tempered by disconcerting new developments. The first of these was the deteriorating situation in the Soviet Union and parts of Eastern Europe and the realization that the transition from communism to free-enterprise democracy was going to be turbulent, long, expensive, and confused. The second was the instability emerging in many parts of the world in the wake of the Cold War and the daunting magnitude of the socioeconomic problems that would have to be tackled if the future was to be assured. It was becoming very clear that as the relationship between East and West improved, the differences of economic status and interest between North and South would be the dominating factor in much of the future work of the United Nations. Finally, Iraq's overnight annexation of Kuwait on August 2 tested the capacity of the world community to deal with a flagrant act of aggression. Although it has recently become fashionable in some Western circles to speak of a "new world order," the future of the United Nations is, at present, anything but clear.

The Main Tasks

The United Nations faces two main tasks—to combine peacemaking, peacekeeping, and collective action into a reliable international security system, and to deal with the great socioeconomic problems of global interdependence. Both tasks are urgent, and neither can be successfully achieved without the other.

Without a reliable system of international peace and security, it will be impossible to devote the necessary attention, energy, resources, and cooperation to the great global problems of our time. This proposition is already foreshadowed in Article 26 of the UN charter, which, in formulating the task of the Security Council in the regulation of armaments, refers to "the establishment and maintenance of international peace and security with the least diversion for armaments of the world's human and economic resources." That goal is still remote today.

If the United Nations is to meet this dual challenge, its member governments and Secretariat will have to make a wholehearted effort to overhaul it and bring it up to date. Its course needs to be carefully and authoritatively charted. It needs to be properly staffed, financed, and supported. It must become professionally competitive with the best in government and with the best in the private sector. Above all, its member governments will need to consider the changes in commitment and in basic attitudes and policies that alone will enable the world organization to respond effectively to the challenges it faces and that can be equitably dealt with only by a universal international system.

Hopes for Peace

In the hopeful early months of 1990 the original design for peace, outlined in 1945 in the charter, seemed to be reemerging. This design contains three main elements—the maintenance of international peace and security, with the related need for arms control and disarmament; a cooperative approach to the great economic and social issues, which also have profound implications for peace and stability; and the development of the role of law and universal respect for human rights. In the last five months of 1990 the Iraq-Kuwait crisis cast a searching light on the organization's actual capacity to make this design a reality.

As previously indicated, the United Nations has recently had considerable success in a variety of operations designed to effect peaceful transitions in situations of instability or conflict. The techniques of both peacemaking and peacekeeping have developed rapidly in the improved international climate of the past two or three years, and it has proved possible to combine them far more effectively than in the Cold War period. This was particularly true in the long delayed, but finally triumphant, supervision of Namibia's transition to independence as well as in UN efforts in Central America, an area from which, in the Cold War period, the UN had been excluded.

The essence of these encouraging experiences was the combination of diplomatic effort, especially by the permanent members of the Security Council, with the operational capacity, both civilian and military, that can be mobilized by the Secretariat. In Namibia this combination allowed for something much more than transitional supervision. The UN Transition Assistance Group (UNTAG) established the workability of democratic procedures in a situation that at first seemed remarkably unpromising. The result, a successful internationally supervised election, proved far more harmonious and provided a much better atmosphere for the future than had seemed possible at the outset. The Namibian development and the spirit in which it was achieved also had important implications for the far more complex situation in South Africa itself, which astonishingly enough appears ready to present—in UN Secretary-General Javier Pérez de Cuéllar's words—"the prospect of a non-racial democracy in South Africa in the not too distant future."

The efforts of the United Nations in Central America also broke new ground, playing a major role in resolving the conflict in Nicaragua. A UN

Observer Mission (ONUVEN) monitored the preparation and holding of free and fair elections, the first such operation authorized and conducted by the UN within a sovereign member state. The UN also played a key role in the voluntary demobilization of the Nicaraguan resistance. The International Commission of Support and Verification (CIAV) was established by the secretaries-general of the UN and the Organization of American States in response to a request by the Central American presidents. It was instrumental in persuading the Nicaraguan resistance to demobilize and in enlisting the support of the UN high commissioner for refugees to help resistance members to resettle in Nicaragua. Another mechanism, the UN Observer Group in Central America (ONUCA) received and destroyed the weapons of the resistance and verified the ceasefire that made its demobilization possible.

The secretary-general and his representative have also been active in searching for solutions to other conflicts in Central America, especially in El Salvador. In this particular case, new ground has also been broken in a partial accord on respect for human rights. The accord provides for an unprecedented long-term nationwide monitoring of human rights by the United Nations.

Such activities, and the United Nations' monitoring of elections in Haiti later in the year, indicate a completely new trend—the involvement of the United Nations in the internal affairs of its member states. This trend has important implications for other prospective tasks of the organization as well as for the future status of the concept of national sovereignty.

In the long-standing problem of the future of Western Sahara, an agreed set of proposals and a timetable were established, and in June the Security Council approved a plan for holding a referendum to enable the people of Western Sahara to determine their future without military or administrative constraints. Contacts with Morocco, the Frente Polisario, Algeria, and Mauritania as well as with the Organization of African Unity and the tribal leaders of Western Sahara continue with a view to realizing the plan as soon as possible.

An even greater challenge awaits the United Nations in Cambodia. At the end of August 1990, the five permanent members of the Security Council agreed on a framework for a comprehensive political settlement based on an enhanced role for the United Nations. The Cambodian parties accepted this framework and agreed to the formation of a Supreme National Council. The final implementation of the peace and reconciliation process, however, remains in the balance as one or another of the parties jockeys for position. If agreement to go ahead is finally reached, there can be no doubt that the eventual UN operation in Cambodia will test to the utmost the organization's capacity in peacekeeping, civilian assistance, and election monitoring.

The combination of UN efforts on some long-standing problems such as Cyprus and Afghanistan have, so far this year, registered less progress. In the Middle East until August 1990, the world organization had played only a peripheral role on the diplomatic stage. Significant efforts to resolve the Israeli-Palestinian problem took place entirely outside the United Nations.

The UN and the Gulf Crisis

The events of August 2, 1990, in Kuwait rudely diverted the United Nations from its relatively promising efforts in peacemaking and peacekeeping under the general terms of the charter's Chapter VI (Pacific Settlement of Disputes). This glaring act of aggression in a particularly sensitive part of the world put to the test—and also raised important questions about—the basic concept of collective security itself. The Security Council invoked, instantly and dramatically, the less familiar Chapter VII of the charter (Action with Respect to Threats to the Peace, Breaches of the Peace and Acts of Aggression). Between August 2 and November 29, 1990, the council adopted twelve resolutions on a wide variety of aspects of the Kuwait crisis. It imposed sanctions and an embargo and on November 29 finally authorized the use of force if Iraq did not comply with its resolutions by January 15, 1991. After that deadline had passed with no response by Iraq, the US-led coalition of some thirty countries with forces in the region—"member states cooperating with the government of Kuwait" as the Council's Resolution 678 puts it—proceeded to forceful measures.

These measures have, in the end, been spectacularly successful in the military sense, and it may therefore seem churlish to raise questions about them and particularly about the role of the United Nations. In the interests of the effective evolution of the world organization, however, it is essential to distill the lessons of the dramatic experience of the Iraq-Kuwait crisis and to consider how to improve the future performance of the United Nations and to develop the concept of collective security.

The truth is that in the Iraq-Kuwait case, collective security, for all its ultimate success, turned out to mean war on a large scale. In the present state of military technology this is a disturbing fact that points urgently to the need to develop a better system of international peace and security. Such a system must include more effective warning systems and better methods of preventing or preempting aggression. Maintaining peace and security must mean more than reacting, however forcefully, to a crisis that has already happened. It will require both the creation of conditions in which peace can be maintained and the capacity to anticipate and prevent breaches of the peace.

Although the coalition forces were ultimately successful in ejecting Iraq from Kuwait, the process of dealing with Iraq's aggression also diverged considerably from the terms of Chapter VII of the United Nations charter, not least because no attention had been given during the Cold War period to providing the means to implement that chapter. Thus the Security Council began at an early stage to relinquish control of the enforcement measures it had voted for when, on August 25, it asked states with naval forces in the Gulf area to monitor shipping and enforce the embargo on Iraq. In Resolution 678 of November 29 it went much farther down this road in virtually giving a blank check to the US-led forces in Saudi Arabia after January 15. The council's Military Staff Committee played no role whatsoever in this crisis, although Article 47.3 of the charter states that it "shall be responsible for the strategic direction of any armed forces placed at the disposal of the Security Council."

The option of sanctions, which were applied at the outset with virtually unanimous worldwide support, was abandoned as the main enforcement measure against Saddam Hussein. The goal of Chapter VII is action short of force if possible, and Article 42 provides that force will be used only when the Security Council determines that sanctions "would be inadequate or have proved to be inadequate." No such determination was made before Resolution 678 was adopted.

Forty years of the Cold War have meant, among many other things, that the steps outlined in the charter for providing the Security Council with the means to enforce its decisions have never been taken. No agreements have been concluded under Article 43 by which member states would make available to the Security Council armed forces, assistance, or facilities. The Military Staff Committee, which was to assist the council in the application of armed force, conducted purely token meetings throughout the Cold War period and, despite recent Soviet suggestions for its revival, to this day remains totally inactive.

Thus, prior to the Iraq-Kuwait crisis, there was no preparation for the deployment of forces under the UN flag, under UN command, or under the direction and control of the Security Council. After the January 15 deadline the Security Council and the secretary-general were virtually marginalized until the end of the military action. Although the outcome was widely acclaimed, the procedure has inevitably raised questions among the broader membership of the United Nations about the control and direction of future actions. These questions will have to be addressed if the world organization is to continue to have universal character and support, which is its main characteristic and strength.

The Gulf crisis highlighted a number of broader issues that are becoming part of a wider concept of international security and will be essential factors in a future common security system. The most obvious of these is the urgent need for progress on the related issues of arms control, arms trade, proliferation of weapons of mass destruction, and the necessity for regional security arrangements that provide equitable security for all states in a region. One of the most striking lessons of World War II was the general conviction, reflected in the UN charter, that disarmament was essential for a peaceful and stable world. This lesson was largely forgotten during the Cold War period, when East and West engaged in an arms race of staggering proportions and the arms trade flourished worldwide as never before. With the world arms trade running at about $1 trillion annually, the indignation recently directed at Saddam Hussein's arms buildup seems, at best, naive. Indeed, some of the members of the coalition against him had been his main suppliers only months before. The question is whether the Gulf crisis will put some serious and urgent resolve into the languid international debate on arms control, disarmament, and proliferation as well as spawn a new and serious effort to curb the arms trade.

The Gulf crisis is also a reminder that virtually throughout the world, largely as a legacy of the age of colonialism, many borders are still controversial, do not represent ethnic, political, or economic realities, and may become sources of conflict. This should be an important consideration in the effort to develop better mechanisms for anticipating and resolving future threats to the peace.

It seems unnecessary to do more than register here the part that oil and the lack of coherent overall energy strategies have played in the origins of the Gulf crisis.

The persistent disparity between rich and poor was claimed by Saddam Hussein, speciously, as one justification for his assault on Kuwait. Nonetheless, it is undeniable that widespread poverty, especially when juxtaposed with enormous wealth, is a sure breeding ground for extremism, instability, and conflict. Related to this worldwide and fundamental problem are the waves of economic migration in all parts of the world from poorer to richer economies, a phenomenon that also added a poignant element to the Gulf crisis. Long after the end of the crisis, massive poverty will remain the greatest and most explosive long-term problem. The concentration of attention on the Gulf crisis and before that on developments in the Soviet Union and Eastern Europe has heightened the feeling of "marginalization" in the countries of the residual "South." The plight of this large part of the world community, whose vast populations see little immediate hope of overcoming poverty and despair, constitutes a tremendous challenge to the concept of a "new world order."

The fact that technological precocity combined with the population explosion has inadvertently produced, for the first time, a threat to the environment and life-support system of the planet itself will also be a dominating challenge long after the Gulf crisis is forgotten. One of the fundamental questions of our time is whether "sustainable development"—development that meets the needs of the present without compromising the ability of future generations to meet their own needs—is an attainable goal.

One thing is certain. These great issues, which will determine the future—perhaps even the survival—of human society, cannot be adequately addressed in the absence of a reasonable degree of international stability, peace, and security and of a system that can provide it.

Future Challenges

The experience of the Iraq-Kuwait crisis provides some useful indications as to how the United Nations, and especially the Security Council, might be developed to become the framework of such a system. Iraq's aggression against Kuwait was, however, an unusually clear and flagrant breach of the UN charter. Future challenges to international peace and stability are unlikely to provide such clear grounds for Security Council action. It is important, therefore, to consider what system of collective security will be best suited to the likely problems of the post-Cold War world.

It seems probable that a period of great instability lies ahead. The reemergence of long-standing international rivalries, border problems, ethnic and religious turmoil, vast flows of arms and military technology, national disintegration, poverty and economic inequality, instantaneous worldwide communication, population pressures, economic migrations, natural and ecological disasters, scarcity of vital resources—these and other elements provide a volatile and restless environment for world peace.

In such a situation no one nation or even a partnership of two or three nations is going to be able to assume the role of world arbitrator and policeman even supposing all the other nations would accept it, which they are most unlikely to do. It would therefore seem only sensible that the United Nations should be developed into a system capable of assuming that role.

Any credible "new world order" must be concerned with disputes and conflicts all over the world, however daunting such a prospect may at first sight appear to be. A convincing response to the Gulf crisis demanded the leadership of the United States in a vast political and diplomatic effort and the mobilization of tremendous resources. It may well prove to have been a unique case, but an international peace and security system worth the name will have to respond to the wide range of disputes, threats to or breaches of the peace, and even acts of aggression, which are likely to occur now that the constraints of the Cold War are removed. Some cases will demand appropriate collective action either through regional or through global organizations. A credible "new world order" will have to be comprehensive and universal, responsive as much to the plight of the weak as to the interests of the strong. Moreover, all members of the community should participate according to their capacity. Many "realists" will denounce such an idea as a dream, but in the ominous conditions of our time, it may be argued even more strongly that it is only political and practical common sense.

The United Nations charter sets out the basic principles of such a system. The Gulf crisis has provided some useful indications of what its main elements should be.

First of all, both the UN and regional organizations should be far more alert to signs of major trouble. The United Nations needs to make a reality of the often suggested global watch on destabilizing developments worldwide including socioeconomic as well as political and military phenomena. It should look especially for dangerous buildups of armaments and for potential threats to weaker nations. Only with such a comprehensive and consistent watch will the words "international security" attain real significance.

It is, however, no good having a global watch if no one pays attention to the sentry. Hitherto, the Security Council has tended to be a reactive body, taking action only after a crisis has developed. Based on the watch system, it should be required as a matter of course to take preventive action in anticipation of a dangerous situation. Such action should include a far more dynamic approach to the flow of arms and military technology and to the proliferation of weapons of mass destruction.

The Security Council has only fifteen members, of which five are permanent. It should develop a procedure for political coordination and consultation that embraces the remainder of the UN membership and ensures the maximum support and understanding for the decisions of the Security Council.

The actual mechanisms for carrying out Security Council decisions need to be developed and made more systematic. Peacemaking activities—concerted diplomatic activity, mediation, conciliation, and good offices—are already fairly well developed, especially regarding the secretary-general's role. Legal recourse on justiciable matters could certainly be used more imaginatively in the future. The International Court of Justice should become a far more active element of the international system. Much closer contact should be maintained with regional agencies and arrangements, both in the maintenance of a security watch and in the taking of preventive action.

Much attention (including the Nobel Peace Prize) has been given in recent years to the technique of peacekeeping, a genuine innovation of the United Nations. The technique is now being diversified into new activities such as election supervision. Financing and logistical support for peacekeeping should be greatly strengthened, and there should be less complaint about its cost. (The cost of one or two days of Operation Desert Storm would have easily covered a whole year of UN peacekeeping operations throughout the world.) Military establishments throughout the world should incorporate training in peacekeeping as part of their regular responsibilities. Standby arrangements should be expanded. Peacekeeping units should be regarded not as an abnormal expense but as a routine and indispensable feature of a new world order. They should be deployed in areas of dispute and potential conflict *before* a crisis occurs to act as a monitor, a warning, and, if the worst comes to the worst, as a trip wire for more forceful action by the Security Council.

Until August 1990, the idea of enforcing Security Council decisions had taken a backseat to peacekeeping, which is a strictly nonforceful technique. Although in 1945 Chapter VII was considered to be the UN charter's greatest innovation, the Cold War largely put this provision on ice for forty years, and as the Kuwait crisis showed, none of the forceful steps envisaged in Chapter VII had been prepared for. The imposition and impact of sanctions, for example, needs a great deal of study, analysis, and preparatory staff work. As for the application of force, the Military Staff Committee should be aroused from its forty-five-year sleep to do preparatory staff work. The committee could start with the idea in Article 43 of agreements for the provision of forces and for their strategic direction and command. It could be asked to determine the extent to which this is still a practical option in the conditions of 1991.

There is another fundamental task in which the Military Staff Committee, which consists in theory of the chiefs of staff of the five permanent members, could be usefully employed. The underlying idea of the charter was the gradual conversion of arms races and military alliances into a worldwide system of common and collective security. In this conversion, the Military Staff Committee was to play an important role, advising and assisting the Security Council on "the regulation of armaments and possible disarmament" (Article 47.1). If the lessons of the Gulf are to be taken seriously, the Military Staff Committee might now be instructed to embark on a study of how to convert the current worldwide military establishment, and especially its deterrent capacity, into a system of international security for a highly unstable world.

There is no denying that the basis for the Military Staff Committee, the institution of the five permanent members of the Security Council who were the leaders of the victorious alliance in World War II, is by now something of an anachronism. Changing this arrangement, however, involves a revision of the charter and will certainly open up many complicated issues. Until the change is made, it is important that the five permanent members avoid resentment of their special status through regular consultations and cooperation with the rest of the membership on important questions.

The UN: Framework or Fig Leaf?

It remains to be seen whether the Gulf experience will be an energizing or a debilitating one for the United Nations. At the time of writing, it is even still an open question to what extent the new champions of a "new world order" have the United Nations in mind. In the future will they regard the United Nations as the essential framework within which to work cooperatively for a more stable and less dangerous world? Or is the United Nations to serve more as a fig leaf, a cover for ostensibly international action which is, in fact, under little or no international control?

For this and other reasons, 1991 is an important year for the development of this world organization. The United Nations has had an unusually dramatic confrontation with its most important task—dealing with aggression. The lessons that its members learn from that experience, and the way in which they apply them, will radically affect the future development of the organization its founders intended "to save succeeding generations from the scourge of war." At the same time, the United Nations is facing a series of global problems with which it has, at the present time, little capacity to deal effectively. Its future is thus in the balance on both major aspects of its activity.

Before the end of 1991 a new secretary-general must be chosen. The appointment of the world's leading international civil servant has hitherto been a haphazard and disorganized affair conducted with a lack of seriousness or method that would be totally unacceptable in any important organization in the private sector. There is now considerable interest in upgrading the process of appointment to take account of the main qualifications required and to include at least some rudimentary search process. It is not clear, however, what kind of appointment the governments who initiate the process, the five permanent members of the Security Council, really have in mind. Will they be looking for a dynamic, innovative, independent internationalist with a flair for communication and for large-scale management? Or will they in the end prefer a safe, low-key functionary who will make no waves and rock no boats?

The answer to these questions will be a good indication of how the more powerful governments view the real place of the United Nations in the turbulent, interdependent world of the twenty-first century.

3

Contrasting Reactions to the Gulf Crisis: Egypt, Syria, Jordan, and the Palestinians

Ann Mosely Lesch

COULD ARAB DIPLOMACY HAVE REVERSED the Iraqi invasion of Kuwait and settled differences between the two countries without external military intervention? Some Arab observers insisted that the rapid deployment of US and other non-Arab forces after August 2 sidetracked regional diplomacy and made an "Arab solution" impossible. The world will never know, yet such evidence as is available points to deep differences existing among Arab countries and within Arab populations that would have severely challenged any diplomatic endeavors.

Saddam Hussein signaled his anger against Kuwait in several ways before the invasion. At that time, efforts by Arab governments including Saudi Arabia, Egypt, and Kuwait itself to resolve Iraq's demands peacefully came to naught. After the invasion and the external intervention, the deep differences in the Arab world became even more pronounced. Jordanians and Palestinians signed up in Amman to fight alongside Iraq, whereas Egyptians volunteered to defend Saudi Arabia. Yemenis stoned the Saudi Arabian embassy in Sanaa to protest the US presence on Saudi soil. Palestinians on the West Bank denounced Egyptian President Hosni Mubarak in their demonstrations, and Egyptians bewailed their treatment by Iraqis and Jordanians as they fled overland from Kuwait. Popular anger

---

This is a revised version of an article that originally appeared in the *Middle East Journal*, Vol. 45, No. 1 (Winter 1991); copyright © 1991 by the *Middle East Journal*. Used by permission.

and anguish underlined the contradictory stances taken by Arab governments and widened the fissures within the region.

Saddam's Appeal

To comprehend the highly polarized reactions, one must assess both the powerful symbolic appeal that Iraqi President Saddam Hussein had among the Arab populace in the months prior to the invasion and the fears that Saddam's appeal and power generated among some Arab rulers. Iraqi leaders have long sought to lead the Arab world, contesting the centrality of Egypt, a nation whose sizable population, homogeneity, and strategic location have enhanced its role. Iraq had hoped to replace Egypt as the pivotal Arab country following Egypt's isolation after signing a peace treaty with Israel in 1979. Baghdad, however, soon found itself requiring Egyptian assistance in its grueling war with Iran. Saddam acknowledged the importance of Egypt's human and military support when he restored diplomatic relations in late 1987 and sponsored the reinstatement of Cairo as the headquarters of the Arab League in the spring of 1990. Saddam also sought to link some of Iraq's and Egypt's policies through the subregional Arab Cooperation Council (ACC).

Despite their reconciliation and cooperation in certain areas, the two governments continued to compete for the loyalties of other Arabs, notably Palestinians and Jordanians. The PLO leaned toward Baghdad when Egypt made peace with Israel but later shifted toward Cairo in the 1980s when the Israeli invasion of Lebanon destroyed its autonomous base in Beirut, when Iraq became preoccupied with fighting Iran, and when Mubarak encouraged Palestinian efforts to achieve diplomatic results through a dialogue with Washington. Meanwhile, Jordan sought enhanced relations with both countries: King Hussein returned his ambassador to Cairo in 1984 to strengthen the Arabs' diplomatic weight with the West while he simultaneously developed a strategic relationship with Iraq to bolster Jordan's eastern front in the event of a military confrontation with Israel. Jordan also joined the ACC. In contrast, Syria was estranged from both Iraq and Egypt during the 1980s. The deep-set antagonism between the two regimes was reinforced by Damascus's active support for Iran in the Iran-Iraq War and Baghdad's effort to undermine Syrian control in Lebanon. Syrian President Hafiz al-Asad also decried Egypt's peace with

Israel, which left Syria exposed strategically and enabled Israel to invade Lebanon unimpeded in 1982.

Iraq and Egypt both sought closer relations with states in the Gulf region, an area Baghdad viewed as its natural sphere of influence, and in the Red Sea region, which served as Cairo's vital flank. The Gulf Cooperation Council (GCC) was founded in 1981 to ward off pressure from Iraq as well as Iran. GCC monarchs feared Saddam's ambitions almost as much as they feared the Islamic republic's goal of exporting its revolution. Moreover, Iraq and Egypt provided political and material favors to the two Yemens and Sudan, all of which experienced internal upheavals in the 1980s. Sanaa sought to benefit from both Iraqi and Egyptian assistance by joining the ACC, whereas Sudan shifted away from Egypt as the two governments differed increasingly over internal Sudanese political issues.

When the Iran-Iraq War ended in August 1988 with Iraqi forces astride the Shatt-al-Arab, Saddam Hussein claimed that he had won a major victory for the Arab world. Saddam challenged the Egyptian model for conflict resolution with Israel when he argued that the world would not take the Arabs seriously so long as they remained militarily and economically weak. An Arab approach to peace, he asserted, lacked credibility if it was not coupled with pan-Arab strategic strength. Saddam argued that Arab oil revenues must, therefore, be invested in the Arab world to underpin Arab industrialization and reduce the glaring inequalities among its peoples. He maintained that Arab wealth was supporting the European and US economies and that their governments were using the funds to manipulate the Arabs and underwrite Israel's occupation of Arab land. Moreover, he contended that the governments of wealthy Muslim countries had a religious obligation to aid their less-endowed neighbors.[1]

Most important, according to Saddam, the Arabs had to create a credible military deterrent to block further Israeli attacks and put muscle behind their peace efforts. On April 1, 1990, Saddam announced that he possessed a binary chemical weapon and asserted that, if Israel were to strike Iraq with its nuclear weapons, Iraq would retaliate with chemical weapons. He added that if Israel commits aggression "against an Arab and that Arab seeks our assistance from afar, we will not fail to come to his assistance."[2] These statements were designed to deter an Israeli air attack comparable to the strike on the Osirak nuclear reactor in 1981, to signal King Hussein that he could count on Baghdad's military support if Israel tried to seize Jordan, and to articulate the regional equivalent of Mutually Assured

Destruction (MAD). MAD, he believed, had restrained the US-Soviet rivalry during the height of the Cold War.

Saddam's tough talk and stress on inter-Arab obligations had tremendous appeal in the Arab world. Palestinians had watched the peace initiative launched by the Palestine National Council (PNC) in November 1988 being frittered away: Israeli Prime Minister Yitzhak Shamir not only stalled on holding talks with Palestinians but also rejected his own proposal for limited Palestinian self-rule in the West Bank and Gaza. The Palestinians' belief that Washington maintained a double standard deepened in the spring of 1990 when both branches of the US Congress affirmed through nonbinding resolutions that unified Jerusalem was Israel's capital. Moreover, the US government vetoed United Nations resolutions that condemned Israel's repressive measures against the intifada and that advocated UN investigations of the situation in the occupied territories. When US President George Bush abruptly suspended the United States' dialogue with the PLO on June 20, 1990—after the Palestine Liberation Front (PLF) attempted a sea raid against Israel—Palestinians' disillusionment with Washington was total. That setback was compounded by the potential political and demographic impact of massive immigration of Soviet Jews to Israel. Palestinians even feared that the hard-line Israeli government, which came to power on June 8, might expel large numbers of Palestinians under cover of a strike against Jordan or Iraq.

In the tense atmosphere of early and mid-1990, with negotiations blocked and the balance of power against Palestinians worsening, Saddam's bravado struck a strong chord. His threats appeared credible because he controlled a powerful battle-hardened army that had already used missiles and chemical weapons in war. Some Arabs spoke apocalyptically of being willing to endure heavy casualties so long as Iraqi retaliation devastated substantial areas of Israel and destroyed its power. Saddam's words also comforted Jordan, which was increasingly concerned that Israel would try to implement the concept that "Jordan is Palestine." Senior Jordanian officials openly expressed their fears that Israel would expel Palestinians across the border and destabilize the newly democratizing Jordanian political system. They recognized that they could not protect their agricultural, mineral, and commercial resources that lay along the border with Israel. Jordanians, therefore, welcomed the prospect that Iraq would provide a strategic rear, and they hoped that Saddam's version of MAD would deter an Israeli attack. Saddam's strategy appealed on the emotional level when viewed as an effort to awaken the dormant "Arab will" and appealed on the practical level when viewed by Palestinian and Jordanian leaders who sought tangible support.

In addition to touching the Palestinian chord, Saddam touched the chord of widespread resentment toward the oil-rich states in the Arabian peninsula. He argued that European colonialism had deliberately fragmented the region in order to deprive the heavily populated areas of access to oil wealth, that current rulers in the Gulf were willing brokers and satellites of the West, and that Gulf states purposely withheld assistance from indebted Arab peoples.[3] Those arguments resonated in such countries as Jordan, Sudan, the newly united Yemen, and among Palestinians. King Hussein had begged for aid from the Gulf states to close a serious budget gap and halt Jordan's mounting debt. "We have exhausted all our material capabilities," he implored at the May 1990 Arab summit in Baghdad.[4] Yemen, the most populous and radical state on the Arabian peninsula, resented its dependence on remittances from Saudi Arabia and shared Iraq's criticism of the lavish lifestyles of the Saudi royal family and Gulf emirs. The perennially poor Sudan, which had squandered substantial development assistance from the Gulf on its unwinnable civil war, joined in the call for an equitable distribution of wealth, hoping to be bailed out one more time. Moreover, Palestinians criticized the failure of some Gulf states to fulfill the financial pledges they announced with fanfare at Arab summits. They also feared that Palestinian professionals were being squeezed out of jobs in the Gulf as governments increasingly filled positions with indigenous personnel, brought in politically malleable Asians, or cut back development projects in response to financial difficulties.

At the Baghdad summit, PLO chairman Yasir Arafat pressed the governments to wield oil as a weapon against Israel by implementing embargoes against countries that aided Israel and by imposing sanctions against institutions that facilitated the transport of Soviet Jews to Israel. Most Arab governments were reluctant, however, to jeopardize relations with the West, and this led Palestinians to argue that they sold out Arab solidarity for financial stability. As a result, Saddam's strident complaints during the summer that Kuwait and the United Arab Emirates (UAE) were waging an economic war against Iraq and were thus serving Washington's interests in keeping the Arabs "backward" seemed credible to many in the Arab world. The Iraqi government claimed that Kuwait stole oil from the Rumaylah oil field, which overlapped their territories; refused to cancel the debts that Iraq had accrued during its war with Iran; and caused the price of oil to plummet by glutting the petroleum market with its own oil. For every one-dollar drop in the price of a barrel of oil, the Iraqi foreign minister complained, Iraq lost $1 billion in annual revenue.[5] Kuwait, he maintained, was not merely exceeding its OPEC quota in order to enrich the royal family but, as a willing tool of the West, was deliberately undermining Iraq's economy and security.

Saddam's shrill and threatening tone profoundly disturbed the governments in Syria and Egypt as well as the GCC. Asad was working systematically to reintegrate Syria into the Arab fold. He applauded the Taif accord as the basis for ending the strife in Lebanon, restoring relations with Egypt after a decade's estrangement, and facilitating the release of Western hostages held by Lebanese factions and hinted at the need for negotiations over the Golan Heights. Although Asad sought strategic parity with Israel in order to put weight behind Arab negotiations, he implicitly supported the nonconfrontational approach fostered by Cairo and the GCC rather than the tough talk emanating from Baghdad. Moreover, Asad could not be certain that Saddam's military might would not be unleashed against him given their undiminished hostility. Even their common concern over Turkey's domination of the waters of the Euphrates failed to overcome their differences.

Mubarak was also wary of Saddam's approach and appeal. At the Baghdad summit, he criticized Saddam's style when he commented that "the Arab message to the outside world should be humane, logical, realistic . . . free of exaggeration and intimidation. . . . The fate of peoples cannot be determined through one-up-manship and self-deception." We do not achieve results by "anger," he averred, but by "confident insistence on the goal."[6] Mubarak underscored Egypt's leadership aspirations by restoring relations with Syria and Libya, welcoming the prospect of returning the Arab League headquarters to Cairo and undertaking well-publicized diplomatic mediation efforts as president of the Organization of African Unity. He also encouraged GCC investment in Egypt's slowly expanding private sector and suggested the creation of a Red Sea security zone. Mubarak did not give high priority to the ACC, in which Iraq played a key role, but instead focused on actions that enabled Egypt to regain its regional strength and simultaneously distance itself from Iraq.

Nonetheless, Mubarak was concerned about Saddam's ability to project himself as the militant defender of Palestinian rights. Cairo had proved unable to achieve an Israeli-Palestinian accord and by late July Mubarak acknowledged that "we're at a loss along with the Palestinians, but we are committed" to a negotiated peace.[7] Those words sounded lame to Palestinians when contrasted with the fiery promises of Saddam. Egyptian-Palestinian tensions were expressed through mutual accusations. When the Egyptian press reported that some PLO officials complained that Cairo had pressured them into the dialogue with Washington and into making concessions to pave the way for talks with Israel, Egyptian officials expressed outrage. They argued that the PLO itself had pressed for dialogue and negotiations with Israel. When the Egyptian foreign minister did not attend a hastily called conference of Arab foreign ministers in Tunis in late June, Iraq joined the PLO in claiming that Egypt had put the Palestinians in a diplomatic bind and was now abdicating responsibility for the failure of its strategy. The heated words underlined the problem that Egypt faced after relinquishing the military option against Israel and aligning itself with the United States: Mubarak could bolster Egypt's regional role, but he could not dispel Iraq's strategic arguments and appeal.

Thus, as the Iraq-Kuwait crisis mounted in late July, the lines of the subsequent schism were already evident. An Egyptian-Syrian-GCC front was emerging, Jordan and the PLO increasingly embraced Iraq, the penniless Sudan welcomed Iraqi oil and arms, and Yemen applauded Baghdad's Arab nationalism. Saddam's dream of becoming the paramount Arab leader may have been stymied by the countercoalition, but his popularity in the street continued to grow. By seizing Kuwait's oil wealth and ports, he must have calculated that he could ensure his strategic hegemony as well as his grassroots support.

Reactions to the Invasion

Iraq's invasion of Kuwait on August 2 surprised the Arab world. Despite the extreme tension between the two governments and despite Iraq's mobilization of forces on the border, Arab leaders thought their differences could be resolved through negotiations and the crisis could be defused. Arafat had just met Saddam in Baghdad and then flown to Kuwait and Amman to reassure their leaders that Iraq's pressure tactics did not mean war. Moreover, Mubarak had won Saddam's agreement to hold a meeting of high-ranking Kuwaiti and Iraqi officials in Jidda that would be followed by meetings in Baghdad and Kuwait. Based on Saddam's assurance that he would not attack Kuwait while they negotiated, Mubarak had calmed the fears of Emir Jabir al-Ahmad al-Sabah. The invasion occurred hours after Iraq's delegation left Jidda on August 1. Saddam claimed later that because the negotiations had aborted, he was free to use force.

Mubarak and Asad immediately sought to help the GCC counter the invasion. The Arab League foreign ministers were already assembled in Cairo as part of a meeting of the Organization of the Islamic Conference (OIC); both groups held emergency sessions to debate Iraq's attack.[8] On August 3, the ministers denounced Iraq's invasion, called for immediate and unconditional withdrawal, and asserted their commitment to preserve the sovereignty and territorial integrity of member states of the Arab League. The foreign ministers opposed foreign intervention in the crisis, but they also rejected Kuwait's demand that they form a joint Arab force to counter Iraq's army. As a result, the ministers from the GCC issued a separate statement claiming that the clause that rejected foreign intervention did not apply to adherence to collective international measures endorsed by the United Nations because the Arab League charter commits members to UN resolutions. The failure of the foreign ministers to call up an Arab force and the GCC addendum opened the door to Kuwait and Saudi Arabia's request for US military support.

The vote of condemnation at the foreign ministers' meeting was significant: Fourteen voted affirmatively (including Egypt and Syria) and five abstained (Jordan, Mauritania, the PLO, Sudan, and Yemen). Iraq was ineligible to vote, and the Libyan minister withdrew on his government's instructions.[9] Those who abstained apparently hesitated to name the aggressor in the resolution, arguing that it would undermine efforts to negotiate a settlement of the conflict. They hoped a minisummit could be convened in Jidda to bring Iraq and Kuwait face-to-face under Saudi and ACC auspices. In this respect, Yemen was in a particularly delicate situation. As the only Arab government seated at the UN Security Council, Yemen sought to represent the Arab consensus at a time when no consensus existed. Moreover, Yemen was inclined toward Iraq on issues of Arab unity, oil prices, and opposition to foreign involvement in the region. Therefore, Yemen abstained in Arab League and UN forums, rather than taking sides, and reluctantly complied with trade sanctions against Iraq.

By the time the emergency Arab summit convened in Cairo on August 10, inter-Arab differences had escalated. The proposed minisummit had fallen through amid sharp recriminations; some claimed that Saddam had refused to sit with the Kuwaiti ruler; others maintained that Mubarak and King Fahd did not want to hold the meeting without a prior commitment from Saddam that he would withdraw from Kuwait. Moreover, Saddam formally annexed Kuwait to Iraq on August 8, just after President Bush had sent the first ground forces to defend Saudi Arabia from an Iraqi attack. Thus, the plausibility of the argument by Arab conciliators that they could persuade Saddam to return to the status quo ante was undercut by Iraq just as the military stakes increased dramatically. For many Arabs, the prospect of a US military presence shifted the political argument from the issue of Iraqi aggression to the issue of Western neocolonialism.

Iraq wanted the summit to focus on the inadmissibility of foreign forces operating on Arab land. Jordan, Libya, the PLO, and Yemen urged the Arab leaders to form a mediation team that would attempt to reconcile the parties without condemning Iraq and that might facilitate the establishment of an Arab peacekeeping presence to separate them during the period of negotiations. The GCC, Egypt, and Syria rejected Iraq's stance as an effort to divert attention from the cause of the crisis. They also derided the proposal for mediation as a move that would delay action and thereby help Iraq consolidate its power position in the Gulf. They did not allow the proposals to be put to a vote. Instead, they insisted that the summit participants pass their own draft resolution that endorsed the earlier Arab League, OIC, and UN Security Council resolutions; denounced Iraq's attack on and annexation of Kuwait; and decried Saddam's threats against the Gulf states. The Egyptian-GCC resolution supported GCC steps to implement "the right of legitimate defense" and agreed to "dispatch Arab forces to support" the GCC "in the defense of their territories . . . against any foreign aggression."[10] The resolution thereby implicitly endorsed the GCC's right to invite US troops to protect them from Iraq. Twelve of the twenty governments attending the summit voted in favor of the tough resolution.[11] Algeria and Yemen abstained; and Jordan, Mauritania, and Sudan expressed reservations. The critics of the resolution sought further mediation before condemning Iraq and strongly opposed the presence of foreign forces in the region. Subsequently, Egypt, Morocco, and Syria sent troops to Saudi Arabia, and Somalia and Djibouti provided staging areas for international forces. The other leaders intensified their criticism of the manner in which the crisis was being handled. The polarization even led to the resignation of Arab League Secretary-General Chedli Klibi and revived questions as to whether the headquarters should move from Tunis to Cairo.

Arab positions were further complicated when Saddam Hussein, by a remarkable sleight of hand, linked the issue of Iraq's presence in Kuwait to the Israeli occupation of Arab lands, Syrian control over Lebanon, and Iraq's territorial disputes with Iran. His initiative on August 12 proposed "that all issues of occupation . . . be resolved in accordance with the same . . . principles . . . set by the UN Security Council." Withdrawal from "the oldest occupation"—Israel's—should take place first, and "arrangements for the situation in Kuwait" must take "into consideration the historical rights of Iraq in its territory and the Kuwaiti people's choice." The UN should impose sanctions and an embargo against "any party that fails to . . . comply with" the request to withdraw.[12] Saddam sidestepped the issue of whether Iraq's presence in Kuwait constituted occupation but highlighted the failure of the international community to respond vigorously to Israel's occupation of the West Bank, Gaza, the Golan Heights, and southern Lebanon. By stressing what was seen as a double standard, Saddam deftly turned the tables on his critics.

Arab differences over the Gulf crisis must, therefore, be analyzed in relation to three issues: Arab governments' and publics' positions on the Iraqi invasion; reactions to the rapid movement of US forces into the region; and responses to the emphasis on the Palestine problem as the fundamental occupation that needed to be resolved. Governments and publics reacted in varying ways to each issue. As a result, policy debates proved extraordinarily complex and bitter.

Egypt: Saddam's Double Cross

The Egyptian government denounced sharply the Iraqi invasion of Kuwait. Mubarak had just reassured the emir that Saddam would not attack, so he was furious at the apparent double cross. He urged Arab countries to respond swiftly to GCC requests for military assistance or, otherwise, "we will be as good as dead bodies. We will be humiliated and dictated to. [Iraq's] military power will impose its will on us in spite of ourselves."[13] Egyptian officials maintained that the basic principles of their policy were the renunciation of force to resolve Arab differences, nonintervention in the domestic politics of Arab countries, and the need to settle Arab differences within an Arab framework. Egypt, therefore, rejected Iraq's invasion and annexation of Kuwait and called for a peaceful solution under the auspices of the Arab League.

Nonetheless, Mubarak viewed the situation as sufficiently grave to warrant international involvement. Because Saddam had lied to the Kuwaiti ruler, Mubarak argued, no one could trust Saddam when he claimed he would not strike Saudi Arabia: "Should [King Fahd] wait until a catastrophe takes place there too?"[14] Mubarak added that the Gulf states were also afraid because no Arab military umbrella existed and they therefore concluded, "I [the Gulf state leaders] will cooperate with the devil for the sake of my country. They are right. Do you then blame those who request US aid?"[15] Mubarak maintained that he would prefer to have Arab or UN forces in the Gulf and that he hoped the crisis would convince Arab states of the importance of forming an Arab defense force. He argued that the Egyptian troops in the Gulf were under Saudi command and that they served a purely defensive purpose. Such comments also deflected potential criticism that many of the troops were sent at the United States' behest as a quid pro quo for writing off Egypt's nearly $7 billion military debt. Mubarak, however, did not deny that Washington anxiously pressed Cairo to provide a credible Arab military presence in Saudi Arabia.

The government was visibly concerned about the negative impact the crisis would have on the Egyptian economy. Egypt could expect to lose substantial sums in foregone remittances, revenue from the Suez Canal, and tourism, not to mention the loss of bank deposits in Iraq and Kuwait, development assistance from Kuwait, and trade with Iraq. An official document submitted to the International Monetary Fund estimated losses at a staggering $9 billion.[16] And yet, the government hoped to offset some of the remittances by sending more workers to Libya and GCC states and by receiving increased aid from oil-rich regimes. Cairo also sought emergency funds from the West and Japan as well as substantial debt forgiveness.

Public support for weathering the economic storm was galvanized by Egyptians' genuine anger at past Iraqi treatment of Egyptian workers. In recent years, resentment had mounted at the severe restrictions on repatriating savings and the mistreatment and even killing of Egyptian workers by demobilized Iraqi soldiers. The Egyptians who poured home from Kuwait and Iraq complained about Iraqi soldiers who stripped money, gold, and consumer goods from them at roadblocks and Jordanian merchants who charged outrageous prices for food and transport. Thus, even though Egyptians criticized the lavish lifestyle that visitors from the Gulf displayed while vacationing in Cairo, they did not respond to Saddam's call for solidarity of poor Arabs against the rich. Moreover, the official media argued that Iraq had itself to blame for its poverty: Saddam had squandered billions on the war with Iran, which he now demonstrated was a pointless venture by agreeing in mid-August to return to pre-1980 borders with Iran.

The invasion occurred at a moment when internal Egyptian politics were unsettled. The constitutional court had just overturned the system of elections to the People's Assembly and politicians were busy maneuvering in anticipation of new elections in the autumn. The government had been frequently arresting Islamist activists and cracking down on potentially violent groups. Nonetheless, virtually all nongovernmental politicians denounced the Iraqi invasion. The general guide of the Muslim Brotherhood, Muhammad Hamid Abu al-Nasr, termed the invasion "terrifying" and urged Muslim leaders to convince Iraq to withdraw its forces before Israel and the West could exploit the situation to their benefit.[17] The liberal secular Wafd party's editor sounded more hawkish than the government when he declared that Saddam had committed a "barbaric crime" and "treacherously stabbed Egypt in the back."[18] On the opposite side of the political spectrum, the left-wing Tagammu party termed the occupation of one Arab country by another an unprecedented act that required immediate Iraqi withdrawal and respect for Kuwaiti self-determination in order to limit the damage to the Arab world and restore Arab solidarity. Cartoons in Tagammu's newspaper portrayed the invasion as a gift to Israel.[19] Such accord across the political spectrum was unprecedented.

Politicians thus found themselves siding with the government in their criticism of Saddam as a ruthless dictator who violated canons of Islamic law and Arab norms by seizing Kuwait. They decried the absence of an Arab or Islamic solution and deplored the damage done to the Palestinian cause. Few trusted Saddam enough to give credence to his August 12 initiative that highlighted Israel's occupation of Arab land. They tended to view it as an attempt to distract attention from his annexation of Kuwait. Nonetheless, they were highly sensitive to the multifaceted US presence in Egypt and, therefore, deplored the entry of American forces into the heart of the Arab world, fearing that Washington would impose a hegemonic order on the region. Some rationalized the US presence as a temporary measure necessitated by Saddam's extreme threat, and all called for a swift replacement of foreign forces by Arab troops. Even Wafd politicians emphasized that Washington had pledged to withdraw as soon as the crisis ended and forcefully rejected the suggestion of US Secretary of State James A. Baker III in early September of a new security structure along the lines of NATO. The Islamist editor of *al-Nur* epitomized the critical reaction when he stated bluntly, "America is a perfidious friend who loves neither the Arabs nor the Muslims" and wants to "swindle" Muslims of their money.[20] Islamist-oriented *al-Sha'b* editorialized:

> the issue has changed from an Iraqi-Kuwaiti confrontation into an Arab-American one. . . . Now the question of who started it and whether he was right is meaningless. Arab and Islamic peoples are concerned now that armies of all the arrogant [powers] are flocking to hit an Arab-Islamic country. . . . How can disgrace and concession go as far as bringing enemies to protect the territory of Islam and its sacred places?[21]

Some Islamists, however, held a less critical perspective on the US role. Observers assumed that Saudi funds helped to ensure their acquiescence in the US presence. A Liberal party newspaper argued, for example, that foreign troops were stationed far from Mecca and Medina and that Saddam, not the foreigners, threatened the holy places.[22] A professor at al-Azhar University maintained that Islam permits Muslims to enlist the help of non-Muslims as long as the purpose is defensive.[23]

The Egyptian government gained freedom to act because of the confusion and consternation within the opposition ranks; Mubarak was encouraged enough to proceed with parliamentary elections under a liberalized election system. Nonetheless, he recognized the volatility of the issue of the foreign presence in Saudi Arabia. Officials muted any pronouncements that might imply coordination with the US troops, and the government banned all demonstrations—even those in support of its policy. Moreover, the assassination on October 12 of Rifaat Mahjoub, the speaker of parliament, underscored the vulnerability of the regime.

Mubarak preferred a peaceful solution to the crisis that would uphold his emphasis on international standards, reinforce Arab diplomacy, and prove that US forces would depart once Gulf security was insured. Egypt would then gain strategic and economic benefits from the GCC and the West for its firm stance. Neither a large-scale offensive war on Iraqi soil nor substantive political concessions to Saddam would serve Mubarak's interests. A full-scale war would arouse widespread popular opposition; concessions would weaken Egypt's stature in the region. Cairo, however, did not have the final say in either the military or diplomatic arenas. Those were in Washington's hands. The American bombing of Baghdad, launched within hours after the January 15, 1991 deadline, caused considerable trepidation in Egypt. By then, the government had committed forces and political will at considerable risk for the regime.

Syria: Pragmatic Partnership

Hafiz al-Asad swiftly denounced Iraq's invasion and called for the unconditional withdrawal of troops from Kuwait.[24] He viewed the crisis as a fundamental threat to the Arab regional system because it violated basic codes of inter-Arab relations and exposed the area to the danger of foreign intervention. Asad argued that Saddam had dragged the Arabs into a side conflict just as he had done in his war with Iran and that he should have focused on Israel instead.

As the first Syrian forces arrived in Saudi Arabia on August 21, the government justified the move with four arguments: Asad had promised King Fahd at the Arab summit in Cairo that he would help him defend his territory; Syrian forces would protect the holy places; as a pan-Arab act, their presence would help prevent further fragmentation of the Arab nation; and Arab forces would gradually replace the foreign forces already in the Gulf. The latter justification was particularly important politically because many observers were startled at the image of Syrian forces fighting alongside US and British troops. Asad firmly blamed Iraq for this painful situation, stating at the summit, "The foreigners who came to the region were not responsible for the event; the event brought them to the region. If we want these foreigners to be out as soon as possible, we have to find a solution to this event . . . so we might not leave a pretext . . . [for them to remain] as unwanted guests."[25]

He noted elsewhere that Gulf rulers had panicked because they lacked military means to protect themselves and, therefore, were compelled to invite foreign forces to help.[26] Nonetheless, Syrian officials insisted that Syrian troops would operate separately from foreign forces on Saudi soil. They became increasingly critical of the immense US military buildup, strongly opposed a US-Iraqi military confrontation, and hoped that economic and diplomatic pressure would oblige Saddam to seek a political solution. Once Iraq withdrew, Syria would join an Arab peacekeeping force in Kuwait that would also provide a buffer between Iraq and Saudi Arabia. US troops would leave, and Arab governments could resolve the remaining issues among themselves.

From the stance they had taken, Syrian leaders saw several potential benefits for their country. On an economic level, the alliance with the GCC guaranteed a major infusion of funds and investments for Syria's struggling economy, promised a resumption of assistance from the European Community, and ensured renewed support from the Soviet Union. If Washington removed Syria from its blacklist as a state that supported terrorist groups, then access to US commercial credits and advanced technology would be possible.

On a political level, Asad deepened his estrangement from Saddam. He hosted meetings of Iraqi opposition groups—Arab nationalist, communist, and Kurdish—who jabbed at Saddam by articulating a program to build a federal democratic state in Iraq. At times, the Syrian press declared that "the people of Iraq should play their role . . . by getting rid of those who imposed this impasse upon them,"[27] a not-so-subtle hint to depose Saddam. Asad may well have viewed the crisis as the optimal moment to remove his nemesis.

Asad also sought to place Syria in a strategically central position in the Middle East to enhance its ability to influence events and resolve central issues. Damascus hoped to use its alliance with Riyadh and Cairo to press for a comprehensive agreement with Israel that would restore Syrian sovereignty to the Golan Heights and resolve the Palestine question in a manner acceptable to Syria. That triad was more appealing than the alternative alignment with Iraq, Jordan, and the PLO in which Iraq would be the dominant partner and the Palestinian movement would remain outside Syrian control.

Syria had already gained benefits from its alignment in the implementation of constitutional reforms in Lebanon during August and September. General Michel Awn, the hold-out against the Taif accord, no longer had access to Iraqi arms and capitulated in October after Syrian forces bombarded his enclave. Syrian officials insisted that their presence in Lebanon could not be compared with Iraq's annexation of Kuwait because Damascus recognized Lebanon as a separate state and sought to reconcile its groups so Lebanon could regain its independence and territorial integrity. Such statements discounted Syria's determination to consolidate paramount influence in Lebanon but reflected the legal distinction that Damascus maintained.

President Asad hoped that Syria's relationship with Egypt and Saudi Arabia could be meshed with his decade-long ties to Iran. He was particularly anxious that Tehran adhere to the UN embargo of Baghdad despite the abrupt Iraqi military pullback from Iranian soil and the exchange of POWs in late August. Asad had helped ameliorate Egyptian-Iranian relations and had urged Tehran to induce the groups it supported in Lebanon to release American hostages. Nonetheless, Iran remained critical of the Saudi regime and denounced the presence of US troops in the Gulf. If Tehran tilted toward Baghdad, Damascus would be relatively vulnerable, caught between Iraq and Israel and committed to a presence alongside Western forces in Saudi Arabia.

As the conflict lengthened, the government had to ward off internal dissent. Although no criticism could be expressed in the open, disagreement with Asad's stance simmered below the surface. Some Syrians viewed Saddam as a pan-Arab hero and welcomed the annexation of Kuwait as a first step toward Arab unity and the liberation of Palestine. Others, such as the long-suppressed Islamist movements, seized the opportunity to vent their anger at Asad by supporting his archenemy. Still, a broad spectrum of citizens opposed the presence of foreign forces in the Gulf and wondered if Asad's arguments were more rationalization than rationale. Reports indicated that even members of the Baath (Arab Renaissance party) and the army were perplexed at Asad's decision to send troops, finding his actions impossible to reconcile with his espousal of Arab nationalism and rejection of entanglement with the West.[28] Asad had survived abrupt policy shifts in the past and had the power to contain expressions of opposition, but he needed tangible economic and political dividends from his pragmatic alignment in the Gulf. His regime could be considerably more vulnerable than Mubarak's if his regional strategy failed.

Jordan: The Double Bind

Jordan presented a stark contrast to Egypt and Syria. The Jordanian public and government were predisposed to support Iraq given their yearning for a strong Arab leader who would stand up to the West, defend them from Israeli attack, and compel the oil-rich regimes to use their wealth to support Arab causes. Political groups of all stripes mounted rallies that praised Saddam and denounced Bush, British Prime Minister Margaret Thatcher, and Mubarak. Some pan-Arab politicians accepted Baghdad's claim that Kuwaitis invited Iraqi forces to enter and remove the Sabahs. They called Saddam the new Salah al-Din who would forcibly unite the Arab world and use its riches to transform it into a major power that would compel Israel to withdraw from the occupied territories and would ward off Western pressures. Muslim Brotherhood members, who had won almost one-half of the seats in the parliament in November 1989, were particularly outspoken. They criticized Saddam's anti-Islamist record and opposed the annexation of Kuwait but denounced vigorously the US military presence. Islamists echoed the Iraqi call for jihad against the unbelievers who trespassed on Muslim soil. Many also joined in the Iraqi jibes at Kuwaitis for living luxuriously and allegedly lording it over other Arabs rather than sharing their fortuitous wealth with them.

The emotional outpourings provided a catharsis for the despair generated by the setbacks facing Palestinians and the pressures on Jordan as well as a release for citizens who had only gained democratic freedoms a few months earlier. Charitable societies and labor unions collected food to send to Iraq; thousands chanted slogans in the Roman amphitheater in Amman, marched on the US and Iraqi embassies, and rallied after Friday prayers. Such demonstrations would have been forbidden a year earlier; in 1990 they were not only condoned but encouraged.

King Hussein expressed considerable sympathy for Saddam's moves. At the Cairo Arab summit following the invasion, he argued "that the [Arab] nation is indebted to Iraq after the latter spent eight years defending it [against Iran]," and he maintained that precisely because "Iraq emerged . . . strong and victorious, . . . other parties . . . initiated campaigns of distortion [and] slander . . . [to] weaken it and to prepare to liquidate it as a promising power in the large Arab homeland."[29] King Hussein argued that the invasion "did not come out of the blue," because Saddam had experienced real difficulties with Kuwait over borders, oil, and debt.[30] The world could not, therefore, expect Iraq to withdraw unconditionally without addressing such legitimate claims. His most scathing remarks were aimed at the United States for mobilizing so rapidly when Iraq invaded Kuwait but failing to apply the same standards to the twenty-three-year Israeli occupation of Jerusalem. The king viewed Israel, not Iraq, as the most dangerous power in the region:

> There are other tigers [aside from Iraq] in the area that have been loose for a long period of time. . . . Such a tiger exists in our neighbor Israel, in its continued occupation . . . and annexation of the Syrian Golan and Jerusalem. . . . Israel represents a very serious threat. . . . I believe that Israel has done a lot to create the present image of Iraq.[31]

Hussein's government, therefore, welcomed Saddam's statement of August 12 that linked withdrawal from Kuwait to Israeli withdrawal from the occupied territories and Syrian withdrawal from Lebanon. Nonetheless, the king described himself as a mediator—not a spokesman for Saddam—in his effort to defuse the crisis. He stressed that he rejected the annexation of Kuwait and still recognized the Sabahs as the lawful rulers.

With the onset of the crisis, Jordan was cornered strategically and economically. Caught between Iraq and Israel, it feared being crushed in a war between the two behemoths. Crown Prince Hassan exclaimed, "tiny Jordan is surrounded by weapons of mass destruction. . . . [I] tremble at the description of a forthcoming massive confrontation between neighboring armies."[32] Jordanian civilians might suffer incalculable harm, he averred, especially if Israel seized the opportunity to destabilize Jordan and create an "alternative homeland"[33] for Palestinians at Jordanian expense. Even without war, Jordan was bound to suffer significant economic damage. Obeying the UN embargo meant that transit trade through 'Aqaba dried up and vital worker remittances vanished. When Jordan also ceased to truck its own produce and manufactured goods to Iraq—its leading trading partner—Jordan's economy was in dire straits. The difficulties were particularly acute because Saudi Arabia retaliated for Jordan's apparent tilt toward Iraq by halting the sale of oil to Amman. Jordanian truckers were harassed at the Saudi border, and Riyadh expelled some Jordanian diplomats and workers. The Jordanian government appealed to the UN for special assistance under Article 50 of the UN charter, which provides for compensation to countries damaged by a UN embargo. Jordan also sought Western and Japanese aid, which would not only help it fend off financial collapse but also help it cope with the massive influx of Arabs and Asians fleeing Iraq and Kuwait. The brunt of the embargo and the burden of sheltering evacuees, however, was borne by Jordan itself, further fueling anger and resentment toward wealthier Arabs and the West.

With the most to lose in a war, the king pressed urgently for military deescalation and relaxation of the sanctions. Caught in a double bind, King Hussein sought an outcome that would leave Iraq's strategic power intact, hasten the evacuation of foreign forces, and lead to serious international pressure on Israel to withdraw from the West Bank and Gaza. The Jordanian public backed him vigorously in those demands, but his unwillingness to distance himself from Saddam undercut his credentials as a mediator, angered the GCC, and irritated the West. The king's internal popularity was at its height just as he faced the greatest external challenge in his thirty-eight-year reign.

Palestine: Dream Versus Reality

If Jordanians were predisposed to favor Saddam Hussein's militant nationalism, then Palestinians had even higher expectations that his tough approach was the correct way to confront Israeli and US "arrogance." Palestinians poured into the streets of the occupied territories and Jordan to support Saddam's violent action to break the noose he claimed was tightening around him. They saw the Kuwaiti oil-price manipulation, Israeli threats to bomb Baghdad's chemical weapons plants, and US naval maneuvers in the Gulf as aspects of a concerted effort to destroy the one Arab leader who could challenge Israel and alter the strategic balance in the region. Saddam's attack on Kuwait was thus perceived as defensive rather than aggressive. If it succeeded, it would put weight behind Palestinian demands. In any event, from their perspective Palestinians had nothing to lose because the route of moderation and negotiations had failed to budge Israel or induce the United States to take their cause seriously.

When US troops landed in Saudi Arabia, the anti-American element of Palestinian protests became pronounced. Arab governments that fought alongside Western forces were derided as Washington's lackeys. Many believed that the United States sought a permanent presence astride the oil fields and strategic waterways and would strangle any signs of independent Arab action. The link between Saddam's stance and the Palestinian cause was confirmed in their minds by his August 12 initiative and by Washington's immediate rejection of the idea of relating one regional occupation with another. That also confirmed the Palestinians' belief that the United States held contradictory standards in regard to Israeli and Iraqi behavior; after all, in the past Washington had vetoed UN efforts to criticize Israeli actions in the occupied territories and Lebanon and had blocked attempts to impose sanctions on Israel. Washington focused on the plight of Western hostages in Iraq but, a Palestinian radio declared, never asked "about the fate of an entire nation which Israel has been holding hostage" for years.[34]

Yasir Arafat quickly supported Saddam's effort to challenge US power. Although the PLO abstained from the vote at the Arab foreign ministers' meeting on August 3, it voted against the summit resolution on August 10. Arafat resented the majority's cavalier rejection of his mediatory delegation to Baghdad, which Mubarak in particular had termed a delaying tactic on behalf of Saddam rather than a serious initiative.

Although PLO leaders were disturbed by the fissures widening in the Arab world, they seized on the opportunity presented by Saddam's initiative on August 12. In his message on the thousandth day of the intifada, Arafat stressed that the PLO's approach—like Saddam's—involved keeping foreign forces out of the region, tackling the Kuwaiti issue within an Arab framework, and highlighting the Palestinian cause as "the crux and core" of the regional conflict.[35] The PLO also floated proposals in conjunction with Jordan, Libya, and Yemen that called for modifications in Kuwait's status in order to accommodate Iraq.

PLO attempts to resolve the crisis thus displayed an underlying sympathy for Iraq rather than a rigorous neutrality. Some Palestinian groups—such as the Popular Front for the Liberation of Palestine (PFLP), the Islamic Resistance Movement (HAMAS), and Abu al-Abbas's Popular Liberation Front—expressed strong solidarity with Iraq and urged violent action to oust US troops from the Gulf. Arafat himself declared in early January that Palestine's fate was linked to Iraq. Other Palestinian officials, however, feared the implications of burning their bridges with the West and wanted to position the PLO as a credible mediator between the two sides; the PLO would then be able to take credit for a negotiated solution and use it as leverage in an international effort to foster Arab-Israeli talks. Indeed, from the start of the crisis, many Palestinians noted the danger of seeming to support the forcible seizure of territory. Professor Hanan Mikhail-Ashrawi voiced that concern: "We do not condemn occupation in one area and condone it in another. We do not condone the acquisition of land by force. We do not have . . . double standards."[36]

As the crisis escalated, Palestinians also expressed concern for the fate of the Palestinian communities in Kuwait and the Gulf that had provided vital financial and moral support to the intifada. The head of the Palestine National Fund, based in Abu Dhabi, attempted to limit the damage by asserting that "the support by the PLO for Iraq's pan-Arab and national position does not mean supporting Iraq in occupying and annexing Kuwait by force . . . [because] this is an illegal measure."[37] Nonetheless, several GCC governments did cut financial support to Palestinian organizations on the West Bank and expelled Palestinian employees. Paradoxically, many West Bank institutions had to appeal to Europe and the United States for substitute funds, and the PLO considered turning to the UN for compensation under Article 50. With remittances to families on the West Bank and Gaza Strip expected nearly to dry up, Palestinians faced extraordinary personal difficulties as they entered the fourth year of the intifada.

As Saddam became increasingly isolated internationally, Palestinians worried that their cause also could be damaged. Washington provisionally agreed to underwrite housing loans for Soviet immigrants to Israel and to provide more advanced weaponry to help compensate for the large-scale US arms sale to Saudi Arabia. The Soviet Union and Europe were cool toward Arafat's efforts to mediate between Iraq and Kuwait and rejected his assertions that Washington was playing a neocolonialist role in the Gulf. Nonetheless, some Palestinians argued that they could win irrespective of the outcome in the Gulf. Sari Nuseibeh, a leading intellectual in Jerusalem, suggested that a US military confrontation with Iraq would cause severe anti-American fallout in the Arab world and thereby restore support for the Palestinians.[38] If, however, there was a political solution, the necessary next step would be international diplomacy concerning Israel's occupation.

During October that perspective gained credibility as world leaders acknowledged the importance of resolving the festering Israeli-Palestinian conflict as well as Iraq's occupation of Kuwait. Moscow stated its commitment to an international conference, and President Bush pledged at the UN to work toward settling the Arab-Israeli conflicts. Most important, the Israeli police's killing of Palestinians in the Muslim holy places in Jerusalem on October 8 underlined the volatility of the unresolved conflict. The violence compelled Washington to alter its decade-long policy of blocking UN criticism of Israel, leading it to support resolutions that not only deplored Israel's actions but also insisted on a UN investigation. Ironically, the October killings may have accelerated American preparations for an offensive war. If an embargo on Iraq was to be maintained indefinitely, Washington feared world attention might return frequently to the Israeli-Palestinian arena, because additional outbursts of violence would undoubtedly occur, thus straining the international coalition in the Gulf and increasing US friction with Israel.

Once the US airstrikes on Iraq began in January, Saddam Hussein carried out his threat to hit Israel with Scud missiles. The United States then had to divert military resources to protect Israel and to eliminate the Scud launchers as part of the effort to persuade Israel to refrain from retaliating on its own. The Israeli government, however, did seize the opportunity to strike hard at Palestinian bases in southern Lebanon and to place Palestinians living in the occupied territories under nearly continuous curfew. Although many Palestinians applauded Iraq's ability to hit Israel from afar, nonetheless, the immediate damage to the Palestinian cause was severe. The prospects for meaningful negotiations appeared even more remote. The gap between dream and reality remained wide.

Fractured Visions

The crisis in the Gulf triggered cataclysmic changes in the Arab world. Shifts in alliance patterns accelerated, and inter-Arab organizations suffered acrimonious discord. Political movements on the left and the religious right struggled to articulate coherent positions. Massive numbers of people were uprooted; they not only included the thousands who fled Kuwait and Iraq but also Jordanians, Sudanese, and Yemenis no longer welcome in Saudi Arabia and the Gulf. Stateless Palestinians in particular had no place to go when expelled or refused entry. The crisis opened old wounds and created new sores.

Depending upon their geographical and ideological outlooks, Arabs placed the crisis in diametrically opposing frameworks that influenced their analysis of the causes of the crisis and of the appropriate resolution. This polarization was strikingly evident in the perspectives taken by Egypt, Syria, Jordan, and the Palestinians.

The Egyptian government, representing a leading regional power with a stake in the contemporary political order, saw Iraq's invasion as a bid to overturn the regional balance of power, impose its will on militarily vulnerable neighbors, and control regional economic resources. Egypt, therefore, sought to contain Iraqi power so that it could not destabilize the region. The Syrian government could not aspire to regional dominance but wanted to consolidate its position in the eastern Mediterranean. Wary of its powerful neighbors, Iraq and Israel, Damascus shared Cairo's concern that Baghdad could fundamentally alter the regional political balance. Syrian officials feared their resultant dependence on Iraq. They therefore sought to enhance their strength by aligning with the wealthy status quo powers rather than with the radical challenger to the regional system. Nonetheless, both Egypt and Syria contended with potentially restive publics that strongly opposed a military alliance with the United States and criticized any diversion of attention from the Arab-Israeli arena. Egyptian citizens could express their views through the press and parliamentary elections, whereas Syrian public opinion was sharply curtailed. Both governments, however, knew their policies had limits. If the United States led an offensive against the Iraqi heartland or Israel became directly involved militarily, popular support could evaporate and the governments would find themselves dangerously isolated. The Egypt-Syria-GCC triad would then be difficult to sustain.

The Jordanian government, in contrast, led a small and vulnerable country with an angry and highly politicized population. Jordanians and Palestinians alike viewed Saddam as an Arab leader who asserted Arab national rights, called attention to the injustices done to Palestinians, sought a strategic balance with Israel, and challenged the inequities in the current state system in the Arab world. Jordanians and Palestinians believed that Iraq should be persuaded, not pressured, to relinquish Kuwait and that Iraq's wider political and economic objectives required urgent attention. They argued that the Palestine problem and the regional gap between rich and poor, if left unattended, would blow up again in highly damaging ways. Both peoples deplored Washington's apparent double standard and resented the status quo regimes' ties to the West. Some hoped that those governments' reliance on external forces would accelerate internal political change and hasten the advent of a new regional order. Meanwhile, Jordanians and Palestinians themselves were gravely affected by the ongoing crisis.

The clash in perspectives about the nature and validity of the regional system led to clashes in policy toward Iraq. That tension, in turn, was exacerbated by the internationalization of the crisis. The leading role played by the United States enhanced the element of unpredictability and increased the risks for the Arab states and peoples. Decisions on waging war, extending the embargo, or proffering a negotiated solution were no longer in Arab hands. For those reasons many feared inviting in foreign troops and transferring decision-making to the UN Security Council. Once again, decisions vital to the very existence of the Arab world were being made by powerful external states. The results of those decisions would, however, have the greatest impact on the Arab world. Each government was vulnerable and risked delegitimization if its approach failed. The people of the region faced painful disruptions in their lives no matter what the outcome. The crisis had unleashed powerful and unpredictable forces whose impact would reverberate for years to come.

Notes

1. Elaborations of Saddam's strategic thinking can be found in the report on his meeting with Palestinian leaders in *al-Muharrir* (Paris), May 7, 1990, as reported in Foreign Broadcasting Information Service (FBIS)-Near East and South Asia (NES) Daily Report, May 9, 1990, p. 3; in his speech at the Arab summit on May 28, 1990, broadcast the same day by Baghdad radio, as reported in FBIS-NES, May 29, 1990, pp. 2-7; and in the full transcript of Saddam's interview with Diane Sawyer of the American Broadcasting Company (ABC) broadcast by the Iraqi News Agency on June 30, 1990, as reported in FBIS-NES, July 2, 1990, pp. 6-15.

2. Speech delivered on April 1, 1990, reported on Baghdad radio April 2, 1990, as reported in FBIS-NES, April 3, 1990, pp. 32-35.

3. Official pronouncements criticizing the Gulf regimes reached their peak in mid-to-late July 1990. They included the letter from Foreign Minister Tariq Aziz to the secretary-general of the Arab League broadcast on Baghdad radio on July 18, 1990, as reported in FBIS-NES, July 18, 1990, pp. 21-24, and Iraqi press statements of July 18-23, 1990, as reported in FBIS-NES, July 19, 1990, pp. 22-23, and July 23, 1990, pp. 28-30.

4. Speech on Baghdad radio, May 28, 1990, as reported in FBIS-NES, May 30, 1990, p. 7.

5. Letter from Foreign Minister Tariq Aziz to the secretary-general of the Arab League broadcast on Baghdad radio on July 18, 1990, as reported in FBIS-NES, July 18, 1990, pp. 21-24, and Iraqi press statements of July 18-23, 1990, as reported in FBIS-NES, July 19, 1990, pp. 22-23, and July 23, 1990, pp. 28-30.

6. Speech on Baghdad radio, May 28, 1990, as reported in FBIS-NES, May 29, 1990, p. 10.

7. Speech on Revolution Day, quoted in *Mayu,* July 23, 1990, translated by *Arab Press Review*, no. 437, July 26, 1990, p. 1.

8. At the OIC, there were five abstentions in the vote of August 4: Jordan, Mauritania, the PLO, Sudan, and Yemen. Iraq opposed it. Djibouti and Libya did not vote. Middle East News Agency (MENA) (Cairo), August 4, 1990, as reported in FBIS-NES, August 6, 1990, p. 12.

9. See text of the resolution translated from MENA, August 3, 1990, in FBIS-NES, August 6, 1990, p. 1. The fourteen affirmative votes were Algeria, Djibouti, Egypt, Lebanon, Morocco, Somalia, Syria, Tunisia, and the six GCC governments.

10. The text from MENA, August 10, 1990, translated in FBIS-NES, August 13, 1990, pp. 1-2.

11. *Ibid.* The twelve affirmative votes were Djibouti, Egypt, Lebanon, Morocco, Somalia, Syria, and the six GCC countries. Tunisia did not attend.

12. Baghdad radio, August 12, 1990, as reported in FBIS-NES, August 13, 1990, p. 48.

13. Press conference on Cairo radio, August 8, 1990, as reported in FBIS-NES, August 8, 1990, p. 10.

14. *Ibid.*

15. *Ibid.*

16. *Middle East International*, No. 384, September 28, 1990, p. 10.
17. *Al-Hakika*, August 4, 1990, translated by *Arab Press Review*, No. 440, August 6, 1990, p. 2.
18. *Al-Wafd*, August 5, 1990, translated by *Arab Press Review*, No. 440, August 6, 1990, p. 13.
19. Tagammu references from *al-Ahali*, August 8, 1990, translated by *Arab Press Review*, No. 442, August 13, 1990, pp. 1-3, 9.
20. *Al-Nur*, August 8, 1990, translated by *Arab Press Review*, No. 442, August 13, 1990, p. 3.
21. Adil Hussein in *al-Sha'b*, August 14, 1990, translated by *Arab Press Review*, No. 443, August 16, 1990, pp. 2-3.
22. *Al-Hakika*, August 18, 1990, translated by *Arab Press Review*, No. 444, August 20, 1990, p. 5.
23. Abd al-Ghaffar Aziz, quoted in *al-Nur*, August 29, 1990, translated by *Arab Press Review*, No. 448, September 3, 1990, p. 2. The official press also embroidered on that theme with one columnist noting that when Muslims were oppressed by relatives in their early years, the Prophet Muhammad urged them to seek refuge with the just Christian ruler in Ethiopia. Ahmad Bahjat quoted in *al-Ahram*, August 20, 1990, as reported in FBIS-NES, August 24, 1990, p. 8.
24. See press reports of August 11, 1990, in FBIS-NES, August 14, 1990, p. 3, and of August 21, 1990, in FBIS-NES, August 22, 1990, p. 47; Damascus radio, August 16, 1990, as reported in FBIS-NES, August 18, 1990, p. 50; and *Middle East International*, No. 382, August 31, 1990, pp. 16-17.
25. Damascus radio, August 20, 1990, as reported in FBIS-NES, August 21, 1990, p. 41.
26. Cited in article by Adil Hussein, *al-Sha'b*, August 14, 1990, translated by *Arab Press Review*, No. 443, August 16, 1990, p. 5.
27. Editorial in *al-Baath*, August 31, 1990, as reported in FBIS-NES, September 6, 1990, p. 49.
28. *Middle East International*, No. 384, September 28, 1990, pp. 11-12.
29. Amman radio, August 12, 1990, as reported in FBIS-NES, August 14, 1990, pp. 1-2.
30. Interview, Jordan television (English), August 4, 1990, as reported in FBIS-NES, August 6, 1990, p. 53.
31. Interview with Dan Rather, Columbia Broadcasting System (CBS), reported on Jordan television (English), August 6, 1990, as reported in FBIS-NES, August 7, 1990, p. 38.
32. Press conference, Jordan television (English), August 15, 1990, as reported in FBIS-NES, August 20, 1990, p. 33.
33. Ibid.
34. Voice of Palestine (Algiers), August 25, 1990, as reported in FBIS-NES, August 28, 1990, p. 2.
35. *Sawt al-Sha'b* (Amman), September 4, 1990, as reported in FBIS-NES, September 5, 1990, p. 6.
36. Interview in *al-Fajr* (Jerusalem), August 20, 1990, p. 16. The assassination of

Salah Khalaf (Abu Iyad) in Tunis in January 1991 appeared the result of his criticism of Saddam's policy.

37. Juwayyid Ghusayn, interview with *al-Ra'y* (Qatar), August 19, 1990, as quoted by Riyadh radio, reported in FBIS-NES, August 20, 1990, p. 2.

38. *Al-Fajr*, September 10, 1990, p. 16.

4

Coalition Diplomacy

David Hoffman

On the night of January 11, 1991, US Secretary of State James A. Baker III stood before 500 American pilots and crews crowded around a makeshift podium in a hanger in Taif, Saudi Arabia. He had come from Geneva and talks with Iraq's foreign minister, Tariq Aziz, hoping to persuade Aziz that Iraq could not prevail in its confrontation with the international coalition seeking to liberate Kuwait. For five-and-a-half months, the coalition had sought to use the threat of force to coerce Iraq into retreat, but to no avail. The January 15 deadline authorizing the actual use of force was drawing near. Aziz again refused to give ground. Baker, looking into the eyes of the men and women who would do the fighting, spoke sadly of the inevitability of war. "Let me be absolutely clear," he said, "We pass the brink at midnight, January 15." He added, "You are the combat crews who will join in the liberation of Kuwait."[1]

Baker's words marked a turning point, the conclusion of an exasperating, strenuous 166-day period of diplomatic maneuvering. In this period before the war, the United States exerted its leadership to create an international coalition of unprecedented scope and durability to oppose Iraq's invasion of Kuwait. The birth of this coalition came at a critical moment, just as the Cold War was giving way to a new cooperation between the United States and the Soviet Union and amid much speculation about which nations would assume leadership roles in the post-Cold War era. To fight Iraq, the twenty-eight-nation coalition eventually sent 700,000 men and women and some of the most accurate and lethal conventional weapons ever used.

There are several reasons why the coalition's diplomatic efforts failed to head off the war. Foremost was the intransigence of Saddam Hussein. He never did pull out when he had the chance—making the war against him inexorable. Second, the United States and its coalition partners adopted a strategy based on the assumption that Saddam's behavior could only be changed through the threat of force. The giant military deployment could not be slowed or reversed without appearing to be a major concession to Saddam. The Iraqi president never gave an inch, and the use of force became even more certain.

In many ways, President George Bush set in motion the decisions that led to war in the very first days of the crisis. He appears to have never even considered trying to talk with Saddam or sending a special envoy in the early days to meet directly with the Iraqi president. At a picture-taking session on August 3, Bush told reporters "we're not discussing intervention." The reason for this comment has never been made clear, but it might well have been calculated not to alarm the American public right away about overseas military deployments. By all accounts, it soon became evident to his advisers that Bush would not be satisfied with sitting back and doing nothing.

Rather, Bush decided at the time on a two-track effort, both tracks employing coercion in an effort to change Saddam's behavior. One was to be global economic sanctions and an arms embargo to try and force Saddam to capitulate; the other was to be a credible military threat, at first for defensive purposes, which would take some time to assemble.

Bush and Baker turned to all the diplomatic tools at their disposal. Much of their effort was coordinated through the Deputies Committee, a group of high-ranking officials who had been given the responsibility for crisis management, which included Under Secretary of State Robert Kimmitt and Assistant Secretary of Defense Paul Wolfowitz. Deputy National Security Adviser Robert Gates chaired the committee.

Immediately, the United States pushed for a meeting of the UN Security Council. The first resolution calling for Iraq's immediate withdrawal from Kuwait was passed within six hours; after a brief pause to allow for an Arab diplomatic effort, economic sanctions were imposed four-and-a-half days later, a maritime embargo three weeks later.[2] The sanctions and embargo were extended to air traffic on September 25.[3]

Diplomacy: Sanctions and Soviet Cooperation

Secretary Baker learned of the Iraqi invasion while meeting in Irkutsk with Soviet Foreign Minister Eduard Shevardnadze. At first, neither Baker nor the Soviets were alarmed at the reports that Iraq was threatening its neighbor. The early intelligence reports apparently did not signal a full-scale invasion, and there were mixed signals from the Kuwaitis about whether they were requesting help. A top aide to Shevardnadze who was in the August 2 meeting with Baker in Irkutsk later recalled that when Baker first got word from Washington that Iraqi troops had crossed the border, he told Shevardnadze that Kuwait was not seeking assistance. "In the past, Iraq had repeatedly crossed the border and gone a couple of kilometers into Kuwait, put forward some demands, and then returned to its own territory. We were not even worried."[4]

Shevardnadze subsequently acknowledged that after hearing the intelligence report from Baker, "I was almost sure there would be no further deterioration."[5]

After the Irkutsk meeting, Baker flew off for a planned visit to Mongolia, and his director of policy planning, Dennis Ross, separately went to Moscow on Shevardnadze's plane for what was to be a few days of relaxed consultations with one of Shevardnadze's aides at a dacha outside of Moscow.

But they never made it to the dacha. The aide heard that Iraqi troops had occupied Kuwait City as he drove to the US embassy in Moscow to see Ross. Thus began the first phase in an unprecedented round of international coalition-building. On hearing of the invasion, Baker decided to come to Moscow immediately. Ross laid the groundwork with Soviet officials for a possible joint statement condemning Saddam's aggression—an enormously complicated task because of the long-standing Soviet role as arms seller and patron of Iraq.

In his office, Shevardnadze convened a group known as the little *Sovnarkom*, or "little collegium," comprised of about two-dozen top foreign ministry officials. Baker's proposal for a joint US-Soviet statement was hotly debated by this group. According to one account, the main point of contention was concern about what would happen to Soviet workers and citizens in Iraq if Moscow decided to join with the United States against Saddam. "The statement was written in blood," according to the Shevardnadze aide.

> Its supporters realized that they bore the entire responsibility for the fate of Soviet citizens in Iraq. Had anything happened, I would have quit the foreign ministry. But our argument was this: We are dealing with a man with whom you can only talk tough. Of course, Saddam might have ordered an attack on a bus carrying our specialists. But there is no policy without risk .... If we did not stop Hussein now, in a few years he would be threatening us with nuclear weapons.[6]

The little collegium decided to go ahead with the joint statement. There was further heated discussion with Ross, who pressed the Soviets for a more strongly worded statement. That evening, at Moscow's Vnukovo-2 Airport, Baker and Shevardnadze huddled briefly and then read the statement to reporters. It included a joint call for an international arms embargo against Iraq, and Shevardnadze emphasized the importance of turning to the UN Security Council for the next steps.

Already exhausted from months of transatlantic diplomacy, Baker returned to Washington on the morning of a critical Camp David meeting with Bush and his top advisers. By this time, Bush's general direction had been set, and Baker's task was to fortify the international coalition against Iraq. The Security Council voted a global economic embargo against Iraq. At great economic peril, Turkey was persuaded to cut off the oil pipeline from Iraq. The United States lurched toward unilaterally implementing a naval blockade of Iraq. On August 12, Baker surprised many other world leaders when he said the United States would proceed with "interdiction" of commerce at sea bound to or from Iraq, citing a request from Kuwaiti authorities and Article 51 of the United Nations charter authorizing acts of individual and collective self-defense.

Baker appeared to be suggesting that the United States would go it alone, and reaction was swift and negative from other members of the Security Council. Baker had stepped too far out in front of the international consensus, and a long series of telephone calls between Baker and Shevardnadze followed in August while Baker was vacationing in Wyoming, leading to approval of a new Security Council resolution on August 25 that had the Soviet blessing. The episode was important in shaping the way the United States, seeking the authorization to use force against Iraq, later approached the Security Council.

At the outset of the crisis, Baker was not inclined to think much of the United Nations, but this episode and others brought home the degree to which the Soviet leadership regarded it as a vital forum. Moreover, Soviet cooperation meant that the prospect of a veto among the five permanent members of the Security Council was reduced.

As the summer ended, President Bush was vacationing in Kennebunkport, Maine. Economic sanctions had been put in place, and some Arab allies in the region thought they would work quickly. Neither the American public nor the allies were yet prepared for offensive military action. A congressional delegation that visited the region reported back that "it did not appear, at least for now, that unilateral military action is being encouraged" but rather that "a show of military force was necessary to make multilateral sanctions and [the] embargo effective."[7] Saddam had started taking Americans and others hostage and moving them to "strategic sites" as insurance against attack, but Bush declared that he would not let his decisions be tied to the emotional issue of the hostages. This was a central lesson he had learned from the Reagan years.

As September began, the administration was committed to the two-track approach Bush had launched in August. But the events of this month would lead Bush and his top advisers to all but give up on sanctions. The administration was also struggling with a problem that persisted throughout the crisis: how to explain its goals to the American people and the rest of the world. An internationally acceptable rationale was essential to the building of a coalition. In his initial televised speech on the crisis in August, Bush had outlined four points to guide US policy: immediate, unconditional, and complete withdrawal of all Iraqi forces from Kuwait; restoration of the legitimate government of Kuwait; commitment to security and stability in the Persian Gulf; and protection of US citizens abroad. But there was a strong sense at the State Department at the end of August that a better job needed to be done explaining to both domestic and foreign audiences what the American goals and stakes were in the crisis. Baker attempted to do this in his September 4 testimony to the House Foreign Affairs Committee.

Baker also used his testimony to urge the nation to be patient for sanctions to work. He asked that the American people "stand firm, be patient and remain united. . . . Our strategy is to lead a global, political alliance to isolate Iraq politically, economically and militarily. We aim to make Iraq pay such a high price for its aggression that it will be forced to withdraw from Kuwait . . . . Time can be on the side of the international community. Diplomacy . . . can be made to work."[8]

On the second track, thousands of American troops were pouring into the region, and this influx created its own waves at home and abroad. General Norman Schwarzkopf, commander of the US forces, said the size of the deployments was actually being exaggerated to the press to deter Iraq from moving into Saudi Arabia. "In the very, very early stages of this operation, when we were over here building up and we didn't have very much on the ground, you all were giving us credit for a whole lot more over here," he said. These same reports, which Schwarzkopf said gave him "confidence," stirred unease in the United States.[9] As he traveled around the country, the president was met with protesters chanting, "No blood for oil!"

Abroad, too, there was still great political and cultural sensitivity to such a sudden and large deployment of American power. Baker suggested in his September 4 testimony that the United States was considering the creation of a new security "structure" in the Gulf if necessary to contain Saddam, and he compared the concept to the way NATO had contained communism. Baker's remark immediately ricocheted around the Arab world and drew shudders from allies and foes alike who were strongly opposed to a permanent US ground presence in the Gulf.

Even the Soviet Union, which had joined the anti-Iraq coalition a month earlier, was watching the second track of military deployments with a cautious eye. The Kremlin was anxious to avoid a military solution. Baker tried to invite them to participate in Operation Desert Shield. One day early in the crisis when the Saudi ambassador to the United States, Prince Bandar bin Sultan, was visiting Baker, the secretary asked him if King Fahd would mind if a Soviet unit joined the Americans. Bandar went into another room and called the king; the answer came back that he would not mind. But the Soviets, traumatized by the Afghanistan conflict, were not willing to send troops abroad.[10] The Soviet leadership and public opinion were still largely dominated by the fate of Soviet workers trapped in Iraq.

At the Helsinki summit of September 9, the coalition further flexed its muscle. Presidents Bush and Gorbachev issued a joint statement saying they wanted a peaceful settlement, but "if the current steps fail to end it, we are prepared to consider additional ones consistent with the UN charter." The statement was the product of intense cooperation between Baker and Shevardnadze. The Soviet foreign minister had proposed an international conference on the Middle East. Baker refused, saying it would reward Saddam for his aggression. But Baker was amenable, he said, to some language referring to a role for the Soviets in the Middle East peace process. The statement said Bush and Gorbachev had directed their ministers "to work with countries in the region and outside it to develop regional security structures and measures to promote peace and stability."

Later, Baker discovered that Shevardnadze may have carried things a little further than the Soviet president had envisioned. But except for minor changes, Gorbachev did not change the Baker-Shevardnadze draft containing the ambiguous but suggestive reference to "additional steps" against Saddam.

The Helsinki summit also cast new light on the larger motivations that were the glue of the international alliance against Saddam. At this point, Gorbachev was still talking enthusiastically about radical reform to a market-oriented economy. The bottom line for the Soviet Union was that it needed help from the West, and Moscow realized that a prolonged war might disrupt the prospects for that help. Thus, Soviet policy was to be cooperative with Washington, but the Soviet's also hoped to avoid a conflagration that could disrupt Western economies. Gorbachev alluded to this in his press conference remarks. "It would be very oversimplified and very superficial to judge that the Soviet Union could be bought for dollars," he said.

But the lure of economic cooperation was strong, and, in fact, after much hesitation Bush offered the Soviet Union emergency food and economic aid a few months later. The view among Bush's senior advisers at the time was optimistic. One of the president's top foreign policy advisers commented, "Look how we have been able to work with the Soviets to our advantage. And the reason is that they have got all these problems. They have obviously decided they want to come in our direction. They want to be part of the West, part of the world."[11]

In his report to Congress after Helsinki, Bush heralded the arrival of a "new world order" out of the allied cooperation against Iraq. But he also hinted at uncertainty about the progress of his two-track effort to reverse Iraq's aggression. He said three regional leaders he had spoken to the day before "told me that these sanctions are working. Iraq is feeling the heat." But, he added, "I cannot predict just how long it will take to convince Iraq to withdraw from Kuwait. Sanctions will take time to have their full intended effect."[12]

Baker also used this period to guard against a political backlash at home by appealing to European and Arab partners for contributions to offset the costs of Operation Desert Shield. Kuwait and Saudi Arabia pledged billions at the outset. But the issue dogged the administration for months as resentment grew in the Congress against Japan and Germany (restricted by their post-World War II constitutions and by their publics from dispatching troops to the region) because of their seeming reluctance to share the costs of the allied military deployment. Both nations eventually pledged billions in aid but did little to ease the animosity toward them in the United States.

In the Middle East, Baker and Bush were also going to great lengths to hold the Arab coalition partners together. Baker broke the ice with Syria by agreeing to travel to Damascus for the first of several meetings with President Hafiz al-Asad, who joined the international coalition against his old foe, Saddam Hussein, and succeeded in easing some of the West's isolation of his country.[13] Egypt, which was also sending troops to the Gulf, was rewarded with a US decision to forgive its $7 billion military sales debt. Turkey received economic concessions. Jordan, which sided with Saddam, suffered severe economic punishment from the global economic embargo of Iraq and Saudi refusal to come to its aid.

Bush devoted the autumn months to midterm congressional campaigns, and his remarks on the stump often underscored the difficulty that he had in offering the country a compelling rationale for the Gulf deployments. He tried saying, delicately, that it was about oil, but polls showed that the American people did not support military action over oil supplies. He several times compared Saddam to Adolph Hitler, but this also seemed hyperbolic. If Saddam were Hitler, then was it enough simply to try and isolate him with sanctions? If he were as evil as Hitler, would he not have to be totally destroyed? At yet another point, Bush emphasized Saddam's nuclear potential, but experts said it was not clear that Iraq was on the verge of obtaining nuclear weapons. Baker, too, stumbled in trying to articulate the stakes, saying at one point that Saddam threatened the world's economic lifeline "and to bring it down to the average American citizen, let me say that means jobs. If you want to sum it up in one word, it's jobs."[14] Baker was widely criticized for the condescending tone of his remark.

As September drew to a close, the prospect that sanctions alone would force Saddam out of Kuwait seemed to wane. So far, at least, Saddam was defying efforts in Washington to modify his behavior, and many senior officials worried that Saddam, who watched the American political debate unfold on Cable News Network (CNN), was getting a skewed picture of US resolve.

In an unusual attempt to persuade Saddam to get out, Bush made a videotape to be broadcast to the people of Iraq in which he sought to demonize their leader. "The pain you now experience is a direct result of the path your leadership has chosen," Bush said. "Perhaps your leaders do not understand the strength of the forces united against them. Let me say clearly, there is no way Iraq can win."[15] Secretly, Bush had ordered a study to determine whether it was feasible for the United States to aid and abet others who wanted to topple Saddam from power.[16] This became part of an unannounced American policy, although many US officials figured it was a long shot. Bush and Baker repeatedly said in public that they would "not shed a tear" if Saddam were deposed.

The threats against Saddam escalated in September. Air Force Chief of Staff General Michael J. Dugan revealed in an interview that the allies were considering a massive bombing campaign against Baghdad and that Saddam would be a target.[17] Dugan was subsequently fired by Secretary of Defense Dick Cheney.

On September 26, at the annual session of the UN General Assembly, Shevardnadze delivered a significant warning to the Iraqi president. "In the context of recent events," he said,

> We should remind those who regard aggression as an acceptable form of behavior that the United Nations has the power to suppress acts of aggression. There is ample evidence that this right can be exercised. It will be, if the illegal occupation of Kuwait continues. There is enough unity in this regard in the Security Council, and there is also the will and a high degree of consensus in the world community.[18]

Saddam in August had called for a settlement in which he would leave Kuwait in exchange for Israel pulling out of the occupied territories, among other demands. This was rejected as "linkage" by the United States. Thus, Bush surprised the world when, in his own address to the General Assembly on October 1, he seemed to suggest some linkage with the Arab-Israeli conflict. "In the aftermath of Iraq's unconditional departure from Kuwait," he said, "I truly believe there may be opportunities—for Iraq and Kuwait to settle their differences permanently, for the states of the gulf themselves to build new arrangements for stability, and for all the states and the peoples of the region to settle the conflicts that divided the Arabs from Israel."[19]

Immediately after giving the speech, Bush insisted that he was not advocating "linkage" and told reporters there had been no change in his policy. In fact, however, the passage was intended for foreign, not domestic, consumption, as a promise to Saudi Arabia and Egypt that their participation in the Gulf coalition would later pay off with renewed US commitment to resolving the Arab-Israeli dispute.

At this point in the crisis, the two-track approach was in full flower. Military deployments were pouring into the region, and there was constant diplomatic activity to keep the coalition intact. But policymakers in Washington could only guess what course Saddam would follow. One senior official who had been involved in much of the decision-making predicted privately at this point that Saddam would begin probing for cracks in the coalition and later in the fall would seek to open a negotiating "bazaar" to get the best deal he could. This official worried whether the emir of Kuwait, who was in exile in a luxury hotel in Taif, would be tempted to make such a deal, whether the Saudis would remain firm, and whether the rest of the coalition could be kept together.[20]

The End of Sanctions, the Beginning of Force

Events soon deepened this concern. A violent clash between Israelis and Palestinians on the Temple Mount in Jerusalem diverted attention from the campaign against Saddam. It set off new tremors in the coalition, which was already getting bogged down in the Security Council in arguments over whether and how to seek reparations from Saddam.

Two major conclusions were dawning on official Washington. One was that sanctions did not appear to be changing Saddam's behavior. The other was that he appeared to be adding to his forces in Kuwait, digging in and preparing to fight. Thousands of tanks, mines, and troops in Kuwait, combined with fresh reports of atrocities against Kuwaitis, spoke volumes about Saddam's intentions.

For all these reasons, the entire complexion of the approach to Saddam began to change. Previously, the United States and its allies had been building a defensive military force to protect Saudi Arabia and trying to force Saddam out of Kuwait by sanctions. Now, Bush and his advisers began to give up on sanctions and turned their attention to making the military force in the desert an offensive one capable of expelling Saddam.

Explaining this shift in emphasis away from sanctions, one of Bush's top advisers recalled later,

> Many of the world leaders were telling us that sanctions would be effective in a matter of weeks. It became obvious through our intelligence and otherwise that this was simply not going to work, in terms of getting him out, before we began to see strains in the coalition. I think we all concluded that sanctions alone—alone, which was an important word in our formulation—were not going to do the job. That they could help as part of an overall integrated plan, but that we really didn't have much chance of getting it done without the application of force, or the threat of force, at that time. Over a period of five and a half months, we saw shortages only in tires, I mean in terms of significant stuff, we saw shortages in tires, we saw the price of a lot of foods go way up, but we didn't see food shortages of signifi-

cance. . . . We saw shortages in gasoline, and we believed there were shortages in spare parts and equipment— military.[21]

This shift did not occur in a vacuum. As the administration began to lose faith in sanctions, many critics began to see the sanctions as a way to avoid a potentially destructive war, and a debate about the effectiveness of the sanctions, past and future, intensified through the autumn months. Some Democrats suspected that the administration was rushing too quickly to bring the crisis to a climax because the White House did not want to wait eight months or a year for the sanctions to work, which would postpone the crisis into the next presidential election cycle.

Within the administration, the conclusion that Saddam was adding to his forces in Kuwait was a powerful reason not to wait any longer for sanctions. Cheney announced on October 5 that Saddam had deployed in excess of 350,000 troops, or about twenty divisions, in Kuwait and southern Iraq. Intelligence reports showed that Saddam was layering his forces, putting the poorly trained troops on the front lines, then the armored and better trained units behind them. "By mid-October we reached the point where the Pentagon was reporting that we were going to have enough on the scene to deter but not to eject them from Kuwait," recalled a policymaker close to Baker. "By October 15, we decided that sanctions plus deterrence would not get him out."[22]

This decision, which seemed unambiguous to policymakers at the time, may actually have been based on faulty assumptions about the size and strength of Iraqi forces. During and after the war, it became apparent that Saddam's forces were never at the maximum strength estimated publicly by the Defense Department. His troops had suffered massive desertions and morale was poor. But this phenomenon could not be detected by satellite photographs.

Bush and his top aides reached three critical decisions in this period. First, they decided to continue pouring thousands of troops into the region, changing the nature of the force from defensive to offensive. Second, they decided to try to win UN Security Council authorization for the use of force. And third, they decided to try to escalate the rhetoric against Saddam. This latter decision was based on intelligence estimates that the Iraqi president was not getting the message that the coalition was serious.[23]

General Colin Powell, chairman of the Joint Chiefs of Staff, flew to Saudi Arabia on October 21 to confer with Schwarzkopf about how much larger the allied force would have to be to expel Iraq from Kuwait. They talked for ten hours, during which time Schwarzkopf appealed to Powell for more troops, promising that the alliance would prevail if it came to war. They discussed the best timing for the offensive—in the first months of 1991.

By late October, unbeknownst to the American people or to most of the government, senior Pentagon officials had prepared a "Phase II" plan for Bush's approval that envisioned sending at least another 200,000 American troops to the region. The plan was known only to a handful of people. Most of the Pentagon bureaucracy saw the buildup as preparation not for reinforcements, in which case they would all stay, but as a troop rotation, under which some would come home. On October 25, Cheney, appearing on four successive television talk shows, hinted broadly that a troop increase might be coming, but he was not specific. On October 30, Powell and Cheney briefed the president on the second wave. Bush approved it shortly thereafter but decided to keep it secret until after the November 6 election.[24]

Baker and the others realized that such a large deployment would take time, and Baker set out to use the interval to lay the political groundwork for the use of force. Under Secretary Kimmitt began working on a three-page strategy memo for Baker covering the period from mid-October to November 30. Kimmitt suggested that to win congressional approval for the use of force, the administration first try to secure authorization from the Security Council. Brent Scowcroft, the president's national security adviser, balked, questioning why a new UN authorization was needed, saying the legal authority was already in place. Baker replied that the United States needed not just the legal authority but also a political consensus, and he departed for another tour of the Middle East, Europe, and the Soviet Union in pursuit of that consensus.

When Baker was in Moscow on November 8, he received an urgent message from Washington that Bush was about to announce the doubling of forces. The message irked him—he thought Bush planned to wait a few more days until he returned to Washington. Baker dashed off an angry note, but the White House decided to go ahead anyway, although there had been little or no consultation with Congress. Senator Sam Nunn, chairman of the Senate Armed Services Committee, was called to a restaurant's public pay phone to be informed of the decision by Cheney only about two hours before the president made his announcement.[25]

Once again, the administration had difficulty in balancing the various constituencies at home and abroad. The decision to double the number of troops was designed to present a credible military threat to Saddam. But the way it was handled only served to create more political questions at home, which then undermined the credibility of the military threat. One reason for this was that the entire American political argument over the Gulf was echoed around the globe on Cable News Network (CNN), watched almost constantly in government offices from Baghdad to Moscow to Washington.

The "augmentation" decision, as it was known inside the government, rekindled a much larger debate about Saddam's intentions and whether the United States was headed to war. The augmentation was a huge step toward the brink. If Saddam would not budge, then war seemed inevitable. This made it even more imperative to understand and change Saddam's behavior. The coalition forces became the fuse; only Saddam could stop the explosion.

One prevalent argument inside the administration was that Saddam knew one language—the use of force—and therefore the augmentation would be a sufficient threat to persuade him to pull out of Kuwait. But there were disturbing unknowns in this argument. First, did Saddam really get the message that the allies were willing to fight him? Some government analysts continued to doubt that he did. One of these analysts commented on November 10 that he saw two levels to Saddam's thinking: "He has gotten the idea that he's surrounded, because he has responded to that by trying to divide the coalition. But he has not realized that he could be crushed—he has not reached that level of fear of being crushed—that would prompt him to capitulate. So we have to get him to that level."[26]

Adding fuel to the debate about dealing with Saddam were Soviet envoy Yevgeniy Primakov's visits to Baghdad made on October 5 and 28. Part of Primakov's mission was to win the release of Soviet citizens held in Iraq, including a number of military specialists who were still under contract to the Iraqi government. But Primakov also subscribed to an approach to Saddam that was at odds with that used by the coalition. The coalition's basic assumption about Saddam was that he was a survivalist, that he would ultimately react to pressure and pull out of Kuwait. This assumption was based in part on Saddam's past behavior showing a pragmatic tendency to cut his losses at the last minute. Thus, the coalition insisted he be allowed no "partial solution" in the belief that with enough pressure Saddam would completely capitulate.

Primakov had a different view of Saddam. He saw the Iraqi leader as proud and suicidal. Instead of a binary choice, yes or no, withdraw or be defeated, Primakov said Saddam needed to be shown the exit, to be given some face-saving way to make a graceful departure. Primakov spelled out this view of Saddam after returning from his second trip to Baghdad. "During my conversations with Saddam Hussein," he said,

> I sensed—and this was not, it seems to me, put on—that he is really charged with the idea that Iraq has become, even following the military victory over Iran, practically a 'fortress under siege.' Saddam Hussein clearly evinced a 'Masada complex,' I would say. This was the last fortress holding out during the Jewish war, and its defenders, realizing the hopelessness of their position, declared their readiness to die, but not surrender.[27]

Primakov also described Saddam as a man consumed with paranoia and still holding to the hope that he could reap some gain—or at least avoid punishment—for his Kuwait adventure:

> As far as I understood it, questions arise for Saddam Hussein in respect to the future also: Will not an attack be launched against Iraq even if it withdraws its forces from Kuwait? Will the economic sanctions be lifted if he withdraws his forces? These misgivings of Iraq's are being fueled by a number of statements from which it may be concluded that some of the people who are making it their goal not only to force Iraq to quit Kuwait but also to eliminate the former's current regime and are 'forecasting' even the dismemberment of Iraq.[28]

The coalition strategy was evolving. The threat of force had replaced sanctions as the chief tool to pressure Saddam into retreat. But there were voices in the coalition who said even this would not influence Saddam. Egyptian President Hosni Mubarak's private advice to the United States was that pride would make it impossible for Saddam to simply turn around and leave. Bush, Baker, and other senior officials began to wonder whether anything would change Saddam's behavior. They had lit the fuse.

In the weeks after the augmentation, two storms were brewing. At home, Senator Nunn held a series of hearings on the Gulf in which former military leaders testified, advising caution. At the same time, Bush and Baker, struggling to keep the pressure on Saddam, were completing a final round of diplomacy designed to produce a UN resolution authorizing the use of force against Saddam.

The congressional hearings were widely televised, and although many of the military leaders were careful to praise Bush's leadership, they also cautioned him to wait for sanctions to work. "We should give sanctions a fair chance before we discard them," said Admiral William Crowe, the former chairman of the Joint Chiefs of Staff. "If in fact the sanctions will work in twelve to eighteen months instead of six months, the trade-off of avoiding war with its attendant sacrifices and uncertainties would, in my view, be more than worth it."[29]

The diplomacy leading to the UN resolution was perhaps the most frenzied and difficult that Bush and Baker had ever attempted. At one point, Bush, then in Paris, telephoned the prime minister of Malaysia, Mahathir Muhammad, who was dining in a Tokyo restaurant, to recruit his Security Council vote. Malaysia voted yes. Baker ventured to Yemen, which had supported Iraq, and held out the promise of American aid if Yemen would support the resolution—but Yemen would not.[30]

As Baker traveled through European and Arab capitals, he discovered the coalition was not united on the use-of-force resolution. Those in Saddam's neighborhood wanted to go to war as soon as possible. British Prime Minister Margaret Thatcher felt that the anti-Iraq alliance already had the necessary authority to fight. She believed a UN resolution might fail and could court disaster if saddled with conditions or vetoes. French President François Mitterrand wanted to avoid "automatic" use of force. But neither Britain nor France would stand in the way. Mitterrand said Bush asked him only one question: "Do you think it necessary to adopt a new resolution in the Security Council possibly authorizing the recourse to force?" and he replied, "Yes."[31]

China's foreign minister, Qian Qichen, indicated that Beijing would not stand in the way of a Security Council resolution, but US officials worried about what appeared to be an intense debate among the Chinese leadership. Chinese officials said they felt acutely the need to normalize relations with the United States. Shevardnadze went to Beijing because the Soviets, too, wanted to make sure they would not be embarrassed by a Chinese veto. Baker invited Qian to Washington, which appears to have been the key factor in persuading China not to veto the resolution. In the end, Beijing abstained.

Following a strategy that had been set earlier, Baker contacted and lobbied every one of the foreign ministers of the other members of the UN Security Council. In some cases, he went to extraordinary lengths to make the US case for the resolution, flying all the way to Colombia from the Middle East, for example. This round of meetings also led to the first such contact with Cuba since 1959—Baker met the Cuban foreign minister in New York City. (The members of the Security Council at this time were

Canada, China, Colombia, Cuba, Ethiopia, Finland, France, the Ivory Coast, Malaysia, Romania, the Soviet Union, the United Kingdom, the United States, Yemen, and Zaire.)

Bush and Baker also went to great lengths to bring the Kremlin along. In lengthy talks with Baker in Moscow, Shevardnadze was initially reluctant to consider the use of force, although his UN speech had broached the possibility. Shevardnadze instead raised other sanctions and pressures that might be used against Saddam. Baker said they were not enough. Baker shared with Shevardnadze secret details of military deployments in the Persian Gulf. Shevardnadze seemed to like the idea of setting a date for Saddam to pull out of Kuwait, emphasizing the importance of a "grace period" before the use of force. He insisted, however, the actual word "force" not be used, just as it was not in an earlier resolution authorizing the naval interceptions, which instead authorized the use of "all necessary means."[32]

Shevardnadze then took Baker to see Gorbachev at his country house outside Moscow, to which few Westerners have ever been invited. In the spirit of the earlier few months, Gorbachev, seated across the table from Baker, crossed his fingers tightly and held them up and said, "We've got to stay together like this."[33]

But Gorbachev did not endorse the use of force. Rather, he started thinking out loud about other possibilities, suggesting to Baker that perhaps there should be two resolutions, one setting a deadline now, another authorizing force later. This struck Baker as a serious mistake that would not pressure Saddam Hussein nearly as much as a single, strong resolution. Baker told Gorbachev two resolutions would be a step backward. Baker feared a second resolution would only give Saddam another chance to split the coalition and delay the day of reckoning.

Recalling Gorbachev's own address to the UN General Assembly in 1988, Baker said Saddam was testing the credibility of the United Nations by flaunting its previous resolutions and thus testing Gorbachev's own vision of how the world should work. "We cannot have the UN go the way of the League of Nations," Baker said. He appealed to Gorbachev's own "canon" that the world community should be governed by the "rule of law." That evening, Shevardnadze surprised Baker by telling reporters, somewhat reluctantly, that force might be required in the Gulf.[34]

Baker left Moscow without Gorbachev's commitment to anything. He and Bush then mounted a campaign in mid-November to persuade Moscow to give up the idea of two resolutions. Bush wrote a letter to Gorbachev in the days before they met at the European summit in Paris on November 19, urging him to abandon the concept of two resolutions. At the Paris summit, Gorbachev proposed to Bush a single "two-tier" resolution close to what Washington wanted. Baker, in words that he later regretted, told reporters to "stay tuned, and you'll get an answer tomorrow"[35] about Gorbachev's endorsement, raising expectations among the reporters that it was imminent. In fact, the Soviet president wanted more time before making his announcement so that he could send Shevardnadze to China and invite Iraqi Foreign Minister Tariq Aziz to Moscow for one last talk. The meeting with Aziz in Moscow went badly, and Gorbachev, apparently irritated by Iraq's refusal to release his citizens, unleashed some of his harshest criticism of Iraq just before the UN vote. According to an American source, Shevardnadze told Aziz in Moscow, "This is the last resolution" the global body would pass.[36]

Over the Thanksgiving holiday, Bush visited American troops in the Gulf. "We are not here on some exercise," he told them. "This is a real world situation and we're not walking away until our mission is done."[37]

On November 29, UN Resolution 678 was adopted by a vote of 12-2. Cuba and Yemen voted no and China abstained. The resolution offered Iraq a "pause of goodwill" until January 15 to evacuate Kuwait. After that, the resolution authorized "all necessary means" to force Iraq out. It was the turning point at which the war became inexorable, as long as Saddam did not douse the burning fuse. Baker knew that once the United States had won the UN resolution, there would be no choice but to use force if Saddam remained unmovable. He hoped to avoid war; he hoped that diplomacy would work; but he also realized that war was more likely than it had ever been before.

Endgame

On the night of the Security Council vote, Baker hosted a dinner with foreign ministers of the other Permanent Five members. There was a general consensus in the discussion that some new bilateral efforts needed to be launched with Baghdad to avert war.

Although Baker did not tell the ministers, this was also what Bush had in mind. Only a handful of officials knew in advance what Bush announced the next morning—an invitation to the Iraqi foreign minister, Tariq Aziz, to come to Washington and a proposal to send Baker to Baghdad, "to go the extra mile for peace."

After months of insisting that Iraq not be rewarded for its aggression, of rejecting such bilateral diplomacy on grounds that it would be a reward, Bush announced a stunning about-face. Bush's offer triggered a spurt of goodwill between Washington and Baghdad. Saddam accepted the proposal, and then, in a surprise of his own, freed all the hostages. The two sides seemed to be heading down the path of negotiation, and, in fact, the jockeying had already begun over the dates and terms of a possible meeting. Outwardly, both sides appeared to be making concessions to the other.

Privately, however, Bush and Baker were growing pessimistic. The overture to Baghdad in their view was necessary only to relieve the domestic pressure that was building on the administration. In the weeks ahead, they came to the conclusion that the overture was going nowhere. Saddam, they felt, was stalling for time, hoping to further delay military action and play on American fears of war.

Those fears were still burning. When Baker appeared before the Senate Foreign Relations Committee on December 5, many senior Democrats spoke out against the early use of force. Senator Paul Sarbanes (D-Md.), in a typical comment, said the augmentation "almost takes you irresistibly down the path of going to war." He said the United States must "sustain the sanctions policy for a period of time sufficiently long to give it a chance to work." Sarbanes added, "Now, I cannot say to a family that loses a son or daughter in a conflict that may well take place in the next sixty to ninety days, that we exhausted every possibility for a peaceful resolution before this happened, because the sanctions option has not been exhausted."

But the two-track policy that Bush had launched in August was now effectively dead. Baker told the panel,

> After four months of a stringent embargo, no one doubts that sanctions are having some effect on the Iraqi economy, but we have to face the difficult fact, I think, that no one can tell you that sanctions alone will ever be able to impose a high enough cost on Saddam Hussein to get him to withdraw. So far, all available evidence suggests that they have had little if any effect on his inclination to withdraw.

As the year ended, Bush's frustration deepened. Saddam continued to stall on the dates Bush had first suggested for the talks. The United States had offered to send Baker to Baghdad on fifteen separate dates, but the only one Saddam proposed was three days before the UN deadline for the use of force. The president felt he was being trapped and expressed chagrin that he had not set a shorter timetable from the start. "I wish now that I'd been a little more explicit in my first announcement on what I meant by mutually convenient dates," he acknowledged.[38]

If Saddam was hoping that time was on his side, the sudden resignation of Soviet Foreign Minister Shevardnadze may have reinforced it. Shevardnadze had been a pillar of the US-Soviet cooperation that had denied Iraq a superpower ally and patron as might have been expected in the past. But Shevardnadze was also under intense pressure at home from hardliners who accused him of making too many concessions to the United States and of following Washington's lead in the Gulf. Although Shevardnadze's resignation was prompted by larger forces—he expressed fear that Gorbachev was abandoning his commitment to reform and turning to authoritarianism—his departure was an acute loss to Baker. The Gulf crisis had coincided exactly with the zenith of Shevardnadze's power and influence. Although Baker realized that Gorbachev could not easily pull back from his commitments to oppose Saddam, the Shevardnadze resignation marked the apogee of cooperation between Washington and Moscow on the Gulf.

Just as Saddam's behavior had been a puzzle for many months, so did many in Washington question whether Bush would take the nation to war. Some felt that Bush, the ultimate pragmatist, still planned to stop short of the brink and strike a deal. But others saw in the president a steely determination traced back to his own service in the Pacific theater and his sense that he was an heir to the tradition of the "wise men"—that elite group of businessmen and diplomats who guided US foreign policy after World War II.

Over the holidays, during a twelve-day stay at Camp David, Bush apparently wrestled with the war decision. When he returned, he was resigned to launching the offensive, if necessary. He offered one last gesture, proposing that Baker and Aziz meet in Geneva. Iraq accepted the offer, and Bush, somewhat unexpectedly, instructed Baker that he could not go on to Baghdad after the Geneva meeting. This decision was important because many analysts believed Aziz could not make any significant concessions by himself—that Baker would have to deal directly with Saddam for war to be averted.

In the early weeks of the crisis, American policymakers felt vulnerable and cheated by Saddam, but as the period before the war drew to a close, they felt superior and confident. They also believed that Saddam did not understand that in dealing with the United States he was facing a superpower, one with enormous resources. Over and over again they had tried to get this message through to him, that he could not possibly win a military conflict, that he was miscalculating on a tragic scale. But the gulf of misunderstanding between Washington and Baghdad was never breached.

In the early period, the United States and its allies had offered no graceful exit, no reward for aggression, no partial solution. This remained the case until the end. However, Baker carried to Geneva a brief that, while emphasizing the importance of an unconditional withdrawal, also sought to underscore for Iraq a number of incentives to do so. The most important was survival: If Saddam pulled out unconditionally, he would not be attacked. Also on the list was a hint that the Arab-Israeli conflict would be addressed after the Gulf crisis was resolved (as Bush had hinted at the UN), that if Saddam pulled out he would spare his country further economic pain, and that the United States and its allies would support some effort to resolve Iraq's border dispute with Kuwait—as the UN resolutions had envisioned.

But because Saddam did not accept the basic premise on which these incentives were offered—that he would be crushed in a war—he did not even get to the point of accepting them.

At the outset of the meeting at Geneva's Intercontinental Hotel, Aziz was offered both a sealed 8x10 manila envelope carrying the original of a letter from Bush to Saddam and a photocopy to read. The letter had been carefully drafted in Washington and encapsulated everything that Bush was trying to get across to Saddam, including the president's uncertainty about whether Saddam was getting the message.

"We stand today at the brink of war between Iraq and the world," it began. The letter went on to say that if Iraq complied with the UN resolutions it would "gain the opportunity to rejoin the international community." But if not, the letter said, the future would be grim. "Unless you withdraw from Kuwait completely and without condition, you will lose more than Kuwait."[39]

Aziz read the copy of the letter. Sitting next to him was Barzan Takriti, Saddam's half brother, who once headed Iraq's internal security service, but he did not look at the letter. Aziz then refused to accept it, complaining that it was not in a tone fit for communication between heads of state.

Baker shot back, "It seems to me you're taking on a heck of a responsibility since you're the only one on your side of the table who's read it."

"You may publish it in your media," Aziz retorted.

"We may publish it in our media, and we may not," Baker said.

Baker and others on his team thought Aziz, a professional diplomat, was flustered at this point. The letter lay in the middle of the table for the six hours and twenty-seven minutes of the talks; even during a break, Baker ordered a security man to guard the room because the letter was still on the table. At the end of the talks, Baker gestured toward the envelope.

"Are you sure, Mr. Minister, that you don't want to take this message?" he asked Aziz. Aziz said he was sure.

In his presentation, Baker said Saddam had made a series of miscalculations and should not miscalculate again. Baker warned the Iraqi minister that the coalition—and not Iraq—would determine the terms of the war. Baker told Aziz it would be nothing like Iraq's eight-year war with Iran.

But once Aziz made his opening presentation, it was clear there was not going to be any breakthrough. Aziz talked at length about Iraq's view of the entire Middle East in terms quite familiar to the US officials, with a heavy emphasis on fear of Israel and laced with references to a conspiracy among Israel, Kuwait, and the United States. Aziz singled out the US decision to suspend the commodity credit grain program with Iraq, subsequent limits on US technology exports, and Iraq's anger over Kuwait's oil production, which Iraq considered excessive.[40]

Finally, Aziz rejected Baker's warning on what kind of a war would ensue. He said, "Your Arab allies will desert you. They will not kill other Arabs. Your alliance will crumble and you will be left lost in the desert. You don't know the desert because you have never ridden on a horse or a camel."[41]

In the aftermath of Geneva, the Senate voted 52-47 and the House 250-183 to authorize the use of force. A last-minute peace mission by UN Secretary-General Javier Pérez de Cuéllar failed. Bush wrote a letter to congressional leaders stating that all efforts to eject Iraq peacefully from Kuwait, including economic sanctions, had failed.[42]

Saddam still believed that it was better to fight the coalition than be humiliated. He was an enigma to the decision-makers in Washington who could not fathom why he would lead his country into war. Two days before the war began, one of these policymakers guessed that Saddam was feeling his oats, that he was a small-time bully who had to make a point and was out parading on the street, flexing his muscles, showing everyone that he had eluded the authorities once again, that he would only wait a day or two and give up.

But like all the other guessing, this, too, was wrong. Saddam had made an even bigger miscalculation. The bombing began—and the coalition held.

Notes

1. David Hoffman, diplomatic correspondent for The *Washington Post*, traveled with US Secretary of State James A. Baker III in the fall and winter of 1990-1991 as the secretary created the coalition of nations that opposed the Iraqi invasion of Kuwait. This account is based on his coverage of Baker's activities and interviews with several of the primary participants.

2. Testimony of US Permanent Representative to the United Nations Thomas Pickering, Senate Foreign Relations Committee, September 20, 1990.

3. UN *Chronicle,* December 1990, p. 21.

4. An account of Soviet decision-making in this period was published in an article in *Komsomolskaya Pravda*, February 16, 1991. The article, titled "Who Determined the Soviet Union's Position in the Conflict Between Iraq and Kuwait and How," relied heavily on a Soviet diplomat identified only as a "member of E. A. Shevardnadze's immediate entourage" who served as Soviet note-taker in these meetings. Others have identified the note-taker as Sergey Tarasenko, a senior aide to Shevardnadze, although he was not named in the article.

5. Transcript of Baker and Shevardnadze remarks to reporters, August 3, 1990.

6. *Komsomolskaya Pravda.*

7. Crisis in the Persian Gulf, hearings and mark up of the House Foreign Affairs Committee, September 4 and 27, October 18, 1990.

8. For many months afterward, this was a source of tension between White House and State Department policymakers. Those at State acknowledged that shaping public opinion was the responsibility of the president, but they felt that the White House staff and the president had not done an adequate job articulating the stakes and bringing along the various publics. Baker repeatedly attempted in his own speeches to do this, but the secretary of state did not have the same impact as the president. Those at the White House naturally resented this attitude as unnecessary interference from Foggy Bottom.

9. Schwarzkopf news conference, February 27, 1991.

10. A senior US official in interview with author.

11. Interview with author.

12. President Bush address to a joint session of Congress, September 11, 1990. *Dispatch,* Vol. 1, No. 3, p. 91. Department of State, Washington, DC

13. In addition to a number of meetings with Baker before and after the war, Asad also met with President Bush in Geneva. However, the United States did not remove Syria from the list of nations sponsoring terrorism, and Baker said he raised the issue every time he met with the Syrian president.

14. *Washington Post*, November 14, 1990, p. A-25.

15. *Dispatch*, State Department Bureau of Public Affairs, September 24, 1990.

16. Woodward, Bob, *The Commanders* (New York: Simon & Schuster, 1991), p. 237.

17. *Washington Post*, September 16, 1990, p. A-1.

18. See note 1.

19. See note 1.

20. See note 1.
21. Interview with author.
22. Interview with author.
23. There continued to be differences in the administration over the tone and content of its rhetorical approach to Saddam. Bush, in the final throes of the campaign, had delivered the most emotional denunciations of Saddam. Eventually, some top Bush advisers, including Baker and Scowcroft, urged the president to halt the references to Hitler and tone down his approach.
24. *Washington Post*, December 2, 1990, p. 1.
25. *Washington Post*, December 16, 1990.
26. Interview with author.
27. *Literaturnaya Gazeta*, November 7, 1990, pp. 1, 10.
28. *Ibid.*
29. Nunn's hearings were followed by another set chaired by House Armed Services Chairman Les Aspin (D-Wis.), who produced a set of influential "white papers" weighing the risks of war and continued sanctions. The white papers proved to be remarkably prescient. Aspin predicted a "phased" military campaign against Iraq relying largely on air power at the outset. He also said the risks were small that American forces would suffer large numbers of casualties. "There is little risk of a long, drawn-out war," he said.
30. This account of UN diplomacy is based on the author's interviews at the time and subsequently. An earlier account appeared in the *Washington Post*, December 2, 1990, p. 1.
31. See note 1.
32. See note 1.
33. Senior official who was present in the talks.
34. See note 1.
35. See note 1.
36. See note 1.
37. See note 1.
38. Bush's original proposal was for Baker to go to Baghdad "at a mutually convenient time between December 15 and January 15 of next year."
39. See full text of letter in Appendix A.
40. This account of the Aziz meeting is based on the author's interviews with three of the six US participants.
41. *New York Times*, Sunday, March 3, 1991, p. A-1.
42. Bush wrote a letter to Congress in mid-January, "Notwithstanding the substantial economic impact of sanctions to date, and even if sanctions were to continue to be enforced for an additional six to twelve months, economic hardship alone is highly unlikely to compel Saddam to retreat from Kuwait or cause regime-threatening popular discontent in Iraq."

5

The Soviet Union and Iraq's Invasion of Kuwait

Carolyn McGiffert Ekedahl

MOSCOW'S UNPRECEDENTED COOPERATION with Washington throughout the Gulf crisis of 1990-1991 dramatically illustrated the Gorbachev leadership's new approach to regional conflict situations. The Soviet Union's endorsement of a major US role in the Gulf and its support for UN initiatives designed to force Saddam Hussein's withdrawal from Kuwait stand in sharp contrast to its previous opposition to any US military deployments and its former exploitation of regional tensions to undermine US interests and further its own.

Soviet cooperation permitted creation of an international coalition and passage of UN resolutions imposing sanctions and endorsing the use of force to compel Iraq's withdrawal. Without that cooperation, allied military action against Iraq would have been far more problematic.

Moscow's policy toward the Gulf War reflected Soviet commitment to the centrality of the US-Soviet relationship and masked a number of fundamental differences with the United States over how the crisis should be resolved. The Soviets consistently urged a peaceful solution achieved through mediation and compromise, and they tried to prevent both the air and ground operations against Iraq.

President Mikhail Gorbachev's efforts in mid-February to mediate an Iraqi withdrawal and thus prevent a land war raised doubts in the West about Moscow's commitment to the coalition. When the initiative failed, however, the Soviets resumed support for coalition policies and endorsed UN Resolution 687, which was passed on April 3; the resolution formally ended the Gulf War and imposed firm conditions on Iraq, requiring payment of reparations and elimination of its weapons of mass destruction. Moscow also contributed military personnel to the UN force deployed to the demilitarized zone between Iraq and Kuwait in the wake of the cease-fire.

New Thinking and the Gulf (1985-1990)

When Gorbachev came to power in March 1985, the Soviet Union's position in the Persian Gulf was weak. Moscow had close ties to only two regional states—Iraq and Kuwait. Its relations with Iran were poor, and it had no diplomatic relations with the conservative Arab states of the Gulf, with the exception of Kuwait. Its position had been adversely affected both by the occupation of Afghanistan and by its ambivalent approach to the Iran-Iraq war.

By early 1991, Moscow's position was significantly better. Soviet relations with Iran had improved considerably, and Moscow had established relations with all the conservative Arab states of the Gulf.[1] Although dramatic regional developments, including the Soviet withdrawal from Afghanistan, were largely responsible for the change in Moscow's position, the policies of new thinking played an important role.

Soviet new thinking is based on the conviction that foreign policy must serve domestic policy, that economic and political restructuring (perestroika) has the highest priority, that Moscow's previous Third World policies had served its interests poorly, and that international stability and improved relations with the United States must take precedence over Moscow's regional interests and clients.

With the advent of new thinking, the Third World, previously considered a safe arena for competition with the United States, was put in a broader context. The linkage between Third World policies and more pressing national interests was recognized. In order to proceed with restructuring, Moscow sought reduced military spending and access to Western capital and technology; for this, it needed improved relations with the West.

In the Persian Gulf, as elsewhere, Gorbachev has pursued a policy based on decreased reliance on military instruments of policy, the pursuit of regional stability, cooperation with the United States on a broad range of issues, and the use of the United Nations to bolster Soviet positions.

Through its new policies, the Soviet Union has tried to enhance its image as a responsible superpower intent on resolving regional disputes peacefully.

Soviet policy toward the Iran-Iraq war (1980-1988) changed only marginally when Gorbachev came to power—and for good reason. The policy had been a pragmatic one, designed to keep Moscow's options open and limit damage to its relations with the warring powers. The conflict had not entailed the risk of confrontation with the United States and had caused no severe strains in superpower relations.

Throughout the war, Moscow and Washington shared the common objectives of avoiding a broader conflict and preventing either Iran or Iraq from emerging as the dominant regional power. Within the parameters imposed by these objectives, however, Moscow maintained its focus on enhancing its own regional position and undermining, or at least limiting, that of the United States.

Seeking to prevent a victory by either antagonist, Moscow shifted its support from one to the other. During the period from late 1980 until mid-1982, when Iraq seemed on the verge of a military victory, the Soviets implemented an arms embargo on both parties. This action was directed far more at Iraq, with which the Soviet Union had an extensive arms-supply relationship, than at Iran. After 1982, when Iran expelled the Iraqis from its territory and moved its own troops into Iraq, the Soviets resumed arms deliveries to Baghdad and supported Iraqi terms for ending the war.

Following Gorbachev's assumption of power, the Soviets tried to improve relations with Iran. During late 1985 and most of 1986, bilateral relations improved as Soviet First Deputy Foreign Minister Georgiy Korniyenko visited Tehran and a number of economic meetings were held. Iranian advances on the ground in Iraq in late 1986, however, led to increased international pressure on Iran, and Soviet-Iranian relations again deteriorated. Moscow supported UN Resolution 598, passed in late 1987 at Iraq's request, calling for an end to the war.

Regional developments during 1987 produced an eventual Soviet tilt back toward Iran. Kuwait, fearing Iranian attacks on its tankers in the Gulf, had requested security assistance from both the United States and the Soviet Union in late 1986. Moscow's agreement to lease three Kuwaiti oil tankers—and, by implication, to provide protection—precipitated US decisions to reflag eleven Kuwaiti tankers and protect them with US naval forces.

As the United States engaged in a naval buildup in the Gulf, the Iranians decided to seek improved relations with Moscow to avoid confronting both superpowers simultaneously. They softened their anti-Soviet rhetoric and upgraded bilateral contacts. The Soviets, also concerned by the increase in the US naval presence, responded positively to Tehran's gestures, expanding trade relations and delaying the imposition of sanctions called for in UN resolution 598. But this policy slowed the pace of the Soviet Union's improving relations with the conservative Arab states of the Gulf and contrasts sharply with Moscow's willingness to support the UN sanctions imposed on Iraq in 1990.

Moscow's concern about the US naval buildup in the Gulf was rooted in a primary tenet of "old thinking"—the need to prevent a shift in the regional military balance in favor of the United States. Although the Soviets did not counter the US action with a buildup of their own, they did become preoccupied with limiting the US buildup. Part of their response, the tilt back toward Iran, suggested a traditional attempt to correct a perceived shift in the balance of power.

At the same time, however, Moscow took initiatives that reflected new thinking. It tried to coordinate policy with the United States, proposing a joint reflagging of Kuwaiti tankers; the Reagan administration flatly rejected the proposal.[2] The Soviets then urged the internationalization of naval forces in the Gulf, suggesting the creation of a UN naval force to replace the US, British, and French fleets there.[3] This proposal, too, failed to generate a favorable response.

Moscow's careful policy toward the Iran-Iraq conflict paid off during the late 1980s. Even before the war ended in 1988, Soviet-Iranian relations had improved considerably. In 1989, the Soviets agreed to sell military equipment to Iran, and the first delivery of MIG 29s arrived in 1990.[4] Soviet-Iraqi relations, which had fluctuated during most of the war in direct opposition to Moscow's policy toward Iran, also improved because of Soviet arms deliveries, credit extensions, and support for Iraqi peace efforts.

Reaction to the Iraqi Invasion (1990-1991)

The Soviet Union's efforts to maintain balance in its relations with Iran and Iraq throughout their war, particularly its equivocation about imposing UN sanctions, made its reaction to Iraq's invasion of Kuwait even more dramatic. Moscow immediately denounced the invasion, suspended military deliveries to Baghdad, and demanded Iraq's unconditional withdrawal.[5] Its unequivocal abandonment of Iraq was the first important aspect of the Soviet approach to the crisis.

The second important policy approach was Moscow's strong backing of UN efforts to force Iraq's withdrawal. On August 2, it voted for UN Resolution 660, which condemned the aggression and demanded Iraq's withdrawal. It subsequently supported all other relevant UN resolutions; the most important of these imposed trade sanctions on Baghdad, permitted the use of force to enforce those sanctions, authorized the use of "all appropriate measures" against Iraq if it did not withdraw from Kuwait by January 15, 1991, and imposed harsh penalties on Iraq at the war's end.

Perhaps most importantly, Moscow moved immediately to coordinate policy with Washington rather than seeking to exploit the crisis to undermine the United States. On August 3, following a meeting at the Moscow airport, US Secretary of State James A. Baker III and Soviet Foreign Minister Eduard Shevardnadze issued a joint statement endorsing the United Nations condemnation of Iraq's invasion and urging the suspension of all arms shipments to Iraq.[6] Baker termed the statement "historic," noting that in the past the two nations would have viewed such a conflict "through an East-West prism."[7] The meeting marked the beginning of a period of frequent communication between the superpowers, including a series of high-level meetings to coordinate policy and prevent misunderstanding.

Reports that Moscow provided the United States with intelligence information about Iraqi military capabilities received considerable attention, not least in Baghdad. The facts are far from clear. Some Soviet officials have indicated that information was provided, some have denied it, some have done both.

In early August, US officials claimed that the Soviet Union had provided the United States with significant details on the operational technology of Scud surface-to-surface missiles and other Soviet weapon systems in the Iraqi arsenal.[8] Soviet Foreign Ministry spokesman Yuriy Gremitskiy denied that intelligence contacts had reached that level.[9]

In a meeting with executives of the Associated Press on September 20, KGB Chief Vladimir Kryuchkov expressed a willingness to share intelligence on Iraq with the United States. He said the Soviets had not made such an offer directly because they had been rebuffed in the past but indicated that if the CIA wanted help, "you can be sure our reaction would be positive."[10]

General Mikhail Moiseyev, chief of the Soviet General Staff, stated in September that he had provided technical information to the US embassy with regard to Soviet weapons used by the Iraqi military.[11] In January, however, Moiseyev denied Western press reports to this effect, saying that to have provided such information would have been a breach of Moscow's friendship treaty with Iraq.[12]

Iraq's concern about the possible transfer of intelligence information from Moscow to Washington was reflected in a harsh warning in October that Soviets remaining in Iraq would not be allowed to return home if Moscow gave military intelligence to the United States.[13] Two days after the Iraqi warning, a Soviet presidential aide flatly rejected allegations that the Soviets would give the United States secret information on Iraq's military potential.[14]

Available evidence strongly suggests that the Soviets did, in fact, provide information early in the crisis but ended this cooperation—at any rate denied it—to ensure the safety of Soviet citizens in Iraq and limit damage to Soviet relations in the Arab world.

Policy Choices

Shortly after the invasion, *Izvestiya* commentator Aleksandr Bovin observed that, had the crisis occurred five or ten years earlier, Moscow would have declared its neutrality and condemned the deployment of US forces to Saudi Arabia; Washington would have accused the Soviets of supporting aggression and indulging the terrorist regime in Baghdad.[15] In view of past Soviet policies, it also seems likely that Moscow would have prevented UN action against Iraq by using, or threatening to use, its Security Council veto and might have continued to supply arms to Baghdad. Such a Soviet policy would have created an entirely different environment for US efforts to reverse the invasion. International backing for its course would have been weakened and Iraq's position strengthened by potential, or actual, Soviet support.

The Soviet Union had maintained good relations with Iraq for decades. The two countries had a Friendship and Cooperation Treaty, signed in 1972, and a mutually beneficial arms supply relationship. In August 1990, the Iraqi debt to Moscow was an estimated $6 billion, and Moscow had from 7,000 to 9,000 military and economic experts and their dependents living in Iraq, earning much-needed hard currency for the Soviet Union.[16]

By siding with the international coalition against Iraq, Moscow risked default on debt repayment and the loss of lucrative contracts. Iraq reportedly did stop payment on the debt shortly after the invasion,[17] and as remaining Soviet specialists were finally allowed to leave Iraq on the eve of the January 15 deadline, Moscow negotiated the "temporary suspension" of their contracts.[18] An article in the Soviet journal *Arguments and Facts* in January 1991 claimed that the Soviet loss as a result of the conflict was already over $1 billion.[19]

The Soviet leadership justified its abandonment of Iraq on grounds of morality and security. In a speech on August 17, Gorbachev called the invasion a "violation of everything the world community now pins its hopes on as it seeks to put civilization on the tracks of peaceful development." He said Moscow had "no other choice" than to join the West in condemning Iraq because the use of force to redraw borders could "set off a perilous chain reaction endangering the entire world community."[20] Gorbachev may well have been thinking about the challenges facing the Soviet Union itself as internal pressures for a return to independence by the Baltic republics intensified.

A TASS release in early August put Soviet policy in the context of East-West relations. It asserted that the unprecedented US-Soviet cooperation was based on the understanding that the two countries "no longer regard each other as military opponents" and that policy can "no longer be determined by obsolete stereotypes like East-West rivalry."[21] Commentator Stanislav Kondrashov elaborated:

> By sacrificing relations with another dictatorship the Soviet Union once again confirms its adherence to the new path—the abandonment of confrontation with the West, which distorted priorities in the foreign and domestic policies of the Soviet leadership and was one of the deep-seated causes of our present historical crisis. The new relations of cooperation and interaction, particularly with the United States, are now seen as one of the chief levers capable of lifting us out of the crisis. The strategic advantage in this area (both political and practical) will more than make up for the loss of friendship with Saddam Hussein.[22]

Cooperation with the United States

Moscow's focus on cooperation with the United States throughout the crisis became clear immediately, although the rapid coordination of policy after the invasion was largely serendipitous. The meeting between Secretary Baker and Foreign Minister Shevardnadze at Moscow airport the day after the Iraqi invasion emerged from previously scheduled meetings

August 1 and 2 in Irkutsk, where the two men agreed to meet immediately if the Gulf situation deteriorated. This agreement set up their emergency meeting at Moscow airport and the issuance of their historic joint statement on August 3.[23]

The Baker-Shevardnadze meeting was the first in a series of high-level meetings including several between President George Bush and President Gorbachev and set the stage for continuous bilateral dialogue throughout the crisis. In spite of fundamental differences, the superpowers were able to sustain a coordinated approach.

Moscow's support for UN Resolution 665, passed on August 25 and authorizing the use of force to enforce sanctions against Iraq, marked the formal reversal of its consistent opposition to the use of US military muscle in Third World regions. The decision was a clear personal victory for Shevardnadze, who had established a close working relationship with Baker and who was a strong proponent of giving US-Soviet relations the highest priority in Soviet foreign policy.

The Bush-Gorbachev summit in Helsinki in early September produced a second joint statement affirming cooperation. The two leaders stressed their preference for peaceful resolution of the crisis but agreed that if peaceful efforts failed, they would consider additional steps "consistent with the UN Charter."[24] Continuing the pattern of high-level contacts, Baker met with Gorbachev and Shevardnadze in Moscow on September 13 and laid the foundation for passage on September 25 of UN Resolution 670, banning passenger and cargo flights into Iraq.[25]

Following Shevardnadze's meetings with Secretary Baker and President Bush at the United Nations in October, a third joint statement was released stressing US-Soviet determination to strengthen the United Nations peace-keeping functions and endorsing continued sanctions against Iraq.[26] And in late January, following a visit to the United States by the new Soviet foreign minister, Aleksandr Bessmertnykh, a fourth joint statement called for Iraqi withdrawal from Kuwait and indicated that in the post-crisis era the two superpowers would work together to resolve other regional issues.

The United States expended considerable diplomatic effort to gain Soviet endorsement for a UN resolution sanctioning the use of force against Iraq if it did not withdraw from Kuwait. Baker visited Moscow in early November but failed to win a Soviet commitment. While Baker was in Moscow, President Bush announced the dispatch of 200,000 additional troops to the Gulf, indicating that the United States was now preparing for offensive action.

On November 19, Baker and Shevardnadze met again in Paris. By this time, the Soviet Union had emerged as the pivotal player in determining whether the United States would obtain passage of the resolution it sought, but Shevardnadze indicated that Moscow still had not decided. The Soviet position was obscured by high-level Soviet statements including one by Gorbachev urging continued pursuit of a peaceful solution.[27] Bush also failed to get a clear commitment to the resolution in a subsequent meeting with Gorbachev in Paris.[28]

By November 26, the Soviets had apparently decided that Saddam was not prepared to be flexible. They demanded that Iraq release the more than 3,000 Soviet citizens still remaining in Iraq and charged for the first time publicly that Baghdad was preventing their departure.[29] In a meeting with Iraqi Foreign Minister Tariq Aziz, Gorbachev reportedly warned that Iraq faced the consequences of a tough UN resolution unless it withdrew from Kuwait. These remarks signaled that Moscow was now prepared to support the UN resolution sought by Washington.

All that remained was for the United States and the Soviet Union to agree on the time frame, and Washington acceded to Moscow's wish for a delayed deadline of January 15.[30] On November 29, 1990, with most of the fifteen members represented by their foreign ministers, the Security Council adopted Resolution 678, permitting the use of "all appropriate measures" to gain Iraq's withdrawal from Kuwait; only Cuba and Yemen were opposed, and China abstained.[31]

Washington's efforts to forge an international coalition in support of its policy toward the Iraqi invasion led it to make numerous gestures toward Moscow. These included suggestions that the Soviet Union contribute forces to the multinational force, that Washington would abandon opposition to a Soviet role in the Middle East peace process, that proposed UN resolutions be modified, and that caution be exercised in linking Iraqi withdrawal from Kuwait with action to address the Arab-Israel conflict.

Seeking Soviet support for the US decision to send troops to Saudi Arabia in early August, Baker invited the Soviet Union to contribute naval or ground units to a multilateral force. On the eve of the Bush-Gorbachev summit in early September 1990, senior officials of the US administration indicated that the United States would be "very happy" if the Soviets agreed to send forces—particularly ground forces—to the Gulf.[32] On December 11, the *Washington Post,* citing informed Soviet sources, reported that during their meetings in Houston, Baker had urged Shevardnadze to commit a token Soviet troop contingent to the multinational force in the Gulf.[33]

Washington had never before approved, much less encouraged, the dispatch of Soviet forces to a Third World area, and its new position contrasted sharply with its refusal to consider cooperating with the Soviets in forming a naval force in the Gulf during the Iran-Iraq war.[34] Administration officials explained that, given the current policy of the Soviet Union, a "cooperative approach is warranted."[35]

At the summit in early September 1990, President Bush sought to calm Soviet fears about US intentions by assuring Gorbachev that American troops in Saudi Arabia would leave after the crisis was over.[36] In subsequent talks, Baker and Shevardnadze discussed the prospect of a realignment of forces in the Persian Gulf. US officials indicated that the two men had begun sketching out ideas for a long-term "regional security structure."[37]

During his September meeting with Gorbachev, Bush explicitly dropped any remaining US opposition to Soviet involvement in a Middle East peace conference; according to administration officials, he invited Moscow to play a greater diplomatic role.[38]

To gain Soviet support for UN Resolution 665 of August 25, allowing UN members with naval forces in the region to enforce sanctions, the United States agreed to changes in the resolution, modifying references to the use of force and referring to the UN's Military Staff Committee as the coordinating body for enforcing the resolution.[39] Washington eventually deferred to Moscow with respect to the date for a deadline for Resolution 678, accepting January 15. The United States reportedly also indicated that it would consult with Moscow before actually giving any order to open fire in the Gulf.[40]

Deferring to Moscow's wishes, the United States participated in a formal meeting of the UN Military Staff Committee in New York in October 1990. The committee is composed of the chiefs of staff of the five permanent members of the Security Council; its functions, as envisaged by the UN's founding members, are to organize and implement the Security Council's military decisions. This was the highest-level meeting ever held by the committee and dealt with the possible expansion of its role in coordinating enforcement of UN economic sanctions against Iraq—although

US sources stressed that there were no plans to put the huge multilateral force in the Gulf region under a unified command.[41]

The US-Soviet joint statement of January 30, 1991, was the most dramatic of Washington's concessions to Moscow. For the first time, by including language both on the Gulf crisis and on the need to resolve other regional issues (particularly Arab-Israeli tensions), the United States implied acknowledgment of linkage between the two, although the statement said only that efforts to resolve other regional issues would be redoubled after the Gulf crisis ended. On the crisis itself, the statement included language more flexible than the United States had used before, indicating that if Iraq made a commitment to pull out of Kuwait and took immediate steps to do so, hostilities could end.[42]

Baker's willingness to accept this language probably reflected growing concern that Moscow's support for the coalition was weakening and that the Soviets might be tempted to join with other nations in calling for a cease-fire. That perception had been reinforced by Bessmertnykh, who, on the eve of his departure for Washington, had expressed concern about the intense US bombing and had indicated a belief that the campaign against Iraq might be going beyond the UN goal of freeing Kuwait. The United States undoubtedly hoped that Washington's agreement to the language of the joint statement would keep Moscow firmly within the alliance by providing assurances that Iraq's destruction was not sought and that the Soviet Union would be a party to any postwar diplomacy in the region.[43] The statement may have led the Soviets to believe, however, that Washington would be receptive to a mediation effort designed to find a compromise and eliminate the need for a ground war.

Finally, in spite of its opposition to the Soviet mediation effort of February 1991 and its commitment to the ground offensive, the United States responded carefully and diplomatically to Moscow's unilateral initiative. President Bush reportedly told Gorbachev in a telephone conversation on February 21 that he considered the quest for peace "useful" in spite of his "serious concerns" about the Soviet formula and his insistence on Iraq's unconditional withdrawal.[44]

The abrupt resignation of Foreign Minister Shevardnadze in late December 1990 raised questions about Moscow's commitment to its policy in the Gulf. Shevardnadze had held productive meetings with Secretary Baker in Houston and with President Bush in Washington in mid-December and submitted his resignation shortly after his return to Moscow. The Soviets quickly assured Washington that the resignation would not affect their policy toward the Iraqi invasion, and the appointment of Aleksandr Bessmertnykh, formerly Soviet ambassador to the United States and a proponent of new thinking, sent a reassuring message of continuity. The pattern of high-level coordination did, in fact, continue. During the Soviet mediation effort in February, Presidents Bush and Gorbachev communicated frequently by telephone. Nonetheless, Shevardnadze's resignation combined with criticism within the Soviet Union of his policies on a variety of issues, including the Gulf crisis, raised concern in the West.

Fundamental Differences with the United States

Beneath public demonstrations of cooperation, there were numerous differences between the US and Soviet approaches to the crisis. Whereas the United States made it increasingly clear that it was prepared to engage Iraq militarily, the Soviet Union emphasized peaceful resolution of the crisis and declined to send its own forces to the Gulf. Whereas Washington was prepared to act unilaterally, Moscow wanted all action to be not only sanctioned but also implemented by the United Nations. Whereas the United States insisted that Iraq withdraw unconditionally, the Soviet Union sought compromise through mediation.

Political Resolution

The Soviets made it clear from the beginning of the crisis that they preferred negotiations to military action and were concerned by Washington's "militant" approach and "impatience." The initial Soviet reaction to the US decision to send troops to Saudi Arabia was negative. Even Shevardnadze, the leading proponent of cooperation with the United States, was reportedly angered when Baker informed him of the decision,[45] and a Soviet Foreign Ministry statement warned that a "buildup in military presence and naval muscle-flexing in such a very tense and very complex situation is not the best line of action."[46]

The Soviets delayed passage of UN Resolutions 665 and 678, which dealt with the use of force to support sanctions and achieve Iraqi withdrawal.[47] And, even while issuing joint statements expressing agreement with Washington, Soviet leaders put their own spin on those statements. Gorbachev agreed at his meeting with Bush in Helsinki in early September

1990, for example, that if economic sanctions did not work, "additional steps" would have to be considered; but during a subsequent press conference, he asserted that it was too early to discuss a military option and that diplomacy had to be given a "real chance" to succeed.[48]

An hour before the allied bombing campaign against Iraq began, Baker reportedly informed Bessmertnykh by telephone. The foreign minister responded with Gorbachev's request that the United States not proceed immediately, and Gorbachev reportedly tried again to persuade Saddam to withdraw from Kuwait—but could not get the message through.[49]

As the bombing intensified, the Soviets increasingly expressed misgivings, emphasizing that the destruction of Iraq was not called for in UN resolutions. In early February, Gorbachev warned that the war was threatening to go beyond the UN mandate and appealed to President Bush to hold off on ground operations to give Moscow's mediation efforts a chance to succeed.[50]

Although eventually moving toward endorsement of the use of force against Iraq, Moscow became increasingly emphatic that its own direct military participation was not a consideration. The original Soviet position as elaborated by Shevardnadze in August 1990 had been that if the United Nations called for a multinational force, the Soviet Union might participate.[51] The foreign minister again raised the possibility in November, when he said that the Soviet Union would not hesitate to use force to protect its citizens in Iraq.[52] As domestic opposition to potential Soviet military involvement became clear, however, Shevardnadze backed away from this formulation.

Many commentators referred to the Soviet Union's counterproductive use of force in Afghanistan to explain this opposition. Vitaliy Naumkin, deputy director of the Oriental Institute in Moscow, expressed a frequently stated position:

> Just as you had a Vietnam syndrome in the United States, so are we now experiencing an Afghanistan syndrome. Gorbachev cannot afford to send troops abroad. The Soviet people would be completely against it. Perhaps we could send two or three ships to the Gulf as a symbolic contribution to a multinational force. But that's all.[53]

But even that turned out to be too much. When the war began in January 1991, the Soviet Union withdrew the two warships that had been in the Gulf and stressed that it would not take part "even symbolically" in hostilities.[54]

Multilateral Enforcement

Throughout the crisis, Moscow tried to lay all responsibility for enforcement of UN resolutions on the United Nations itself, principally by reviving the Military Staff Committee.[55] A Soviet military analyst, describing the committee as "still-born" because of the cold war, urged that the Gulf crisis serve as the first practical arena in which the committee could function.[56]

While the Soviets urged collective action by the United Nations to force Iraqi compliance with the resolutions, the United States preferred to rely on its own strength as leader of a multinational coalition. In part, the US approach was based on concern that the UN approach was time consuming and ineffective; but as President Bush indicated, it also rested on the position that although the United Nations might be useful, the United States was not willing to surrender any of its own authority to it.[57]

Mediation

The Soviets may have hoped at the beginning of the crisis that their relationship with Iraq would enable them to mediate a solution. In his earliest statement concerning the conflict, Shevardnadze emphasized Moscow's close relations with both Iraq and Kuwait and indicated that he saw "no reason that would make it impossible to end this conflict."[58]

Iraq, for its part, tried to use its relationship with the Soviet Union to create a rift between Moscow and Washington. From the beginning of the crisis, the Iraqis indicated their desire for increased Soviet involvement. In early September 1990, Iraqi Foreign Minister Tariq Aziz told Gorbachev that Iraq would welcome a more active Soviet role and held out the prospect that Soviets in Iraq would be treated better than citizens of other nations.[59] In late October, a senior Iraqi official stated that Iraq would release all foreign nationals held as a deterrent against attack in return for a Soviet-French commitment that the crisis would be resolved through political means.[60]

Moscow maintained its contacts with Iraq throughout the crisis period, sending messages to Saddam and making direct representations to other Iraqi officials.[61] When Moscow had no success in talking Iraq into a more conciliatory position, it warned Baghdad that stronger measures would follow. On the eve of the UN vote on Resolution 665, for example, Gorbachev sent an "urgent personal message" to Saddam, warning him of additional international sanctions if he did not withdraw from Kuwait and release the foreign nationals under his control.[62]

Moscow made its most serious efforts to mediate in October and in February, using Yevgeniy Primakov, a long-time Arabist and adviser to Gorbachev, as its representative. In October, Primakov met twice in Baghdad with the Iraqi president. After the first visit, the Soviet envoy purported to have received indications of Iraqi willingness to negotiate and to have reached agreement on a timetable for the departure of the Soviet citizens remaining in Iraq.[63] After consultations in the United States, Europe, and the Middle East, Primakov returned to Iraq. Subsequently, both he and Gorbachev reported "signs emerging that Iraq's leadership might at last heed the voice of the United Nations."[64]

Within days of these statements, however, Gorbachev concluded that Primakov's visits had not accomplished their objectives. A senior State Department official reported that the Soviet president told Baker in early November that Primakov had been "basically stiffed" by Saddam. Gorbachev also indicated, the official said, that Saddam's efforts to split the international coalition had failed and called the crisis a "test" of the post-Cold War world order.[65]

After the war began, the Soviet Union supported various mediation efforts. In early February, Deputy Foreign Minister Aleksandr Bolonogov visited Tehran in a gesture of support for an Iranian attempt to present a compromise package; Tehran's initiative was rejected by Baghdad.[66] Several days later, warning that military operations in the Gulf were going beyond the UN mandate, Gorbachev announced that he was again sending Primakov to Baghdad in an effort to gain a compromise and prevent a ground offensive against Iraq.[67]

The Primakov mediation effort continued until the eve of the ground war on February 24, 1991, and involved a series of formulas designed to achieve an Iraqi withdrawal from Kuwait while enabling Saddam to remain in power. The initiative was undertaken without coordination with coalition members and was widely criticized in the West as an effort to undermine coalition policy and distance Moscow from the negative consequences of a ground war. It was also cited as an indicator of a Soviet "turn to the right" and a faltering commitment to the centrality of the US relationship.

The Soviets reluctantly returned to support for the coalition after the failure of the Primakov effort. By focusing attention on differences between Moscow and Washington, however, this episode altered perceptions of Moscow's position and raised suspicions about the game it was playing. The episode may well have been one result of the departure of Shevardnadze, who had given the highest priority to maintaining the dialogue with Washington and had not permitted other Soviet interests to intervene.

Moscow was consistently more willing than Washington to consider and urge a compromise solution to the crisis. Shevardnadze professed to see some hope in a proposal made by Saddam on August 19, 1990 linking resolution of the Kuwait situation to resolution of the Palestinian problem and suggesting that Saudi Arabia's security be guaranteed by multinational forces.[68]

On September 4, in a speech in Vladivostok, Shevardnadze called for fresh UN efforts to resolve the crisis, including the rapid convening of a Middle East peace conference to settle the Arab-Israeli conflict. He did not directly link the two issues, but by referring to a set of "highly complex, interlocking problems" in the Middle East and by reviving the longstanding Soviet proposal for an Arab-Israeli peace conference, he appeared to support the Iraqi president's earlier linkage. Baker responded coolly, saying that given all the action in the United Nations, "we almost have an international conference."[69]

During the summit meeting of early September 1990, President Bush continued to assert that the issues of the Iraqi invasion and an international conference on the Middle East were not linked and that any effort to link them was "an effort to dilute the resolutions of the United Nations." Gorbachev, however, argued that the Gulf crisis and other disputes in the region were of "equal concern."[70]

President Bush did state, however, that the United States was open to a peace conference provided the Gulf crisis not be on the agenda—in other words that there be no obvious linkage.[71] In his speech to the United Nations on October 1, the president again held out the possibility of movement on Arab-Israeli negotiations, indicating that Iraqi withdrawal from Kuwait could lead to "opportunities" to resolve other regional disputes, including the Arab-Israeli conflict. But he subsequently insisted that no linkage had been implied.[72]

In his speech to the United Nations on November 29, Shevardnadze challenged the United States to accept movement toward an international conference on the Arab-Israeli issue and not reject it out of "some occult fear of the word linkage." To do so, he said, would be not a reward for Saddam but simply a sensible policy.[73]

The repeated Primakov mediation efforts reflected Moscow's desire for a compromise solution—and Washington's unwillingness to consider any compromise with Saddam Hussein. The Soviet Union was prepared to accept a longer timetable for Iraqi withdrawal than was the United States, to initiate a cease-fire before the withdrawal, and to lift UN sanctions against Iraq immediately after a withdrawal. The United States insisted on Iraq's immediate and unconditional withdrawal and on continued imposition of all UN sanctions.[74]

Concern About US Intentions

Even many Soviets who supported US policy in the Gulf expressed concern about Washington's long-term intentions. Commentator Kondrashov, for example, argued that Washington's

> gigantic military mechanism is working like clockwork, inevitably making Soviet generals and politicians bristle: after all, this is alongside our borders. After all, this is a show of US power, which we have opposed for decades. Are we now to welcome it? . . . What if the Americans stay even after Saddam Hussein is gone?[75]

Kondrashov argued that US lack of patience and temptation to use force required Moscow's emphasis on peaceful, political means of resolving the crisis.[76]

Naumkin of the Oriental Institute predicted that massive military action in the Gulf would aggravate fundamentalist movements throughout the region and asked, "How would that serve either US or Soviet interests?" He said a prolonged US military presence in the Gulf could undermine antifundamentalist regimes in Saudi Arabia, Jordan, and elsewhere.[77]

Soviet concern was heightened by Secretary Baker's suggestion in early September 1990 that the United States and Arab nations should establish a new "regional security structure" for the Persian Gulf to contain and roll back Saddam Hussein. Baker indicated that such an effort might require a sustained US naval presence in the region.[78]

After the war began, Soviet expressions of concern intensified as numerous commentators and officials criticized the extent of the US attack on Iraq. Former Chief of the Soviet Armed Forces Marshal Sergey Akhromeyev, now an adviser to Gorbachev, charged in an article in *Pravda* that the United States had moved too soon and suggested that Washington had not abandoned the idea of military superiority.[79]

During this period, the Soviets made it clear that the liberation of Kuwait—and only that—was the spirit and letter of Security Council resolutions. Concern was increasingly expressed about US rhetoric stressing the need to punish Saddam Hussein and destroy his regime. On January 22, 1991, in an interview on Soviet television, Gorbachev indicated reservations about the course of the war and Foreign Minister Bessmertnykh subsequently did the same.[80]

Stanislav Kondrashov again expressed the growing disenchantment of those Soviets who supported action against Iraq:

> We feel that we have somehow been deceived and taken in. But we also deceived ourselves . . . . The Americans . . . want to safeguard their soldiers' lives and to that end they are prepared to bomb Iraq's military and industrial potential to dust, not sparing Iraqis in military uniform, or even those in civilian dress when they happen to get in the way of their "smart" bombs. There is nothing new in this. It is the traditional strategy and tactics of American democracy when it goes to war . . . . Those who voted in the Security Council 19 November for "all necessary measures" against the Iraqi aggression might have guessed that, for Iraq, the Americans would not rule out a kind of apocalypse.[81]

Domestic Pressures in the Soviet Union

Although Moscow reacted quickly following the Iraqi invasion and there was apparently little questioning of its basic approach, there were differences within the Soviet hierarchy about aspects of the policy. Articles in the government newspaper *Izvestiya* were more supportive of US actions and Soviet policy than those in the party paper *Pravda* or the Defense Ministry paper *Krasnaya Zvezda*. Those papers, while condemning the Iraqi invasion, emphasized Washington's "use" of the crisis to build political influence and strategic presence in the Middle East.[82] A *Newsweek* article in September 1990 cited such conflicting Soviet statements to argue that both the foreign and defense ministry bureaucracies were lagging behind the leadership in supporting cooperation with the coalition.[83]

A number of Soviet officials expressed concern about the American force buildup and long-term US intentions. Appearing before a Soviet legislative committee in late August, General Vladimir Lobov, commander in chief of Warsaw Pact forces, portrayed the US buildup as a potential threat to the Soviet Union's southern borders that might jeopardize East-West talks on cutting conventional weapons in Europe.[84] Deputy Foreign Minister Aleksandr Bolonogov told a parliamentary committee that there were "no guarantees that the United States will ever leave Saudi Arabia.[85] Colonel Anatoliy Petrushenko, one of the military officers whose constant criticism of Soviet policy would later be cited by Shevardnadze as a factor in his resignation, warned that the United States was "moving into the Middle East without relaxing its grip on Europe."[86]

Soviet Major Aleksey Vashchenko, writing in *Literaturnaya Gazeta* in late November, strongly criticized Shevardnadze's approach to the crisis. He asserted that the United States was conducting a major mobilization and assault landing operation at the same time the Soviet Union was withdrawing its forces from Eastern Europe and asked how Moscow could justify defending US political and economic interests so strongly. He suggested that Moscow was abandoning its proclaimed principles of foreign policy in an effort to get credits from the West.[87]

There were hints of differences within the leadership itself. Statements made by Primakov suggested that he hoped to salvage relations with Iraq; Soviet academician Georgiy Mirskiy described Primakov as a person "susceptible to Baghdad's point of view, someone who is more inclined to give Saddam a way out" than had been Shevardnadze,[88] who consistently placed harmony between the Soviet Union and the United States above other policy considerations.

Even after Gorbachev indicated that Primakov's October missions to Iraq had been unsuccessful, the envoy continued to urge negotiation and compromise. In an interview on November 15, Primakov called for a delay in the introduction of Resolution 678 and urged continued pursuit of a political solution that would give Saddam a face-saving way out of the crisis.[89]

In a demonstration of the new political realities within the Soviet Union, Gulf crisis policy was debated and eventually endorsed by the Soviet legislature. After the Bush-Gorbachev summit of mid-September, the Soviet parliament voted its approval of the Kremlin's handling of the crisis. Following Shevardnadze's resignation, the Supreme Soviet again endorsed Gorbachev's policy while insisting that it be constantly informed about developments.[90]

The Soviet leadership had to endure rigorous questioning about its policy. In an appearance before the Supreme Soviet on October 15, for example, Shevardnadze responded to concerns about possible Soviet military action and about the treatment of Soviet citizens in Iraq. He said the leadership had no plans to use military force and that any decision to do so would be made by the legislative body.[91]

Several events raised questions in the West about the possibility of ongoing covert Soviet support for Iraq. The first of these, Moscow's reluctance to pull its military experts out of Iraq, created misunderstanding both at home and abroad. Some Western press articles charged that the continued presence in Iraq proved the Soviet military was helping the Iraqi war machine.

There was also internal pressure on the leadership to recall the specialists. In September, both the Russian Republic's Supreme Soviet and the Soviet Union's Supreme Soviet's Foreign Affairs Committee urged the immediate recall of "all Soviet military specialists" from Iraq.[92] One Soviet commentator reported that neither the Defense Ministry nor the Foreign Ministry wanted to take responsibility for withdrawing the experts and suggested that the reason for hesitation was concern that Iraq would retaliate by canceling payment of its debt.[93]

Primakov's visits to Baghdad in October were designed in part to respond to these domestic pressures by negotiating the departure of the Soviets remaining there. Between the two visits, the Iraqis issued their threat to detain the Soviets if Moscow gave intelligence information to Washington.[94] On October 12, Soviet Foreign Ministry spokesman Gennadiy Gerasimov accused the Iraqis of failing to live up to previous promises to allow Soviet citizens to leave the country freely;[95] the Iraqi threat prompted Shevardnadze's warning that Moscow would use force to protect its citizens if necessary.

In mid-December, a Soviet delegation led by Deputy Prime Minister Igor Belousov arrived in Baghdad to negotiate the departure of the experts, and agreement reportedly was reached to suspend contracts temporarily. Soviet workers in Iraq were given the option of leaving by January 10. Some workers remained behind "voluntarily" to monitor projects,[96] but by the beginning of the war in mid-January, the Soviet Foreign Ministry said there were only 112 Soviet nationals left in Iraq, 34 of them specialists closing down equipment.[97] Only embassy personnel remained in Iraq when the ground war began in February.

The second episode that provoked charges of continued Soviet military support for Iraq was the seizure in January of a Soviet freighter carrying military equipment possibly intended for Iraq. The freighter, detained in the Red Sea, was carrying tank parts, detonators, and other military equipment. The military cargo was unlisted and part of it was found stacked in the captain's stateroom. This event has not been adequately explained but appears to have been an unsanctioned smuggling operation. At most it was an aberration in Moscow's adherence to the international embargo on arms shipments to Iraq.

Soviet Policy: Long-Term Implications

The Soviet Union's approach to the Iraqi invasion was unprecedented, though consistent with the themes of new thinking. Moscow demonstrated that relations with the West, particularly with the United States, are, in fact, central to its foreign policy. It also demonstrated that its frequently expressed commitment to a stable world order and to the enhanced role of the United Nations is genuine.

Beneath the public demonstrations of US-Soviet cooperation, however, differences remained. The United States was prepared to use force and to act unilaterally if necessary, although it sought the backing of the international community. The Soviet Union, weakened at home and disengaging from its military commitments abroad, sought to define its role and relevance through its position as a permanent member of the United Nations Security Council and its developing partnership with the United States.

Moscow's importance as a player in the Gulf crisis was magnified by the search for a peaceful solution and diminished when the use of force began because it was not a military participant. To the greatest possible extent, therefore, Moscow tried to slow movement toward a military solution, urging restraint and focusing on peaceful resolution of the crisis. The Soviets made important political and economic gains in the Persian Gulf as a result of their policy. Most important, on September 17, 1990, they reestablished relations with Saudi Arabia. In late November, a Saudi official announced that Saudi Arabia would lend the Soviets as much as $1 billion, and in early December the Kuwaiti ambassador to the Soviet Union indicated that a group of Gulf countries had agreed to grant Moscow more than $3 billion in loans.[98]

The dramatic cooperation between Washington and Moscow during the Gulf crisis does not signify the complete congruence of US and Soviet interests in the region. Stanislav Kondrashov has warned that those interests remain very different:

> America wants to dominate a region where there is so much oil, where Israeli interests . . . are still more important to it than Saudi interests, and which lies strategically close to the Soviet Union. What has changed in these principles of US policy? It still relies on force and on assurances that force will be used in the interests of peace and stability. There are no grounds for doubting the sincerity of the assurances, but Washington reserves the right to determine what the interests of peace and stability are. Despite the level of cooperation reached between the United States and the USSR, the policies of the two powers are not and cannot be identical."[99]

The abrupt resignation of Shevardnadze raised questions about the durability of Moscow's policies. The intensifying national crisis within the Soviet Union, the departure of other key backers of new thinking, and President Gorbachev's apparent move to the right reinforce Western concerns about the future of new thinking. Certainly, there is no doubt that the Soviet leader is embattled, that military and conservative political forces have gained strength, and that the backers of perestroika and glasnost are on the defensive. Yet there seem to be few strong challenges to the basic orientation of Soviet foreign policy. Moscow's continuing commitment to the international coalition suggests that it will continue efforts to reinforce its relations with the West, particularly with the United States.

With the end of military action against Iraq and the ejection of Iraqi forces from Kuwait, new regional alignments and security arrangements are emerging. The Soviets will resist the long-term deployment of US forces in the Gulf and will seek to capitalize on the increased receptivity of Gulf states to Soviet political and economic expansion in the area. Although Soviet and US interests need not clash directly and the old competition is unlikely to be renewed, differing perceptions and objectives are inevitable and will test the diplomatic creativity of both Moscow and Washington.

Notes

1. The Soviets had maintained good relations with Kuwait since the early 1970s. Moscow concluded several arms agreements with Kuwait, in 1974 and 1976, which involved weapon sales, military training, and help in constructing naval and air facilities. Relations with Oman and the United Arab Emirates had been established in late 1985, with Qatar in 1988, and with Saudi Arabia and Bahrain in 1990 after the Iraqi invasion of Kuwait.

2. Elaine Sciolino, "Peacekeeping in a New Era: The Superpowers Act in Harmony," *New York Times*, August 28, 1990, p. A-13.

3. *Pravda*, July 4, 1987, and October 18, 1987.

4. TASS, June 22, 1989, and Tehran TV, September 22, 1990.

5. TASS, August 2, 1990.

6. TASS, August 3, 1990.

7. Michael Dobbs and Al Kamen, "U.S., Soviets Call For World Cutoff of Arms to Iraq," *Washington Post*, August 4, 1990, p. A-13.

8. *US News and World Report*, September 10, 1990, p. 25.

9. Carey Goldberg, "Moscow Denies Advisers Help Iraq," *Los Angeles Times*, August 14, 1990, p. A-7.

10. Bryan Brumley, "KGB Willing to Share Intelligence on Iraq," *Wall Street Journal*, September 20, 1990, p. A-14.

11. Gary Lee and Rick Atkinson, "Soviet General Warns of World War," *Washington Post*, September 28, 1990, p. A-20.

12. Michael Dobbs and David Remnick, "Soviets Hail Mideast Statement as an Important Shift in U.S. Policy," *Washington Post*, January 31, 1991, p. A-15.

13. Edward Cody, "Iraq Warns Soviets Against Giving U.S. Military Information," *Washington Post*, October 13, 1990, p. A-17.

14. TASS, October 16, 1990.

15. Aleksandr Bovin, "Political Observer's Opinion," *Izvestiya*, August 24, 1990, p. 4.

16. Patrick E. Tyler, "Iraq Is Delaying Soviet Departure," *New York Times*, December 17, 1990, p. A-1.

17. David Hoffman and David Remnick, "Soviets Resist Using Force," *Washington Post*, August 23, 1990, pp. A-1, A-38.

18. Tod Robberson, "Iraq, U.S.S.R. Set Terms for Departure of Soviets," *Washington Post*, December 30, 1990, p. A-36.

19. A. Konoplyanik, "Persian Gulf Crisis: Our Profit and Loss," *Argumenty i Fakty* (Arguments and Facts) No. #1, January 1991 (Moscow), p. 6.

20. David Remnick, "Gorbachev Cautious About Gulf," *Washington Post*, August 18, 1990, p. A-13.

21. *Pravda*, August 3, 1990.

22. Stanislav Kondrashov, "Together Against the Aggressor, What Then?" *Izvestiya*, August 15, 1990, p. 4.

23. TASS, August 3, 1990. Shevardnadze stated at a press conference on August 3 that he had responded to Baker's concern about Saddam Hussein's intentions by expressing confidence that Iraq would not resort to an overt invasion. He and Baker agreed at that time that they would meet again if the situation became aggravated. At this press conference, Shevardnadze emphasized that it was not easy for the Soviet Union to take the steps it was taking given its decades-long relationship with Iraq.

24. Bill Keller, "Bush and Gorbachev Say Iraqis Must Obey UN and Quit Kuwait," *New York Times*, September 10, 1990, pp. A-1, A-6.

25. David Hoffman, "U.S. May Seek Tougher Sanctions Against Iraq," *Washington Post*, September 14, 1990, p. A-24.

26. TASS, October 3, 1990.

27. R. W. Apple, Jr., "Moscow Holds Off on Backing Move for Use of Force," *New York Times*, November 19, 1990, pp. A-1, A-13.

28. Andrew Rosenthal, "Bush Fails to Gain Soviet Agreement on Gulf Force Use," *New York Times*, November 20, 1990, p. A-1.

29. Bill Keller, "Kremlin Insists that Iraqis Let Russians Leave," *New York Times*, November 27, 1990, pp. A-1, A-16.

30. John M. Goshko, "U.S. Gains Backing for Use of Force," *Washington Post*, November 27, 1990, pp. A-1, A-18.

31. Paul Lewis, "U.N. Gives Iraq Until January 15 to Retreat or Face Force: Hussein Says He Will Fight," *New York Times*, November 30, 1990, p. A-1.

32. Margaret Garrard Warner, "The Moscow Connection," *Newsweek*, September 17, 1990, p. 24.

33. David Hoffman, "Soviet Said to Reject Baker Plea on Gulf," *Washington Post*, December 11, 1990, p. A-1.

34. Thomas L. Friedman, "U.S. is Ready to Ask Soviets to Help With Naval Blockade of Iraq," *New York Times*, August 8, 1990, p. A-8.

35. Andrew Rosenthal, "Bush Wants a Rise in Moscow's Force," *New York Times*, September 8, 1990, pp. A-1, A-5.

36. Keller, "Bush and Gorbachev Say Iraqis Must Obey UN and Quit Kuwait."

37. *Ibid.*

38. *Ibid.*

39. Text of UN Resolution 665, *New York Times*, August 26, 1990, p. 15.

40. M. Yusin, "James Baker's 'Moscow Marathon,'" *Izvestiya*, November 10, 1990, p. 4.

41. John M. Goshko, "U.N. Boosts Pressure on Baghdad," *Washington Post*, October 30, 1990, p. 1.

42. Rick Atkinson and David Hoffman, "Commitment in Pullout From Kuwait Sought," *Washington Post*, January 30, 1991, p. A-1.

43. Andrew Rosenthal, "Gulf Concession That Wasn't; U.S. Moves to Quell a Furor," *New York Times*, January 31, 1991, pp. A-1, A-15.

44. Maureen Dowd, "Allies to Consult," *New York Times*, February 22, 1991, p. A-1.

45. Warner, "The Moscow Connection."

46. Thomas L. Friedman, "U.S. Ready to Ask Soviets to Help Form Naval Force," *New York Times*, August 8, 1990, p. A-8.

47. Elaine Sciolino with Eric Pace, "How U.S. Got U.N. Backing for Use of Force in the Gulf," *New York Times*, August 30, 1990, p. A-1.

48. Thomas L. Friedman, "Soviets Warning to Iraqis on War Praised by West," *New York Times*, September 27, 1990, pp. A-1, A-11.

49. Craig Whitney, "Three Peace Proposals Offered to Iraqis," *New York Times*, January 18, 1991, p. A-6.

50. Serge Schmemann, "Gorbachev Gives Iraqi a Peace Proposal," *New York Times*, February 19, 1991, p. A-1.
51. Remnick, "Gorbachev Cautious About Gulf."
52. David Remnick, "Soviets Would Stay Out of Gulf War."
53. Michael Dobbs, "Soviet 'New Thinking' Faces Major Test in Persian Gulf Crisis," *Washington Post*, September 9, 1990, p. A-31.
54. Berlin, *Allgemeine Deutsche Nachrichen* (ADN), January 22, 1991; Paris, *Agence France-Press* (AFP), January 18, 1991.
55. Paul Lewis, "U.N. Council Declares Void Iraqi Annexation of Kuwait," *New York Times*, August 10, 1990, p. A-11.
56. Vladimir Chernyshev, TASS, August 14, 1990.
57. Sciolino, "Peacekeeping in a New Era."
58. TASS, August 2, 1990.
59. TASS, September 6, 1990; Michael Dobbs, "Iraqi Envoy Asks Moscow to Seek Gulf Settlement," *Washington Post*, September 7, 1990, p. A-27.
60. *Jordan Times* (Amman) October 30, 1990, p. 1.
61. TASS, August 5, 1990, Moscow Domestic Service, August 6, 1990.
62. TASS, August 24, 1990; Bill Keller, "Gorbachev Warning Iraqi on Kuwait and Foreigners," *New York Times*, August 25, 1990, p. 4.
63. "Russian Sees Hussein and Is Hopeful," *New York Times*, October 7, 1990, p. 21.
64. Alan Riding, "Gorbachev, in France, Says His Envoy Found Signs of Shift in Iraq," *New York Times*, October 30, 1990, p. A-13.
65. David Hoffman, "Buildup Timed to Sway Saddam: Baker Says Iraq Let Down Soviets," *Washington Post*, November 10, 1990, pp. A-1, A-26.
66. Michael Dobbs, "Kremlin Seeks Distance from U.S. on War," *Washington Post*, February 6, 1991, pp. A-19, A-23.
67. David Remnick, "Gorbachev Says War Risks Going Too Far," *Washington Post*, February 10, 1991, p. A-23.
68. TASS, August 20 and 21, 1990.
69. Francis X. Clines, "Soviets Suggest Conference Combining Issues of Mideast," *New York Times*, September 5, 1990, p. A-17.
70. Keller, "Bush and Gorbachev Say Iraqis Must Obey UN and Quit Kuwait."
71. Andrew Rosenthal, "Bush, Reversing US Policy, Won't Oppose a Soviet Role in Middle East Peace Talks," *New York Times*, September 11, 1990, pp. A-1, A-18.
72. Ann Devroy, "Bush Offers U.N. Hope on Gulf," *Washington Post*, October 2, 1990, p. A-1.
73. TASS, November 30, 1990.
74. Michael Dobbs, "Soviets Press for Iraqi Pullout Within Three Weeks," *Washington Post*, February 23, 1991, pp. A-10, A-16.
75. Stanislav Kondrashov, "And This Time in Helsinki," *Izvestiya*, September 4, 1990, p. 1.
76. *Ibid.*
77. Hoffman and Remnick, "Soviets Resist Using Force."

78. David Hoffman, "Baker Proposes New Alliance to Contain Iraqi Aggression," *Washington Post*, September 5, 1990, pp. A-1, A-25.

79. Esther Fein, "Senior Soviet Official Says U.S. Rushed Into War," *New York Times*, January 22, 1991, p. A-9.

80. Moscow Central Television, January 26, 1991.

81. Stanislav Kondrashov, "Political Observer's Notes: Desert Carnage," *Izvestiya*, February 15, 1991, p. 5.

82. Francis X. Clines, "Soviets Say Crisis Won't Mar U.S. Tie," *New York Times*, September 4, 1990, p. A-9; Michael Dobbs, "Soviet Spokesman Rebukes Military, Defends U.S. Presence in Persian Gulf," *Washington Post*, September 4, 1990, pp. A-1, A-24.

83. Warner, "The Moscow Connection."

84. TASS, August 30, 1990.

85. Clines, "Soviets Say Crisis Won't Mar U.S. Tie."

86. David Hoffman, "Long-Term Gulf Security Arrangement Sought," *Washington Post*, September 12, 1990, pp. A-29, A-31.

87. Aleksey Vashchenko, "The Persian Gulf: It is Right Alongside," *Literaturnaya Gazeta*, November 30, 1990, p. 3. Access to credit and technology has been one of the main objectives of Soviet foreign policy and a major rationale of new thinking. Moscow's recognition that its activist Third World policy had undermined relations with the West led to the cooperative Soviet approach most dramatically demonstrated by its Gulf policy. The Soviet Union has gained increased access to Western capital in the past few years as a result of its domestic reforms, its policies toward Eastern Europe, and its retreat from the Third World. Its crackdown in the Baltics in early 1991, however, produced a negative reaction in the West and resulted in the temporary suspension of food aid and technical assistance programs by the European Community.

88. David Remnick, "Hard-Liners Criticize Gorbachev on Gulf," *Washington Post*, February 13, 1991, p. A-21.

89. Paul Lewis, "Soviet Aid Urges Delay of U.N. Move on Force in Gulf," *New York Times*, November 16, 1990, pp. A-1, A-12.

90. TASS, December 28, 1990.

91. Moscow Television Service, October 15, 1990.

92. TASS, September 12, 1990.

93. Kondrashov, "And This Time in Helsinki."

94. "Persian Gulf: Requests and Threats," *Izvestiya*, October 14, 1990, p. 1.

95. Cody, "Iraq Warns Soviets Against Giving U.S. Military Information."

96. *Moscow Domestic Service*, December 29, 1990; Robberson, "Iraq, U.S.S.R. Set Terms for Departure of Soviets."

97. TASS, January 17, 1991.

98. Moscow International Service, December 5, 1990.

99. Kondrashov, "Together Against the Aggressor. What Then?"

6

OPEC in 1990: The Failure of Oil Diplomacy

Charles K. Ebinger and John P. Banks

THE DANGERS AND COMPLEXITIES of maintaining a cohesive and functioning oil cartel were never more apparent than in 1990. The Iraqi invasion of Kuwait was oil politics taken to its most brutal extreme and will fundamentally alter the structure and traditional role of the Organization of Petroleum Exporting Counties (OPEC) in global oil markets. Nevertheless, rumors of OPEC's demise are premature. Despite the violent consequences of OPEC's political failure to resolve the problem of Saddam Hussein and his search for economic security, regional political dominance, and oil market hegemony, OPEC will emerge from this turmoil strengthened, albeit in a very different form.

OPEC in the 1980s

1980-1986: The Downward Spiral. The oil price shocks of the 1970s boosted oil prices to unprecedented levels and set the stage for dramatic changes in the global oil market in the 1980s. Higher prices stimulated additional non-OPEC oil production, increased conservation and fuel switching, and prompted greater utilization of alternative fuels such as coal, natural gas, and nuclear power. Indeed, it is estimated that on a worldwide basis in the period 1979-1985, primarily in industrial boiler and electric power markets, coal backed out (replaced) 5 million barrels per day (mmbd) of oil equivalent, nuclear 4 mmbd, natural gas 1 mmbd, and end-use efficiency and conservation 5.5 mmbd. Together these factors had a severe impact on OPEC; from 1979 to 1985, the cartel's production plummeted from 31 mmbd to 15.5 mmbd, and the value of OPEC's petroleum exports decreased from $284 billion to $127 billion. As the 1980s began, OPEC accounted for 57 percent of total free world oil production, but by 1985 OPEC's share dropped to 41 percent.

Prices moved steadily downward in the period 1980-1985 as it became evident that OPEC could not maintain control over a fixed-price regime in the wake of cascading oil demand and massive fuel substitution. The cartel began to lose cohesion as most OPEC members unofficially adopted a flexible pricing system whereby they accepted current market prices in lieu of fixed prices. Saudi Arabia, however, sought to moderate price and production fluctuations by assuming the role of swing producer, increasing production when demand rose, and decreasing output if overall OPEC production threatened to glut the market. The net effect of these trends was a steady erosion of oil prices as other OPEC members cheated on their quotas, offsetting much of the market-stabilizing impact of Saudi actions.

Consequently, this one-sided effort to shore up the market became increasingly intolerable to Saudi Arabia. The kingdom accounted for more than 40 percent of the total decrease in OPEC production between 1979 and 1985, suffered the largest decline in oil revenues of any other cartel member (from $116 billion in 1981 to $17 billion in 1986), and continued to lose market share to other OPEC countries. These factors drastically limited Riyadh's ability to fund its own national development plans and meet the kingdom's other foreign policy obligations.

In an attempt to regain market share lost to other OPEC and non-OPEC producers, alternative fuels, and conservation as well as to recapture a larger portion of the OPEC pie, the Saudis introduced "netback" pricing in 1986. Instead of a fixed price regime, under the new netback arrangement the pricing of crude oil at the wellhead was based on the value of the products produced from the crude oil in the marketplace. The move toward netback pricing represented a complete reversal of OPEC policy. The effect of this change was to shift market risk away from the end-use consumer and to place it squarely on the shoulders of the oil producers. The Saudis realized that the near-term effect of this policy would be to force prices down. Because the Saudis had the lowest cost to produce oil reserves as well as the largest share of underutilized production capacity, they hoped to regain market share while their less well-endowed OPEC brothers would begin to feel real economic pain.

The ensuing intra-OPEC competition led to a collapse in oil prices as some OPEC members continued to overproduce relative to global oil demand in a desperate attempt to maintain state revenue. The resulting price free-for-all briefly drove oil prices below $10/barrel before they recovered to the $13-$14/barrel price range and then moved slowly up to the mid- to upper teens.

Quotas and the Hawks and Doves. The netback pricing regime that dominated in 1986 and led to the devastating downward price spiral prompted OPEC in August 1986 to introduce a new system of production quotas in order to provide a mechanism to regulate production and arrest the price decline. It was believed that by following strict production quotas (to be periodically reviewed and adjusted when market conditions warranted), OPEC supply could be matched with demand and a target price level of $18/barrel sustained.

Almost from the beginning, however, maintaining an efficient and manageable production regime proved a difficult task. Individual member quotas were determined by a complicated formula based on such variables as oil reserves, production capacity, export capacity, population, GNP, and per capita income of each OPEC country. The quota system was never able to satisfy each country's needs, and contending interests among OPEC's membership often resulted in blatant cheating on official quotas in the name of national self-interest.

Owing to the diverse resource base and particular social, economic, and political characteristics of each OPEC country, the new quota system fostered the emergence of two camps within OPEC. The large production capacity and vast oil reserves of the Persian Gulf states of Saudi Arabia, Kuwait, Qatar, and the United Arab Emirates (UAE) as well as Venezuela guarantee that they will be major producers and exporters over the long-term. They understood that the 1986 oil price collapse occurred because OPEC raised prices too high in the 1970s and thus sought oil price moderation and stable oil markets in an effort to maintain demand for their resources over the long term. These countries emphasized market forces to determine prices and avoided excessive market management.

Even within this camp, there were seriously divergent opinions. Whereas Saudi Arabia and Venezuela generally favored the adoption of policies to defend the $18/barrel target price, the Kuwaitis realized that to recapture the industrial boiler and electric power markets lost between 1979 and 1985, oil would have to be priced competitively with coal and natural gas, suggesting a crude oil price closer to $15/barrel. Likewise, the Kuwaitis realized that the fastest growing market was no longer found in the Organization for Economic Cooperation and Development (OECD) nations, but rather in the burgeoning economies of the Asian Tigers and the other large nations of the Third World. To keep these countries from using coal and natural gas, fuel oil had to be competitively priced to penetrate these rapidly expanding markets.

The other camp comprised the low-reserve, small-volume producers such as Algeria, Libya, Indonesia, Ecuador, Gabon, and Nigeria. Given a more limited resource base and output capacity, this group will become increasingly insignificant in global oil markets over the long term and thus emphasizes higher prices to maximize revenues in the short term. These countries did not focus on quota increases because they do not possess the capacity to increase production to any significant degree and often, as in the case of Algeria and Indonesia, cannot even produce at their allotted quota levels. Inability to raise production to capture market share leaves these countries more price sensitive. This group continually attempted to pressure the large-volume, high-reserve countries to exercise output restraint while arguing for higher quota allotments for themselves in the interests of protecting high prices.

In addition, several of these "price hawks"—especially Indonesia and Nigeria—are low-income, high-population countries often burdened with massive foreign debt and costly infrastructure needs common in developing countries. In addition, high economic and population growth rates in these countries have resulted in rising domestic oil demand, absorbing potential exports and limiting revenues. This group also consists of some of the more radical Islamic countries—Algeria, Iran, Iraq, and Libya—that view moderate pricing policies as bowing to the interests of the industrialized, oil-consuming countries at the expense of the Islamic nation. Saddam Hussein, in his attack on Kuwait and the UAE for their overproduction during the first half of 1990, stressed the threat of their practices to the "Arab nation."

Although Iran and Iraq are large-volume, high-reserve countries, their emphasis since the end of the Iran-Iraq War in 1988 has not been on quotas and price moderation to preserve their markets in the long term. Rather, both countries have embarked on rebuilding their war-ravaged economies. To do so, however, requires large revenues generated through oil exports, a goal not achievable by adhering to strict production quotas and a modest reference price. Prior to the invasion of Kuwait, Iraq generated 98 percent of the country's export revenues from oil.

Given their economic situation and redevelopment programs, both Baghdad and Tehran joined the ranks of the price hawks, consistently arguing for higher production quotas for themselves and production restraint from others in order to maintain high prices. Iran and Iraq expected their demands to be met not only on the basis of economic need but also in recognition that in the long term both are expected to parlay their significant reserves—a combined 19 percent of the world's total and 25 percent of OPEC's total—into expanded output capacity, increased market share, and a more prominent status within OPEC and global petroleum councils.

An equally important development since the establishment of the quota regime has been the emergence of Kuwait and the UAE as the principal culprits responsible for OPEC overproduction. Both countries not only have flagrantly violated their respective output restrictions but also have publicly dismissed their responsibility to adhere to assigned quotas. This situation reached a critical stage during and after the June 1989 OPEC meeting. Although Kuwait signed the production accord negotiated during that gathering, its oil minister, Sheikh Ali Khalifa al-Sabah, added a written reservation to the text of the agreement stating that Kuwait refused to be bound by any production limits. The UAE also publicly dismissed its quota and declared that it would continue to produce at a self-determined "appropriate" level.

What lay behind this renegade behavior was each country's attempt to carve out a more independent role, increase revenues, and strengthen its market position. Each believed that the primary factors determining quota allocations should be reserves and spare production capacity. In the case of Kuwait, it justified its demands partly on a need to maintain its vast network of downstream activities. Kuwait is foremost among OPEC countries in that it diversified its operations with substantial investments in downstream activities. Kuwait Petroleum International (KPI) is the downstream division of the government-owned oil company Kuwait Petroleum Corporation (KPC), operating three refineries in Europe with a total capacity of 234,000 barrels per day as well as 6,500 service stations throughout the continent under the logo of "Q8." This downstream network not only provides Kuwait with an outlet for its crude output but also with a cushion in times of lower crude prices because lower raw material costs give it an advantage over its competitors. Kuwait thus has the luxury of utilizing excess production as a weapon to argue for higher quotas and a larger market share.

The oil policy of the UAE is complicated by the fact that technically only Abu Dhabi is a member of OPEC. This posed no unique problems until Dubai and Sharjah emerged as significant oil producers. Because the other emirates ignore the OPEC quota for the UAE, Abu Dhabi either has to restrict its own production to make way for the oil output of the other emirates to be included in the OPEC quota or produce at quota, leading to chronic overproduction by the emirates at large and generating great animosity inside OPEC. The problem is further exacerbated by dynastic family rivalries in the emirates that make any agreement difficult, if not impossible, to effect.

Rising Oil Demand. Despite statements by many OPEC observers that the oil price collapse in 1986 would have little impact on global oil consumption, demand for OPEC oil has soared as lower oil prices have led to a surge in consumption in industrial boilers, electric power generation, and Third World transportation markets. With low oil prices, OPEC recaptured nearly 6.5 mmbd of its market share between 1985 and the eve of the Iraqi invasion of Kuwait. Demand for OPEC oil was rising in excess of 1 mmbd per annum prior to August 1990, and OPEC production had increased from 17 mmbd in 1988 to nearly 24 mmbd in early 1990.

The implications of this were not lost on the OPEC Secretariat. OPEC Secretary-General Subroto indicated that the cartel would be required to increase production capacity by 6 mmbd above the estimated OPEC capacity of 26 mmbd by the year 2000 just to keep global oil supply and demand in balance at a staggering cost of $60-$70 billion, although there is considerable uncertainty about where this capital is to originate.

Indeed, in anticipation of increasing oil demand in the 1990s, many OPEC producers, especially the large-volume and high-reserve Gulf states, commenced plans to increase capacity in order to stake a claim for a bigger piece of an expanding OPEC pie. In December 1989, Saudi Arabia announced a 10-year, $15 billion program to raise production capacity from 6.5 mmbd to 10 mmbd. Abu Dhabi declared its intentions to raise onshore capacity from 1 mmbd to 1.25 mmbd through 1995. In December 1989, Iran claimed it could increase capacity by 1 mmbd over the next two years; Iraq planned to add 1 mmbd by mid-1991.

Increasing demand for OPEC oil, however, exacerbated the competition between the two camps. The large-volume and high-reserve countries realized that as demand increases and the capacity of other OPEC states dwindles throughout the course of the decade, the locus of oil power and intra-OPEC decision-making will shift toward the Persian Gulf. This realization has created a situation in which no country is willing to forego increases in quotas or cutbacks in production for fear of losing market share at a time when the market is expected to expand. No country will unilaterally restrain output unless the cutbacks are shared across the board with all OPEC producers. Since 1987, Kuwait and the UAE in particular have forcefully argued for higher quotas and have produced well above official limits.

Thus, as 1990 began, there were several converging forces already in motion that would have a profound impact on OPEC: (1) the emergence and growing polarization of competing subgroups within OPEC; (2) the drive by Kuwait and the UAE to achieve greater prominence and higher quotas, exhibited through their disregard for official production limits; (3) the increased quotas and higher prices sought by Iran and Iraq to generate enhanced revenues necessary to rebuild their economies; (4) the increase in demand for OPEC oil and the competition to capture the expanding market; and (5) Saudi Arabia's unwillingness to play the role of swing producer. The ingredients for a crisis were all in the pot and beginning to boil.

Economic Warfare—January to July 1990

Passive Spring. During the first six months of 1990, OPEC was confronted by a steady deterioration in oil market conditions and a growing policy paralysis. Although official OPEC production quotas (established during the December 1989 meeting) were set at 22.086 mmbd for the first half of the year, overproduction was rampant. In the first quarter of 1990, OPEC output averaged 23.7 mmbd, with Kuwait and the UAE accounting for 75 percent of the excess production.

Despite the recognition that eventually some action would be required to address the situation, there was little sense of urgency with the approach of the scheduled Monitoring Committee meeting in March. During this uneventful gathering, OPEC examined the status of the current market characterized by excess supply and softening prices as well as potential actions that could be taken at the full OPEC conference in July. These included raising the reference price and changing or scrapping the quota system—the latter favored by Kuwait. Despite the looming crisis, the committee determined that a definitive policy decision on these thorny matters could wait until the July conference.

This was to be the turning point for OPEC in 1990. Although the cartel was surely aware of an emerging problem (OPEC production reached 24 mmbd and prices had dropped below the $18/barrel reference mark in March), it chose not to take action and instead passively allowed the market to resolve any imbalances. The de facto result was that there was little incentive for producers to restrain production until July, if then. Certainly no country would be willing unilaterally to apply the brakes to output in light of anticipated increases in demand for OPEC oil in the long term and fears of losing market share to overproducers in the short term. Thus, the March meeting provided a self-fulfilling prophecy—postponing critical policy decisions on price and production in a soft market prompted further disregard for quotas.

By April the situation was serious; total OPEC production remained at 24 mmbd, and the OPEC basket price, which had peaked at $20.56/barrel in the last week of January, tumbled 25 percent to $15.50/barrel by the second week of April, the lowest level in fourteen months and well below the OPEC reference price. The situation was compounded by seasonal factors such as stock drawdowns, refinery maintenance, and warmer weather, all of which lowered the demand for OPEC oil.

The worsening situation prompted OPEC to scramble for solutions. Clearly OPEC overproduction was the primary reason for current market conditions, and the UAE and Kuwait were the primary, though not the only, quota violators. In effect, however, OPEC had no real mechanism to enforce quota adherence except peer pressure, and this is exactly what was used along with an intensified campaign to convince Kuwait and the UAE to reduce production. The Saudis issued the first official statement calling for a return to quota adherence but also indicated that Riyadh would not lower production unless others agreed to reduce output simultaneously. Saudi Arabia also reiterated that it would not return to the role of swing producer.

On April 12, Secretary General Subroto issued a statement that OPEC was considering an Emergency Monitoring Committee meeting to address market conditions. Instead, on April 19, Kuwait, Saudi Arabia, and the UAE met in Riyadh to discuss the issue and released a communiqué calling for all OPEC members to adhere to their quotas. Then on May 2, OPEC convened a gathering in Jeddah, Saudi Arabia, which, according to

Subroto, would not address quota increases but rather the "specific problem of over-production."[1] This meeting resulted in a temporary and informal agreement that there would be production cuts totaling 1.5 mmbd for all thirteen OPEC members in the period May to July and that Kuwait, Saudi Arabia, and the UAE would together reduce output by 1 mmbd. Many industry observers were skeptical of the effectiveness of the arrangement given its informal nature and the recent behavior of the main quota violators. In addition, Iraq's bellicosity at this meeting shocked OPEC colleagues and members of the international oil community alike. Indeed, it appeared that nothing could stop the inexorable wave of excess oil production coming into the market.

Then on May 30, Saddam Hussein addressed the Arab League summit in Baghdad, stepping up the rhetoric and threatening the OPEC overproducers. He declared that the principal cause of the current market disruption was "non-adherence by some of our Arab brothers to OPEC resolutions" and claimed that a drop of $1/barrel resulted in a loss of $1 billion per year for Iraq. He bluntly stated that "we cannot tolerate this type of economic warfare which is being waged against Iraq . . . and we have reached a state of affairs where we cannot take the pressure" and went on to call for full adherence to OPEC quotas.[2]

June: Calling the Bluff. Saddam's speech dramatically altered the traditional parameters of OPEC decision-making, characterizing an oil-policy dispute in terms of "warfare" and subtly introducing the threat of force as a bargaining tool in the oil-policy process. He had raised the political stakes and created an ominous sense of urgency and uncertainty. Although at this time no OPEC member believed that Iraq would actually use force to achieve higher oil prices, during the month of June OPEC continued its frantic attempt to pressure Kuwait and the UAE to restrain production in efforts to defuse further confrontation. On June 11, OPEC President Sadek Boussena circulated a letter to all OPEC ministers warning that a continued rapid price decline could lead "to a serious price collapse akin to the one experienced in 1986."[3] He then traveled to Iran, Iraq, Saudi Arabia, Kuwait, and the UAE in an attempt to bolster prices. King Fahd of Saudi Arabia reiterated Riyadh's intentions to adhere to the May 2 arrangement and called upon other producers to exercise production restraint.

On June 20, Kuwait's oil minister, Sheikh Ali Khalifah al-Sabah, was replaced by Dr. Rashid Salim al-Ameeri. Despite many observers' claims that this represented a shift to a more conciliatory approach on oil policy, in effect it was a superficial move to placate Kuwait's critics. Al-Sabah had been oil minister for twelve years and was associated with the emirate's confrontational positions within OPEC. Any illusions that policy would change, however, were shattered by an interview with al-Ameeri shortly after his appointment. He flatly stated, "I would like to emphasize that there will be no change in Kuwait's oil policy. In any case, oil policy in Kuwait is determined not by the Oil Minister but by the cabinet as a whole and higher authorities."[4]

More important, there were other clear and direct signals that both Kuwait and the UAE had no intention of changing their policies. During a mid-June press conference, incoming Kuwaiti Oil Minister al-Ameeri spelled out in no uncertain terms his country's oil policy: moderate price levels to foster long term demand for oil, a production level for Kuwait commensurate with its vast oil reserves and the needs of its domestic and international oil network, and expansion and consolidation of its downstream activities. Al-Ameeri also stated, perhaps not so diplomatically in light of Iraq's economic woes, that Kuwait's demand for higher quotas was due to the country's large budget deficit. UAE Oil Minister Dr. Mana Saed Otaiba chimed in, "I want to make it clear that the UAE rejects threats and pressure from any source."[5]

Despite the effort to structure a makeshift agreement on May 2 to reign in excess output as well as the flurry of high-level diplomatic and political activity, perennial pleading, veiled and direct threats, and high-minded calls for solidarity and adherence to formal agreements, persistent and chronic overproduction continued. OPEC output dipped only slightly to 23.6 mmbd in the second quarter 1990, and although Kuwait and the UAE trimmed production, they continued to produce 1.1 mmbd above their quotas. Moreover, the OPEC basket price dropped to $13.99/barrel in the second week of June.

Under these circumstances Iraq stepped up its high-profile and vociferous barrage of criticism against Kuwait and the UAE in June. Baghdad reserved its harshest attacks for its neighbor, arguing that Kuwait's extensive downstream activities would more than compensate for reducing production. In addition, Iraq noted that Kuwait exercised greater control over its oil operations than the UAE owing to the latter's political structure that allows each emirate to pursue independent oil policies.

Iraqi Oil Minister Isam al-Chalabi stated that "one can easily imagine the intentional harm caused to the interests of oil producing states."[6] At a press conference in Kuwait in late June al-Chalabi recited recent Kuwaiti production figures (all well above quotas), embarrassing his hosts. During the last week in June, Iraqi Deputy Prime Minister Saddoun Hammadi traveled to the UAE, Qatar, Saudi Arabia, and Kuwait to make Iraq's case that plunging oil prices were causing serious damage to the Iraqi economy and that "our financial and economic situation motivates us to speak loudly."[7] He hand-delivered letters from Saddam Hussein to the leaders of each country stressing that overproduction had led to the fall in oil prices.

It was during this trip that Iraq outlined its proposed oil policy. Baghdad sought a minimum reference price of $25/barrel with quotas to remain at current levels, with the exception of the UAE, which would see its quota raised to 1.5 mmbd in line with Kuwait. This production ceiling would remain in place until the $18/barrel reference price was restored. If this did not occur, there would be appropriate reductions in the quota ceiling with pro rata cuts for all countries. Al-Chalabi added that there should not be an increase in the ceiling until prices firmed up and rose above the $18/barrel level. Not surprisingly, the Iranians, Algerians, and Libya voiced support for raising the reference price.

July: Raising the Stakes. By July, the situation was becoming catastrophic, with OPEC appearing on the brink of collapse. Something had to be done. On July 10-11, Saudi Arabia, Qatar, Kuwait, the UAE, and Iraq met in Jidda and once again attempted to fashion some makeshift arrangement to address continued excess production and placate a restless and increasingly belligerent Iraq. The Jidda agreement in effect implemented the Iraqi proposal with the understanding that the full OPEC conference on July 25 would provide the venue for more detailed discussions on the future framework of OPEC, including the possibility of formally raising the reference price. Thus, for the time being, the "price-firsters" gained the upper hand; the large-volume, high-reserve Gulf producers and Venezuela temporarily placed their goal of higher quotas on the back burner. Once again, all parties praised unity and promised to adhere to all agreements.

Saddam Hussein was not impressed. On July 17, in a speech commemorating the anniversary of the 1958 and 1968 Baath revolutions in Iraq, he raised the stakes to the point of no return. In reference to the downward spiral of prices and the rampant overproduction of the first two quarters of 1990, he declared "the policy followed by some Arab rulers is an American policy, on American advice" and that "if words cannot provide its people

[Iraq] with protection, then action will have to be taken to restore matters to their normal course and regain the rights which have been usurped."[8] Remarkably, and regrettably, this speech was never noted by the American news media.

The following day, Iraqi Foreign Minister Tariq Aziz delivered a letter to the Arab League in which he provided a detailed outline of Iraqi grievances against Kuwait beyond the issue of overproduction. Iraq claimed that Kuwait had been intransigent on discussions concerning territorial disputes, including the prospect of leasing the strategic islands of Bubiyan and Warba to Iraq; that Kuwait had been producing oil from the southern end of the Rumaylah oil field since the early 1980s, and consequently owed Baghdad $2.4 billion; and that Kuwait committed an affront to all Arabs by categorizing its $12-$13 billion in assistance to Iraq during the Iran-Iraq War as a loan.

Saddam Hussein drastically changed the parameters of intra-OPEC politics. He now depicted the policies of fellow Arab members of OPEC as "a campaign launched by imperialist and Zionist circles against Iraq and the Arab nation."[9] Introducing a broader political dimension to what had been a fundamentally economic question clearly raised the stakes and provided convenient justification for what had become direct threats. More ominously, in July Iraq had begun moving troops, artillery, aircraft, and armor to positions in southern Iraq near the Kuwaiti border. Despite these provocations, Kuwaitis appeared profoundly complacent with the Iraqi threat. Indeed, almost across the board Kuwaitis saw Iraq's mobilization as a bluff. Nevertheless, to soothe the Iraqis, the KPC announced on July 18 that production would be cut by at least 300,000 barrels/day to meet its commitment to reduce output to 1.5 mmbd in accordance with the Jidda agreement. In addition, Kuwait entered into negotiations with Iraq concerning several issues, even offering Baghdad $1 billion for pumping Rumaylah oil, an offer that was summarily rejected.

But the time for defusing the situation had long since passed. By the time of the July 25 OPEC meeting, Iraq had 70,000 members of the Republican Guard with 350 tanks and 350 armored personnel carriers positioned on the Kuwaiti border. Iraq's muscle-flexing loomed over the meeting as Iraq, Iran, and several other price hawks argued for a reference price of $25/barrel and Saudi Arabia, Kuwait, the UAE, and Venezuela favored a more modest increase to $20/barrel. After days of negotiating, with Saudi Arabia playing a major mediating role, OPEC decided to raise the reference price to $21/barrel and increase the quota ceiling to 22.491

mmbd, effectively formalizing the Jidda agreement's stipulation that only the UAE's quota would be raised to parallel that of Kuwait. OPEC hoped to restrict production to this quota level over the next several months, boosting prices to the new reference price; as oil demand increased in the fourth quarter and into 1991, production levels could be adjusted. This arrangement was acceptable to countries that sought higher prices (Iran, Iraq, Libya, Algeria), the Gulf states (Saudi Arabia, Kuwait, and the UAE), and Venezuela. The latter group accepted the short-term appeasement not only to assuage Iraqi demands but also owing to the perception that as the only members capable of boosting capacity to meet growing demand, they could afford to wait for the day when they would usurp the lion's share of quota increases.

It appeared that a crisis had been averted, but the Kuwaitis now took a step that was intolerable to Iraq. The ink was hardly dry on the agreement when the Kuwaiti oil minister stated rudely and publicly to the Iraqi oil minister that the agreement meant nothing and that Kuwait would continue to produce at a level commensurate with its own interests.[10]

The old method to enforce quota adherence—the threat of a price war, primarily wielded by Saudi Arabia—had been replaced. There was a new enforcement mechanism—the threat of war, as wielded by Iraq—and Baghdad was willing to use its weapon.

The Unthinkable—Why Did It Happen? OPEC had grossly underestimated the willingness of Saddam Hussein to utilize force as an oil policy weapon. Kuwait and the UAE, in particular, engaging in a kind of oil market brinkmanship, called Saddam Hussein's bluff and went too far.

The underlying impetus for the invasion was economic. In 1988, with Iraq's defeat of Iran in the Gulf War, Iraq clearly emerged as the dominant military power in the Gulf. The war, however, left Iraq deeply in debt and in need of generating revenue to rebuild its society. In addition, Iraq had been plagued by rampant financial mismanagement in recent years—Baghdad's non-Arab external debt of $60 billion is the world's third largest behind Mexico and Brazil, and its annual short-term debt service has been estimated at $6-$7 billion. Just prior to the invasion, Iraq had failed to meet payments on its debt, some of which had been rescheduled for a third time only six to nine months earlier.

The chronic OPEC overproduction and the steady fall in prices over the first two quarters of 1990 posed a grave threat to Iraq's financial and economic health. The outcome of the July 25 OPEC meeting was the final straw; though the trade press made much of the differences between Iraq's demand for oil at $25/barrel and the rest of OPEC supporting $20/barrel until a compromise was worked out at $21/barrel, in reality Iraq knew that prices could not be sustained at $20/barrel in the wake of previous OPEC overproduction and the likelihood that cheating would continue. At the time of the meeting, it was difficult to achieve stability for spot prices at $15-16/barrel. Indeed, during the first seven months of 1990, the spot price for OPEC's seven most widely traded crudes averaged $16.84/barrel versus the $18.00/barrel target price. In July, the spot price had fallen to $15.68/barrel with the prospect of further decline. This prospect was clearly intolerable to Iraq, especially in light of the fact that recent sources have indicated that Baghdad's post-Iran-Iraq War long-term development plans had been drawn up based on an oil price level of at least $20/barrel.

Baghdad knew that in addition to Iraq's preponderant military power in OPEC councils its 100 billion barrels of oil reserves placed it on a par with the UAE (98 billion), Iran (93 billion), and Kuwait (97 billion, including its share of the Neutral Zone). Nevertheless, it was still far behind Saudi Arabia'a official figure of 255 billion barrels (at least 285, if recent discoveries of light crude reserves are included).[11]

Thus, although Iraq offered immediate reasons for the invasion of Kuwait—repudiation of war debt, gaining direct access to the Persian Gulf, disgruntlement over Kuwait producing Iraqi oil, and the desire to recover the nineteenth province—there can be no doubt that Iraq's primary motivations were first, to stop cheating on oil quotas by Kuwait and the UAE, which threatened to collapse the price of oil, and second, to emerge as the principal challenger to Saudi Arabia's domination of the world petroleum market in the 1990s, thus guaranteeing some degree of financial and economic security. Although Iraq clearly miscalculated the impact that the invasion of Kuwait would have on galvanizing world opinion against it, the invasion was not the act of a "madman" but a cold, calculated decision that by a single stroke Iraq would achieve its long-standing goal of becoming the dominant force in the Gulf.

Saddam Hussein's gambit did not work, but surely he must have decided that the opportunities were worth the risk. With the acquisition of Kuwait, Iraq overnight would have boosted its reserves to 194.5 billion barrels, nearly 20 percent of the world's total; acquired a near-term production capability of 5.7 mmbd and the prospect of being a 9.5 mmbd producer in the 1990s versus 10 mmbd for Saudi Arabia; gained control of 5.2

billion barrels of oil reserves in the neutral zone and 400,000 barrels/day of production—output that in the current market was Japan's single largest crude supply source. Iraq also would have gained control of significant upstream investments in a dozen countries, major downstream world class refineries, significant retail markets in Western Europe, and sizeable investments in petrochemicals and tankers, not to mention the prospect of solving its debt problem by seizing an estimated $100 billion in Kuwaiti assets abroad.

Iraq realized that during the 1990s at least five and possibly more OPEC countries would cease being significant oil exporters and that the locus of world oil power would reside clearly in the Gulf. The acquisition of Kuwait combined with Iraq's raw military power would enable Iraq to emerge as the dominant power in the Middle East and as a significant world actor never to be held economic hostage again.

An Emerging OPEC Order: August-December 1990

OPEC to the Rescue. The United Nations trade embargo on Baghdad removed an estimated 4 mmbd from world oil markets (including Kuwaiti output).[12] In the immediate aftermath of the invasion and subsequent embargo, there was concern over potential supply shortages. With the approaching winter heating season, there was a perception that a shortfall would emerge, and the fear of a severe market imbalance jolted prices to $31/barrel by August 22.

In OPEC's quest to determine from where additional supplies would come, it was not clear in the several weeks following the invasion whether other oil producers, principally OPEC members Saudi Arabia, Venezuela, and the UAE, had the spare capacity to increase production in order to replace the supply shortfall. Not only were there questions concerning the technical capability of these countries to boost production but there were also doubts concerning the political will to undertake such an endeavor. Iraqi Foreign Minister Tariq Aziz warned OPEC against raising production and the Iraqi government newspaper *al-Jumhuriya* bluntly stated on August 22 that "the new Iraq owns a big share of the world oil reserves that will establish it as a regional power that is worth taking into consideration.[13]

Simultaneously, Saudi Arabia took provocative steps against Iraq, and US and other Western forces began arriving in the kingdom; Riyadh shut down the IPSA II pipeline, which transported Iraqi oil to the Red Sea. In fact, Saudi Arabia privately had already set in motion contingency plans to increase production. On August 16, Saudi Arabia publicly called for an OPEC meeting to authorize member countries to boost oil output, and Venezuela announced its support on the following day. Riyadh's proposal called for an increase in production to meet the supply shortfall and stabilize markets.

Once again, however, OPEC was divided. The price hawks were opposed to any production increase—they were reaping benefits from the higher prices, as were all member countries. They saw no economic reason to jeopardize the windfall. Algeria, Indonesia, and Nigeria all claimed that it was too early to consider a production increase, that no unilateral decisions should be taken, and that oil stocks should be drawn down first. Venezuela declared that it would temporarily raise production by 500,000 barrels/day to help offset the supply shortfall, but this additional output would be placed in storage and await official OPEC approval to export.

The most severe attack on the Saudi's proposal, however, came from Iran. Iranian President Ali Akbar Hashemi-Rafsanjani stated that "OPEC members have no right to commit treachery against their people in favor of the global oil devourers" and called on the industrialized world to use huge oil stockpiles instead of increased OPEC production to meet the expected demand/supply shortfall.[14] Large oil stocks throughout the OECD nations had contributed to the downward pressure on OPEC prices all through 1990, and some OPEC members hoped that if these stocks were drawn down during the crisis, OPEC would have fewer prorationing problems following the crisis.

Nevertheless, the simple fact was that those who possessed the spare capacity were in favor of raising production. Saudi Arabia was estimated to have extra output capacity in the short term of 7.65 mmbd and 8.2-8.5 mmbd in the long term. By year-end, it was estimated that the UAE could increase production 600,000 barrels/day above quota, Venezuela 500,000 barrels/day, Libya 217,000 barrels/day, and Nigeria 289,000 barrels/day.

Indeed, near the end of August, without an official meeting to sanction increased production, any country with the spare capacity to raise output was doing so. Saudis were producing 6-6.5 mmbd and were rumored to have concluded September contracts for 7.4 mmbd. Nigerian production reached 1.8 mmbd (quota of 1.61 mmbd), and Libya's output neared 120,000 barrels/day in excess of its quota.

Riyadh was attempting to preserve some semblance of a united and operational OPEC by going through official OPEC procedures and succeeded in convening a meeting in Vienna from August 26 to 29. Under the leadership of the Saudis, the UAE, and Venezuela, OPEC fashioned an agreement in which members were allowed to increase output according to excess capacity with no specified volume limitations. Priority for the additional output was given to the developing countries owing to their greater susceptibility to oil price and supply disruptions. The agreement, however, was only temporary and specific provisions mandated that OPEC revert back to the July 1990 resolutions "only until such time as the present crisis is deemed to be over."[15] Iraq and Libya refused to participate.

Pumping up the Volume. Despite initial opposition, OPEC increased production significantly after the August agreement. Following a decrease in output to 21.9 mmbd in the third quarter, production averaged 23 mmbd in the fourth quarter of 1990. In December, OPEC crude oil production averaged 23.86 mmbd, with Saudi Arabia's production reaching 8.3 mmbd—in August the kingdom's output was 5.5 mmbd. In early November, the Saudis announced that they were accelerating their expansion program, increasing production capacity to 10 mmbd by 1995 instead of by 2000 at a cost of $75 billion, five times the original cost estimate.

By the end of the year, the UAE and Venezuela were producing at 2.35 mmbd, and Libya and Nigeria also increased production during the fourth quarter of 1990. Even Iran had joined in boosting output, despite earlier strenuous objections. Tehran increased the volume of oil shipped to the Far East by 760,000 barrels/day in the fourth quarter and also secured substantially improved price terms for increased volumes shipped to Japan. Iranian light was increased by $0.60/barrel, and Iranian heavy was increased by $1.40/barrel.

The New Order. How will the events of 1990 affect OPEC? Three fundamental factors will probably characterize the new OPEC: the rising dominance of the Saudi-led subgroup; a growing focus on economic considerations in OPEC decision-making; and increasing producer-consumer cooperation.

Although the locus of power within OPEC has been shifting toward the high-reserve, large-volume, market-oriented Gulf states and Venezuela since 1986—driven primarily by increasing demand for OPEC oil—Iraq's invasion of Kuwait and the Gulf War have inexorably accelerated this process. The market destabilization and volatile price fluctuations resulting from the recent crisis in the Gulf are anathema to this coalition. The

August accord was an attempt to reinstitute some stability and predictability to markets and symbolized the solidarity and prominence of this coalition, presenting the low-volume, limited-reserve members with a fait accompli. The August accord was fundamentally an economic decision.

Moreover, from an intra-OPEC political standpoint, the August agreement signaled that the Saudi-led group was willing to abandon the traditional unanimity required in all OPEC policy decisions. The meeting was procedurely converted to the status of a Monitoring Committee meeting, thus removing the requirement that any action be approved by every member. The Saudis gave notice that they were willing to discard their consensus-building modus operandi. In addition, the weak opposition of price hawks such as Algeria, Libya, and Iran to Iraq's actions in 1990 will serve to discredit these players and diminish their influence at least in the near term.

The August agreement represented a political as well as an economic decision. Saudi Arabia and the UAE were directly threatened by Iraq's willingness to resort to brutal force. Their decision to support wholeheartedly the worldwide condemnation of Iraq, to allow hundreds of thousands of foreign troops into the Gulf, to cut off Iraqi pipeline exports, and to increase production in order to stave off a potential serious shortfall in supplies were clearly provocative to Iraq but were calculated political decisions to confront Baghdad and guarantee their own survival. The invasion and subsequent war forced the market-oriented Gulf states to band together and abandon the nonconfrontational, consensus-building approach. The close cooperation and mutual assistance that emerged among Kuwait, Saudi Arabia, Qatar, and the UAE further enhances the power of this OPEC subgroup.

Clearly, such provocative steps were contemplated only under the diplomatic and military aegis of the United Nations coalition. With strong international support, the high-reserve, large-volume coalition has gained significant stature. With Saddam's military machine devastated, the willingness and ability to undertake economic decisions without intimidation, fear of reprisals, or political-military repercussions are likely to continue.

The new OPEC focus on economic and market factors in setting policy will have an impact on its relationship with the consumer countries. Since August, OPEC (minus Iraq) and the industrialized consumer countries have moved closer together. The widespread military and political support that Western nations have provided to Saudi Arabia, Qatar, the UAE, and Kuwait have linked the interests of producers and consumers in confronting a common enemy and attempting to restore stability to the troubled Persian Gulf. Support from the consumer countries was not limited to the political and military realms. On January 11, 1991, members of the International Energy Agency (IEA) representing the major industrialized countries agreed to a plan designed to stabilize the global oil market in the event of a shortfall caused by hostilities. The plan includes a drawdown from government and private company stocks of 2 mmbd, with another 400,000 barrels/day to be backed out by conservation measures and 100,000 barrels/day to be made available from fuel switching and surge capacity. IEA member countries were to arrange their own plans to meet the overall 2.5 mmbd target. After the outbreak of the Gulf War, the IEA announced that its members were ready to implement this contingency plan, releasing 2.5 mmbd of oil to world oil markets within fifteen days.

For its part, OPEC demonstrated a willingness to bolster the new-found cooperation through increased production in an attempt to stabilize prices as well as through Saudi and Kuwaiti pledges to contribute $27 billion to the US costs of operations Desert Shield and Desert Storm. In addition, the industrialized countries participating in the liberation of Kuwait are playing a significant role in the rebuilding of that country, cementing the relationship even further.

Cooperation is a theme that had been raised frequently in the course of 1990, owing in part to the deteriorating market conditions. Secretary-General Subroto indicated early in the year that the financial requirements of expanding OPEC capacity in the 1990s would necessitate investment from the consumer countries. In October, OPEC President Boussena called on greater cooperation between producers and consumers to achieve a consensus on appropriate oil price levels in the future. Even Iran, in the midst of criticizing the OPEC decision to boost production after the invasion, called for a meeting between the IEA and OPEC to work out a shared plan to address market concerns. Sheikh Ahmad Zaki Yamani, the former Saudi oil minister, in a speech delivered in March 1990, took the call for a new cooperative spirit one step further, arguing for a "trilateral dialogue between the governments of the consuming countries, the producers—members and non-members of OPEC—and the oil companies."[16]

Whither Prices? How will these developments affect price levels? The interests of the consumer and producer countries will move closer together, and the support of the United Nations coalition, including most of the major consumer countries, will vastly improve the stature of the high-reserve, large-volume producers, making it easier for them to dominate the price hawks whose influence is on the wane. The interests of the ascendant

OPEC sub-group—stable oil markets and moderate price levels—coincide with those of the consumer nations. Thus, the Saudi-led subgroup will enjoy growing influence and will be empowered to pursue policies designed to achieve these goals.

This is exactly what has evolved in the several months after the Gulf War. With Saudi Arabia, Venezuela, and other producers having invested large sums of money to raise production capacity in order to stabilize oil markets and capture a larger share of the rising demand for OPEC oil, there is little incentive for them to roll back their production and have it sit idle. Indeed, although Saudi Arabia has professed its desire to see strict quota adherence and prices at the established $21/barrel reference mark, it also has indicated that it will not unilaterally sacrifice production increases and revenue for the good of OPEC, thus tending to depress the price below the $21 target. An estimated $50 billion in war-related costs provides Riyadh with an additional incentive to preserve prices at this level.

Saudi Arabia wasted no time in wielding its new-found power in OPEC councils. At the March 12, 1991, OPEC Monitoring Committee meeting, Saudi Arabia orchestrated an agreement to reduce the cartel's output by 5 percent and set the quota ceiling at 22.3 mmbd (down from 22.49 mmbd) in an effort to bolster prices. In addition, prior to the March meeting, Saudi production was estimated at 8.4 mmbd, and officials indicated that they would not accept any quota below 8 mmbd—a quota that Saudi Arabia was ultimately assigned and that was significantly above its prior quota of 5.38 mmbd. More important, the agreement appears to have worked: Preliminary estimates from the IEA indicate that OPEC production decreased in April by 600,000 bd.

Although much has been made of the potential destabilizing impact of returning oil production from Iraq and Kuwait, it appears that output from these former combatants will not return to world markets in any significant volumes in the near term. Ongoing damage assessment of Kuwait's wells, reservoirs, and infrastructure indicates that the emirate's production is not likely to reach notable levels until late 1992 or early 1993.

For Iraq, the return of oil exports to the world market is being delayed indefinitely by the continuation of the UN embargo. Until the debate in the Security Council concerning the mechanics of allocating a certain percentage of Iraqi oil export revenues to reparations is resolved, Iraqi production will not have an impact on prices. In fact, some estimates suggest that, even with outside financing, it will take two years to rebuild its oil infrastructure to prewar levels.

In addition, as discussed, Iraq will not likely pose problems for the new OPEC in the near- to midterm (through 1993). Baghdad will be militarily defanged, and when Iraqi exports do resume, Saudi Arabia and the Gulf states are in a stronger position within OPEC to force Baghdad to comply with conservative pricing and production policies. Indeed, the Saudis are in the unique position of being able to control 300,000 bd to 400,000 bd of Iraqi export capacity through the Saudi pipeline system. If current discussions concerning post-war security arrangements lead to the permanent presence of Western allied forces in the region, the political standing of Saudi Arabia and its Gulf allies will be even further enhanced. It is most ironic that Saddam's move into Kuwait, initially designed to catapult Iraq into a leadership role in OPEC and world oil markets, will in the end create an OPEC in which it has little, if any influence in the near term.

In the longer term, however, both Iraq and Kuwait face the daunting task of rebuilding their war-ravaged societies, and reestablishing oil production and export capacity will be the only route to generating sufficient revenues to accomplish this. Ironically, if Iraq is forced to pay war reparations, it will have an even stronger incentive to raise production. Eventually, therefore, increased Iraqi and Kuwaiti production could place downward pressure on prices.

The behavior of Iran is another important variable in determining the direction of oil prices. The destruction of most of Iraq's military and Iran's neutrality and efforts at mediation during the war will improve Tehran's stature in the Gulf and the Middle East at large. Initially, there was considerable concern that Tehran might decide to parlay this new-found influence into a campaign to gain more power within OPEC, boosting output and forcing the subgroup to contend with more overproduction. In addition, it was feared that Iran might also attempt to bolster its standing by drawing attention to the close relationship of the Arab and Western members of the UN coalition and rouse the anti-Western, anti–Gulf state sentiments of the Arab world.

None of this has materialized, however, as Iran has shown increasing signs of moderation over the first several months of 1991. Iran and Saudi Arabia have recently commenced discussions on reestablishing diplomatic relations, and Riyadh received great cooperation from Tehran in arranging the March 1991 Geneva agreement. Other signs of moderate behavior include the decision by Iran to increase diplomatic contacts with Egypt, ending years of cool relations between the two countries; Tehran's reticence to take any overt military role in the rebellion inside Iraq following the end of the Gulf War even though Saddam Hussein's forces were killing Shiite brethren; and Iran's willingness to ask for and accept assistance from the West—especially US military forces—in dealing with the Kurdish refugee problem.

Clearly, Iran is cooperating with the Gulf War victors in a concerted effort to guarantee a political role in the postwar balance of power. This portends stable oil prices in the near term as Tehran adheres to the policy direction of the Saudi-led subgroup and indeed becomes more incorporated into the OPEC locus of decision-making. Longer term, Iran still needs to generate revenues to rebuild its shattered economy in the aftermath of the Iran-Iraq War, and there remains considerable debate about the outcome of an internal political power struggle between the Islamic fundamentalists and the more Western-oriented moderates. These factors could translate into more aggressive posturing by Iran and lobbying for higher quotas, thus increasing supply and depressing prices.

Despite the potential for intra-OPEC political divisions and OPEC over-supply, the political and market forces described above should combine to maintain prices in the $18-$22 per barrel range until 1993. Sluggish demand owing to a weak global economy also will help maintain prices in this range. In fact, the IEA forecasts that global demand for oil will increase only marginally in 1991, by 0.3 percent. But the call on OPEC oil will remain strong owing to expected non-OPEC production declines, particularly in the United States and the Soviet Union. The Independent Petroleum Association of America (IPAA) has forecast US production to continue its recent downward trend, dropping another 0.5 percent in 1991. The IPAA also projected that US crude output would decrease 11.9 percent in the period 1991-1995 and 10.9 percent in 1995-2000. The IEA has projected Soviet production to decrease to 10.9 mmbd in 1991, from 11.5 mmbd in 1990 and 12.3 mmbd in 1989.

A near- to midterm price in the $18-$22 per barrel range for OPEC oil not only looms on the horizon but is in OPEC's long-term interest. Prices much above this range would stimulate a response similar to that exhibited in the period 1980-1985: increased non-OPEC production, rising use of alternate fuels, and greater utilization of energy conservation. Price levels below this range would depress revenues and cause intolerable financial and economic pain for all players, similar to the effects experienced in the 1986 price collapse.

If OPEC pushes for a higher price without a number of producers cutting back on current output to make room for Kuwaiti and Iraqi reentry into the market, the specter of a price collapse below $15 per barrel will become a reality. In addition, although both Iran and Iraq have been relatively docile and noncontentious forces within OPEC in the immediate aftermath of the Gulf War, the internal political situation and foreign policy of each country is in a state of flux. Over the longer term, a real potential exists for Baghdad and Tehran to exert greater influence over production and pricing policies, a role they believe is justified owing to huge oil resources and high output capacity. The almost certain divisions within OPEC that might follow such a revival of the influence of Iraq and Iran would lessen the organization's control over prices and lead inevitably to a decline in prices.

Thus, there remain myriad unresolved diplomatic, economic, and political issues that could lead to other confrontations. The world has witnessed the human, financial, and environmental consequences of failed oil diplomacy: It is incumbent upon the international community, particularly the Persian Gulf states, to guarantee that oil politics do not again deteriorate to such a violent conclusion. In particular, assured access to Middle Eastern oil reserves will never be secure unless the United States uses all its diplomatic leverage to help effect a comprehensive peace plan for the region. If projections of US oil import dependency materialize—11 to 12 mmbd by the year 2000, coming increasingly from the Persian Gulf—future crises of ever greater magnitude will be the result.

Notes

1. *Oil Daily*, May 1, 1990, p. 1.
2. From Saddam Hussein's speech at the closed session of the Baghdad Emergency Summit Conference. Reprinted in *Middle East Economic Survey* (*MEES*), July 23, 1990, p. D-7.
3. MEES, June 18, 1990, p. A-1.
4. From the text of an *MEES* interview with al-Ameeri, reprinted in *MEES*, July 2, 1990, p. A-3.
5. *MEES*, July 2, 1990, p. A-6.
6. *Oil Daily*, June 28, 1990, p. 2.
7. *MEES*, July 2, 1990, p. A-4.
8. *MEES*, July 23, 1990, p. D-2.
9. *MEES*, July 23, 1990, p. D-1, reprint of July 19 speech.
10. Confidential conversations with officials present at the meeting.
11. Reserve figures are not absolute and are subject to debate. The figures cited here are accepted industry estimates.

12. *MEES*, August 13, 1990, p. A-2.
13. *MEES*, August 27, 1990, p. A-6.
14. *MEES*, August 27, 1990, p. A-4.
15. Text of OPEC's Vienna Agreement, August 29, 1990. Reprinted in *MEES*, September 3, 1990, p. A-4.
16. Address by Sheikh Yamani to a meeting of the Institute of Petroleum in Glasgow on March 8, 1990, reprinted in *MEES*, April 2, 1990, p. D-1.

7

Diplomacy of German Unification

Berndt von Staden

THE EUROPEAN DIPLOMATIC SCENE in 1990 was largely dominated by the issue of German unification and, more particularly, by negotiations between the two German states and the Four Powers—Britain, France, the Soviet Union, and the United States. These negotiations led to the signing of the Treaty on the Final Settlement with Respect to Germany on September 12. The unification of Germany—or, to be more precise, the union of the German Democratic Republic (GDR) with the Federal Republic of Germany under Article 23 of the Federal Republic's constitution—the Basic Law—took place on October 3. It brought a development of truly revolutionary character to its conclusion: one of the rare instances in modern history where upheavals of such scope could be channeled through and kept under the control of diplomacy.

To understand these events properly one must look back to 1989. It is always difficult, if not impossible, to determine a precise date at which events began to unfold, but with regard to German unification, May 5, 1989, was undoubtedly of crucial importance. On this day Hungary began to open its border with Austria, creating the first gap in the Iron Curtain since the Berlin Wall was erected in 1961. The effects of this action, by itself an expression of growing liberalization in Hungary, were soon felt, and events began to accelerate until in the end they moved with the speed of a tidal wave. In July and August growing numbers of people from the GDR began to take refuge in the diplomatic missions of the Federal Republic in Budapest, Prague, and East Berlin to force permission for them to emigrate to West Germany. On September 10, Hungary permitted more than

6,000 refugees to cross the Austrian border, waiving its agreement with the GDR not to let each other's citizens emigrate to third countries. On October 5, the GDR felt compelled to permit more than 10,000 East Germans sojourning in Czechoslovakia to leave for the Federal Republic. Finally, on November 9 the GDR leadership took the fateful decision to open the border of the country, evidently hoping to lessen the pressure by opening the safety valves. This hope, however, proved vain. On the contrary, a veritable exodus set in, until by the end of the year more than 340,000 refugees had left for the West—more than 2 percent of the entire population, most of them young, active, and well trained.

This movement, rightly called a "vote with the feet," was of decisive importance. The GDR could neither endure such a hemorrhage for any length of time nor, in the long run, could the Federal Republic cope with an influx of such magnitude; the GDR was not able to close the border again, and the Federal Republic could not afford to erect a wall of its own. The mass exodus, which continued in 1990, increasingly forced the hand of the two German states and ultimately of the Four Powers, accelerating the pace of the German internal process of unification as well as that of the international community.

Parallel and connected developments within the GDR had similar effects. The country had developed into a gerontocracy, with such leaders as Erich Honecker, Willi Stoph, Horst Sindermann, and Erich Mielke in their late seventies or early eighties. They were inflexible, increasingly remote from reality, unwilling and unable to initiate overdue reform. Categorically refusing to follow Soviet President Mikhail Gorbachev's policies of perestroika and glasnost, they were not only confronted with mounting internal pressure but had also lost Soviet support—a development that became obvious at the fortieth anniversary of the GDR on October 10 and 11, 1989. It was on this occasion that Gorbachev, in his keynote address, coined the phrase, "Those being late will be punished by life itself." This remark, understood by everyone, had an electrifying effect. Demonstrations began: 15,000 people in Leipzig on October 8, 70,000 the next day, hundreds of thousands in the weeks to come. On October 18 Prime Minister Honecker was forced to resign and was replaced by Egon Krenz, his "crown prince." Hans Modrow, only recently criticized by the conservatives for being a liberal dissenter, was appointed prime minister on November 13. On December 1, the phrase concerning the leading role of the party was dropped from the constitution of the GDR. Krenz was in turn forced out as secretary-general of the Socialist Unity Party (SED) on

December 8, to be replaced by Gregor Gysi. On December 17 the party was renamed the Party of Democratic Socialism (PDS). Free elections were then scheduled for May 6, 1990, a date later advanced to March 18. They were the first free elections in the GDR since 1933, when Hitler came to power.

It was increasingly evident that the GDR was caught in an accelerating process of dissolution. The demonstrations had begun with the slogan "we are the people," which soon changed to "we are one people" and "*Deutschland einig Vaterland*" (Germany, united fatherland). Clearly, what the vast majority of the people really wanted was not only radical reform in the GDR but unification with the Federal Republic as well. That appropriate action had to be taken lest developments should get out of hand and elude diplomatic control became more apparent each day to the government of the Federal Republic and, ultimately, to the governments of the Four Powers.

Preliminary Steps

Thus, at the end of 1989 German unification was unavoidable and would have to be accomplished sooner rather than later. But it was some time before the governments concerned and their leadership could assess the situation realistically; so many plans had been overtaken by events that could not have been predicted.

In legal terms, the situation was simple, at least for the Federal Republic and its three Western allies—Britain, France, and the United States. The Federal Republic's Basic Law required the government to pursue a policy aiming at the reestablishment of German unity. The three Western powers were bound by Article 7 of the Convention on Relations between the Three Powers and the Federal Republic of Germany of May 26, 1952, amended on October 23, 1954, in which they had committed themselves to "cooperate to achieve by peaceful means their common aim of a reunified Germany, enjoying a liberal-democratic constitution, like that of the Federal Republic, and integrated within the European Community."[1]

Politically speaking, however, unification was more complex and difficult to manage for the parties concerned—less so for the Federal Republic and the United States, somewhat more for Britain and France, and most of all for the Soviet Union.

The Federal Republic's chancellor, Helmut Kohl, was the first one to take action, launching in the Bundestag on November 28, 1989, a ten-point program for German unification covering internal as well as external aspects of the problem. Kohl's approach, which at that time was considered overly bold, was actually cautious, providing for a step-by-step process without any fixed time schedule. He was particularly anxious to link it to progress in European integration, the development of East-West relations in Europe, and the CSCE process (the Conference on Security and Cooperation in Europe, or the Helsinki process) as the "heart piece" of the "All-European structure."[2]

German unification was to be imbedded in the All-European process. Germany, in Foreign Minister Hans Dietrich Genscher's words, was seeking a "united Germany in a European framework under a European roof."[3] Throughout the process of unification, this multilayered linkage was to become one of the keynotes of German diplomacy.

Kohl's statement caused considerable irritation: It failed to mention future membership of a united Germany in NATO and passed over the question of Germany's eastern border with Poland; President François Mitterrand of France, who on the terms of the Elysée Treaty of 1963 could at least have expected to be notified in advance, was not even consulted. Mitterrand's visit, made on short notice, with Soviet President Mikhail Gorbachev in Kiev on December 6 and his state visit to the dissolving GDR from December 20 to 22, 1989—where he was received by the acting head of state, Professor Manfred Gerlach—were probably expressions of French irritation. The meeting in East Berlin may also have been a belated attempt to stabilize the crumbling East German state.

Paris soon realized, however, that unification had become inevitable. Although France still wanted to move slowly and proceed step-by-step, French diplomacy began to define the conditions under which unification could take place. France first would insist that a united Germany unconditionally recognize its current borders—in particular its border with Poland—remain in NATO, and continue to renounce the national possession of nuclear weapons. To compensate for the increased weight of an enlarged Germany, the French leadership began to press for accelerated European integration and especially for the creation of an "economic and monetary union." Paris also stressed its interest in an early conclusion of the Viennese negotiations on conventional arms control and in the "ratification" of any agreement on German unification by a CSCE summit conference to be held in Paris at the end of 1990.

British reactions were similar, but with one marked difference. Prime Minister Margaret Thatcher for a time insisted that German unification was not on the agenda. But under the impact of events London "changed course"—as Foreign Secretary Douglas Hurd put it after a meeting with his French colleague Roland Dumas—coming to conclusions rather similar to those of France.[4] The difference, which turned out to be an important one, referred to the link between German unification and European integration. For France, as was mentioned, deepening of the European Community—that is, acceleration of integration—was and still is the means to master the delicate problem of German enlargement or, in other terms, the future balance within the European Community. Prime Minister Thatcher, however, drew the inverse conclusion; to her, the widest possible enlargement of the community was the answer. On visits to Prague and Budapest, and even to Bern, she consequently encouraged host governments to seek membership as early as possible. France clearly wanted to tighten the bonds; Mrs. Thatcher seemingly intended to loosen them.

The situation of the United States was in many respects easier than that of its Western European allies. Geographically remote and being of a different size, the United States was not haunted by anxieties regarding Germany's enlarged size or increased weight. For the United States, questions of balance between itself and Germany did not come into play. Washington's main interests were to assure the future of the Atlantic alliance, to maintain stability in Europe, to secure recognition of the Polish border by Germany, and to make the process at the same time bearable to the regime of Mikhail Gorbachev.

The US position was spelled out by President George Bush at a NATO summit meeting in Paris in December 1989 and by Secretary of State James A. Baker III in an address to the Berlin Press Club on December 12, 1989. They both summed it up in four points, which Secretary Baker, quoting the president, formulated as follows:

- Self-determination must be pursued without prejudice to its outcome. We should not at this time endorse nor should we exclude any particular vision of unity.
- Unification should occur in the context of Germany's continued commitment to NATO and an increasingly integrated European Community and with due regard, of course, for the legal role and responsibilities of the allied powers.
- In the interests of general European stability, moves toward unification must be peaceful, they must be gradual, and part of a step-by-step process.

- Finally, on the question of borders, we should reiterate our support for the principles of the Helsinki Final Act.

President Bush concluded that "an end of the unnatural division of Europe, and of Germany, must proceed in accordance with and be based upon the values that are becoming universal ideals, as all the countries of Europe become part of a commonwealth of free nations."

Furthermore, Secretary Baker came out strongly in favor of what he called a new architecture of Europe: a new and more political role for NATO based on a conventional forces agreement as the keystone of European security; a new institutional and consultative line between the United States and the European Community; and a strengthened, although not institutionalized, Helsinki process as the one forum "that brings all the nations of the East and West together in Europe."[5]

Of all the parties concerned, the Soviet Union undoubtedly faced the most difficult situation. Gorbachev's "new thinking"—his attempt to base the position of the Soviet Union in world politics on cooperative instead of confrontational relationships and on a sound economy instead of military power alone—had brought about sweeping changes in his country's foreign policy. These changes included a much more liberal attitude toward reform within the former satellite countries of Eastern Europe. Originally, however, the foreign policy changes were meant to lead to the dissolution of the Warsaw Pact or the Council for Mutual Economic Assistance or, more important, to the collapse of the communist regimes. But developments turned out to be unforeseeable and uncontrollable. The gradual erosion of the communist regimes in Poland and Hungary could have been stopped only by brutal force. To do so, however, would have robbed Gorbachev of all the benefits of his new policy toward the West. Thus, by 1989, the Brezhnev doctrine of limited sovereignty of socialist countries had virtually been abandoned.

The accelerating collapse of the communist regime of the GDR must have been the most painful of all these developments for Moscow. Since 1955, when the Kremlin definitely abandoned the hope to have all of Germany neutralized and under Soviet codetermination, the GDR had been considered the cornerstone of Soviet influence in Central Europe and a bedrock of stability. During a state visit to Moscow in 1987, the Federal Republic's president, Richard von Weizsäcker, was told by Gorbachev that with regard to German unity only history could decide how things would look in a hundred years.

Only two years later, however, events began to move. Gorbachev's attempt to press publicly for reform at the SED party congress in October 1989 came, as it turned out, too late. His historic decision finally to keep the more than 300,000 Soviet troops in their barracks when ever-growing mass demonstrations for freedom—and increasingly for unity as well—took place between October 6 to 16 was probably decisive for ultimate developments.

But the Soviet leader was nevertheless not yet willing to face the prospect of German unity. As late as December 3, in his joint press conference with President Bush, he insisted that German unification was not a question of actuality, that history should judge, that one should not artificially accelerate developments. Only on December 19, in an address to the political committee of the European Parliament in Brussels, did Soviet Foreign Minister Eduard Shevardnadze outline the conditions under which German unification could be envisaged by Moscow. He formulated seven points:

- Political and legal guarantees that German unity would not constitute a threat to the security of other states and to peace in Europe.
- The recognition by a united Germany of existing borders and German willingness to renounce any territorial claims.
- The place Germany would occupy within European military structures—as Shevardnadze observed, one could not expect the GDR to change its status radically while the status of the Federal Republic remained unchanged.
- The military potential and doctrine of a united Germany, the acceptance by it of a status of neutrality, and its willingness to restructure German economic relations with Eastern Europe.
- Its attitude toward the presence of allied forces on German soil and toward the quadripartite agreement on Berlin.
- Whether German unity would fit into and further the CSCE process.
- Whether the two German states—should they opt for unity—would be ready to take the interests of the other European states into account and be willing collectively to seek mutually acceptable

solutions for all problems that might emerge in this context, including a European peace agreement.[6]

The Two Plus Four Process

It is neither within the framework of this essay nor necessary to retrace the hectic diplomatic activities at the end of 1989 and the beginning of 1990 leading to the decision on February 14, 1990, to initiate the Two plus Four talks on unification between the two German states and the Four Powers.[7] The plan launched by the Federal Republic on February 7 for an economic and monetary union between the two German states and the visit by Chancellor Kohl and Foreign Minister Genscher to Moscow from February 10 to 11 were, however, particularly important.

The idea to form an economic and monetary union between the two German states within only a couple of months was, from an economic and financial point of view, obviously risky and, accordingly, was criticized by experts. But in view of the accelerating erosion of the economy and currency of the GDR, the plan corresponded to a political necessity. It largely anticipated full political unification and made it even more unavoidable. That Gorbachev did not veto it during Kohl's visit a few days later clearly indicated that Moscow had resigned itself to German unification. The readiness that the Kremlin showed on this occasion to participate in the Two plus Four talks proposed by Bonn pointed in the same direction. This at least was the clear impression of the German delegation and was not contradicted by the Soviet side. Gorbachev, the chancellor said, had agreed that it was for Germans only to decide on the timing of unification and on the way to reach the goal.[8]

As a consequence, the decision to initiate such talks could be made by the foreign ministers of the two German states and the Four Powers at the margin of a conference between NATO and Warsaw Pact members held in Ottawa, Canada, on February 13 and 14. The designation Two plus Four instead of Four-plus-Two was incidentally of symbolic significance, symbols being on occasion meaningful in diplomacy. It expressed the fact, to which the German side attached importance, that this time, different from the postwar years, negotiations were not between the Four Powers *about* Germany but *with* Germany. Negotiations, as Genscher pointed out, were to be confined to external aspects of German unity, internal ones concerning only the Germans.[9] They were to cover the issue of the Polish border, military and security aspects, Berlin, and the termination of the special rights of the Four Powers.

About the definite recognition of the Polish border by Germany there could never be serious doubt. But the issue had acquired a significance out of proportion because of a tactical error by Chancellor Kohl. The Potsdam Agreement of July 1945 between the Four Powers had stipulated that the final delimitation of the Western frontier of Poland should await the peace settlement.[10] That stipulation had been taken up by the Convention on Relations between the Federal Republic of Germany and the Three Western Powers of 1952 and 1954.[11] But except for a tiny though vociferous minority among expellees and refugees in Germany, no one had any doubt about the finality of the so-called Oder-Neisse line, which had been accepted through international treaties by both German states as Poland's western border.

The chancellor, however, basing his views on the stipulations mentioned previously, persistently refused to commit Germany formally. In strictly legal terms he had a point; politically, however, he was mistaken and came under increasing international and domestic pressure. His motive probably was mostly tactical. Facing elections at the end of 1990, he was, it seems, anxious to keep the radical right-wing party, "the Republicans," out of parliament. Polls gave them between 2 to 3 percent of the vote. The chancellor was apparently concerned that they might win the 5 percent required to enter parliament should he recognize without reservation that one-fifth of former national territory was definitely lost. That he himself should have had any doubts about the finality of the Polish western border is most unlikely. Domestically the issue was finally settled on March 6, 1990, by an agreement between the parties forming the coalition government in Bonn. The international settlement took place in the course of the third round of the Two plus Four talks at the ministerial level in Paris on July 17, 1990, which the Polish foreign minister, Krzysztof Skubiszewski, attended. The German side committed itself to concluding a border treaty with Poland as soon as possible after unification and to the regaining of full German sovereignty. The treaty was ultimately to be signed on November 14 in Warsaw by the foreign ministers of Germany and Poland. Ratification is scheduled for late 1991 after the conclusion of a second treaty, signed June 17, 1991, on good neighborliness, partnership, and cooperation.

The Two plus Four negotiations were to take place on two levels. High officials were to plan ministerial meetings of which ultimately four took place on May 5 in Bonn, June 22 in East Berlin, July 17 in Paris, and September 12 in Moscow, where the treaty was signed. From its inception in Ottawa in February to its end, the negotiating process lasted almost seven months to the day—an incredibly short time in view of the underlying revolutionary changes, all of which needed attention.

The military status of the united Germany was clearly the central issue of the negotiations. Here the starting positions were entirely contradictory. The two German states and the three Western powers insisted on the right of united Germany to take over the membership of the Federal Republic in the Atlantic alliance and to remain within the North Atlantic Treaty Organization, its integrated structure. Taking over this membership implied the union of the GDR with the Federal Republic under Article 23 of the Basic Law instead of a merger under a corresponding treaty. In other words, the German and Western governments categorically rejected neutralization.

The Soviet Union, which at the outset had significantly rejected unification under Article 23, insisted on neutralization by contractual obligation. In taking this position, Moscow actually reverted to the pattern of 1952, when Stalin, in his famous note to the Western powers, offered unification at the price of neutralization in order to prevent German rearmament.

A number of interconnected steps were needed to reconcile these two contradictory positions, largely in favor of the position taken by the West. The main and most convincing Western argument against neutrality referred to the question of stability in Europe. Could not an enlarged Germany untied to any alliance and alone responsible for its own defense be forced to arm itself heavily and end up as a "loose cannon?" Significantly, this argument was adopted by Moscow's partners to the west in the Warsaw Pact—Poland, Czechoslovakia, and Hungary—leaving the Kremlin virtually isolated.

Moscow's most convincing argument referred to the balance of forces. The extension of NATO to the territory of the GDR would constitute an unacceptable shift of balance to the disadvantage of the Warsaw Pact members. This was a most serious argument indeed, for not only the military balance was involved. To evacuate its stronghold in the heart of Europe was for Moscow virtually equivalent to the surrendering of its outer eastern European empire. Would Gorbachev be able to make the Soviet power elite—the party and the military in particular—face facts and convince them that this was inevitable? Could he survive politically? It may have been this question that for a moment led to an apparent wavering in the US attitude. During a visit to Moscow from February 7 to 10, on the eve of the Ottawa conference, Secretary Baker suggested a possible associated or otherwise reduced membership of Germany in NATO.[12] Afterward, this was never again mentioned.

A proposal made by Foreign Minister Genscher, however, became a key to the solution of the problem. In an address to the academy at Tutzing in Bavaria on January 31, the very day when East German Prime Minister Hans Modrow visited Moscow, Genscher first advanced the idea that Germany should stay in NATO but that NATO structures should not be extended to the territory of the GDR.[13]

For the time being, however, Moscow persisted in rejecting NATO membership of a united Germany. But the idea was launched by one of Gorbachev's policy advisers, Viacheslav Dashitshev,[14] to be taken up by the Soviet president's military adviser, Marshal Sergey Akhromeyev. Germany, they indicated, might eventually stay in NATO after the transformation of the military alliances into political organizations. This trial balloon should probably be seen in the context of the endeavors of the Atlantic alliance to redefine its own role, efforts that culminated in the London Declaration of the NATO summit of July 8, 1990.

Nonetheless, the basic Soviet attitude remained unchanged throughout the first ministerial round of the Two plus Four talks held in Bonn in the beginning of May. There was, instead, an attempt by Moscow to elude the problem. As has been mentioned, the Soviet side was, for obvious reasons, opposed to a simple adhesion of the GDR to the Federal Republic under Article 23 of the republic's constitution. This opposition had been confirmed and strongly underlined by a statement issued by the Soviet Foreign Ministry on March 14.[15] Moscow's opposition was in clear contradiction to the acknowledged principle that to decide on the inner aspects of unification was up to the Germans alone.

After communist rule was brought to an end in the GDR through free elections on March 18, however, the two German states agreed to proceed according to Article 23. Furthermore, this became unavoidable in view of the ever-accelerating disintegration of the GDR. The Western powers, who initially also favored a step-by-step approach, had for some time already accepted that unification must quickly be realized. Now it was the Soviet Union that silently dropped its opposition against instant unification under Article 23. Instead, Moscow suggested a decoupling of the internal and external aspects of unification. According to this proposal, unification could be accomplished before a final settlement of the external aspects was obtained. United Germany, in other words, would not immediately regain full sovereignty, and the Four Powers would retain their rights at least for a transitional period.

This proposal was first welcomed by Foreign Minister Genscher but was shortly afterward rejected by Chancellor Kohl. As the *Neue Züricher Zeitung* commented, it would have been tantamount to a partial neutralization of Germany.[16] Nor did the Western powers accept the idea, and it was not to be brought up again.

One further move by Moscow on the occasion of the first ministerial ground was the acceptance, in Secretary Baker's words, of "a final settlement under international law"[17] instead of a peace treaty, which the Kremlin initially demanded. The question was of some importance. The Protocol of the Proceedings of the Potsdam Conference of 1945[18] as well as the Convention Between the Three Powers and the Federal Republic[19] use the term *peace settlement*. In the ensuing years, however, the term *peace treaty* had been used in many official statements. The Federal Republic, with the concurrence of its Western allies, was interested in reverting to the notion of a "settlement" to avoid the immensely complex and virtually unsolvable issue of reparations. In announcing the agenda on which the Two plus Four had agreed for their talks, Foreign Minister Genscher listed as point four "a final settlement under international law,"[20] thus indicating that the Soviet Union had changed its position.

Regarding the central issue of the future military status of Germany, the Soviet Union launched further trial balloons. According to press reports, Gorbachev, during consultations with President Mitterrand, indicated Soviet willingness to accept membership of Germany in the Atlantic alliance provided it, like France, stayed out of NATO.[21] At the US-Soviet summit in Washington from May 31 to June 3, 1990, Gorbachev raised the possibility of a dual membership of Germany in both military alliances for a transitional period. Both ideas were rejected by the Federal Republic as well as by its Western allies. "Decoupling" the internal and external aspects of German unification came up again at the second ministerial round of the Two plus Four talks when Foreign Minister Shevardnadze surprisingly proposed to delay German sovereignty for a transitional period of five years.

But despite such maneuvers, generally considered as rear-guard actions, a package deal began gradually to emerge. It included the following elements: Genscher's idea, accepted by the Western powers, not to advance

NATO forces and structures into the territory of the GDR; German acceptance of a Soviet military presence on the territory of the GDR for a transitional period; a solution for the problems connected with Soviet withdrawal from Germany, in particular, the extremely difficult problem of housing for families of officers and commissioned officers; limitation of the strength of the armed forces of a united Germany; agreement on a ceiling for US and Soviet forces in Europe and an assured conclusion of the Viennese talks on conventional arms reductions; changes in NATO strategy; transformation of NATO into a more political alliance; and institutionalization of the CSCE. This package deal could ultimately be put together because of a combination of firmness and flexibility on the Western side, particularly in Washington and Bonn. The West adamantly insisted on the undeniable right of sovereign Germany under the UN charter as well as the Helsinki Final Act to decide alone the question of its membership in the alliance. It was willing at the same time to go a long way toward meeting understandable Soviet concerns.

During his meeting with President Bush in Washington on May 17, Chancellor Kohl indicated flexibility on the question of the presence of Soviet troops in the eastern part of Germany for a transitional period.[22] As to the crucial issue of the future limitation of German armed forces, in the view of the Federal Republic and its Western allies that would be dealt with in Vienna. Foreign Minister Genscher nevertheless indicated German readiness to reduce the forces of a united Germany within three to four years to 370,000, a statement formally confirmed at the negotiating table in Vienna on August 30.[23] Appropriate signals concerning the adaptation of NATO policy and strategy to post–Cold War conditions were sent out to Moscow first by the regular council meeting at the ministerial level in Turnberry, Scotland, on June 5 and 6—the so-called Turnberry signal—and then by the London Declaration by heads of state and government on July 6.

In this declaration, the Atlantic alliance offered friendship to the countries of Central and Eastern Europe and proposed a solemn joint statement on the renunciation of force; invited Gorbachev and other Eastern leaders to visit Brussels to address the council; proposed military contacts between NATO and Eastern Europe; offered a continuation of talks on military doctrine; attached highest priority to the Viennese talks on conventional disarmament; proposed to initiate immediately afterward a second round of negotiations aiming at the limitation of European forces; indicated its willingness to negotiate considerable reductions of short-range nuclear weapons; announced the elaboration of a new strategy, the revision of its doctrine of flexible response with a view to reducing the role of its nuclear means to weapons of last resort; proposed a CSCE summit to be held at the end of the year and the institutionalization of the CSCE process, including a center for conflict prevention.[24]

The last point constituted a marked concession on the part of the United States. Washington had initially been reluctant to accept institutionalization of the CSCE, probably out of concern that the alliance might ultimately be absorbed into some kind of ill-defined collective security system.

Breakthrough

The breakthrough came only a few days after the London Declaration in the course of a visit by Chancellor Kohl to the Soviet Union from July 14 to 16. Kohl and Gorbachev reached complete agreement regarding the external aspects of German unification, announced by the chancellor in a statement before the press in Shelesnovodsk (Caucasus). Most important, Germany would regain unrestricted sovereignty upon unification, and in accordance with the Helsinki Final Act it would be free to decide by itself whether it wanted to belong to a military alliance. The chancellor made it clear that in the opinion of his government united Germany was to be a member of the Atlantic alliance. An agreement should be concluded with the Soviet Union regarding the modalities of the withdrawal of Soviet troops from Germany within three to four years. NATO structures would not be extended to the territory of the former GDR as long as Soviet troops were still present, and Germany, as the chancellor confirmed, would agree in Vienna to reduce its forces to 370,000. Finally, Kohl again committed Germany to renounce atomic, biological, and chemical weapons and pledged continued German membership in the Non-Proliferation Treaty.[25]

Thus, for the fourth time in the process of German unification, Gorbachev had made a decision of historic importance. First, he had publicly dissociated himself from Honecker on the fortieth anniversary of the GDR, bringing about the latter's downfall. Then he had refused to let Soviet troops support (by force) the crumbling SED regimes. At the chancellor's visit to Moscow in February 1990 he had accepted that it was up to the Germans themselves to decide when and how they wanted to be united. Now he had recognized the sovereign right of united Germany to stay in NATO and agreed to withdraw Soviet troops. When making the first two of these decisions Gorbachev in all probability did not yet foresee that they would lead not only to the end of communist rule in East Germany but also to the absorption of the GDR by the Federal Republic. With the third one, he drew the conclusion from the realization that rapid unification had become inevitable.

The fourth decision must have been the most difficult. True, the West had made concessions, notably regarding the policy of the alliance, the institutionalization of the CSCE, and the limitation of German armed forces. Furthermore, Gorbachev was isolated within his own crumbling alliance—Poland, Czechoslovakia, and Hungary being against the neutralization of Germany. Finally, the right of Germany under the Helsinki Final Act to decide for itself was undeniable. But still, resistance within the Soviet leadership, particularly among the military, must have been exceedingly strong. Gorbachev's decision thus remains an act of true statesmanship.

In his report to the parliament on the agreement reached with the Soviet Union, Chancellor Kohl mentioned two more elements of the understanding—a comprehensive treaty of cooperation between united Germany and the Soviet Union as well as economic and financial cooperation.[26] It had further been agreed, as Gorbachev mentioned in his press conference on July 16,[27] that the considerable cost of Soviet troop withdrawals, in particular with regard to housing for military personnel, would be shared. The treaty on cooperation was ultimately initialed in Moscow on September 13, one day after the signing of the Treaty on the Final Settlement with Respect to Germany and was signed on November 9, 1990 after unification was realized.

Two treaties regarding the Soviet troops in Germany were signed in Bonn on October 9 and 12, respectively, the first covering the financial, the second the political and organizational aspects of the temporary stationing and the gradual withdrawal of the forces. The financial arrangement, worth noting, provided for German payments in the amount of DM13 billion, approximately $8.2 billion.[28] All the treaties have meanwhile been ratified.

The results obtained at Shelesnovodsk definitely paved the way to the conclusion of the Two plus Four talks at the fourth ministerial round. The Treaty on the Final Settlement with Respect to Germany was signed in Moscow on September 12, 1990. Among other agreements it stipulated in particular these terms: United Germany would comprise the territory of the Federal Republic, the GDR, and Berlin; Germany and Poland would confirm the frontier between them by a treaty; united Germany would never use its weapons except in conformity with its constitution and the charter of the United Nations; Germany would renounce the production, possession, and control of nuclear, biological, and chemical weapons; the rights and obligations under the Non-Proliferation Treaty would continue to apply for the united Germany; German forces would be reduced to 370,000 within three or four years; Soviet troops would withdraw from Germany by the end of 1994; until the completion of Soviet withdrawal only German forces not integrated in NATO would be stationed on the territory of the former GDR and no nuclear weapons would be deployed on that territory afterward; the right of united Germany to belong to an alliance would not be affected by the present treaty; the Four Powers would terminate their rights and responsibilities; and united Germany accordingly would enjoy full sovereignty in its internal and external affairs.[29] Pending ratification, the Four Powers agreed to suspend their rights on the eve of the realization of German unity—October 2. Thus, a process of truly revolutionary character was brought to a successful conclusion by skillful diplomacy.

A kind of All-European "ratification" of the outcome took place at the summit conference of the thirty-four (thirty-five minus the GDR) member countries of the CSCE in Paris from November 19 to 21, 1990. On this occasion a treaty on conventional disarmament in Europe between the member states of NATO and the Warsaw Pact was signed as well as a joint statement of these twenty-two states regarding the new East-West relations in Europe. Finally, a declaration of the CSCE meeting of heads of state and government was issued on November 21, 1990—the Paris Charter for a New Europe.

The year 1990 ended with great hope, but the shadows of the crisis in the Persian Gulf and in the Soviet Union were beginning to loom large on the horizon.

Notes

1. Documents on Germany 1944-1985, Department of State Publication 9446 (Documents), p. 428.
2. *Europa Archiv* (*EA*), No. 24, 1989, p. D 728 ff.
3. Translation of speech at Sipri/IDW Conference in Potsdam on February 9, 1990, released by Auswärtiges Amt, Bonn.

4. *EA*, No. 1, 1990, p. Z 3.
5. "Baker: Outlines Blueprint for New Era in Europe," text of address to Berlin Press Club. Released by US Embassy, Bonn, December 12, 1989.
6. *EA*, No. 5, 1990, p. D 132.
7. See the Chronology in this volume.
8. *Neue Züricher Zeitung* (*NZZ*), February 14, 1990, p. 1.
9. *NZZ*, February 16, 1990, p. 1.
10. Documents, p. 63.
11. Documents, pp. 427-428.
12. *NZZ*, February 14, 1990, p. 3.
13. *EA*, No. 4, 1990, p. Z 30; NZZ, February 4-5, 1990, p. 1.
14. *NZZ*, March 20, 1990, p. 2.
15. *EA*, No. 19, 1990, p. D 492.
16. *NZZ*, May 10, 1990, p. 2.
17. *NZZ*, May 8, 1990, p. 2.
18. Documents, p. 54.
19. Documents, p. 425.
20. *EA*, No. 19, 1990, p. D 502.
21. *NZZ*, May 29, 1990, p. 1.
22. *NZZ*, May 20-21, 1990, p. 2.
23. Translation of advance text, issued by Auswärtiges Amt, Bonn, August 30, 1990, p. 4.
24. *EA*, No. 17, 1990, p. D 456 ff.
25. *EA*, No. 18, 1990, p. D 480.
26. *EA*, No. 18, 1990, pp. D 488-489.
27. *EA*, No. 18, 1990, p. D 483.
28. *EA*, No. 21, 1990, p. Z 214.
29. Text *EA*, No. 19, 1990, p. D 509-512.

8

The Problem of Security in Post-containment Europe

James E. Goodby

THE COLD WAR IMPOSED a bipolar order on Europe and divided the most powerful of the European states. Consequently, so it is argued, the "normal" laws of behavior of the European state system have been suspended for the past forty years. The division of Germany and of Europe ended in 1990 and the bipolar system is rapidly disappearing; so inevitably a new specter is being conjured up to haunt US-European relations. It is the fear that the old order will return and, with it, the heightened risk of war in Europe. To take counsel from this fear could destroy the unity of the democratic commonwealth that has emerged in Europe and North America, and US foreign policy and public opinion would be focused on the wrong security issue.

The security problems confronting Europe today are not the traditional balance-of-power issues among the most powerful of the European states. The security threats now and for the next decade will stem from ethnic disputes and from claims of autonomy from central authorities in Eastern Europe and the Soviet Union. These are *internal* problems; they pose new questions about state sovereignty. For this reason, there is an urgent need to develop mechanisms for dealing collectively with such issues. Even though all disputes may not be resolved through such procedures, they can be contained, and the process would help to define and reinforce the rules and norms of international and even internal behavior.

The traditional pattern of European *interstate* relations has been broken, and the causes for this transcend the Cold War. The engagement of the United States in the political and security affairs of Europe and the continuing advance of the European Community (EC) toward a confederal status have created a new European order. This order should persist beyond the Cold War because its survival is not dependent on Cold War conditions. The new European interstate order should be quite resistant to change, but it cannot be immune to the corrosive effects of protracted public confusion, doubt, or hostility in Europe and North America. The steadiness of purpose that was the unexpected hallmark of US policy during the Cold War could be lost if the essential principles of US policy in Europe cannot gain a consensus among the American people.

An American foreign policy consensus could be built around several points. First, positive changes in the structure of European state relations have resulted from the rise of the United States as a European power and the drive toward unity by the members of the European Community. This Euroamerican Commonwealth is essential to peace and stability in Europe. Second, through the process of concerting policies regarding German unification, the inclusion of the Soviet Union in the new European order has begun. This process should be encouraged. Third, new procedures must be developed to deal with the most likely threats to stability in Europe, which are internal to states, not traditional balance-of-power issues, which will be less important in the next decade.

New Problems, Old Answers

Will the disciplines imposed by the Cold War cease to exist as the Cold War recedes into memory? Probably, and the nature of nation-states and of the anarchical states system, as exemplified by centuries of European history, could lead to the conclusion that conflict among the European states is inevitable sooner or later. If it is assumed that war was prevented by the bipolar stalemate represented by the Cold War in Europe, then the collapse of bipolarity should be accompanied by a renewal of rivalries and eventually of conflicts. This gloomy conclusion is based on the assumption that democratic governments are as prone to conflict as governments of any other persuasion and that Europeans by and large are like the Bourbons: They forget nothing and they learn nothing. However, even without hegemony or empire, it is conceivable that patterns of cooperation can be learned and can persist that may temper or even prevent conflict among nation-states. Perhaps it is possible that cooperation strategies can be institutionalized in the form of international regimes—a set of norms, rules, and expectations about behavior. The nineteenth-century Concert of

Europe can be thought of as an international regime. The twentieth-century Conference on Security and Cooperation in Europe (CSCE) is beginning to take on the characteristics of an international regime. States that are linked by a common set of norms, rules, procedures, and expectations—a common constitution, in effect—can be called a *society of states* to signify that a certain order exists among them.[1] Any "new world order" would be a society of states premised on some sort of unwritten constitution that postulates accepted rules of international behavior. Order in Europe clearly requires an interstate constitution, and this must be one of the main tasks of US diplomacy.

The weight of European experience with the states system since the Peace of Westphalia in 1648 is on the side of those who doubt that cooperation will replace conflict. There are elements that may be more important today than in the past, but these should not be overrated. Flaws can be found in theories that seek to prove that war as an institution is on the wane. International regimes can be feeble institutions when up against strong national ambitions. Democratic governments may not always remain democratic. The impediments to major war in Europe, nonetheless, appear to be formidable. Two quite specific new phenomena clearly have altered the circumstances that led to wars in Europe in the past. These two factors—the United States as a European power and the rise of the European Community—can serve to prevent a return to the power rivalries and conflicts of the past. The conceptual and ultimately the political framework within which the United States and the European Community will interact in the future has been well developed in the past forty years. The new challenges to the system are not the theoretical instabilities of multipolarity but the real problems of a Europe struggling toward a supranational identity in the West and toward democracy and market economies in the East while being beset, especially in the East, by the claims of ethnic particularism. These are problems about which classic balance-of-power prescriptions say little of value.

The Constitution of Order in Europe

A set of common rules and institutions—a regime, or what is called in this chapter a constitution—is what links and defines a society of states and is what this society of states uses to bring order out of chaos in interstate relations. Rules can be as basic as the notion that nuclear war should be avoided and institutions can be as fundamental as war and diplomacy. As a society of states evolves, its set of rules and institutions should become increasingly complex and affect more aspects of the life of states within it. An example of this is the European Community. It is obvious that several societies of states currently exist in Europe, each with a somewhat distinct set of rules and institutions. Two of these societies are of special interest to the United States: the group of democratic market-economy nations—essentially the North Atlantic Treaty Organization (NATO), the European Community, and Western-oriented neutrals—and the larger society of all those nations, including the Soviet Union, that are linked more loosely by a common set of rules and institutions related mainly to their common purpose of survival in the nuclear age. The first of these societies, comprising the democratic market-economy nations, could be described as the Euroamerican Commonwealth because of the high degree of cohesion and interdependence these states already have achieved. Its structure is strong and well tested. The second could be described as the European Concert because these states have achieved some success in concerting their policies, albeit for limited purposes.

Priority should be given to developing the concept and the infrastructure of these two societies of states. In this regard, US policy toward Europe, especially toward Europe as a whole, is not well thought through. The end of a bitter ideological struggle is an ideal time to reemphasize the ideas that unite these nations rather than those that divide them.[2] Perhaps, also, greater attention in American foreign policy to building a commonwealth and a concert will prove to be more inspirational for the American people than the idea of simply being Europe's "cop on the beat." The motivational factor cannot be ignored if the United States is to remain as steady in its purpose in Europe as it has been for the past forty years. Being an "off-shore balancer" or a proliferator of nuclear weapons to nations that have no interest in having them are ideas that are not likely to be in tune with the American style.[3]

The idea of societies of states in Europe has many facets. Four are examined in this chapter: the durability of the United States as a European power; the impact of the European Community; the place of the Soviet Union in the Euroamerican society of nations; and an institutional response to the most likely type of security problems of the next decade, which will be overwhelmingly internal to states, rather than to classical balance-of-power struggles.

Will the United States Remain a Part of the Commonwealth?

The rules, norms, and expectations associated with the society of states that existed in Europe in the eighteenth and nineteenth centuries did not prevent war, although they had their successes, too. History teaches us that exaggerated hopes for the beneficent effects of a society of states would be misplaced. Some conditions exist today, however, that were not foreseen in earlier centuries. Through the Monroe Doctrine, the United States and Britain collaborated after the Napoleonic Wars in deterring the spread of European imperialism in the Western Hemisphere, but the United States at that time played no direct role in Europe. World War II changed all that. The United States has become something new under the European sun in power terms, but only in this century and really only since the 1950s. Since then, the United States has become a significant force influencing the equilibrium of Europe.

Those who have suggested that the European states system has been changed forever by the events of the 1940s and 1950s may have been right, even though the division of Germany, on which their assumptions and predictions were largely based, is no longer a factor.[4] The division of Germany probably was a less important element in creating a stable order in Europe than the advent of the United States as an active player in nearly every aspect of European life. This can be seen more clearly now with the collapse of Soviet power in Europe and the end of the confrontation that obscured the real character of the changes in Europe. The United States, no longer so critical in the defense of Western Europe, still is seen by Europeans as a stabilizing force in Europe, a powerful economic motor for all developed nations, and the only multipurpose global superpower. The presence of the United States as a European power changes the basis for measuring and judging the nature of an equilibrium in Europe and for estimating the chances that order will win out over anarchy.

Will that remain so? The United States could free itself from the links that have been forged between the new and the old worlds, but it would take quite a sustained effort to do so. This is not a matter of American forces in Europe but of an economic, political, and cultural network that has become so intertwined that the nations of Europe and North America have become linked at many levels, not just the governmental. This fact is what gives meaning to the notion that a commonwealth already exists. It is not an overt military threat that still brings forth "the New World to redress the balance of the Old" but the more benign pressures of a strong tradition of cooperation, the idea of a commonwealth.[5]

Paul Kennedy's analysis of imperial overstretch and the obvious economic difficulties the United States is facing have to be taken seriously.[6] A failure to solve these problems could inflict permanent damage on the transatlantic connection. Joseph Nye, Samuel Huntington, and others have made persuasive arguments, however, that the United States is the fortunate possessor of a variety of advantages that should preserve its leadership role.[7] It can, at the same time, avoid imperial overstretch unless the new world order requires the United States to play the policing role on a large scale.

The European Community

The rise of the European Community is another important reason that history cannot be a complete guide to the prospects for replacing anarchy with order. There have been alliances and ententes aplenty in the past 400 years of European history. There has been nothing like the European Community as it exists today, to say nothing of the community of the future that is now being planned and constructed. Institutionalized economic cooperation already has subordinated national laws and prerogatives to those of the EC. The fiscal and monetary policies of the EC countries—matters still jealously guarded by national governments—increasingly are bound together. Political cooperation has reached the point where common EC policies on the Middle East and relations with Moscow are the rule rather than the exception despite the disarray during the Gulf War. Defense cooperation has been more difficult to achieve, but it, too, is beginning to be actively discussed among EC countries.

The Great Illusion, Norman Angell's well-known book, first published in 1909, used economic arguments to attack the idea that war was a profitable venture.[8] His predictions were so wrong that economic interdependence has been discredited ever since as a disincentive to war. If the EC were merely interdependence writ large, its effect on war and peace could be assessed in terms of historical experience with economic interdependence and its impact discounted correspondingly. The community is more than that. States in Western Europe no longer are fully sovereign, and this change clearly has introduced a new factor into European relations. Members of the community have learned a strategy of cooperation out of which they have created order.

The European Community will not be, for the next decade, a sufficient answer to the problem of creating order in Europe. The European society of states must include the United States, at least for this period, if the conditions for order in Europe are to be met. The EC's political, economic, and defense institutions are still being built. Its internal structure lacks a democratic system of governance, and progress toward deeper integration may slow down after 1992. Furthermore, the community's weak foreign policy and security machinery limit what it can do externally.

Arguments that the EC can help to avert anarchy in Eastern Europe and extend the commonwealth into that region carry considerable force.[9] Much depends, however, on the course the EC charts for itself. It has been divided in its counsels between those who would broaden its membership and those who would deepen the extent of cooperation among the present members. Broadening almost certainly will be deferred until after the next phase of deepening has been accomplished in 1992. But after that, it would not be surprising to find, by the year 2000, a community of eighteen members. Austria, Sweden, and possibly Finland may be admitted by 1995. Czechoslovakia, Hungary, and Poland might achieve full membership by the end of the century. Associate membership may be the best that the rest of Europe can achieve by that time or, in some cases, would want. The decade ahead, therefore, could see the EC making a substantial contribution to stability in Eastern Europe and creating a much larger commonwealth. Obviously, expansion of the community's eastward reach would not solve all the foreseeable problems if one considers only the countries left out of the list of candidate members. Yugoslavia, Romania, and Bulgaria could be the sources of considerable unrest. Nor should it be inferred from this discussion that the nations of Eastern Europe are incapable of self-help. They can do a great deal for themselves, but the next decade is all too short a time for them to shake off the burdens of the past without external assistance.

And what about Western Europe? There is only so much that can be done in a given time under the procedures that must be followed by the EC. The expansion of the community would delay the process of federation. But this is the process that is creating a Europe different from the one that existed in previous centuries and that must influence the outlook for order within the European society of states. The loss in the momentum toward deeper integration affects precisely those EC nations—Britain, France, Germany, and Italy—whose relations, according to traditional theory, are critical to the avoidance of general conflict in Europe and whose cooperation is essential to the strengthening of the commonwealth. The argument that historical experience cannot be a reliable guide to the outlook for order in Europe is weakened by this anticipated slowdown, but not by much because truly impressive steps toward integration will already have been made by 1992.

The Soviet Question and Concert Diplomacy

Should the Soviet Union, too, be a member of a Euroamerican society of states? How would the common rules and institutions of this society of states be affected by Moscow's participation in it? Russia's presence in European affairs in the past century was not a source of comfort to the Western powers. However, its absence in the period after World War I—and the absence of the United States as well—was partially the reason that another bloody war began in 1939. If the United States remains a part of the European society of states, it could be argued that the inclusion of the Soviet Union in it is not essential. Indeed, there are good arguments to support the view that Russia's history, its governmental traditions, and its Asian territory mean that the commonwealth ends at Poland's eastern frontier.[10] In many respects this situation will be confronted for a long time to come. It means that a society of states that includes the Soviet Union will be linked by a set of rules and institutions rather different from that which links the United States and the European democracies, old and new. Although the EC may expand to include Poland, it is unlikely ever to include the Soviet Union, or even Russia. For decades, the economic ties between the United States and the EC are likely to be far stronger, even though occasionally strained, than the EC's ties with Moscow. Political turbulence in the Soviet Union also is likely to persist for some time, making links between Moscow and the West difficult to nurture. The Soviet Union, in whatever form it emerges from the current struggles, cannot and will not be ignored by the Europeans. In one way or another, a common set of rules by which the Soviet Union, North America, and the European states pursue their international goals will be constructed.

The diplomacy of 1990 may have set a pattern for Soviet relationships with the European states that will persist for the rest of the 1990s. The central event of 1990 was the unification of Germany, a unique event but one that illustrates how Moscow and the Western capitals may interact in the future.[11] This diplomacy is reminiscent of concert diplomacy in the nineteenth century except that the big powers are no longer the sole arbiters of Europe's fate. The principle is the same: Concerted policies are likely to protect the interests of each state within the society of states better than unilateral action. No one should expect that the effort to accommodate differing interests will always succeed. It did not in the nineteenth century; it will not today.

Even in the brief heyday of the Concert of Europe, dealings among the European partners were as difficult as those faced by today's governments. The concert offered a *process* for resolving problems, not ready-made answers. Castlereagh's prescription for Alexander I, Czar of All the Russias, was succinct: "He ought to be grouped."[12] A closet liberal in his youth, Alexander became something of a religious visionary in his later years. His concept of the Holy Alliance was rooted in Christian brotherhood and a conviction that any threat to the established monarchical order anywhere in Europe ought to be stamped out. Other members of the concert—France, Prussia, Austria, and Britain—found life with czarist Russia disquieting at times. But, as Henry Kissinger recently has pointed out, "it did not have the ideological fervor of its Communist successors, and it proved possible for long periods to deal with it as an important member of the European concert powers."[13]

Concert diplomacy in the period after the Napoleonic wars appealed to the self-interest of the great powers of the European society of states in avoiding another hegemonic war and in maintaining an equilibrium among them. It worked for their benefit, not necessarily for the smaller states whose fates were decided by the concert. Castlereagh's verb "grouped" captured the essence of the idea: To the extent possible the great powers should forswear unilateral action and work to achieve common policies. The idea was attacked in the nineteenth century by British politicians especially, and its sponsors were derided just as those who would renounce global unilateralism in twentieth-century America have found themselves accused of selling out American interests. Maintaining an equilibrium within the concert required constant adjustments of policy and some coercion of governments showing signs of contemplating defection. It was a difficult system to manage and was not especially popular among politicians. Castlereagh's successor in Whitehall, George Canning, gladly abandoned the concert with the comment, "Every nation for itself, and God for all of us!" And yet the idea, if not the original mechanisms, persisted through much of the nineteenth century.

Contemporary Concert Diplomacy

In the past forty years, the idea that nations should be grouped—their policies coordinated rather than independently formed and conducted—has survived and even prospered. Concerts are no longer limited to great powers. The Atlantic alliance has been a success not just because it linked US forces to the defense of Western Europe. Despite overtones of hegemony created on the one hand by the huge disparity between US and West European military power and on the other by Washington's occasionally heavy-handed diplomacy, there has been a genuine process of accommodation. The policies and preferences of the United States were altered by Washington's basic desire to group and to be grouped within the Atlantic alliance. The perception of mutual interests in some semblance of free trade and even in a limited degree of coordination of monetary policy has prompted the leading economic powers—North America, Japan, and Western Europe—to allow themselves to be grouped. These societies of nations have not been totally successful in concerting their policies or even in preventing disputes among their members. Neither was the nineteenth-century Concert of Europe. But these twentieth-century concerts have not yet had a falling out so serious as to lead to armed conflict within their ranks.

Robert Jervis has suggested that concert systems arise under conditions when two of the generally accepted assumptions of the balance-of-power have been altered: Instead of being able to shift alliances fairly rapidly as in a pure balance of power system, there are inhibitions that slow down or prevent such shifts. And in place of a belief that they can resort to war fairly readily, states conclude that war is not an acceptable policy under almost any circumstances. Jervis also suggests that in a bipolar system a high level of cooperation is difficult to maintain because of fear that exploitation might be the reward of attempts to cooperate. In a multipolar system, he argues, one state's attempt at exploitation is likely to be restrained by others, especially in a concert system where there is some mutual interest in preserving the system.[14]

In the Europe of 1989-1990, alliance patterns have changed, but obviously not with the avowed purpose of maintaining a balance of power. In fact, it is unlikely that realignments will occur for this reason over the next decade. Open, democratic forms of statecraft are likely to have more difficulties in conducting policies of realignments than are aristocratic or autocratic diplomatic establishments. Neither is war in Europe regarded by any of the participants in the European society of states as a reasonable exercise of statecraft. The bipolar system has not quite disappeared from the European scene, but already it is clear that fear of exploitation has decreased and a greater willingness to cooperate is slowly growing. Some of the conditions for reemergence of a European-wide concert system that would include North America seem to be at hand. At the very least, the conditions seem propitious for strengthening the rules and institutions of the society of states that includes all these nations.

In 1990, as in the period after the Napoleonic wars, the great powers allowed themselves to be grouped. Britain, France, the Soviet Union, and the United States, the four states with special responsibilities in Berlin and Germany, joined with Germany in concerting major elements of their European policies. The Soviets were offered a nine-point plan by Bonn and Washington to meet their concerns.[15] The plan promised that NATO would revamp its strategy and force structure, no NATO forces would be stationed in East Germany, Soviet troops would remain in East Germany for a transition period, and the Conference on Security and Cooperation in Europe would be endowed with permanent organizations to allow it to play a larger role in the affairs of Europe. Germany also would renounce any territorial claims and give economic assistance to the Soviet Union. On July 6, 1990, a NATO summit meeting in London formalized the multilateral aspects of these promises to Moscow.[16] This was followed by a meeting between German Chancellor Helmut Kohl and Soviet President Mikhail Gorbachev in Stavropol, USSR, on July 15-16, which yielded a series of German-Soviet commitments.[17] Included among them was a German promise to limit personnel strength of the armed forces in a unified Germany to 370,000 and to negotiate a comprehensive bilateral German-Soviet treaty of friendship and cooperation. In return, Gorbachev promised to give up all four power rights and responsibilities in Germany and dropped objections to a unified Germany joining NATO. Finally, a summit meeting of the Conference on Security and Cooperation in Europe adopted an agreement on November 21, 1990, on conventional force reductions in Europe, a package of new confidence-building measures, and a nonuse of force agreement among members of NATO and of the Warsaw Treaty Organization. The summit participants also decided to strengthen the Conference on Security and Cooperation in Europe.[18] In so doing, the states of Europe and North America established mechanisms not unlike those that supported the concert diplomacy of the nineteenth century.

What was seen in 1990 within the society of European states that includes the Soviet Union was the diplomacy of restraint and of compensation for losses, conducted jointly, to the extent possible. This diplomacy, even though frequently conducted bilaterally and in small groups, eventually and at various stages became the diplomacy of consensus—all members of the European society of states were involved and gave consent. The diplomacy of 1990 differed from the European concert diplomacy of the nineteenth century in its relative openness and observance of democratic principles. It was inspired, however, by the same idea that motivated the leaders of the nineteenth-century concert: The interests of each of the powers are better served by joint decisions than by unilateral actions.

Institutional Responses to Post-Cold War Security Problems

The rules and institutions that the Paris summit of November 1990 sought to impose on the states that will be practicing concert diplomacy say something about how the process may work. They cannot say everything, because not all the security problems of Europe are going to be handled by the institutions created in Paris in November 1990. It would be advisable to regard the formal apparatus established at Paris as pseudo-institutions because they will be essentially empty of content until the concert develops procedures and customary law that give this machinery real meaning.[19] The mechanisms that are now being put in place, however, will begin to shape how governments deal with critical European issues and, in time, may become the preferred method.

The following are the institutions created within the framework of the Conference on Security and Cooperation in Europe by the 1990 Paris summit:

- Council of Ministers, which will meet at least once a year.
- Committee of Senior Officials to assist the Council of Ministers. A mechanism for convening emergency meetings of the committee is to be discussed by the council.
- Secretariat, to be located in Prague, that will provide administrative support to the council and Committee of Senior Officials.
- Conflict Prevention Center, accountable to the council and located in Vienna, which in its initial stage of operations is to be concerned with the implementation of agreed confidence-building measures such as

consultations concerning unusual military activities. In time, other responsibilities might be assigned to the center in the area of dispute settlement. The substantive work of the center is to be accomplished by a consultative committee composed of representatives from all participating states.

- Office for Free Elections, accountable to the council and located in Warsaw, which will facilitate contacts and the exchange of information on elections.

The Paris summit made perhaps its most important decision when it established the Council of Ministers that would meet regularly and at least once a year. The council, supported by the Committee of Senior Officials, should become the principal element of the CSCE. At this stage of the CSCE, cooperation is likely to operate most effectively if ministers are directly involved and feel directly responsible for the main business of the CSCE, many aspects of which cannot be predicted with any certainty in the current highly fluid situation. The other organizational elements of the CSCE established by the Paris summit are potentially useful and evidently are seen by many members of the CSCE as the nuclei of what might become larger and more powerful centralized authorities.

With these decisions, the Conference on Security and Cooperation in Europe has entered a phase of institution-building not unlike that which has accompanied other major European convulsions. A significant difference, however, is that now, for the first time in history, Moscow and Washington are both involved in creating institutions that will link North America and all of the states of Europe. This is one reason why special emphasis in US diplomacy should be placed on developing the rules and institutions of the larger European society of states.

Whether the CSCE, or some other institution yet to be improvised, will become the main framework for strengthening the constitution of the concert cannot now be predicted. Washington's near-term interests have been well served by its policy of endorsing the creation of a formal CSCE structure to augment the loosely organized process that the CSCE has been until recently. Germany has become united and is still in NATO; NATO itself has not been challenged by the new version of the CSCE and is still broadly viewed in Europe as a powerful stabilizing factor. Washington, however, has considered the CSCE relatively marginal to its own basic interests. Its current view of the CSCE is colored by a tendency to think that Moscow and the East European nations need a strengthened

European platform, and no other European organizations are currently open to them. The United States and many West European governments hope that NATO will continue to be the main institutional linkage between the United States and Europe for the foreseeable future. Moscow, however, clearly conceives the CSCE to be only part of a network connecting it to Europe. Although the Soviet Union favors more robust CSCE mechanisms, its interest in European connections is not limited to the CSCE. A number of conceivable bilateral arrangements are probably at least as attractive to Soviet policymakers as the CSCE, and Soviet spokespersons have even suggested that NATO should be opened to membership by the Soviet Union.[20] NATO, however, is likely to remain what it is—a military alliance among the Western industrialized democracies that serves to hedge against uncertainty in Eastern Europe and in the Middle East.

As a commonly accepted set of understandings about the behavior of governments toward their own people and toward each other spreads throughout the continent, the "pseudo-institutions" can begin to become more congruent with the way Europe really works. The Concert of Europe was the diplomatic manifestation of the acceptance by the great powers of a limited set of principles, norms, assumptions, and expectations that bound them together as a society of states. For a time, concert diplomacy was an effective instrumentality for harmonizing the policies of most of the European states on security-threatening issues. For fifteen years the CSCE has provided a framework for establishing principles and defining norms among the member states. The massive changes in Central and Eastern Europe have begun to create the basis for building common assumptions and expectations. The CSCE member states, including the most powerful among them, will probably find it convenient to use the machinery they established at Paris. The basic question, however, is whether the underlying regime—the set of rules, assumptions, and expectations that the member states accept—will continue to be strengthened. How the CSCE is used can reinforce the regimes' development or injure it.

European Security and the CSCE

Peacekeeping operations in Europe can be performed by several international institutions. Some of them—NATO, for example—will be better able than the CSCE for many years to come to fulfill basic tasks such as deterrence or the use of force to restore the territorial integrity of a state. There may be some dispute-settlement, humanitarian, and peacekeeping operations in Europe, however, that the CSCE could potentially manage well if it were given a mandate and the tools. The conditions that would make the CSCE the ideal choice for such operations may not happen very often, but the probability is sufficiently high to justify some contingency planning. One important advantage of the CSCE, not shared by other institutions, is that its political structure gives all European states their due weight in European affairs. There are many conceivable contingencies in Eastern Europe where some kind of collective all-European response would be the best possible solution, better by far than a NATO, West European Union (WEU), or UN response. These contingencies are mainly in the area where all parties to a dispute want to avoid conflict and settle the dispute. In such cases, third-party intervention in the form of the CSCE, properly constituted, could be of real value.

The operational responsibilities of the CSCE in the security field will become meaningful only in connection with a strengthening of the international regime—the set of rules and institutions—that the CSCE embodies. This will occur as the CSCE becomes responsible for the peaceful settlement of disputes and peacekeeping operations. The CSCE has had no experience with either of these functions. Although the member states of the CSCE have developed general procedures for the peaceful settlement of disputes, no disputes have been taken for resolution to the CSCE. Member states of the CSCE have extensive experience in peacekeeping, but not within the framework of that institution; not one of them is evidencing much enthusiasm for transposing UN experience in this area into the CSCE context. Yet how dispute settlement and peacekeeping are managed in Europe will be crucial to building rules and institutions that will strengthen the concert.

Potential or actual disputes litter the landscape of Eastern Europe and the Soviet Union. Many disputes in the new Europe are internal or may be portrayed as such—treatment of minorities or relations between states within a federation. New conceptions of sovereignty may evolve to permit the international community to deal with massive human tragedies. The CSCE has had considerable success in encouraging improved behavior in the area of human rights; it should adopt a similar approach with regard to internal disputes. The basic principles involved are the same as those characteristic of any international regime—enhance communications among its members and use rewards and punishments to develop and reinforce certain norms of behavior. Even if the prospects for resolving an internal dispute through the mechanisms of the CSCE are fairly dim, efforts should be made to do so, in the first place for humanitarian reasons and secondarily to promote the acceptance of a strengthened international regime in Europe.

The use of the CSCE as a mechanism for settling disputes and defining rules of behavior will be accompanied by changes in the long-standing consensus procedure. Traditional CSCE procedures would not permit urgent or special meetings of the Council of Ministers or Committee of Senior Officials to be convened if even a single government objected. Procedures like those of the UN Security Council will be adapted to CSCE needs to permit emergency meetings when requested by CSCE states. The unanimity rule is likely to be retained only for some time with regard to most decisions that emergency meetings would be called upon to make.

This process of dispute settlement would not be complete unless it contemplated and provided for authorization and use of military forces. Military forces may very well be needed for humanitarian purposes in some situations in Europe. Events in northern Iraq have shown that if the international community is not ready to mount large-scale logistical efforts to meet humanitarian needs, resort to national military forces may be the only answer and may not be the best answer. Planning for and, if necessary, getting experience in the use of military forces for humanitarian and peacekeeping purposes will be an essential part of the "regime"-building function of the CSCE. In addition to basic humanitarian functions, three types of peacekeeping operations might be needed and could be feasible even under the rule of unanimity. These are

- Use of military or paramilitary units to observe a situation that contains some risk of conflict.
- Use of such units to control borders or other sensitive areas.
- Use of such forces to establish a buffer zone between adversarial military forces.

In each of these cases, it is possible that no objection would be raised by states involved in situations that seemed to threaten conflict, and they might even actively seek such help. These applications of peacekeeping forces might be relevant to many of the possible crises that one can envisage in Eastern Europe: ethnic disputes within one state, political subunits of one state on the verge of conflict with one another, and two states that are on a collision course over some unresolved issue.

The Next Decade

The Cold War in Europe had many kinds of costs—bitter hostility, sterile confrontation, violent struggle, and damaged societies—but it offered relative stability for a long time. Elsewhere in the world, wars fought in the name of containment cost the lives of more then 100,000 Americans and many more of other nationalities. Europe may be both safer and more unstable after the Cold War. Ethnic and nationalistic claims driven underground for decades by communist repression already are sparking conflicts. There is uncertainty, too, stemming from the difficult and disorderly transition from authoritarian political systems and command economies in Eastern Europe. The situation in the Soviet Union is unpredictable, but even civil war on a significant scale cannot be ruled out.

Somewhere near the bottom of this list of stability-threatening situations should appear the question of whether West European nations will return to their old habits of internecine warfare. It is not very probable, and there are more imminent threats to stability and security in Europe that demand more serious attention and creative solutions to contradictory demands of sovereignty and humanitarian needs. The nations of Europe and North America need to confront these new threats and learn how to deal with them. If these more proximate threats are not handled well, Europe, and indeed the world, will suffer for it. There are plenty of troubles to go around in what can already plainly be seen. The last decade of the twentieth century will be full of turmoil, but not because eighteenth-century power politics will make a comeback in Europe.

Notes

1. Robert Axelrod, *The Evolution of Cooperation* (New York: Basic Books, 1984); through repeated plays of "The Prisoner's Dilemma," Axelrod demonstrated that strategies of cooperation could be learned. Robert O. Keohane, *After Hegemony: Cooperation and Discord in the World Political Economy* (Princeton: Princeton University Press, 1984); one of the classic studies of cooperation and international regimes. Hedley Bull, *The Anarchical Society: A Study of Order in World Politics* (New York: Columbia University Press, 1977), p. 315; Bull's viewpoint was that "the states system can

remain viable only if the element in it of international society is preserved and strengthened."

2. Bull, *The Anarchical Society*, p. 42ff. Bull did not really make this case but his analysis is consistent with it and with historical experience.

3. John Mearsheimer, "Back to the Future," *International Security*, Vol. 15, No. 1 (Summer 1990), pp. 37-38, 55.

4. Anton DePorte, *Europe Between The Superpowers: The Enduring Balance*, Second Edition. (New Haven: Yale University Press, 1986).

5. Keohane, *After Hegemony*, p. 43. Writing of the world political economy, the author contends "that the common interests of the leading capitalist states, bolstered by the effects of existing international regimes (mostly created during a period of American hegemony), are strong enough to make sustained cooperation possible, though not inevitable."

6. Paul Kennedy, *The Rise and Fall of the Great Powers; Economic Change and Military Conflict from 1500 to 2000* (New York: Random House, 1987).

7. Joseph Nye, *Bound to Lead: The Changing Nature of American Power* (New York: Basic Books, 1990). Samuel Huntington, "The U.S.—Decline or Renewal?" *Foreign Affairs*, Vol. 67, No. 2 (Winter 1988/1989), pp. 76-96.

8. Norman Angell, *The Great Illusion: A Study of the Relation of Military Power in Nations to their Economic and Social Advantage*, Third Edition (London: William Heinemann, 1912).

9. Jack Snyder, "Averting Anarchy in the New Europe," *International Security*, Vol. 14, No. 4 (Spring 1990).

10. Henry Kissinger, "No Illusions About the USSR," *Washington Post*, January 22, 1991, p. A-13.

11. See Chapter 7 of this volume for a review of the diplomacy of German reunification.

12. Walter Alison Phillips, *The Confederation of Europe: A Study of the European Alliance, 1813-1823 as an Experiment in the International Organization of Peace* (New York: Howard Fertig, reprinted in 1966 from the 1920 Second Edition), p. 155.

13. Kissinger, "No Illusions About the USSR."

14. Robert Jervis, "From Balance to Concert: A Study of International Security Cooperation," *World Politics*, Vol. 38, No. 1 (October 1985), pp. 58-79.

15. Thomas L. Friedman, "U.S. Will Press the Soviets to Accept Plan on Germany," *New York Times*, June 5, 1990, p. A-17.

16. The text of the London declaration was published in the *New York Times*, July 7, 1990, p. A-5. A statement by Soviet Foreign Minister Eduard Shevardnadze, responding favorably to the London declaration, appeared on the same page.

17. Serge Schmemann, "Gorbachev Clears Way for German Unity, Dropping Objection to NATO Membership," *New York Times*, July 17, 1990, p. A-1.

18. R. W. Apple, "34 Leaders Adopt Pact Proclaiming A United Europe," *New York Times*, November 22, 1990, p. A-1. Excerpts from the Charter of Paris for a New Europe appeared on p. A-16 of this edition. The full text of the Charter of Paris is available from the Bureau of Public Affairs, U.S. Department of State, Washington, DC.

19. Bull, *The Anarchical Society*, p. xiv. The term *pseudo-institutions* is attributed to Martin Wight. Bull seeks to distinguish between *international organizations* and the *institutions* of international society, which he sees as balance of power, international law, diplomacy, the role of the great powers, and war.

20. Thomas L. Friedman, "Soviets Promise to Pull Back Some Tactical Nuclear Arms," *New York Times*, June 6, 1990, p. A-10. Soviet membership in NATO was broached in conversations between Presidents Gorbachev and Bush during the Washington summit, May 31-June 3, 1990, in the context of a united Germany's entrance into NATO.

9

The CSCE in Transition

Andrei V. Zagorski

THE END OF THE POSTWAR PERIOD in Europe was marked by the second summit meeting of the participating states of the Conference on Security and Cooperation in Europe (CSCE). The Charter of Paris for a New Europe, signed at the summit, reflects a wide range of common values now shared by all CSCE countries. It contains guidelines for future efforts within the Helsinki Process and provides an unprecedented set of new CSCE institutions.

Agreement was reached on holding biannual meetings of heads of state or government. A council consisting of ministers of foreign affairs is meeting at least once a year. The Committee of Senior Officials is preparing the work of the council. The small CSCE Secretariat is situated in Prague, the Conflict Prevention Center in Vienna, and the Office for Free Elections in Warsaw.

Decisions on the establishment of new pan-European structures have become the subject of comment in various countries, and the emergence of a new "superstructure" in Europe, designed to replace the still existing blocs and become *the* foundation of a system of collective security, is also a topic of speculation. Nevertheless, the CSCE summit put forward more questions than answers. It provided for new mechanisms of multilateral cooperation, but as of this writing, it is still unclear whether these mechanisms really will become the core of a new European architecture. The Charter of Paris formally opened a period of transition and adjustment of the CSCE to the dramatic changes without having defined its final place in the emerging "great Europe." It is clear that the Helsinki Process will evolve, as will Europe itself. The end of this evolution and the implementing of the new features of the CSCE will depend both on long-term trends of European developments as well as on the model of European security and cooperation that may result from recent and future developments.

Profound Changes

An assessment of the recent changes and development in Europe is the point of departure for an analysis of the future of the CSCE. The environment in Europe has altered, presumably irreversibly, since the end of 1989. The postwar confrontation of East and West has ended. Even the very notions of East and West have become obsolete with the East no longer existing in its previous form.

Although several features of the East-West confrontation still exist—for instance, the bloc-to-bloc Conventional Forces in Europe (CFE) negotiations in Vienna—the main issue on the current European security agenda is no longer the management of the conflict between the countries of the North Atlantic Treaty Organization (NATO) and those of the Warsaw Treaty Organization but the new causes of instability in Europe. The internal developments in the Soviet Union are still the most unknown and unpredictable factor of European evolution. The fate of perestroika in the Soviet Union—its progress or regression—is, of course, one of the crucial issues determining the ongoing transformation of Europe. The surprisingly rapid unification of Germany confronted Europe with new challenges with regard to the emergence of a power capable of dominating the European scene politically, economically, and, potentially, even militarily.

Thus, profound changes have marked the end of the "Yalta order." The postwar system in Europe has collapsed, but another one is just begining to emerge. The summit in Paris in November 1990 contributed significantly to the management of this process—specially by endorsing the first CFE treaty as well as by establishing new CSCE structures that can and will be instrumental in helping Europe through the transition period. But the summit cannot pretend to have established a new system of European relations.

Major Interests Behind CSCE Institutionalization

The ongoing transformation of Eastern Europe, and indeed of all of Europe, has changed the traditional distribution of interests within the CSCE. This change opened the way for achieving consensus on the institutionalization of the Helsinki Process twenty years after the issue was first raised in the CSCE context.

In May 1990, the Soviet Union officially initiated the establishment of permanent CSCE bodies in a letter Soviet Foreign Minister Eduard Shevardnadze addressed to his colleagues from other participating states. This letter followed a number of proposals expressed in several political forums during previous months.

At the CSCE Copenhagen meeting of the Conference on the Human Dimension (CHD), June 5-29, 1990, the problem of the institutionalization of the CSCE had already begun to dominate the opening statements of many foreign ministers from both East and West. The declaration approved by the North Atlantic Treaty Organization (NATO) summit meeting in London, July 5-6, 1990, promoted this idea by proposing "that the CSCE summit in Paris decide how the CSCE can be institutionalized to provide a forum for wider political dialogue in a more united Europe" and recommended the establishment of a number of institutions.[1]

By the summer of 1990, there was a growing understanding on the feasibility and methods of CSCE institutionalization, but the reasons for this understanding differed from country to country. In Moscow, the position favoring the establishment of permanent CSCE bodies grows, in part, out of internal Soviet divisions. Since early 1990, confrontation between orthodox conservatives and the reformists in the Communist party and in the state apparatus has increased. During the spring and summer of 1990, foreign policy issues for the first time became controversial in domestic debates as the conservatives accused President Mikhail Gorbachev and Foreign Minister Shevardnadze of having "lost" Eastern Europe and the German Democratic Republic—the former "socialist community of states"—and of damaging the national security of the Soviet Union through progressive disintegration of the Warsaw Treaty and the geographic expansion of NATO. Thus, the demonstration of "positive" trends—the evolution and politicization of the Warsaw Treaty and NATO as well as the emergence of a collective security system based on new pan-European structures (CSCE institutions) instead of bloc structures—became crucial in the domestic arguments of reformist circles in the Soviet Union.

Long-Term Soviet Policy

Beyond its value to reformists in the domestic debate, the institutionalization of the CSCE can also meet long-term Soviet interests. The

Helsinki Process ensures participation of the Soviet Union in European affairs. And this link becomes even more important because the disintegration of the socialist community of states makes the CSCE a unique and valuable multilateral forum within which the Soviet Union is fully integrated into the decision-making process. Enhancing the role of the CSCE will no doubt remain a long-term Soviet priority that will be increasingly important in the coming years.

Recognition of this interest by the Soviet authorities would contribute significantly to consolidating the recent trend in Moscow's European policy—a growing acceptance of the need to improve multilateral structures of cooperation in Europe.[2] This general trend in Soviet policy can be seen in the greater openness toward the far-reaching initiatives of the thirty-five (and now thirty-four) CSCE participating states in practically all areas, including that of human rights. In that context, the emerging institutionalization of not only economic but also political cooperation of the Soviet Union with the European Community (EC) since 1989 should be considered as well as the development of contacts and cooperation with the Council of Europe and dialogue with the Western European Union (WEU) and NATO. The initiative to institutionalize the CSCE has been the culmination of the trend in Soviet policy that seeks a greater engagement in multilateral endeavors in Europe.

An uninterrupted continuation of this trend cannot be taken for granted, however. The unpredictable future of domestic developments in the Soviet Union makes it necessary to consider the possibility of a reverse direction of its European policy: backward to a neo-ideological isolationism as the result of a restoration of an orthodox regime or a dissolution of the Soviet Union with the appearance of smaller states with different priorities.

The US Attitude

A growing recognition on the part of the United States of the importance of the CSCE in the future European architecture appears also to be developing. Previously, US policy emphasized the centrality of the bilateral dialogue with the Soviet Union and East European countries. This downgrading of multilateral East-West negotiations prevailed during the elaboration of the Helsinki Final Act and resulted in a low level of US diplomatic activity at the Geneva stage of the CSCE (1973-1975).

Although further US participation in the multilateral process in Europe, beginning with the Belgrade follow-up meeting of 1977-1978, became more active, the CSCE did not immediately move up on the list of American priorities in Europe. Furthermore, in the mid-1980s the US approach to the CSCE was to some extent negative. Ten years after Helsinki it was widely believed in Washington that the impact of the whole endeavor—especially with regard to the implementation of the human rights accords—was not sufficient to justify an American commitment to the CSCE.

Speaking at a conference in Bonn on November 24, 1985, US Ambassador Richard Burt concluded, "Generally regarded, the CSCE process has proved itself in the past twelve years as a diplomatic instrument of limited use."[3]

Nevertheless, profound changes in Europe seem to have paved the way for at least partial changes in American approaches. As a study of the Congressional Research Service states,

> The apparent disintegration of the Warsaw Treaty and the political and economic weakness of the Soviet Union have naturally raised serious questions about NATO's future .... The question of what future European security system would be in the interest of the United States has provoked a debate both within and outside the US government . . . the debate has focussed on the question of whether the United States should emphasize the need to preserve NATO while adapting it to the new European circumstances or should begin preparing a shift toward a much greater role for the CSCE.[4]

Although this discussion has demonstrated that divisions still exist within the US government—the Department of State is more receptive to strengthening the CSCE and the National Security Council (NSC) is more skeptical— the debate has, in fact, echoed several previous warnings from the late 1980s as expressed, for instance, by Jonathan Greenwald: Under conditions of the emerging substantial demilitarization of European politics connected with at least partial transformation of blocs' functions, the CSCE was expected eventually to become a crucial instrument of US participation and influence in European affairs.[5]

US foreign policy seems to follow a "parallel path" strategy of both keeping NATO and partially strengthening the CSCE. Nevertheless, American interest in the Helsinki Process possibly has risen during 1990 and may rise further. This growing interest was manifested in the proposal to convene a meeting of foreign ministers of the thirty-five states in New York on October 1 and 2, 1990, thus drawing the attention of the American public to the then "non-existent" multilateral instrument that might become a new symbol of transatlantic links in the future. Even though it was the first CSCE event to be held in the United States, the ministerial meeting in New York did not succeed in attracting much attention because the American news media, overwhelmed by reports about developments in the Gulf, did not take sufficient note of it. The meeting nonetheless reflected a visible shift in US policy toward a growing commitment to pan-European instruments including the CSCE, making possible a more receptive attitude toward institutionalizing the CSCE.

Other National Views

Other countries also had reasons to accept or promote the CSCE institutionalization.[6] A clear commitment to strengthen the CSCE was regarded by practically all of the West European governments as well as by the United States as reassuring Moscow that the Soviet Union would be a participant in future European security discussions. This commitment was also regarded as one of the keys to ultimate Soviet acceptance of the membership of a united Germany in NATO. The West seems also to have recognized the domestic problems Gorbachev faced in the summer of 1990 in his debate with orthodox conservatives and supported him in his proposal for CSCE institutionalization at the London NATO summit.

For Germany, the CSCE provided a much more acceptable framework in which to discuss constraints on its future force levels than did the Two plus Four talks on bilateral negotiations with the Soviet Union.

The Neutral and Nonaligned countries (NN) supported CSCE institutionalization long before 1990. Most of them had been receptive to the concept since the early 1970s because it would ensure their active participation in discussions on European security and cooperation.

Finally, institutionalizing the CSCE opened further opportunities for freeing East European countries from their former security dependence on the Warsaw Treaty without provoking the Soviet Union, as closer ties with NATO might do. At times, many members of the Warsaw Treaty—primarily Hungary, Poland, and Czechoslovakia—have emphasized the collective-security functions of the new CSCE institutions, making the existence of the military structures of the Warsaw Treaty unnecessary. They have also actively proposed similar language during negotiations on the Charter of Paris.

Recent Trends Within the CSCE Negotiations

Diplomatic preparations for the summit in Paris began in Vienna on July 10, 1990, in accordance with the decision made by the foreign ministers of the thirty-five at their meeting in Copenhagen on June 5. The Preparatory Committee for the summit—*Prepcom* in CSCE diplomatic jargon—completed its work in two sessions: July 10 to July 27 and September 4 to November 17, 1990. During the first session two documents were completed and adopted by consensus: the agenda for the Paris summit and the so-called coordinator's nonpaper, which was, in fact, a "shopping list" enumerating draft elements to be included in the document or documents of the summit.[7] The second session was devoted to the elaboration of the document named, at the very last moment, the Charter of Paris.

Negotiations within the Prepcom reflected several new trends and a new constellation of interest groups within the CSCE. Many of those trends are significant symbols of the changing nature of the CSCE as well as of some important directions for further evolution of the original "baskets" features of the CSCE. It is important to state before illustrating those new trends that most of the former "coalitions" within the CSCE have not been discarded and replaced with other ones. Instead, the whole picture of intra-CSCE relationships has become more comprehensive and dynamic than before.

One of the most remarkable of the new features of the CSCE is the change from its former nature as an East-West dialogue forum. Practically all of the CSCE forums in 1990 have demonstrated that the previous pattern of negotiations based on the interaction of the three major groups of states—NATO and the EC, the Warsaw Treaty members, and the NN group—becomes more and more obsolete. The Bonn Conference on Economic Cooperation in Europe (March 19-April 11, 1990) and the Copenhagen meeting of the Conference on the Human Dimension of the CSCE (June 5-29, 1990) were already characterized by a wide-ranging consensus on the principles of market economy, human rights, and democracy beyond all previous differences among East and West. Even the bloc-to-bloc CFE negotiations in Vienna in practice changed their nature since the Warsaw Treaty caucus ceased to exist in 1990.

The growing common understanding of shared values has been confirmed and even expanded by the heads of state or government in the Charter of Paris. The first section of the charter reflects this wide spectrum of common values ranging from human rights and democracy to economic liberty and responsibility. Discussions on most of the "difficult" issues in the Prepcom, however, brought together an unusual intermixture of interest groups across previous and still existing "traditional" caucuses.

The Soviet idea of the elaboration of a joint declaration of the twenty-two member states of the Warsaw Treaty and NATO, raised during the first session in July, was met with skepticism by France and Hungary; they confronted this idea with another one elaborating a declaration of all thirty-five[8] CSCE states instead of the declaration of twenty-two, which to them emphasized rather than diminished the role of the blocs. These contradictions even complicated Soviet-French negotiations at the political level when the foreign minister of France, Roland Dumas, visited Moscow in August 1990. Although the French delegation became more receptive to the idea of the declaration of twenty-two in September, at this time Poland and Czechoslovakia joined those delegations that were cool-minded toward the declaration. Most of the NATO countries, and in particular the United States, Germany, and Great Britain, promoted the Soviet idea, however, and contributed much to its elaboration following the London NATO declaration of July 1990.

Different concepts were raised with regard to the establishment of the Conflict Prevention Center (CPC). Both the Canadian and German nonpapers on the center, introduced in July 1990, suggested a broad concept for the CPC to serve as a tool for preventing and resolving a wide range of conflicts, both military and political, that might arise in connection with the implementation of the CSCE commitments. This dual function of the CPC was actively promoted by the Soviet delegation; the US delegation facilitated the monitoring and the implementation of the confidence- and security-building measures elaborated within the CSCE. Some other countries—including Switzerland, the Netherlands, and Denmark—suggested postponing the structuring of the political functions of the CPC at least until the end of the Valletta meeting of experts on the peaceful settlement of disputes in early 1991.[9]

Earlier interest groups still exist within the CSCE. The discussion of the "traditional" issue of the framework for continuing CFE negotiations reflected not only positions taken at the follow-up meeting of 1986-1989 in Vienna but also those laid out at the origins of the CSCE in the early

1970s: The neutral and nonaligned countries supported by most Eastern delegations promoted the idea of merging the CFE and Confidence- and Security-Building Measures (CSBM) negotiations in one forum with the participation of all CSCE states at least until after the Helsinki follow-up in 1992. It was the US delegation that opposed that decision, preferring to continue both negotiations separately until Washington then agreed to the NN idea at the New York ministerial meeting of October 1 to 2, 1990.

Nevertheless, negotiations in the Prepcom clearly confirmed that the former division of the CSCE participants into West and East belongs to the past. Even though separate caucuses of the twelve (EC), sixteen (NATO), and nine (NN) still coordinate individual positions of their members, controversial issues are not being discussed solely within those caucuses but to a larger extent are the subject of much more open discussions at the meetings of all thirty-four CSCE participants.

Another important trend of 1990 was the growing role of the European Community caucus within the CSCE. EC members have played a remarkably cooperative role all through the history of the CSCE. At the beginning of the Helsinki Process, however, the NATO caucus played the central role in the coordination of the Western positions on the CSCE agenda.[10]

The situation changed remarkably during 1990. The NATO caucus in the Prepcom did not manage to coordinate successfully the positions of its sixteen delegations on most of the controversial issues. Among the numerous nonpapers introduced within the Prepcom, only one was submitted on behalf of the sixteen members of NATO—a nonpaper on the development of the structures of the CSCE process introduced by the British delegation on September 14, 1990.

On most of the other issues, the twelve produced their own nonpapers, which failed to agree with the US delegation within the NATO caucus on several issues. In many cases, the introduction of a proposal of the group of twelve was generally regarded as a crucial precondition to moving forward in the substantial drafting work. The lengthy internal consultations of the EC delegations often delayed other agenda items, however, promoting criticism within the Prepcom. Nevertheless, no delegation could ignore the EC presence.

Of course, other delegations succeeded in opposing several positions of the EC countries. The proposed elevation of the Helsinki provision for the modification of borders of the participating states, "in accordance with international law, by peaceful means and by agreement,"[11] was firmly rejected by the delegations of Poland, the Soviet Union, and the United States as a collective revision of the ten principles of Helsinki. The US and Soviet delegations dropped the ambitious language of the twelve, suggesting that "the European Community will continue to play a central role in the political and economic development in Europe."[12]

The EC caucus was active and successful, however, in shaping many parts of the Charter of Paris as well as in pushing through several decisions innovative to previous CSCE practice. The twelve succeeded despite the initial opposition of the Soviet Union and the United States in gaining acknowledgment of the EC through an agreement provided that Jacques Delors, the president of the Commission of the European Communities, would endorse the charter and issue a statement at the summit meeting officially as a member of the delegation of Italy, then holding the EC presidency. Both decisions initially were opposed by the Soviet Union and the United States.

Thus the experience in the Prepcom as well as during the CSCE conferences in Bonn and Copenhagen made it clear that the EC is becoming one of the major interest groups within the CSCE, capable of successfully challenging the previous role of the NATO caucus.

Diminished Role for the Neutrals

One of the most remarkable recent trends, to some extent related to others, is the decreasing mediating role of the NN group. Mediating efforts of the nine neutral and nonaligned countries have been somewhat successful and thus crucial in the history of the CSCE. Although this role was sometimes challenged with regard to negotiations on political-military issues—at the Stockholm Conference on Confidence- and Security-Building Measures and Disarmament (1984-1986) the most delicate problems of on-site inspections were negotiated primarily among NATO and the Warsaw Treaty members, the Soviet Union, and the United States—the efforts of the nine were appreciated by both East and West and enabled them psychologically to accept compromise decisions coming from "neutral" negotiators.

In 1990 the situation changed. The EC group attempted several times to play a key role in consolidating CSCE decision-making. At the Bonn Conference on Economic Cooperation in Europe it was the group of twelve, not the NN countries, that tabled the draft providing the basis for the document of the conference. Although the draft document of the Copenhagen CHD meeting in June 1990 was officially submitted by a representative of the NN group— Austria—the twelve played a significant role in achieving a consolidated text both by procedural initiatives and by introducing carefully elaborated drafts on such crucial items as the EC's nonpaper on the rule of law.

The EC group did not succeed in keeping this role in the Prepcom. Nevertheless, the NN countries did not play a mediating role as before. Several neutral countries were rather ambitious in promoting their own positions. They insisted, for example, on enlarging the participation of the CFE negotiations to all thirty-four CSCE states—this possibility with regard to the period after 1991 is reflected in the Charter of Paris. Several NN countries, in particular Austria, also insisted on the possibility of convening emergency meetings of the Committee of Senior Officials—initially of the ministerial council as well—at the request of any participating state even if there was no consensus.[13]

However—and this factor might be more important—the CSCE environment has changed so much that at least the previous role of NN mediating efforts has become obsolete. In the 1970s and 1980s this group helped to ease confrontation between East and West both by providing mutually acceptable compromises and by making them psychologically acceptable—the initiative came not from the "opposite" side of the table but from a mediator. This role was critical in the CSCE negotiations because both East and West were overly sensitive with regard to each other's proposals, presuming that they were initially mutually unacceptable.[14]

In 1990 the situation changed radically. Although all major CSCE actors continued to study each other's proposals thoroughly, they apparently became much more receptive to them. Thus the specific form of previous East-West mediation is being replaced by usual mediation, which can be pursued not only by NN states.

Although NN countries formally still enjoy their traditional privilege of coordinating the drafting work—few exceptions to this rule have occurred since 1990—at the Copenhagen CHD meeting Hungary was appointed to coordinate one of the drafting groups and Canada was appointed to coordinate a subgroup within the drafting group on national minorities. At the Valletta meeting of experts on the peaceful settlement of disputes in January-February 1991 a Norwegian representative coordinated the elaboration of the document—most of the controversial issues in the Prepcom have been resolved in informal consultations among "most interested" delegations. The most successful draft of the first chapter of the Charter of Paris—"New Era of Democracy, Peace and Unity"—was, for example, elaborated in regular consultations among the heads of the delegations of France, Germany, Hungary, Italy, the Soviet Union, the United Kingdom, and the United States as well as with the Swedish coordinator of drafting group 1.

In the future, the mediating role of the NN countries will be challenged by other powerful factors as well. The most crucial is the prospect for further expansion of the European Community. Most of the members of the NN group are already looking forward to joining the EC. Austria applied for full membership a few years ago and will probably become an EC member soon after 1992. In the fall of 1990, the Swedish *riksdag* adopted a decision favoring an EC membership. Finland is clearly in the process of revising its previous position on this issue as well. Malta's ruling National party proclaimed its aim of full membership in the EC. Even in Switzerland, there are signs of serious considerations of the challenges the country will confront in the future if it fails to adapt to the deepening process of integration in Europe.

This trend will develop further when several of the most active members of the NN group—Austria, Finland, Sweden—become members of the EC caucus. The new constellation could noticeably limit the opportunities for the style of mediation previously employed by those countries and enhance the role of the EC group.

East European Countries in Transition

The relatively low level of activity of most East European countries is remarkable among recent trends within the CSCE. The level of independent activity of the "small" Warsaw Treaty members has differed all through the history of the CSCE. They were active in the mid-1960s when Poland launched the proposal to convene a conference of European states with US participation in December 1964 and when Romania, in December 1965, initiated UN General Assembly Resolution 2129 (XX), "Actions on the regional level with a view to improving good neighborly relations among European States having different social and political systems." Then, after a long period of Soviet domination of the "collective" position of the East—the only remarkable exception was Romania—several East European countries expanded their own profile during the

Vienna follow-up meeting and just after it in 1989. The active performance of these countries—specifically that of Romania, the German Democratic Republic, and, to some extent, Czechoslovakia and Bulgaria—was primarily aimed at preventing the adoption of new and ever more ambitious standards. Romania questioned the outcome of the Vienna follow-up and refused implementation of a number of its provisions with regard to the human rights dimension of the CSCE. Romania was one of the major forces preventing the adoption of any kind of even symbolic document—a communiqué or a chairman's statement—at the London Information Forum of April-May 1989 and at the Paris CHD meeting in late May-June 1989. It was also Romania that prevented consensus on the draft document of the Sofia meeting of experts on environmental issues in October-November 1989, cosponsored by all the other thirty-four delegations.[15]

The situation changed in 1990 following the democratic revolutions in Eastern Europe. After resisting consensus for so long on several issues related first of all to human rights, these countries noticeably reduced their activity within the CSCE and were prepared to accept most of the decisions emerging from discussions in several 1990 CSCE forums. Hungary and Czechoslovakia pretended to play an active role. At the Copenhagen CHD meeting, for example, Hungary, together with its partners from the Pentagonale group,[16] insisted on the adoption of far-reaching decisions recognizing collective rights of national minorities, and Czechoslovakia initiated procedural moves enabling the fast elaboration of the Copenhagen document. In general, however, the East European countries reduced their role primarily to resisting decisions that were unacceptable to them. Bulgaria and Romania, together with France, Greece, and Turkey, for example, opposed the conception of collective rights of national minorities in Copenhagen.

A similar pattern of behavior was repeated during the work of the Prepcom. At the beginning of the July session, Czechoslovakia, Hungary, and the German Democratic Republic demonstrated their desire for a greater role within the CSCE while introducing a draft of the Paris document,[17] but they did not succeed in this effort. Their draft did not influence discussions within the Prepcom or the language of the Charter of Paris to any extent.

Hungary and Poland were active with regard to some of their specific concerns—Hungary with regard to the issue of national minorities and Poland on the issue of easing immigration barriers. Looking for a new role in Europe, both countries attempted to elicit a political commitment from the West to assist their economic reforms and to convert the CSCE into a system of collective security. Both failed to achieve any clear language on those issues. Bulgaria, Romania, and, to some extent, Czechoslovakia kept a low profile through the elaboration of the Charter of Paris.

One of the most remarkable new features of the CSCE negotiations in 1990 was the (at least temporarily) lowered profile of Soviet diplomacy. Active in negotiating CSCE issues on the political level—initiatives on convening the CSCE summit as well as on its institutionalization—the Soviet delegations at the expert level in most of the CSCE forums of 1990 in Bonn, Copenhagen, and at Prepcom were receptive to Western proposals and followed the principle of common sense.

Even though the concept of the Paris summit was one of the most ambitious initiatives of the Soviet Union in the previous two years, proceedings in the Prepcom did not make it necessary for the Soviet delegation to take a leading role. Most of the decisions on the new CSCE institutions to be established already reflected the initial Soviet proposals expressed in Shevardnadze's letter of May 1990. The Soviet delegation, therefore, concentrated its activity on a few items of special concern to them where controversy existed—the elaboration of the declaration of the twenty-two NATO and Warsaw Treaty states and the establishment of the Conflict Prevention Center. Beyond these, the Soviets were prepared to accept the emerging consensus on the modalities of the new institutions.

The trends described here do not exhaust all the new developments that occurred during the CSCE negotiations in 1990 and, in particular, during the negotiations on the Charter of Paris. But they seem the most noticeable manifestations of the changing nature of the Helsinki Process. The evidence of change in the CSCE negotiations thus raises the question of what may be the main direction of this change.

Future Options for the CSCE

From its beginning the CSCE has been primarily concerned with regulating East-West relations in Europe and resolving several problems arising in this context. Formerly, all CSCE commitments were equally applicable to all participating states, but in practice, they mostly covered issues that were controversial between East and West. Problems with regard to the implementation of human rights provisions were raised as an

East-West issue, and only in the past two to three years as an East-East issue—Hungary-Romania. All the complaints coming from West European countries on this topic, for example, were dealt with in the Council of Europe or in the UN framework. Similarly, provisions on confidence-building measures were used mostly between NATO and the Warsaw Treaty countries because no one seriously considered sending observers or on-site inspectors to neutral states.

The current transformation of the CSCE reflects the erosion of its prior nature as an East-West forum because, as stated earlier, the former East-West confrontation disappeared in Europe. To answer the question of what other functions the CSCE can fulfill beyond its previous tasks requires an analysis of the major options of pan-European development itself.

Theoretically, major alternative security conceptions can be defined for Europe. There can be an attempt to restore the collective security concept that has its intellectual and political sources in the League of Nations as well as in the postwar activities of the United Nations. One should recognize, however, that this concept failed to achieve its end because neither of its major premises—a mechanism can be devised to contain militarily an actual or potential aggressor, and it is possible to resolve disputes arising between states by arbitration only—could be realized.

The events prior to World War II as well as the postwar experience of the UN have demonstrated that it is idealistic to hope that international disputes can be resolved solely on the basis of international law without providing the instruments to enforce a state's adherence to its international obligations. This was recently reaffirmed by Iraq's invasion of Kuwait.

After World War II, bloc confrontation and mutual nuclear deterrence effectively restrained states from crude violations of international order and status quo. Beyond being costly and dangerous, those methods were useful primarily at the macrolevel of East-West relations in Europe. They cannot be as efficient at the microlevel, which now is so crucial in maintaining European stability with regard to potential "Balkanization" or renationalization of the security politics of several states, specifically in southern Europe. Thus to prevent the Hobbesian "war of all against all" during the weakening of the bloc structures, new and more reliable instruments are required that are capable of effectively managing interstate relations at the microlevel.

That is why an integrative model based on growing interdependence within the CSCE area seems to be the most promising one for building a new system of European security. This model should ensure a reintegration of the former East into the European and global economy while developing mechanisms that enable gradual harmonization of national economic principles, legislation, and standards. The mechanisms must also strengthen specific political, economic, and legal institutions capable of providing effective means for coordinating domestic policies and resolving disputes arising among the participating states. The pan-European process should not copy the EC structures and history. The political experience of the EC demonstrates, however, that a deep and institutionalized integration makes a war between West European states unthinkable and mutual deterrence unnecessary. Integration does not preclude contradictions and disputes between states, but it makes political compromises more efficient and forcible actions irrational.

If this evaluation is correct and the integration model—institutionalized interdependence—is the one with the best prospects, any attempt to build up the CSCE as a collective security system establishing some kind of a regional "mini-UN" for Europe could result in a marginalization of the CSCE while bringing it away from the mainstream of European development. This assessment means also that in reality there is no dilemma of "NATO or CSCE" in European politics. The functions of the blocs that are now being reduced will not pass to the CSCE.

What instrument will become the main integrator of the "great" Europe?—this is the more acute question. At least in 1990 it was still thinkable that the CSCE could pretend to fulfill this function.[18] But in 1990, the disintegration of the Warsaw Treaty and the Council for Mutual Economic Assistance (CMEA) accelerated. Under current conditions there is a remarkable trend of strengthening the EC positions as the eventual core of the emerging great Europe. Not only the NN countries but also the East European governments are looking forward to joining the community. It is clear that at least for such countries as Czechoslovakia, Hungary, and Poland, the status of "associated" states, which they will soon have, will be the first step toward a closer integration with the community.

Thus the prospect of a "Europe from Portugal to Poland" formed on the basis of the geographically expanding European Community becomes more and more possible. This great Europe would include most of the CSCE participating states, except the Soviet Union and the North American states. If this trend continues, the CSCE will fail to become the primary instrument of an integrated Europe.

This failure of the CSCE, however, would not mean that the Helsinki Process loses ground if EC integration develops as dynamically as now. The integrative model of European security cannot be reduced to EC integration even if it is expanding and tends to cover most of Europe. "Traditional" European integration is not sufficient to build up a new European security architecture because it leaves out such major European actors as the Soviet Union and the United States. That is why there will be a constant need to add to the expanding EC area another integrative dimension that will involve the Soviet Union and North America. This integration need not be as deep and as institutionalized as is the EC, but it should provide instruments to manage their common as well as diverging interests and achieve a greater cohesion among them.

In that sense, the CSCE might be transformed into some kind of "European triangle" mechanism. Its prior task would be to ensure effective means of managing interest conflicts among the three "centers of power" within Europe and partially outside of it. It also may result in a growing cohesion and interaction between NATO and the CSCE institutions. And if this assessment is correct, this option specifically would ensure a growing convergence of Soviet and American geopolitical interests with regard to the CSCE.

Four major functional options for the future role of the CSCE can be defined:

- Regulation of East-West relations in Europe.
- Establishment of a collective security system.
- Institutionalization of interdependence (integration) of the former East and West in Europe.
- Common decision-making between Europe, the Soviet Union, and North America on key issues of common interest.

Two major observations with regard to these options should be mentioned. First, it is not necessarily a choice of only one option for the CSCE. Rather, the Helsinki Process could combine several of those functions, at least during the transition period.

Second, in projecting recent trends on the future of the CSCE one should consider that none of these trends can be taken as irreversible. The situation in Europe is still dynamic and will depend on the interplay of several powerful factors. The escalation of confrontation in the Baltics and the attempt of a military takeover in Lithuania in January 1991 were signs of the existing threat to further democratization in the Soviet Union. This is only one example of how events can influence future development in Europe.

Uwe Nerlich has demonstrated how much the future of Europe will depend on the choice between internationalism and unilateralism of the five major European powers—France, Germany, Great Britain, the Soviet Union, and the United States.[19] The situation is much more complex, however, and its evolution will depend on more factors. With regard to the future options for the CSCE, the following ones seem to be crucial.

The internal development of the Soviet Union will be decisive for defining the future of the CSCE. In case of a consolidation of perestroika, both collective security and, primarily, "triangle" models are thinkable. If perestroika fails and a modernized orthodox socialist regime is restored, the CSCE could return to the regulation of East-West relations in Europe, but the meaning of the notion East will be reduced to the Soviet Union. Various scenarios from developing mechanisms of integration to building a collective security system, as well as East-West regulation and integration, can be imagined if the Soviet Union splits into a number of smaller states.

The focus on integration or on the triangle model also will crucially depend on the future of the countries of Eastern Europe. If those countries fail to join the West European integration in the coming decade, there might be a trend toward combining their efforts to create their own economic, and perhaps also political, "space" in order to overcome the current crisis and manage the ongoing reforms. The emerging cooperation among Poland, Czechoslovakia, and Hungary might then become a prototype for that kind of subregional cooperation. If development takes this path, the "great Europe" will remain split in two or even more regions partially separated from each other's economic and political spaces. The CSCE could then become instrumental in bridging them.

The development of Eastern Europe will depend largely on the concept that will prevail within the EC: that of a deeper or that of a wider integration. The deeper concept, combined with the enhancement of the authority of the community, would be instrumental in overcoming existing fears of a dominant Germany in Europe but would slow down the integration of East European countries into the EC. The wider concept would accelerate integration into the community, thus challenging the potential integrative role of the CSCE. Although EC decisions of late 1990 demonstrate attempts to combine both approaches, the success of this strategy will depend to a great extent on the willingness of Germany, first of all, and Great Britain to agree to more confederative structures of the EC.

Necessary Adjustment

It may be clearer now why the Paris summit has not yet established any new European order. First, the CSCE is not developing into *the* European architecture. This architecture will be multi-institutional in the foreseeable future. Different institutions will not form a hierarchy but will independently fulfill their specific functions, overlapping only partially. Second, it is not known yet which of those functions will be taken primarily by the CSCE.

That is why the Paris summit created only proto-institutions, confirming the legitimacy of the CSCE as one of the major European instruments in the future, but one that must still be appropriately adapted to changing circumstances. The adjustment must be both substantive and institutional. The former is necessary to make the CSCE agenda more flexible in regard to the dynamics of European developments—the calendar of the CSCE Vienna meetings adopted in January 1989 does not anymore reflect the whole complexity and the evolving content of the problems under consideration. The substantive adjustment was partially accomplished in Paris and is reflected in the guidelines chapter of the charter. But most of the work to be done has been postponed until the Helsinki follow-up meeting in the spring of 1992.

More important was the institutional adjustment providing the CSCE with "flexible response" capability. This response is accomplished primarily with scheduled follow-up meetings and the meetings of heads of state or government (every two years) but specifically with regular (at least once a year) meetings of the Council of Ministers, assisted by the Committee of Senior Officials.

Several critical points should be raised, however, with regard to the methods of the current and potential CSCE institutionalization. In making plans for the future one should consider that the establishment of permanent CSCE bodies under certain conditions could have not only positive ramifications but also negative ones. A scholar from Finland, Esko Antola, observes,

> In the framework of the CSCE, institutionalization means that there should be a proliferation of permanent methods of cooperation instead of ad hoc-type forums in various areas. It would also mean an increase in the autonomy of these forums, which could lead to the disintegration of the process. It would be much more difficult to coordinate the process or to balance its various elements. But on the other hand, institutionalization would increase the stability of cooperation and disengage it from the problems of the political-military dimension. This would probably favor

collaboration in areas that are sufficiently far away from the hard core of national security interests.[20]

One of the most important sources of CSCE's previous effectiveness was the fact that it operated on the basis of the asymmetric interests of its participants, thus enabling the negotiations to exchange concessions in different fields of cooperation—for example, the traditional CSCE linkage of human rights and security issues. Another important feature of the Helsinki Process was the ad hoc character of the "smaller" expert meetings, conferences, and seminars devoted to specific issues on the CSCE agenda. These meetings enabled the follow-up meetings to examine thoroughly the balance of progress in different "baskets" and to maintain it both through complex concluding documents and the structure of specific ad hoc forums to be convened. The establishment of autonomous permanent CSCE bodies not governed by this balance could thus bring about a fragmentation, and even disintegration, of the entire process while making the overall balancing of its development more difficult.

Several scholars question the efficiency of the traditional "package deal" method with regard to the future of CSCE negotiations as well as to the feasibility of elaborating large concluding documents as did the Vienna follow-up.[21] But their argumentation does not imply the necessity of changing the very method of previous CSCE negotiations: balanced progress on the basis of asymmetric, or simply different, interests of the participants.

The linkages between specific baskets and issues may, and surely will, change because of the changes in interests. The major task of the follow-up meetings may be to ensure the overall balance of progress. Such a task could evaluate the results of previous expert meetings and structure future activities within the CSCE without elaborating large and substantative documents. But this change in the appearance of the CSCE would not change the method of negotiation that in the past has proved to be efficient.

A thorough analysis of the institutional decisions of the Paris summit reveals that it has not yet dismantled the previous mechanism of the follow-up meetings and specific CSCE forums. The summit only added a parallel structure operating largely on the basis of the Council of Ministers, which provides the process with the necessary flexible response capability. Decisions of the summit made more spontaneously than intentionally, however, might harm the efficiency of the Helsinki Process in the future.

At several places in the Charter of Paris and in its annexes[22] are provisions stating that the Council of Ministers will take into account the report or the summing up of two meetings of experts and one seminar—peaceful settlement of disputes, Valletta, January-February 1991; national minorities, Geneva, July 1991; and democratic institutions, Oslo, November 1991. At first glance these harmless provisions, corresponding with the whole spirit of the CSCE institutionalization, raise an important issue. Previously, the follow-up meetings had the explicit privilege of evaluating or taking into account the results of all the expert meetings held between regular meetings in order to maintain the balance of the entire process. With the decision made in Paris, this privilege passes to the Council of Ministers, thereby partially undermining the role of the follow-up meetings.

This "dual authority" within the CSCE could create an unusual situation. The follow-up meetings might be limited in their capacity to maintain the overall balance of the CSCE (the council may enact recommendations of specific forums before the next meeting), although the council is not yet in the position to fulfill this function because it is designed largely to make decisions on single issues. Meetings of the Committee of Senior Officials authorized to prepare the work of the council are limited to two days unless otherwise agreed, which is not enough time to prepare decisions on a broad agenda; the so-called working sessions both of the ministerial meeting in New York and of the Paris summit proved inefficient and need more thorough preparation.

In that regard, two major solutions are possible. Either the follow-up meetings will regain their authority to take care of the entire balance of the CSCE progress and the Council of Ministers will reduce its functions primarily to consultations and flexible interventions if the situation requires it, or the council and the Committee of Senior Officials will assume the whole responsibility for keeping the process intact and balanced, thus challenging the further existence of the follow-up meetings. The latter solution provides a further strengthening specifically of the functions and procedures of the Committee of Senior Officials, making it practically a full-time working body elaborating and negotiating decisions on a wide range of issues.

The resolution of the "internal" CSCE problem appears to be postponed until the Helsinki follow-up. And the choice between the two options will, to a great extent, depend on those options for the CSCE that will be realized in the near future: whether changes in Europe and its regions will make it feasible to enhance the role of the new institutions or will freeze their development.

Notes

1. "Text of the Declaration After the NATO Talks," *New York Times*, July 7, 1990, p. 5.

2. Contrary to the general belief that the Soviet Union was always eager to develop permanent pan-European institutions, the Soviet Union has been rather cool to that kind of endeavor since 1975 and specifically since the late 1970s after it recognized the human rights implications of the CSCE. This was one of the reasons why bilateral cooperation with European countries prevailed in Soviet policies all through the 1970s and most of the 1980s regardless of official statements emphasizing the importance of the Helsinki Process.

3. *"10 Jahre Helsinki—die Herausforderung bleibt." 78. Bergedorfer Gesprächskreis am 24. und 25. November 1985 in der Bad Godesberger Redoute, Bonn* (10 Years of Helsinki—The Challenge Remains." 78th Bergedorf Conversations on November 24 and 25, 1985, in the Redoute of Bad Godesberg, Bonn) (Hamburg: Kröber Stiftung, 1986), p. 12.

4. Stanley R. Sloan, "The United States and a New Europe: Strategy for the Future," Congressional Research Service Report for Congress, May 14, 1990 (Washington, DC: Government Printing Office, 1990), pp. 21, 23.

5. Jonathan Greenwald, "Wien—Herausforderung für das NATO-Bündnis" (Vienna—A Challenge to the NATO Alliance), *Aussenpolitik*, No. 2, 1987, pp. 155-169.

6. See *inter alia*, Sloan, "The United States and a New Europe," pp. 33-34.

7. A nonpaper (Fr. *bout de papier*) is an unofficial and personal adjunct to oral diplomatic communications.

8. In Paris, there were thirty-four states. The GDR, on October 3, 1990, disappeared from the political landscape of Europe. Since June 1991, there are again thirty-five CSCE participating states after the first meeting of the CSCE council in Berlin approved the participation of Albania.

9. The Valletta meeting of experts (January 15-February 8, 1991) approved a document providing a CSCE dispute settlement mechanism. This document was the subject of discussions at the CSCE council in Berlin on June 19-20, 1991, which officially approved the enactment of this mechanism.

10. See John J. Maresca, *To Helsinki—The Conference on Security and Cooperation in Europe 1973-1975* (Durham, NC, and London: Duke University Press, 1987), p. 20.

11. Nonpaper on friendly relations among the CSCE states, introduced by Italy on behalf of the twelve EC countries on September 24, 1990.

12. Nonpaper "Guidelines for the Future," introduced by Italy on behalf of the twelve on September 26, 1990.

13. This issue was not resolved in the Prepcom because neither the proponents nor the opponents of the proposal gave up their positions. It was therefore postponed, and the Council of Ministers was authorized "to discuss the possibility of establishing a mechanism for convening meetings of the Committee of Senior Officials in emergency situations." (See the Supplementary Document, which gives effect to certain provisions contained in the Charter of Paris for a New Europe, Paris, 1990, p. 16.) During the spring of 1991, the major opponents of the idea—the Soviet Union,

Turkey, and the United States—changed their position, and the Council of Ministers approved the emergency meeting procedures in Berlin on June 19-20, 1991.

14. See, for example, Hans-Heinrich Wrede, *KSZE in Wien. Kursbestimmung für Europas Zukunft* (CSCE in Vienna. Defining the Course for Europe's Future) Cologne: Wissenschaft und Politik, 1990), p. 78.

15. The Sofia Document was officially adopted as a CSCE document by consensus one year later at a special ad hoc meeting of representatives of the participating states of the CSCE in Vienna on November 5, 1990.

16. Austria, Czechoslovakia, Hungary, Italy, and Yugoslavia.

17. Document CSCE/GVA.1 (This is an official CSCE index in which GVA stands for "Gipfelvorbereitungsausschuss"—Preparatory Committee for the Summit—and "1" is the number of the proposal.)

18. "Das gemeinsame Haus Europa." (The Common European House. Excerpts from a statement by Andrei Zagorski), *Deutsche Volkszeitung/die tat* (German People's Newspaper), No. 17, April 29, 1988, p. 4.

19. Uwe Nerlich, "Europa zwischen alten Ängsten und neuen Hoffnungen" (Europe Between Old Fears and New Hopes), *Europa-Archiv*, No. 16, 1990, pp. 481-492.

20. Esko Antola, "The CSCE as a Collaborative Order," in Frances Mautner-Markhof, ed., *Process of International Negotiations* (Boulder, CO: Westview Press, 1989), p. 47.

21. See Stefan Lehne, "Vom Prozess zur Institutition. Zur aktuellen Debatte über die Weiterentwicklung des KSZE-Prozesses" (From the Process to the Institution. On the Present Debate about the Further Development of the CSCE Process), *Europa-Archiv*, No. 16, 1990, p. 503.

22. Security section of the "Guidelines for the Future" in the Charter and in Annex II, point 7, and Annex III, point 8.

10

The Non-Proliferation Treaty Review Conference of 1990

George Bunn

THE NON-PROLIFERATION TREATY (NPT) provides for a conference every five years to review its operation and determine whether its "purposes" and "provisions" are "being realized."[1] The fourth such conference broke up at 5:30 AM Saturday, September 15, 1990, because a consensus could not be reached on the final declaration. The central disagreement was a dispute over the significance of continuing nuclear weapons tests by the nuclear-weapons powers who are parties to the NPT: the Soviet Union, the United Kingdom, and the United States. Because the Soviet Union had not tested the year before the review conference and had expressed its willingness to ban future tests, the onus for testing fell on the United Kingdom and the United States.

The purpose of this chapter is to describe what led to the disagreement over testing, what it means for the NPT's future, and what the conference declaration would probably have codified if the disagreement could have been papered over.

The Breakup over Testing

Article VI of the treaty requires that parties undertake "negotiations in good faith on effective measures relating to the cessation of the nuclear arms race at an early date and to nuclear disarmament."[2] A purpose stated in the NPT's preamble is "to seek to achieve the discontinuance of all test explosions of nuclear weapons for all time and to continue negotiations to this end."[3] Putting these two provisions together, Mexico and many other developing countries argued at the 1990 review conference that the United States and the United Kingdom had breached their obligation to negotiate in good faith to achieve a comprehensive test ban treaty or other measures toward a "cessation of the *nuclear* arms race."[4] They contended that no American-British-Soviet negotiations to end all testing had been held for some years despite Soviet willingness; that no nuclear bombs or missile warheads would be eliminated by either the Intermediate Nuclear Forces (INF) or the Strategic Arms Reduction Talks (START) treaties; and that the total number of deliverable strategic warheads after START's implementation would, in fact, be far greater than the number in 1968 when the NPT was signed. For these developing countries, progress toward a halt in all nuclear-weapons testing and in the nuclear-weapons arms race are the key standards by which compliance with Article VI by Britain and the United States is to be judged.[5]

Britain and the United States were alone in their opposition to the prompt conclusion of a comprehensive test ban. Responding to the charge of treaty violation, the US representative took credit for completion of the verification annexes for the 1974 Threshold Test Ban and its 1975 companion, the Peaceful Nuclear Explosions Treaty. Completion of these annexes meant that these US-Soviet treaties, which establish a 150-kiloton threshold maximum for underground tests, could go into effect. (The US Senate gave its consent to the US-Soviet treaties in 1990.) The US statement called for "a step-by-step approach to further nuclear testing limitations and to a comprehensive test ban as a long-term objective." But, the statement continued, "so long as the United States must rely upon nuclear weapons for deterrence, we must have a sensible test program to maintain the safety, security, survivability, and reliability of those weapons."[6] The British representative expressed similar views.

The United Kingdom and the United States thus opposed an end to their tests before that distant day when nuclear weapons are no longer needed for deterrence. The Soviet Union, as indicated, favored an immediate end to testing. So did all or almost all non-nuclear-weapon NPT states that attended the conference and spoke on the subject. But the European NPT parties who were there—except Cyprus, Yugoslavia, and perhaps Romania—were such strong supporters of the NPT that they seemed to side with Britain and the United States to the extent of refusing to put language in the final declaration *linking* a future extension of the NPT to a prompt halt in nuclear-weapons tests—the goal of Mexico and its followers. Australia, Canada, Japan, New Zealand, and the Republic of Korea also sided with Britain and the United States. Thus the strongest support for the NPT as it stood seemed to come from the industrialized Northern Hemisphere plus Australia and New Zealand. If a vote to extend the NPT had taken place at the end of the review conference in September 1990 rather than in 1995 when it is scheduled, the chances are good that all thirty-four of these states would have voted for a significant extension of the treaty without conditioning their vote on a prompt end to all testing.[7]

The developing countries had different views—though they were by no means in complete agreement among themselves. A September 1989 summit conference of nonaligned countries had concluded that a comprehensive test ban treaty was essential for the preservation of the nonproliferation agenda embedded in the NPT.[8] One hundred and twenty-seven UN members voted in 1989—over the opposition of Britain and the United States—for a special conference to amend the existing Partial Test Ban Treaty (PTBT) to make it comprehensive.[9] At the 1990 review conference, the caucus of nonaligned and other developing NPT parties agreed "that the possibility of a significant extension of the" NPT "will be enhanced by the effective implementation of the [NPT] by 1995 and in particular on obligations laid down in it relating to nuclear disarmament."[10] Listed in this caucus statement as the first three steps to satisfy these obligations were a moratorium on nuclear tests, support for the special Partial Test Ban Treaty amendment conference to make that treaty cover all tests, and agreement to negotiations toward a comprehensive ban.

A draft nonaligned resolution from this caucus went further. It urged the Soviet Union, the United Kingdom, and the United States to negotiate in good faith "with a view to achieving a comprehensive test ban treaty prior to 1995, as an *indispensable step* towards implementing their obligations under Article VI of the Non-Proliferation Treaty" to end the nuclear arms race.[11] Mexico and several others went still further in arguing, for example, that the final document of the 1990 review conference should state that "the continuing testing of nuclear weapons by the nuclear-weapon States Parties to the [NPT] would put the future of the [NPT] beyond 1995 in grave doubt."[12]

In private negotiations over the final report, the United Kingdom and the United States went a long way toward agreement with Mexico and its backers, on one condition—that another *partial* test ban treaty before 1995 be recognized as possibly sufficient to justify a significant extension of the

NPT beyond 1995. In the drafting committee, Britain and the United States were prepared to have the review conference recognize "that the discontinuance of nuclear testing would play a central role in the future of the NPT."[13] But a condition of their agreement to this language was parallel recognition of the existing US-Soviet agreement on "step-by-step negotiations on further intermediate limitations on nuclear testing"—such as lowering the threshold for underground tests below the 150-kiloton level agreed in the Threshold Test Ban Treaty.[14] Britain and the United States thus wanted to hold open the option that another partial ban on testing by 1995 would justify a significant extension of the NPT at that time.

Mexico and the seven other nonaligned delegations serving on the drafting committee rejected this idea. They objected to the US-UK added language because it seemed to imply that gradual, step-by-step moves *toward* a halt in testing between then and 1995 would suffice. For them, only a complete stop in UK-US-Soviet testing by 1995 seemed enough to support a significant extension.[15]

If a vote on extending the NPT had been taken at the end of the 1990 review conference, how many of the developing countries would have voted with Mexico and the others espousing this position and how many would have voted with Britain and the United States? Because of the rules of the conference, there were no votes of all the participants on language proposed by Mexico and others. In the end, one or two objections were sufficient to prevent consensus, and not even a straw vote was taken on the issue. But some estimate of the problem facing the United States and others supporting a significant extension of the NPT can be gained from looking at votes of the developing countries in other forums (Table 10.1) and from watching what they did and said at the 1990 review conference.

Table 10.1 contains only those states who came to the 1990 review conference and whose support for an extension cannot be assumed. New additions including Albania, Mozambique, Tanzania, and Zambia, which make up the over one hundred and forty NPT parties, are not included. The thirty-four Eastern, Western, and formerly "neutral" states listed in Note 7 that appear to be the NPT's strongest supporters are not listed in the table because their support for a significant extension is assumed.

It is indeed sobering to realize that if a vote on extending the NPT for a substantial period without further constraints on nuclear-weapon testing had been required at the 1990 review conference, its passage would have required the affirmative votes of thirty-nine of these fifty NPT developing countries, which would have been highly improbable.

Of the one hundred and forty-four parties to the NPT, more than one hundred are developing countries. Of the fifty present at the 1990 review conference, more than fifteen seemed to be active in supporting Mexico's position at one time or another during the conference. These included Cameroon, Columbia, Ghana, Indonesia, Iran, Jamaica, Kenya, Malaysia, Morocco, Nigeria, Peru, the Philippines, Sri Lanka, Syria, Uganda, Venezuela, and Yugoslavia. The depth of support for Mexico's position beyond this was difficult to judge, and even some of those listed might have voted for a significant extension despite criticism of the UK-US position on testing. Readers can draw their own conclusions from the table. Support for a comprehensive test ban is widespread. The real question is, how many supporters will be willing to run the risk of ending the NPT soon after 1995 if they fail to achieve their aim of a comprehensive test ban?

The industrialized countries do not seem prepared to take such a risk. What impressed American NPT negotiators present at the 1990 review conference was the depth of support has among industrialized countries—including those the United States or the Soviet Union worried about in the 1960s as being potential nuclear-weapons countries of the future—Australia, Germany, Italy, Japan, Sweden, and Switzerland, for example. Former Soviet bloc countries about whom there might now be concern following the removal of Soviet control seem also to be strong NPT supporters—Hungary, for example. In Europe, once the two German states committed a united Germany to the NPT and support for its continuation at the 1995 extension conference, the treaty became an essential part of the foundation for European stability. At the review conference the two German states joined in the following statement: "Rights and obligations under the instruments [of the NPT] will continue to apply to the united Germany. The united Germany will seek the continued validity of the [NPT] and support the strengthening of the non-proliferation regime."[16]

Significant Agreements that Could Have Been Recorded

At the conference, progress was made on several issues of interest to the developing and industrialized countries.

"Security Assurances" for Non-Nuclear-Weapons Countries. Nigeria had proposed a new treaty in which the nuclear-weapons countries

Table 10.1 Views of Developing Countries at 1990 Review Conference

Developing NPT Parties Attending 1990 NPT Review Conference	*Voted for 1989 UNGA Resolution on PTBT Amendment Conference**	*Signed 1990 Request to Convene PTBT Amendment Conference***	*Linked extension of NPT beyond 1995 to an end to nuclear tests****
Bahrain	Y		
Bangladesh	Y	Y	
Bhutan	Y		
Brunei	Y		
Bolivia	Y	Y	
Cameroon	Y		
Colombia	Y	Y	
Costa Rica	Y	Y	
Cyprus	Y	Y	
Ecuador	Y		
Egypt	Y	Y	
Ethiopia	Y		
Ghana	Y	Y	Y
Honduras	Y	Y	
Indonesia	Y	Y	Y
Iran	Y	Y	Y
Iraq	Y	Y	
Ivory Coast	Y		
Jamaica	Y		
Jordan	Y	Y	
Kenya	Y		Y
Kuwait	Y		
Libya	Y		
Malaysia	Y		
Mexico	Y	Y	Y
Mongolia	Y	Y	
Morocco	Y		
Nicaragua	Y	Y	
Nigeria	Y	Y	Y
North Korea			
Peru	Y	Y	Y
Philippines	Y	Y	
Romania	Y	Y	
Qatar	Y		
Sao Tome and Principe			
Saudi Arabia	Y		
Senegal	Y		
Singapore	Y		
Somalia	Y		
Sri Lanka	Y	Y	Y

Table 10.1 (continued)

Developing NPT Parties Attending 1990 NPT Review Conference	*Voted for 1989 UNGA Resolution on PTBT Amendment Conference*[a]	*Signed 1990 Request to Convene PTBT Amendment Conference*[b]	*Linked extension of NPT beyond 1995 to an end to nuclear tests*[c]
Sudan	Y	Y	
Syria	Y		Y
Thailand	Y	Y	
Tunisia	Y		
Uganda	Y		
Uruguay	Y	Y	
Venezuela	Y	Y	Y
Viet Nam	Y		
Yemen	Y	Y	
Yugoslavia	Y	Y	Y
	48	26	11

*This resolution was adopted over UK-US objection by 127 votes with Western and other US allies abstaining. UN General Assembly Resolution 44/106 recommending the convening of a special conference to amend the Partial Test Ban Treaty to make it comprehensive—that is, to ban nuclear weapons tests underground as well as in the atmosphere, in space, and underwater.

**Over UK-US objections, forty-one states (the necessary special majority) petitioned for convening the special conference to amend the LTBT to make it comprehensive.

***Linkage was expressed in language such as that quoted in the text by Mexico and others. The language appeared either in drafts such as those cited in notes 11 and 12, in conference statements, or in both.

would promise not to use or threaten to use nuclear weapons on countries that had forsworn nuclear weapons in the NPT or a similar agreement—such as the Latin American nuclear free–zone treaty. This type of promise is often called a security assurance. The United States had agreed, with qualifications, to such an obligation to the parties to the Latin American treaty and had made a unilateral statement to the same effect in 1978, a statement that the Reagan and Bush administrations have both reaffirmed. This is the statement, with its qualifications:

> [T]he United States will not use nuclear weapons against any non-nuclear-weapon states party to the NPT or any comparable internationally binding commitment not to acquire nuclear explosive devices, except in the case of an attack on the United States, its territories or armed forces, or its allies, by such a state allied to a nuclear-weapons state or associated with a nuclear-weapons state in carrying out or sustaining the attack.[17]

Other nuclear-weapons countries had also made unilateral statements that they would not use nuclear weapons against non-nuclear-weapons countries. Some statements, particularly those of China and the Soviet Union, were less qualified than the US statement. The United States had, however, refused in the 1960s to include in the NPT a promise not to use or threaten to use nuclear weapons against non-nuclear-weapons parties. Ever since, it has resisted proposals for a new legally binding treaty obligation on the subject when they were made at the Geneva multilateral disarmament conference.

The Nigerians have urged a new effort for a treaty on this subject separate from the NPT. They were supported at the review conference by most of the developing country NPT parties. For the first time, the US delegation seemed to have instructions permitting some flexibility on this issue. The American and Nigerian delegations were reported to have come close to agreement on language for the final declarataion; this language also appeared to have the general support of other participants. Because of the breakdown of negotiations over the comprehensive test ban issue, however, no agreed language was made public. The United States may feel relieved of any commitment to help organize the conference that Nigerians and others want. But the widespread interest and the new US flexibility suggest that this issue will be pursued again.

"Full-scope" International Atomic Energy Agency (IAEA) Safeguards. A second significant agreement that was not recorded, because there was no final declaration, concerned "full-scope safeguards." The NPT treaty requires all non-nuclear-weapons countries that are NPT parties to accept IAEA safeguards on *all* their peaceful nuclear activities (that is, full-scope safeguards). But it does not prohibit any party from exporting nuclear materials and equipment to non-nuclear-weapons countries that are *not* NPT parties (India and Pakistan, for example) that have activities not under safeguards, *provided* that the exports and the nuclear materials derived from them are to be subject to safeguards. In other words, non-nuclear-weapons NPT parties have to have full-scope safeguards, but non-parties do not. This requirement has resulted in discrimination against NPT parties, which many developing countries have complained. To deal with the problem, Australia, Canada, Japan, the Netherlands, and the United States now require full-scope safeguards on all their exports to non-nuclear-weapons countries, whether NPT parties or not. At the conference, the Federal Republic of Germany (on behalf of united Germany) made an important promise to adopt the same practice. Belgium, Italy, the Soviet Union, and the United Kingdom hesitated at first. In the end, however, there was consensus on declaration language urging full-scope safeguards: "the nuclear supplier states to require henceforth, as a necessary condition for the transfer of relevant nuclear supplies to non-nuclear-weapon States under new supply arrangements." [18] This long-time US goal was welcomed by many other NPT parties represented at the conference. What will happen to the agreement without a final declaration recording it is not clear. Since the conference, several suppliers have indicated that they would not require full-scope safeguards unless all supplier countries agreed to do so. Unless some new efforts toward agreement are successful, this consensus may come apart.

Acceptance of IAEA Safeguards by Nuclear-Weapons Countries. A third issue important to non-nuclear-weapons states was the NPT's discriminatory application of safeguards to the peaceful nuclear activities of non-nuclear-weapons countries as compared with nuclear-weapons countries. Because the treaty's first purpose was to prevent the bomb from spreading to other countries and because the Soviets then resisted on-site inspection on their territory, the NPT required IAEA safeguards only on the peaceful activities of non-nuclear-weapons states. In 1964, President Lyndon Johnson first invited the IAEA to apply its safeguards to an American electric power reactor operated by a utility. He did this to help persuade reluctant non-nuclear-weapons countries to accept IAEA safeguards by leading the way and removing a little of the discrimination. Since then, the IAEA has also inspected peaceful nuclear activities in Britain, France, and the Soviet Union, all of which eventually followed the US example. Not long ago China agreed to do so as well. At the conference, the Soviet Union announced that more of its facilities would be offered for safeguarding.

The draft declaration welcomed these developments and pushed for more. It recorded agreement to a "goal of the universal application of IAEA safeguards to all peaceful nuclear activities in all States."[19] It suggested that the IAEA adopt a system seeking reports on all nuclear-weapons state peaceful activities but selecting those to inspect on a random basis. In addition, it asked the nuclear-weapons powers to move toward separation of their peaceful from their military activities. Plutonium production reactors for weapons would no longer be used to produce electricity, for example. If this recommendation were followed by the

Soviet Union, it would remove one of the criticisms of the verification system suggested for a cutoff of the production of fissionable materials for nuclear weapons, a proposal long advocated by the United States and opposed by the Soviet Union—though now their positions are reversed. This language of the draft declaration, accepted by American and Soviet delegations as well as others, may have little effect because disagreement prevented final adoption.

Participants, Nonparties, and Problem Countries

Who came to the 1990 review conference? This is a question of considerable interest. Attending were eighty-four of the NPT's parties, slightly fewer proportionally than at the 1985 review conference. The average attendance for the four review conferences held since the treaty began is just under two-thirds of the parties. Under Article X of the NPT, a 1995 decision on the length of any treaty extension must be made by a majority of the *parties*, not just of those attending. If only two-thirds attend, three-quarters of those attending will have to agree on the length of an extension in order to produce a simple majority of all parties to a specific extension.

Because the decision to extend is more important than a review of the NPT's operation, a higher proportion than two-thirds may attend. But a look at the list of the countries *not* attending in 1990 suggests that most of them are small countries that do not have nuclear facilities of significance and may not have much interest in sending delegates to a 1995 NPT extension conference.

All of the avowed nuclear-weapons countries came to the 1990 review conference either as NPT parties—the Soviet Union, the United Kingdom, and the United States—or as nonparty observers—China and France. For China and France, this conference was a first. They had not attended any prior review conference. As observers this time, they did not participate actively in the negotiations over the declaration. But both submitted messages to the conference showing support for nonproliferation. Observers speculated, based on these messages and private talks, that China and France might eventually join the NPT (both have since promised to do so). The treaty permits them to come in as nuclear-weapons countries with treaty obligations similar to those of Britain, the Soviet Union, and the United States. In other words, they would not have to give up their nuclear weapons to become parties.

The French statement recalled earlier French declarations that France would behave as if it were a party to the NPT. It then said that France was engaged in "rigorous" nonproliferation efforts, had a "keen interest" in the outcome of the 1990 review conference as well as of the 1995 extension conference, and would "continue to work for the broadest possible consensus in favor of an equitable and stable non-proliferation regime."[20] For years, the Chinese had been hostile to the NPT. But they submitted a paper acknowledging that the treaty "has played some positive role in preventing the proliferation of nuclear weapons and maintaining world peace and stability." The paper pledged "not to advocate, encourage or engage in nuclear proliferation and not to help any country to develop nuclear weapons." On testing, the paper seemed close to the UK-US position. It argued that testing should be ended "in the context of an effective nuclear disarmament process."[21]

Threshold nuclear-weapons countries—India, Israel, Pakistan, and South Africa—are not NPT parties and cannot join as nuclear-weapons states as can China and France. But Israel and Pakistan attended the conference as observers. Israel's representative roamed the corridors seeking information but submitted no statement. Pakistan submitted a message saying Pakistan had complied with the NPT's obligation "not to manufacture or otherwise acquire nuclear explosive devices." The message expressed Pakistan's willingness to accede to the NPT *if* "credible security assurances were given to the non-nuclear weapon states against the use or threat of use of nuclear weapons and if the treaty attracted the universal adherence of the so-called 'threshold' nuclear powers, including India."[22]

Neither India nor South Africa sent observers to the conference, and neither submitted a statement to it. But rumors circulated at the conference that South Africa and some front-line African state were about to accede to the NPT. Since the conference South Africa has promised to do so and Madagascar, Tanzania, and Zambia have, in fact, done so.

Of less concern as NPT holdouts than India, Israel, and Pakistan, are Argentina and Brazil. They both sent observers and together submitted two statements, one urging a ban on all underground nuclear tests and the other supporting the goal of nonproliferation and continuance of the Latin American nuclear free-zone treaty, which both have signed but neither has brought into force for itself. What was remarkable about their statements is not so much their language as that they were jointly made. With similar cooperation in economic matters and in their nuclear programs, the two countries appear to have reduced the perception each seemed to have of the other as a potential enemy in pursuit of nuclear weapons.

Much concern about Iraq's nuclear progaram was expressed at the conference, mostly in the corridors. Although Iraq is a party to the NPT, many suspected that it had a secret nuclear-weapons program using nuclear materials in facilities not subject to IAEA inspections. The conference took place a few weeks after Iraq's invasion of Kuwait. Iraq said little except to question Kuwait's participation, an objection that was promptly rejected.

Sometime before the invasion, the IAEA had inspected Iraq's declared fissionable material. It did so again in November 1990. Inspection of other Iraqi suspected facilities did not take place then because Iraq had not declared them as nuclear and therefore subject to IAEA inspection. The draft declaration's response was to tell the IAEA "not to hesitate to take full advantage of its rights, including the use of special inspections" provided in the agreements that the IAEA has with Iraq and other NPT parties.[23]

What this means is that there was consensus that the IAEA has the authority to ask Iraq to permit inspection of the facilities where clandestine nuclear activities are suspected even though Iraq has not declared those facilities as nuclear. If Iraq then refused, the refusal should be reported to the IAEA board of governors and, if the board so ordered, it would be the basis for IAEA sanctions and possibly a report to the UN Security Council.

This would be a major new step for the IAEA. So far, it has only inspected facilities declared (by the states to be inspected) to contain nuclear material or facilities subject to inspection. The argument for the new authority was of course not published at the review conference for it, too, would have been in the final declaration. After the cease-fire in the Gulf War, however, the UN Security Council directed Iraq to accept on-site inspection by the IAEA of all its nuclear weapon-usable materials wherever located.[24]

At the review conference, North Korea was criticized for its failure to sign a safeguards agreement with the IAEA covering safeguards on its nuclear facilities. North Korea joined the NPT at the end of 1995, and its deadline for signing such an agreement has long since passed. Its argument was that it had acceded to the NPT in part "to remove the grave nuclear threat" emanating from US nuclear weapons deployed in South Korea. North Korea added that this threat had not been removed after its accession to the NPT, and it offered to sign an IAEA safeguards agreement only when the nuclear-weapons powers signed a legal obligation to assure North Korea against the use or threat of use of these weapons. After the conference it announced that it would sign an IAEA safeguards agreement but would not permit IAEA inspections until the US removed its nuclear weapons from South Korea and signed a nonuse agreement.

As noted earlier, one of the things that the draft declaration would probably have included was agreement to recommend another conference to consider negotiating a new treaty prohibiting the threat or use of nuclear weapons against non-nuclear-weapons countries that have joined the NPT, or a similar agreement. But North Korea stands in violation of its NPT obligation to sign a safeguards agreement whether or not a new nonuse treaty is negotiated.

Impact on the NPT's Future

What will be the impact of the breakdown of negotiations at the 1990 review conference on the parties to the NPT and on the likelihood of a significant extension of the NPT at the 1995 extension conference?

This review conference is not the first to fail to produce agreement. The same thing happened in 1980, mostly over the same issue—ending all nuclear weapons tests. President Ronald Reagan was elected two months later, and his administration was far more hostile to a ban on all nuclear weapons tests than was President Jimmy Carter's. The failure of the 1980 review conference to produce a consensus had no impact on the US position opposing renewal of negotiations for a comprehensive test ban. It probably did help produce a serious two-year US effort to consult with important countries in preparation for the 1985 review conference. At that conference, a compromise was reached early in the morning after the last scheduled day of the conference. The compromise was that a large majority—not, of course, including the United States—thought a ban on all tests was a first priority, but a few—including the United States—felt that reductions of strategic weapons systems were more important. That time, this type of agreement was unacceptable to the Mexicans and their associates.

If Britain and the United States do not at least begin serious negotiations with the Soviet Union toward a comprehensive test ban by 1995, two things are possible. First, the Mexicans, or perhaps others, could withdraw from the NPT on the grounds that the treaty has been breached by the failure of Britain and the United States to negotiate to achieve a comprehensive test ban. The Mexicans say they considered withdrawal in 1975.

For them, the NPT may be redundant because the Latin American nuclear free-zone treaty is in effect for their territory. But Mexican withdrawal could have the effect of legitimizing the withdrawal of others who might want an excuse to get out—Iraq or North Korea, for example. This development could begin an unraveling of the NPT regime.

No state has so far withrawn from the NPT, and none threatened to do so at the review conference. Indeed, almost every speaker expressed support for the treaty—despite criticisms of the nuclear-weapons states for failing to negotiate a comprehensive test ban. The danger of withdrawal does not seem imminent.

Second, in their anger at the "non-compliance" of Britain and the United States with their obligation to negotiate in good faith toward a cessation of the nuclear arms race—including, they say, a halt in all nuclear testing—Mexico and others might organize opposition to any extension of the NPT of more than a year or so. Could the NPT's strongest supporters then get three-quarters of those present at the extension conference to vote for an extension of twenty-five years? That will be difficult, as the attempt to estimate a 1990 vote reported earlier suggests. The result might be a single five-year extension. As many read the NPT, it would terminate at the end of that extension. Only one extension conference—that in 1995—is provided for in the treaty's text.

The NPT could be extended after the five-year extension only by a treaty amendment—which is almost impossible as a practical matter. Or it could be extended by a new treaty—which, given the hostility of many non-nuclear-weapons countries to the NPT's "discriminatory" application to nuclear-weapons and non-nuclear-weapons countries, is unlikly to produce a new NPT, at least not without greater obligations toward nuclear disarmament by the nuclear-weapons states than appear in the current NPT.

Alternatives for Winning Votes in 1995

What alternatives to a halt on all nuclear weapons tests might help produce a large enough vote in 1995 to extend the NPT for at least twenty-five years? Steps to limit testing by cutting the size or number of tests such as recommended by the 1988 Belmont Conference might help a little.[25] But this step-by-step approach is what was rejected by Mexico and its associates at the 1990 review conference. And such steps would not likely limit the testing of any countries other than the Soviet Union, the United Kingdom, and the United States. The steps would not therefore contribute to nonproliferation except perhaps by picking up a few votes at the 1995 conference.

The virtue of amending the Partial Test Ban Treaty to make it comprehensive is that India, Israel, Pakistan, Argentina, and Brazil, for example, would be forced to accept a ban on all tests—or to withdraw from the amended treaty, an embarrassing and unlikely move. Even a new comprehensive treaty that these countries helped negotiate would be more likely to slow proliferation independently of the NPT than a new step-by-step treaty that only nuclear-weapons countries signed.

Another helpful US-Soviet step would be agreement on a cutoff of production of fissionable materials for nuclear weapons and/or the transfer of at least the fissionable materials from the INF and START warheads to peaceful purposes. The cutoff was also discussed when the NPT was negotiated as one of the measures that the nuclear-weapons powers should negotiate in good faith to satisfy their obligation under the treaty's Article VI. So far, however, though this proposal has attracted interest in the Congress, it has not in the Bush administration.

Clearly, credible legally binding security assurances against the threat or use of nuclear weapons on non-nuclear-weapons NPT parties would receive support from developing countries whose votes are needed at a 1995 extension conference. Many countries at the 1990 review conference supported the Nigerian effort to start negotiations on a new treaty on this subject. Moreover, two problem countries—North Korea and Pakistan—expressed a desire for security assurances. Security assurances may become central to the expected US effort to rally support for a significant extension of the treaty. START and the Conventional Forces in Europe (CFE) treaties will also help. But the Mexicans and many of their associates have already discounted these agreements because they do not reduce the numbers of nuclear weapons. How many countries Mexico and its associates will carry with them at the 1995 NPT review conference is impossible to predict.

For many of these developing countries, a ban on all nuclear weapons tests has become the ultimate test of whether the NPT should be extended for a significant period. An agreement similar in that it froze an aspect of nuclear weapons development or growth—a cutoff of fissionable-material production, for example—might substitute. But another partial test ban would not.

Notes

1. Treaty on the Non-Proliferation of Nuclear Weapons, signed July 1, 1968, Article VII. 3. See US Arms Control and Disarmament Agency (ACDA), *Arms Control and Disarmament Agreements: Texts and Histories of the Negotiations* (Washington, DC: ACDA, 1990), pp. 98-102.

2. *Ibid.*, p. 100.

3. *Ibid.*, p. 98.

4. *Ibid.*, p. 100 (emphasis added).

5. For more detail, see Charles N. Van Doren and George Bunn, "Progress and Peril at the Fourth NPT Review Conference," *Arms Control Today* Vol. 20, No. 8 (October 1990), pp. 8-12.

6. Van Doren and Bunn, "The Fourth NPT Review Conference," p. 9.

7. Australia, Austria, Belgium, Bulgaria, Canada, Czechoslovakia, Denmark, the Federal Republic of Germany, the German Democratic Republic, Finland, Greece, the Holy See, Hungary, Iceland, Ireland, Italy, Japan, Liechtenstein, Luxembourg, Malta, the Netherlands, New Zealand, Norway, Poland, Portugal, the Republic of Korea, San Marino, the Soviet Union, Spain, Sweden, Switzerland, Turkey, the United Kingdom, and the United States.

8. Official Records of the UN General Assembly, 44th Session, Document A/44/551, section entitled "International Security and Disarmament," paragraphs 10 and 11.

9. The resolution is the same as that in the second column of Table 10.1. Except for the Soviet Union and the former Warsaw Pact states, the European and other industrialized supporters of the NPT listed in Note 7 abstained on this resolution.

10. Statement of August 1990 by "the Non-Aligned and Other States Parties to the NPT not taking part in the East European or Western Groups," Fourth NPT Review Conference, Document 30.

11. Fourth NPT Review Conference, Document L.1, August 24, 1990 (emphasis added).

12. See Fourth NPT Review Conference Document MC.I/GG.3 /CRP 5, "Compendium of Proposals Received in Writing Regarding Chairman's Paper on Art. VI," suggestion by six countries led by Mexico. Essentially this same language appeared earlier in Document MC.I/ WP.4, "Suggested Paragraphs for Inclusion in the Final Declaration on Article VI and Preambular paragraphs 8 and 12," submitted by Ghana, Kenya, Mexico, the Philippines, and Venezuela.

13. "An Assessment by the Delegation of Mexico," September 20, 1990, quoting two drafts to which Britain and the United States agreed, on the condition stated in the text. See letter of October 1, 1990, from Ambassador Miguel Marin Bosch, permanent representative of Mexico to the European Office of the UN, on file with the author.

14. *Ibid.*

15. *Ibid.* Besides Mexico, the nonaligned countries serving on the drafting committee were Indonesia, Iran, Nigeria, Peru, Sri Lanka, Venezuela, and Yugoslavia.

16. Fourth NPT Review Conference, joint declaration of August 23, 1990, Document 28.

17. *ACDA Documents on Disarmament* (Washington, DC: Government Printing Office, 1980), p. 384.

18. Fourth NPT Review Conference, Report of Main Committee II, September 10, 1990, p. 8.

19. Fourth NPT Review Conference, Report of Drafting Committee, Document DC/1/Add. 3(A), September 13, 1990, p. 4.

20. The French statement is quoted in somewhat more detail in Van Doren and Bunn, "The Fourth NPT Review Conference," pp. 10-11.

21. *Ibid.* The Chinese statement is also quoted in this article.

22. Fourth NPT Review Conference, letter dated September 16, 1990, Document 35.

23. Language from the draft resolution.

24. "Excerpts from Draft Resolution on the Cease-Fire in the Gulf," *New York Times*, April 3, 1981, p. A-7.

25. Report to President-elect George Bush from the Belmont Conference on Nuclear Test Ban Policy by many nongovernmental experts (December 1988); see David A. Koplow, "The Step-by-Step Approach," *Arms Control Today* Vol. 20, No. 9 (November 1990), pp. 3, 6-8; compare in the same issue Wolfgang K. H. Panofsky, "Straight to a CTB," pp. 3-5, and Spurgeon M. Keeny, Jr., "The Comprehensive Test Ban," p. 2.

11

Regional Peacemaking: ECOWAS and the Liberian Civil War

Abiodun Williams

ON AUGUST 24, 1990, while the international community was still stunned by the recent invasion of Kuwait by Iraq, an important and unprecedented development took place in West Africa that was largely overshadowed by events in the Persian Gulf. The Economic Community of West African States (ECOWAS) decided in the wake of abortive peace talks to send ground and naval forces to Liberia comprising contingents from five of its sixteen member states: Gambia, Ghana, Guinea, Nigeria, and Sierra Leone.[1] For independent African states to organize a multinational force to intervene militarily in the affairs of another African state is a rare phenomenon. That this action was sanctioned by an entity whose cardinal function is to promote regional economic integration was equally extraordinary—and appeared to some even as a contradiction in terms. The civil war that has plagued Liberia since December 1989 and that prompted the intervention by ECOWAS had historical roots.

Historical Background

Liberia has an unusual historical experience among African countries. In 1822 it became a haven for former American slaves whose descendants, known as "Americo-Liberians," formed a distinct cultural and social group. In 1847 it became an independent republic and, besides Ethiopia, was the only country in Africa not to be colonized by European powers. The

Map 11.1 Liberia and Its African Neighbors, with County Boundaries, 1984–present

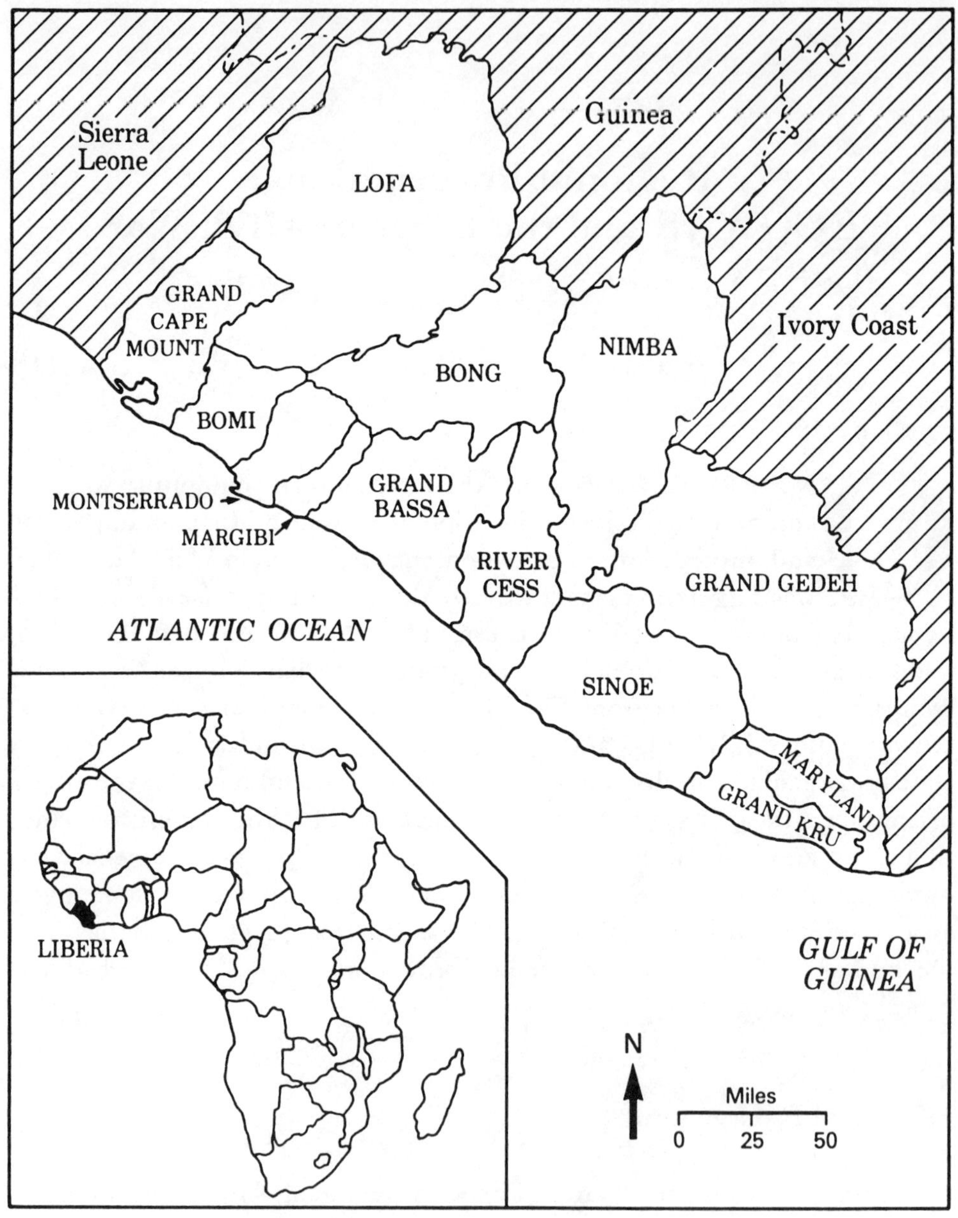

Source: J. Gus Liebenow, *Liberia: The Quest for Democracy* (Bloomington: Indiana University Press, 1987). Copyright © 1987 by J. Gus Liebenow; reprinted by permission of Indiana University Press.

Americo-Liberian minority dominated all aspects of national life—political, economic, cultural, and social—for more than a century.[2] They were the unchallenged elite of a society that also included sixteen indigenous ethnic groups. The formal political structures in Liberia were strongly influenced by those in the United States, with governmental authority being divided between the legislative, executive, and judicial branches. The True Whig party, formed in 1870, was the main political organ through which Americo-Liberians maintained political control.[3] The Christian churches and the Masonic Order—to which the major political leaders belonged—were also vehicles of influence. Liberia enjoyed a brief period of two-party democracy in the late nineteenth century, after which the True Whig party held a monopoly of power under successive presidents until the end of the First Republic in 1980.

From 1945 to 1971, Liberia's president was William V. S. Tubman, who introduced two major policies during his tenure: the Open Door Policy and the National Unification Policy. The Open Door Policy was intended to attract foreign investment and increase trade and encourage the exploitation of Liberia's natural resources. Large deposits of iron ore had been discovered in Bomi Hills, Nimba Mountain, and with rubber soon became the country's primary export and source of foreign exchange earnings. As a result of foreign investment and favorable international prices for its primary export commodities, Liberia experienced significant economic growth in the 1950s. The National Unification Policy was designed to ameliorate the tensions between Americo-Liberians and the indigenous peoples. For example, amendments to the constitution were made that gave indigenous ethnic groups and women the right to vote, provided they owned real estate or other property. Nevertheless, political power remained firmly in the hands of the elite, and challenges to presidential authority and control were suppressed.

When William R. Tolbert succeeded President Tubman as chief executive on Tubman's death in 1971, he had served as vice president for nineteen years. The country was soon faced with economic problems as prices for its primary exports fell on world markets. These economic difficulties were compounded by widespread mismanagement and graft. The national treasury was not always distinguishable from Tolbert's personal exchequer, as the president and his family engaged in blatant corruption. The Tolbert family gained significant influence in and often complete control of many business enterprises. In spite of the severe economic depths to which the country had plunged, President Tolbert spent an inordinate amount of money to host the Organization of African Unity (OAU) Summit Meeting in Monrovia, the capital, in 1979.

The political performance of the Tolbert regime was no better than its record in the economic realm. On assuming the presidency, Tolbert embraced a populist style of government that was in sharp contrast to the formality of the Tubman years. Slogans he adopted, such as Rallytime and Total Involvement, were given wide currency. This new populism was short-lived however, and President Tolbert became increasingly authoritarian, brooking no political dissent or opposition. The long tradition of patron-client relations that had formed the basis of the political system continued, and the news media became mouthpieces for the government. General opposition to the regime, long suppressed but never extinguished, found an outlet in two main opposition movements formed in the late seventies: the Progressive Alliance of Liberia (PAL), subsequently renamed the Progressive People's party (PPP), and the Movement for Justice in Africa (MOJA). After the government announced a 50-percent increase in the price of a bag of rice in 1979, the PAL called for a demonstration to protest the proposed increase. The rice riots that ensued revealed starkly the vulnerability of the Tolbert regime, which had to seek help from President Sekou Toure of Guinea for additional troops to quell the demonstrations. There was an uneasy hush across Liberia—the proverbial calm before the storm. The stage was set for the most momentous and turbulent drama the country had witnessed since the arrival of the first settlers more than 150 years earlier.

The Coup d'Etat: Enter Master Sergeant Doe

Early in the morning of April 12, 1980, a group of seventeen army officers led by a young master sergeant, Samuel Doe, entered the Executive Mansion and assassinated President Tolbert.[4] The coup d'état shattered the long Liberian tradition of peaceful transitions of power and ended the equally long dominance of its political life by the True Whig party. The seventeen soldiers established the People's Redemption Council (PRC) and selected Doe—the highest-ranking soldier among the group—as its chairman. Doe was not gentle in victory, and ten days after the successful coup d'état the PRC ordered the summary execution of thirteen prominent officials on a public beach in Monrovia.[5]

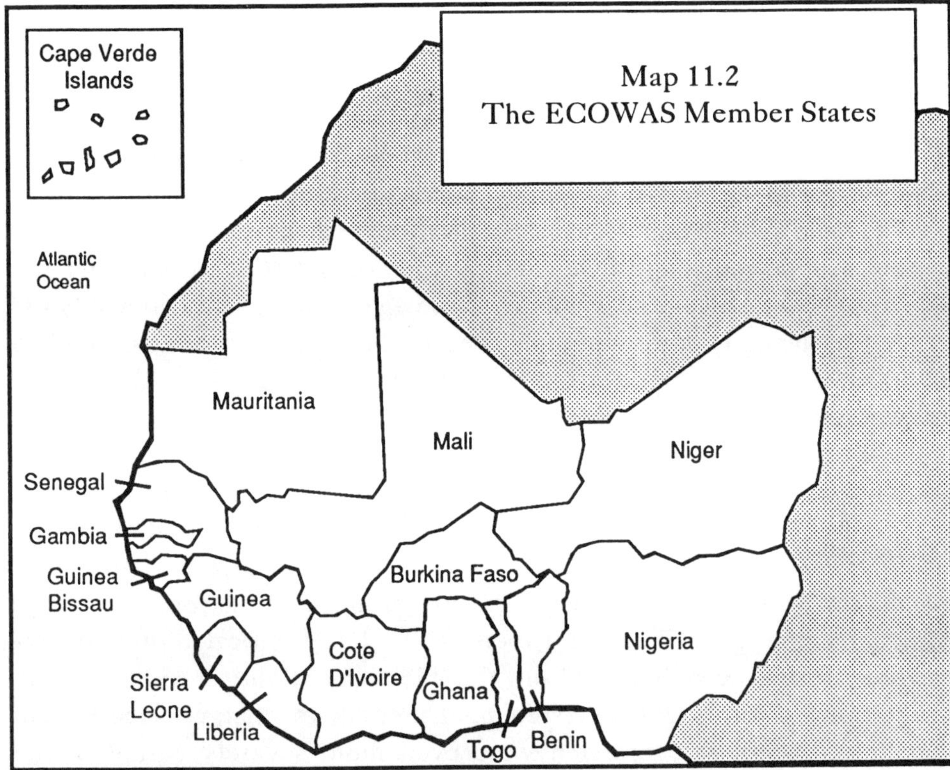

Source: Becky Kohler, Africa News Service, Inc. © 1988.

Doe and the other members of the PRC were welcomed heartily by many Liberians, who rejoiced at the toppling of the Americo-Liberian oligarchy and the end of the True Whig party's repression. The PRC, which regarded itself as the "guardian of the revolution," embraced the rhetoric of revolution and struck a responsive chord in many Liberian hearts. Expectations were great that significant improvement would take place not only in the political climate but also in the economic and social fortunes of the average Liberian.

Doe, however, was an unlikely candidate for the role of founding father of a new Liberia. A man of rudimentary education, he demonstrated in a short time that he lacked the capacity, willingness, and vision to implement meaningful reform. Initially, he sought national legitimacy and international recognition by forming a coalition cabinet that included civilian members. Among the civilians were four members of the PPP, three representing MOJA, and some former members of the Tolbert regime such as Rudolph Grimes, who had served as foreign minister, and Ellen

Johnson-Sirleaf, the former finance minister. The Constitutional Commission, with some prominent academics among its ranks, was later established to revise and draft a new constitution.

But the would-be liberator gradually showed his true colors. Doe installed many members of his own small ethnic group, the Krahn, in positions of authority and increasingly surrounded himself with bands of courtiers and sycophants. He and his cronies used their political positions to prosper financially, and Doe's military combat fatigues were exchanged for trappings of power and symbols of prestige that he had ostensibly eschewed in the early days of his rule. Before the 1985 elections, contenders for political office in the government were asked to resign from their posts, but when the chairman of the Constitutional Commission, Amos Sawyer, a professor at the University of Liberia, suggested that Doe should also tender his resignation Sawyer was arrested and subsequently went into exile in the United States. After much fraud, manipulation, intimidation of voters, and vote-rigging, Doe claimed victory with 50.9 percent of the votes cast for the presidency and a majority of seats in the legislature won by his National Democratic Party of Liberia (NDPL).[6] Political repression increased after Doe's "victory" in the elections. Political parties were banned and their leaders arrested on trumped up charges; freedom of speech and political expression were even more severely curtailed; the Liberian National Student Union was banned and intervention by the army on campuses was now permitted. Opponents of his regime were routinely imprisoned or murdered, and international human rights organizations consistently drew attention to Doe's human rights abuses. The high expectations of 1980 were dashed as Doe repeatedly spiked hopes for a new political and social order. Continued favoritism shown toward the Krahn exacerbated ethnic tensions and exposed the fissures among the indigenous peoples that had long been subsumed under the Americo-Liberian oligarchy. The dramatis personae had changed, the ancien régime had been disbanded, but the drama remained essentially the same and, indeed, had worsened in many respects. As Malcolm lamented for his beloved Scotland in Shakespeare's *Macbeth*, Liberia continued "to sink beneath the yoke . . . and each new day a gash was added to her wounds."[7]

Liberia's political problems were compounded by severe economic difficulties. Since the coup in 1980, its economy has declined steadily at an annual rate of 3.4 percent. Its export volume fell from $600 million in 1980 to $430 million in 1985, and from 1980 to 1990 its external debt doubled to more than $1.6 billion.[8] The World Bank closed its office in Monrovia in

1986, and the International Monetary Fund followed suit in February 1988, the latter maintaining that the government had made no serious attempts to reform the economy along the lines it had recommended.

The Advent of Civil War

The Doe regime was plagued with instability from its inception, and there were a number of abortive coups to topple it. A year after overthrowing the Tolbert government, Doe survived the first coup attempt against him. Punishment was not only swift but dire, and eighteen soldiers—including five members of the PRC—were executed for their alleged role in the plot. The sword of retribution remained unsheathed, and another unsuccessful coup in April 1985 resulted in the execution of the deputy commander of the presidential guard. But the most serious challenge to Doe's authority occurred in November 1985, when Thomas Quiwonkpa, a member of the Gio ethnic group and former army commander, led an unsuccessful coup. The killings carried out by government troops were not only extensive but had a disturbing ethnic dimension: "Krahn soldiers, moreover, in one of the worst manifestations of the 'new tribalism' . . . were given almost carte blanche to carry out a brutal campaign against the Gio and Mano areas of Nimba County, where the support for Jackson Doe and Quiwonkpa was the strongest. Charges of ethnic genocide toward the Gio were being raised against the Krahn within the military."[9]

On Christmas Eve of 1989, Charles Taylor led a band of armed rebels and Liberian exiles known as the National Patriotic Front of Liberia (NPFL) and invaded Nimba County from the neighboring Ivory Coast. A former government employee, Taylor had been charged with theft of national funds, after which he fled to the United States. He succeeded in escaping from the United States while awaiting the outcome of extradition proceedings. President Doe took strong measures to repel the invasion, but the brutal counterattacks of his army served only to alienate the inhabitants of Nimba County even further, and they began joining the rebel forces in increasing numbers. Liberia was divided against itself. Ethnic antagonism reared its ugly head once more, with the NPFL drawing the bulk of its support and membership from the Gio and Mano, while the government soldiers who were predominantly Krahn were supported by the Mandingos. By March, an estimated 200,000 refugees had fled to the Ivory Coast and Guinea, and the rebels were in control of the southeastern section of the national highway. By May, the rebel forces had made significant advances, gaining control of Nimba and Bassa counties, including Yekepa, the country's second-largest city.

Intervention by ECOWAS

When the sixteen members of ECOWAS met in Banjul, the Gambian capital, in May 1990, the fifteenth anniversary of the organization's creation was overshadowed by unresolved conflicts in the region including the raging civil war in Liberia.[10] Although the Liberian situation was not included as a formal item on the agenda, the heads of state discussed it and subsequently adopted a resolution that called for an end to hostilities and the holding of elections.[11] On the recommendation of President Ibrahim Babangida of Nigeria, the leaders also decided to set up a standing mediation committee that would intervene promptly whenever a conflict threatened the stability of the region. Gambia, Ghana, Togo, Mali, and Nigeria were elected members of the committee.

Meanwhile, the war intensified, and by the end of May the NDFL forces were in control of Buchanan, the second port, about 100 kilometers southeast of Monrovia; Buchanan would serve as a base from which they would launch future offensives. Early in June, the large Japanese-owned and US-managed Firestone Tire and Rubber plantation, 55 kilometers southeast of Monrovia, also fell to the rebels, and all international flights to and from nearby Robertsfield Airport were temporarily suspended.

The Liberian Council of Churches attempted to act as a mediator between Doe's government and Taylor's rebel forces by sponsoring peace talks in neighboring Freetown, Sierra Leone, in mid-June. The main area of contention was the future role of Doe himself. His intention was to stay on as president in a transitional administration pending the election of a new government; the NPFL insisted on Doe's immediate resignation as a precondition for a cease-fire. Their positions proved irreconcilable, the conflict was not "ripe for resolution,"[12] and the talks broke down. Although the Council of Churches attempted to revive the mediation process it had initiated, the NPFL refused to attend a second week of meetings.

Taylor's success on the battlefield had been rapid, and with his increasing military strength he felt that ultimately he would be able to pressure President Doe to step down. Similarly, Doe viewed the demand for his resignation as a test of strength. Safe, at least for a time, within the confines of the Executive Mansion and increasingly isolated from much of the country, he was convinced that he still maintained sufficient authority to rebuff calls for his abdication.

The small amount of optimism that had been engendered by the talks in Freetown quickly dissipated as the rebels launched a two-pronged attack on Monrovia, cutting off the capital's electric power, water, and fuel supplies. The government troops responded by intensifying their harassment of civilians, even murdering some, and pillaging and looting shops. The United Nations withdrew its personnel after government soldiers entered its grounds, killed four people, and abducted another forty who had sought refuge there. The United States also began evacuating Americans and other foreign nationals after having stationed six warships off the Liberian coast. A development that was to complicate the situation still further also occurred with a rift in the ranks of the NPFL. Prince Yormie Johnson, a Gio from Nimba County and former commander of the NPFL's special forces, formed a rival group known as the Independent National Patriotic Front of Liberia (INPFL).[13] Johnson had left the NPFL early in the year following accusations that he had executed a number of his own soldiers. Both rebel leaders—Charles Taylor and Prince Johnson—were committed to ousting President Doe, but neither man wanted the other to gain power. Doe offered to resign if he and the Krahn people were offered immunity, but the offer was rejected by the NPFL.[14] The already low morale among the government forces was worsened by desertions of top military officers who fled to neighboring countries as well as by many in the rank and file of the army.

In the wake of the unsuccessful talks organized by the Liberian Council of Churches, ECOWAS became more actively engaged in trying to find a peaceful solution to the war. The increased involvement by the organization was prompted by four factors. First, the tragic brutality and ethnic bloodletting of the civil war that had been going on for six months was simply appalling, and the country was degenerating into a virtual state of anarchy. The humanitarian concerns that influenced the decision to take action were stressed by President Babangida of Nigeria when he observed, "We believe that it would have been morally reprehensible and politically indefensible to stand by and watch while citizens of [Liberia] decimate themselves."[15] Second, the conflict threatened stability in the region, primarily because enormous numbers of refugees fled to the neighboring countries of Guinea, the Ivory Coast, and Sierra Leone. Third, no peace proposals or solutions to the civil war came from either the OAU or the UN. (The OAU has a mixed record in dealing with civil wars and internal conflicts; in some cases governments have opposed OAU intervention on the basis of the principles of sovereignty and territorial integrity as happened during the Nigerian civil war. The UN is also prohibited by its charter from intervening in situations of civil conflict, and the organization did not consider the Liberian civil war until January 1991 when the Security Council adopted a resolution on the matter.) Fourth, the United States, Liberia's historic ally, steadfastly maintained that it had no intention of intervening militarily to halt the continuing carnage despite requests from many quarters for US intervention. The United States apparently viewed military intervention as a "no-win" proposition because it could be interpreted as support for one of the warring factions. Furthermore, there were concerns that such overt military action might be viewed in certain parts of Africa as an unwelcome precedent. Equally important, the end of the Cold War may have weakened the rationale previous US administrations have used to intervene in African states.

The legal basis for ECOWAS intervention involved an ingenious and elastic interpretation of its treaty. The Defense Protocol adopted in 1981 provides only a collective security system, under which member states pledge to give mutual aid and assistance against an armed attack or aggression from a nonmember state and provide a peacekeeping force in cases of conflict between member states.[16] No provision is made for military intervention in cases of civil war or domestic conflict. During discussions among the heads of state, however, "reference was made to the ECOWAS mutual defence protocol. . . . By extension this decision was considered applicable to the situation in Liberia. The situation had deteriorated so much that it was considered necessary for the member states to do something to prevent Liberia [from] sinking into anarchy and destruction."[17]

The foreign ministers of the countries comprising the ECOWAS standing mediation committee held an emergency meeting in Freetown in early July to fashion a "peace formula." Its essential elements were the declaration of a cease-fire, the deployment of a regional peacekeeping force, the resignation of President Doe, and the establishment of an interim government before general elections were to be held. According to the formula, members of the interim government would not be eligible to run in the general elections. The timetable for accomplishing the goals of the proposal was twelve months. On the request of the standing mediation committee, Abbas Bundu, the ECOWAS executive secretary, embarked on a fact-finding mission to Liberia. It was one of several shuttle diplomatic trips he would make to the warring factions and to neighboring countries to gain support for the ECOWAS peace plan.[18]

When Bundu met with Charles Taylor, it was clear that Taylor opposed the ECOWAS plan on several grounds. The main source of his disapproval was his wish to have Doe resign and leave the country before a cease-fire would go into effect. ECOWAS, on the other hand, feared that making a cease-fire conditional on Doe's resignation would result in a power vacuum that would be detrimental to the peace process.[19] Taylor was also displeased that there was no role for him in the transitional government that he wished to head. In addition, he was not receptive to the idea that members of the interim government would be precluded from being candidates in the general elections, as this would frustrate his own presidential ambitions. ECOWAS, for its part, regarded this restriction as necessary to ensure that the elections would be free and fair with no intimidation by rebel leaders and their supporters. Bundu explained to Taylor the reasoning behind the different elements of the formula, and Taylor seemed to have been sufficiently persuaded to endorse it. The Doe government was in favor of the proposal and indicated that it was prepared to accept it.

Two rounds of talks were held in Freetown between representatives of the government and the NPFL between July 10 and 20 to discuss the specifics of the proposal, especially the modalities of the cease-fire. There were some encouraging signs at the outset; it seemed that both sides were committed to finding a peaceful solution to the conflict. Events took a turn for the worse, however, when Tom Woiweyu, head of the NPFL delegation, returned to Freetown after consulting with Taylor and announced that the NPFL could not sign a cease-fire agreement because they were not convinced that ECOWAS would be able to persuade Doe to resign. He said that the NPFL "was only interested in getting a military solution to the problem and they were going right ahead to flush Doe out of the Executive Mansion."[20] Taylor seemed to think also that the peacekeeping force would be a cover for certain countries such as Nigeria and Guinea to bolster Doe's failing regime by insulating government soldiers from attack by rebel forces.[21] The only difference in the outcome of these discussions from those sponsored the previous month by the Liberian Council of Churches was that now there was a peace plan—but only one party was willing to accept it. In a desperate attempt to break the deadlock, Liberia's minister of information, Emmanuel Bowier, advised Doe to resign "in order to save Liberia from further destruction . . . and also to ensure his personal safety."[22]

The NPFL forces had meanwhile made significant advances in the past few weeks and were now in control of two-thirds of the country. The area around Monrovia, however, was the stronghold of the rival group led by Prince Johnson, and at the end of July he attacked the capital itself, seizing control from Doe's troops. On July 30, government troops massacred about 600 people who had sought refuge on the grounds of a Lutheran church in Monrovia. It was the worst single massacre in the seven-month-long civil war. Many of the victims were women and children of the Mano and Gio groups, and this brutal action evoked widespread international condemnation.

Although Taylor had rejected the ECOWAS peace plan, the heads of state of the mediation committee nevertheless met in Banjul in early August and formally adopted the organization's broad framework for peace. Not all member countries specifically supported the peace formula, especially the provision calling for the intervention of a peacekeeping force. President Blaise Compaore of Burkina Faso, a strong supporter of the NPFL, publicly opposed the intervention because he felt it would weaken Taylor's attempts to oust President Doe. Senegal and the Ivory Coast also had reservations about the peacekeeping force, and Togo, a member of the mediation committee, declined at the eleventh hour to contribute troops. These disagreements raised fears about the resurgence of old Anglophone-Francophone divisions and threatened to undermine the ECOWAS initiative.[23] Although some leaders such as President Dawda Jawara of Gambia, the current chairman of ECOWAS, tried to downplay the differences, they were nonetheless quite real.[24] Eventually, the differences were subsumed through tactful diplomacy and in the overall interest of achieving peace in Liberia. By late August it was estimated that more than 5,000 people had been killed and about 300,000 had taken refuge in neighboring countries.

On August 24, a peacekeeping force known as the ECOWAS Monitoring Group (ECOMOG) and under the command of General Arnold Quainoo of Ghana left Freetown for Liberia. Composed of 3,000 troops from Gambia, Ghana, Guinea, Nigeria, and Sierra Leone, its mandate was that of "keeping the peace, restoring law and order and ensuring that the cease-fire is respected."[25] Charles Taylor's opposition to ECOWAS intervention was well known by now, and he threatened reprisals against nationals of the countries providing contingents for ECOMOG.[26] President

Doe as well as Prince Johnson welcomed the intervention by ECOMOG—the latter having previously taken twelve foreigners hostage in an attempt to provoke outside intervention.

ECOMOG adopted two distinct strategies in fulfilling its mandate. From the end of August when it arrived in Monrovia to mid-September, its strategy was one of passive resistance. It interpreted its mandate strictly, not waging any attacks and refusing to retaliate even when attacked by rebel forces. At the same time, it did not retreat. As a result its troops were vulnerable, especially from raids by the NPFL, who still refused to accept a cease-fire. ECOMOG also had little success in accomplishing another goal—that of preventing arms and ammunition from getting through to the rival factions. After mid-September, ECOMOG adopted a strategy of "limited offensive." This change in strategy was prompted by the heavy shelling of the port area, where ECOMOG was based, by NPFL forces on September 14. Two Ghanaian sailors and three Nigerian nurses were killed, and many others were injured. ECOMOG aircraft responded by bombing the NPFL's artillery positions; another 1,000 troops were sent from Nigeria to augment the now 4,000-strong ECOMOG force.

ECOMOG'S efforts to halt the military conflict were complemented by continuing attempts by ECOWAS to advance a political solution to the civil war. It convened the Liberian National Conference in Banjul at the end of August attended by more than fifty delegates representing various political parties and interest groups. Of the three warring factions, Prince Johnson's INPFL was the only one that took part, although Johnson himself did not attend. Liberian Liberal Party (LLP) leader Amos Sawyer was elected president of the interim administration, and Bishop Ronald Diggs, the head of the Liberian Lutheran Church, was elected vice president.[27] An interim legislative assembly was elected, and although the NPFL was not represented at the conference, six of the thirty seats in the assembly, including the post of speaker, were reserved for Taylor's faction. The dynamics of the situation changed soon after with the death of President Doe at the hands of Johnson's rebels following his capture at ECOMOG headquarters on September 10. Although his death removed a major obstacle to the peace process, it also complicated the situation. Four factions now contended for the leadership of Liberia: the Interim Government of National Unity (IGNU) led by Amos Sawyer; the Armed Forces of Liberia (AFL), including the remnants of Doe's presidential guard, led by General David Nimley and subsequently replaced by General Hezekiah Brown;

the NPFL led by Charles Taylor; and the INPFL led by Prince Johnson.

During the next two months, a combination of political pressure from ECOWAS, the NPFL's supporters, and the United States and military pressure from ECOMOG was required to bring Charles Taylor to the bargaining table. At the first extraordinary summit of ECOWAS, held in Bamako, Mali, on November 27-28, a cease-fire agreement was finally signed between Charles Taylor, Prince Johnson, and the Liberian armed forces. An interim government was installed in Monrovia, and it was agreed that a National Conference would be held within sixty days, following talks in Banjul in late December.

A Divided National Conference

The long-awaited All-Liberian conference opened in Monrovia on March 15 under the auspices of ECOWAS. Represented were the two rebel factions—the NPFL and the INPFL—the AFL, six political parties, and fourteen professional, religious, and civic interest groups. The hopes engendered by the start of the conference were dampened by the conspicuous absence of Charles Taylor, who cited "security reasons" for his failure to attend. Because President Doe had been killed following his capture by Prince Johnson's forces, Taylor declared that he could be a target for the INPFL. Many of the delegates believed, however, that this excuse was a deliberate attempt by Taylor to stall deliberations and strengthen his claim to the interim presidency. Several attempts were made by Nigeria's foreign minister, Ike Nwachukwu, ECOWAS Executive Secretary Abbas Bundu, and Togolese Foreign Minister Yaovi Adodo to persuade Charles Taylor to join the conference. Although they gave assurances that ECOMOG would be responsible for his safety and that special security arrangements would be made to assuage his fears, the mediators were unable to convince Taylor to travel to Monrovia.

Taylor was a major player in this conflict and his absence was a setback, but because delegates from his faction were at the conference, an attempt was made to proceed even without his direct participation. Three Liberians were selected to chair the sessions: Roman Catholic Archbishop Michael Francis, Sheikh Kafumba Konneh of the Muslim Congress, and a former ambassador to the United States, Herbert Brewer. The early sessions of the conference were dominated by debates over procedure, credentials, and voting powers, not unusual in negotiations of this nature. Greater conflict erupted over the substance of the ECOWAS peace plan. Representatives of ECOWAS hoped the plan they had adopted at Banjul in August would be acceptable to the major factions so that the conference could then pave the way for the formation of a broad-based interim government and eventual national elections.

A week after the start of the conference, the NPFL delegation proposed that a three-member council be established to replace the interim government and govern the country until elections were held. Later in a BBC interview, Taylor stated that this triumvirate should include himself, a representative of the interim government, and a "neutral" person of "credibility and distinction" acceptable to both sides.[28] Under this proposal, the three members of the ruling council would be eligible to run for the presidency. Taylor's plan was thus in direct opposition to the ECOWAS peace plan, which prohibited a leader of any armed faction from leading the interim government; it also stated that the interim president and vice president would be barred from being candidates in the presidential elections.

Taylor's proposal was severely criticized by most of the delegates, who viewed it as his latest ploy to secure the presidency. A nine-member conference committee was established to find a compromise between the ECOWAS plan and Taylor's "troika" proposal. It recommended that two vice presidents should serve in the interim government, chosen from both rebel groups. As in the Banjul peace plan, the committee also proposed that Taylor should serve as speaker of the legislative assembly. It further recommended that national elections be held in October and that the interim government's term should end in January 1992. Nevertheless, after nearly two weeks of often bitter and acrimonious debate, the NPFL delegation walked out.

The Continuing Stalemate

After nearly seventeen months of a brutal civil war that has killed thousands of Liberians, displaced an even greater number, and reduced the country to ashes and ruins, the efforts at a political settlement to the conflict have reached a deadlock. Repeated attempts to bring Charles Taylor, a key figure in the conflict, to the negotiating table have failed. His intransigence has made an already difficult situation more intractable. Although currently in control of twelve of Liberia's thirteen counties, his reckless ambition and the widespread atrocities of his NPFL forces cast serious doubts about his suitability for leadership of a new Liberia.

In March, Taylor's NPFL forces took the war beyond Liberia's borders when they began a series of attacks against border towns in the southern and eastern provinces of Sierra Leone. A number of civilians and soldiers were killed, the NPFL looted and damaged property, and the government of Sierra Leone had to request military reinforcements from Guinea and Nigeria. This act of aggression and violation of Sierra Leone's sovereignty seemed part of a deliberate attempt by Charles Taylor to destabilize Sierra Leone and sabotage the Liberian peace process initiated by ECOWAS.[29]

As of this writing, prospects of a peaceful and early resolution of the civil war seem bleak. Unless Charles Taylor's principal supporters—Libya, Burkina Faso, and the Ivory Coast—can be persuaded to use their leverage and end support for the NPFL, Taylor will remain a formidable foe. The possibility of a full-scale military offensive led by ECOMOG forces, which now number nearly 9,000, has been raised. Although this scenario cannot be ruled out, it will most likely result in enormous loss of life in an already war-torn and ravaged country. Liberia is going through the darkest period it has experienced in its history, and when the carnage and bloodletting ends, its people will face a formidable task of national reconciliation and reconstruction.

Lessons and Future Possibilities

A final resolution of the Civil War is not yet a reality, but certain conclusions can be drawn about the effects of the ECOWAS initiative and the future role the organization can play in peacekeeping and the resolution of regional conflicts.

The Importance of Leadership. The first lesson of the ECOWAS involvement is the important role of governmental leadership. On the suggestion of President Babangida, leaders decided to take the bold step of establishing the standing mediation committee, which played a central role in trying to find a peaceful solution. ECOWAS now has a body that can monitor disputes and take preventive action before they spin out of control. It could potentially play a role in settling conflicts in Senegal, Mauritania, and Guinea-Bissau. Its small size also means that it might be free from some of the difficulties that often confront a more unwieldy body.

Strengthening the Role of the Executive Secretary. Under the ECOWAS Treaty, the executive secretary is responsible for the "day-to-day administration of the Community and all its institutions." The current executive secretary has been actively involved in the search for a diplomatic solution to the Liberian civil war, and this involvement may signal the start of a greater role in peacemaking for the organization's senior official. If this role is to continue, the position of the executive secretary needs to be strengthened and enhanced.

Establishment of New Norms. One of the most important norms governing relations among African states is respect for territorial integrity and nonintervention in the domestic affairs of states. This principle is contained in the charter of the OAU and has limited its ability to play a significant role in many intra-African disputes.[30] With the ECOWAS intervention, an important precedent has been set for intervention on humanitarian grounds in cases of civil strife. Other regional organizations—such as the Southern African Development Coordination Conference (SADCC)—could play similar roles in their own regions in the future. It is also time that the OAU reconsider its interpretation of the principle of nonintervention. ECOWAS was, after all, established primarily as an organization to promote regional economic integration; the OAU was given a broader mandate, as its name itself implies. Such a reevaluation will necessitate establishing uniform standards and criteria to govern situations in which intervention would be permissible.

The performance of ECOMOG also offers instructive guidelines for future peacekeeping operations:

- Clear and Feasible Mandate. ECOMOG operated within the framework of a broad peace formula. Peacekeeping in a vacuum without a diplomatic and political framework can lead to stalemate and even disaster. ECOMOG's operating instructions, however, were amorphous: Should the troops remain passive or should they return fire?
- Neutrality. ECOMOG in the early stages managed to remain neutral, but after the capture of President Doe at its headquarters and his

subsequent death, its image and prestige were affected. Reports that soldiers from Johnson's rebel group were supporting ECOMOG created the impression of an alliance between the two. Also important in this regard is the quality of command and the discipline of the troops. Following this incident, the command structure of ECOMOG had to be reorganized, and a field commander, Joshua Dogonyaro, was appointed.

- Comprehensive Multinational Representation. It is important to have a broad representation of member countries in any future peacekeeping force to emphasize in fact as well as symbolically united and concerted action on the part of ECOWAS.
- Respecting Rights of Noncombatants. When ECOMOG adopted a strategy of "limited offensive," there were several reports that its troops shelled civilians in Monrovia and its suburbs.[31] Future peacekeeping forces will need to observe international conventions on human rights and standards governing armed conflict.

Notes

1. ECOWAS (CEDEAO in French) was established in 1975 and its sixteen members are Benin, Burkina Faso, Cape Verde, Gambia, Ghana, Guinea-Bissau, Guinea, the Ivory Coast, Liberia, Mali, Mauritania, Niger, Nigeria, Senegal, Sierra Leone, and Togo. The literature on ECOWAS is extensive, but a useful introduction is Uka Ezenwe, *ECOWAS and the Economic Integration of West Africa* (New York: St. Martin's Press, 1983).

2. For an introduction to the Liberian political system and the role of Americo-Liberians, see J. Gus Liebenow, *Liberia: The Evolution of Privilege* (Ithaca, NY: Cornell University Press, 1969).

3. For a fuller discussion, see Katherine Harris, *African and American Values: Liberia and West Africa* (Lanham, MD: University Press of America, 1988).

4. After seizing power, Doe quickly promoted himself to the rank of general and, later, commander in chief of the armed forces.

5. The executions evoked widespread international condemnation. Nigeria refused to permit the Liberian delegation to attend an OAU summit it hosted the month of the coup because President Tolbert was the chairman of the OAU at the time of his assassination.

6. The other main political parties that were established before the 1985 elections were the United People's Party (UPP), the Liberian Unification Party (LUP), the Liberian People's Party (LPP), the Liberian Action Party (LAP), and the Unity Party (UP).

7. *Macbeth*, Act 4, Scene 3.

8. See Esther L. Guluma, "The Trouble with Liberia," University Field Staff International, *Field Staff Reports: Africa/Middle East*, No. 4, 1990-91, p. 4.

9. J. Gus Liebenow, *Liberia: The Quest For Democracy* (Bloomington: Indiana University Press, 1987), pp. 302-303. Jackson Doe, no relation of the president, had been the presidential candidate of the Liberian Action Party (LAP) during the 1985 elections.

10. An indication of the extent of the domestic problems faced by many leaders is the fact that less than half of the heads of state attended the summit.

11. *Keesing's Record of World Events*, Vol. 36, No. 5 (1990), pp. 37446-37447.

12. See I. William Zartman, *Ripe for Resolution: Conflict and Intervention in Africa* (New York: Oxford University Press, 1989).

13. "Prince" is a common first name in Liberia and in this case not an indication of royal status.

14. President Doe offered to resign on July 3, but by the next day he reversed his position and refused an offer of US assistance to leave the country.

15. Quoted in *West Africa*, February 4-10, 1991, p. 140.

16. ECOWAS Defense Protocol, A/SP3/5/81.

17. See interview by Sir Dawda Jawara in *West Africa*, November 26-December 2, 1990, p. 2894.

18. Details of the executive secretary's shuttle diplomacy are from *West Africa*, August 6-12, 1990, p. 2236.

19. *Ibid.*, July 16-22, 1990, p. 2120.

20. *Ibid.*, August 6-12, 1990, p. 2236.

21. *Ibid.*

22. *Keesing's Record of World Events*, News Digest for July 1990, p. 37602.

23. Libya also supported the NPFL by providing training for its troops, weapons, and military supplies.

24. See interview by President Dawda Jawara in *West Africa*, November 26-December 2, 1990, p. 2895.

25. *Ibid.*, September 24-30, 1990, p. 2510.

26. The NPFL forces carried out Taylor's threat on August 31, when they killed an estimated 200 civilian nationals of countries who had contributed troops to ECOMOG.

27. *West Africa*, September 10-16, 1990, p. 2438.

28. *Ibid.*, April 8-14, 1991, p. 510.

29. See Letter and Annex from the Permanent Representative of Sierra Leone to the United Nations, addressed to the UN Secretary-General, April 10, 1991, S/22474.

30. For a study of the OAU, see Yassin El-Ayouty and I. William Zartman, eds., *The O.A.U. After Twenty Years* (New York: Praeger, 1984).

31. Africa Watch, *Liberia: A Human Rights Disaster*, October 26, 1990, p. 4.

12

Diplomacy and the Western Sahara Conflict

Charles Michael Brown

ON APRIL 29, 1991, the United Nations Security Council established a peacekeeping force designed to bring to an end the fifteen-year conflict between the Kingdom of Morocco and the independence group Polisario (Popular Front for the Liberation of Saguia al-Hamra and Rio de Oro)[1] in the northwest African territory known as the Western Sahara. This Security Council action marked a new departure for the UN. The peacekeeping force dispatched to the Sahara will have more complex duties and greater responsibilities than any previous peacekeeping force has seen. Whereas earlier forces have supervised votes or referenda organized by others, the UN Mission for the Referendum in the Western Sahara, or MINURSO from its French acronym, will organize and conduct a self-determination referendum in the disputed territory. With MINURSO, the UN will be moving from the realm of peacekeeping into the realm of peacemaking—a significant step that may help define the role of this organization in the post–Cold War—and post–Gulf War—order.

The conflict in the Sahara has not yet been resolved, but a mechanism now exists for its peaceful resolution. That MINURSO exists is no small accomplishment, but the real success of the UN so far can only be understood when compared to the failures of other parties to resolve the conflict thorough negotiation or mediation. These failures can be best understood only when placed in the context of the conflict's complexity. Though the issue may seem relatively simple—a dispute over the sovereignty of a barren, Britain-sized former Spanish colony with only 120,000-180,000 nomadic inhabitants, called Sahrawis[2]—it is in fact complex. The conflict involves competing nationalisms, ideologies, and geostrategic interests.

Map 12.1 The Western Sahara

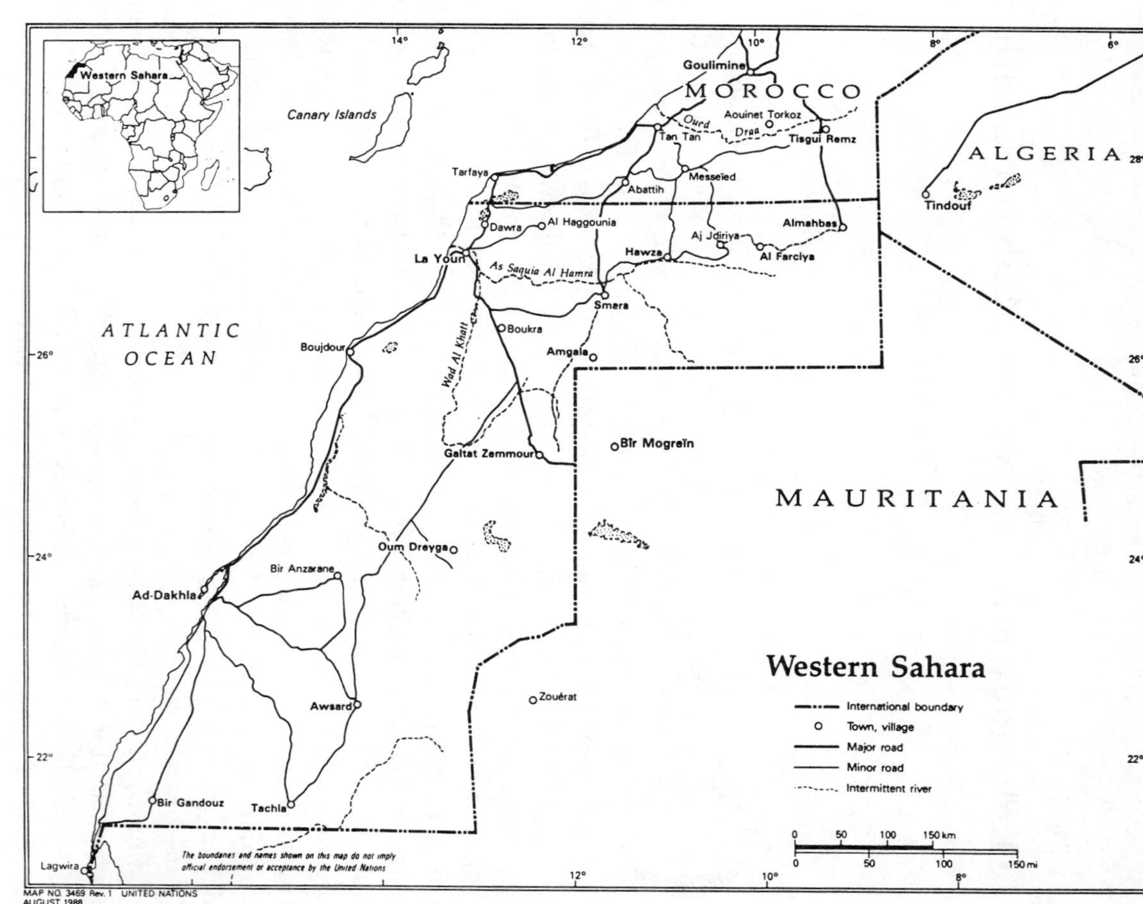

The 1975 Madrid Agreement: A Lost Opportunity

The path to the UN Security Council action of April 1991 began with an agreement signed in Madrid in November 1975 by Spain, Morocco, and Mauritania. With this accord, Spain began to turn control of the then-Spanish Sahara over to Morocco, which borders the territory on the north, and Mauritania, which borders on the west and south—with the expectation that they would jointly administer it only long enough to prepare a self-determination referendum for the Sahrawi population. Although the negotiation had important regional implications, the Polisario, formed in 1973 to pursue Saharan independence, and Algeria, the Polisario's principal creator and backer, were excluded, carrying important negative consequences.

The Spanish position in the 1975 talks was a weak one. Despite Spain's formidable military and administrative forces in the territory and the general crackdown it had undertaken after the 1970 outbreak of insurgency, internal and external political problems—Franco's imminent death and the succession question and Portuguese instability following the 1974 revolution—dictated that it was time for the Spanish presence in the Sahara to end. Spain's principal objective in holding the 1975 Madrid talks was therefore to find a face-saving method of withdrawing from the territory to deal with other problems, domestic and external.

The Spanish saw that without negotiating they could face an expensive, protracted insurgency, as happened in Lusophone Africa, contributing to Portugal's political turmoil. A defeat in the Sahara could jeopardize Spanish control of the Canary Islands off the Saharan coast and the Ceuta and Melilla enclaves on Morocco's north coast. Negotiating the end of their presence had further value for the Spanish: It would cede to other parties the responsibility of combating the insurgency and organizing a territorial referendum. Spain's own attempts at organizing a self-determination referendum as specified in several United Nations and Organization of African Unity (OAU) resolutions had been frustrated by Polisario attacks and successive Moroccan objections to the inclusion of the independence option for the territory.[3]

Morocco's overriding regional objective in 1975 was the "integration of the Sahara with the motherland."[4] A first step toward this goal would be the removal of the Spanish presence, for which Morocco followed a dual path of diplomacy—by sponsoring regional talks and Saharan-related UN resolutions and by subversion through support of anti-Spanish military efforts in the territory. With a 1975 International Court of Justice ruling that Morocco did not have unquestioned sovereignty over the Sahara, however, Morocco's diplomatic path diminished in importance, and a more assertive military effort was launched. King Hassan II also initiated a pro-integration popular mobilization, resulting in the 1975 "Green March," in which 350,000 unarmed Moroccans "peacefully invaded" the territory as a sign of national unity and nationalistic ambitions.

Realizing Spain's weakening Saharan position, Morocco entered the 1975 negotiations with the hope of hastening Spanish withdrawal. Additionally, the Polisario's emergence precipitated Moroccan negotiating efforts. Morocco hoped to reach an agreement, deploy its forces, and thwart what it began to see as the new threat to its control over the territory.

Mauritania's principal Saharan objective in 1975, like Morocco's, was control over and eventual absorption of the territory. Mauritania talked of "reunification" of the Sahrawi people—stemming from the related ethnicity of the Saharan and northern Mauritanian populations. Mauritania did indeed have strong ethnic links to the territory, and it believed that geographically and socioeconomically it had the best claim to annex the Western Sahara. But its "quest" to control the Sahara was never as strong as Morocco's, because Mauritanian territorial claims date so far back—it cited 1,000-year-old conquests—and because it had experienced severe economic difficulties since independence in 1960.

Negotiations offered bright prospects for Mauritania in 1975: It would most likely receive at least partial control of the Sahara, and this meant that Mauritania could possibly exploit the iron ore and phosphate deposits in the southern part of the territory—an attractive prospect for its desperate economy. With only 2,500 soldiers it could hardly afford, or win, a fight with Morocco for control of the territory. And joint control with Morocco meant, in theory at least, that Morocco would assist the weak Mauritanian army in case the Polisario attacked its Saharan positions.

A final party—Algeria—played an important role in the pre-1975 Saharan settlement process but was excluded in the 1975 Madrid talks. None of the parties trusted Algeria's intentions because of Algerian help in creating and arming the Polisario. Additionally, Algeria had no formal claims to the Sahara, suggesting that its support for the Polisario was more out of a desire to deny the territory to Mauritania and especially to Morocco. The establishment of a Polisario-led state in the Sahara, however, would definitely benefit Algeria by permitting Algerian access to the Atlantic Ocean, which would facilitate the transport of iron ore mined in western Algeria. A

Polisario victory would also mean a Moroccan loss, and revenge was important for Algeria after its 1963 military defeat to Morocco in a border war. And, with Algeria's socialist regime ideologically opposed to Morocco's conservative monarchy, a Polisario victory would surround Morocco with socialist states and weaken its regime domestically.

The Madrid agreement represented a synthesis of the positions of the parties to the negotiations. With its military strength and "national will" to reclaim the Sahara, Morocco entered the 1975 negotiations with definite leverage. In fact, Morocco was the only participant for whom non-negotiation seemed possible: It could have attempted, with reasonable chance of success, to force the Spaniards and Mauritanians out of the territory. For Spain, however, internal problems and loss of control in the territory left no face-saving option but negotiation. As for Mauritania, military force was not an option; its only possible alternative to negotiation was to throw in its lot with the Polisario in the hopes that a victory by the latter over Morocco might lead to negotiations on a Sahrawi state in a Mauritanian federation—a risky and unlikely prospect.

The agreement created a tripartite administration to run the territory until Spanish withdrawal. Moroccan and Mauritanian troops also began their move into the territory. An analysis of this agreement shows that all parties made partial gains in their overall objectives. Though Spain lost its largest remaining colony, it turned over to others the burden of organizing a referendum and combating the Polisario insurgency. It was also able to focus on internal problems and avoid a protracted desert war. Morocco and Mauritania gained administrative control over the territory and would now be the arbiters of the Sahara's future. Additionally, by cooperating these two were able to deny Algeria and the Polisario any territorial gains. Algeria could thus be considered the "loser" here: By its exclusion from the Madrid negotiations, it was relegated to a spectator role; to increase its voice in the Sahara's future, it would have to support a guerrilla movement—or take military action itself.

1976 to 1981: The Question of Sovereignty

The 1975 Madrid Agreement actually created new problems. The day after Spanish rule ended, the Polisario rejected joint Moroccan-Mauritanian administration and proclaimed an independent state, the Sahrawi Arab Democratic Republic (SADR). Immediately thereafter, Morocco severed relations with the Polisario's main backer, Algeria. War erupted in the territory, with the much smaller Polisario pursuing hit-and-run tactics against Moroccan and Mauritanian positions. Peaceful settlement prospects were diminished further when just six weeks after Spain withdrew its forces, Morocco and Mauritania partitioned the territory, with Morocco receiving its northern two-thirds and Mauritania the southern third.

The key issue during this stage was the question of sovereignty over the Western Sahara: The Polisario sought an independent state, and Morocco and Mauritania each sought to integrate the Sahara into its national territory. Primary parties were Morocco, the Polisario, and Mauritania, though Mauritania would cease to be a party after 1979. Key secondary parties were the Polisario's main backer, Algeria, and major international organizations that began to seek to mediate the conflict.

After February 1976, Morocco pursued a two-pronged strategy to attain its goal of integrating the Sahara into the kingdom. To defeat the Polisario militarily, Morocco deployed troops—more than 85,000 by mid-1976—and equipment into the territory, including Mauritania's sector. And to win the "hearts and minds" of the Sahrawis, Morocco enacted the Urgency Plan (*Plan d'Urgence*), consisting of large-scale infrastructure construction in the territory including hospitals, water management facilities, roads, and schools. The plan was designed to urbanize and settle the nomadic Sahrawis, raise their living standards, and render them less accessible to the Polisario.[5]

To achieve its goal of an independent state, the Polisario also had a two-pronged strategy: a national liberation war within the territory and a diplomatic campaign for international recognition. For its armed struggle, the Polisario received much support in the form of weapons, bases, and training from Algeria. Libya, too, made major early contributions. Other "radical" or "socialist" states—Cuba, Mozambique, Vietnam, and the countries of the Soviet bloc, for example—also provided various types of political or financial support. On the diplomatic front, the SADR soon gained recognition from seventy-one countries, more than thirty in Africa alone. It also applied for OAU membership as the legitimate Saharan government and sought UN observer status.

Mauritania's post-partition goals and strategy were more tenuous. It wanted to maintain control over and eventually annex the portion of the Sahara it received in the partition, especially because this area contained mineral deposits, but it did not have the financial resources to undertake a development program there. Its strategy was therefore limited to trying to defeat the Polisario militarily, and the size of its army accordingly grew sixfold (to 15,000) after the partition. But the Polisario's hit-and-run sabotage campaign caused major losses for Mauritania. The strain of the war, militarily and economically, fostered internal discontent, and in May 1978 a military coup overthrew the civilian government. Further political and economic turmoil led the Mauritanians to sign a peace agreement with the Polisario in August 1979. In this agreement, Mauritania withdrew from the Sahara and renounced its territorial claims, recognized the Polisario as the legitimate representative of the Sahrawi people, and declared neutrality in the conflict. Morocco promptly rejected this agreement and moved to occupy—"liberate" in Moroccan language[6]—the Mauritanian zone.

In the same period, the UN and the OAU—which both had the Saharan question on their agendas since the early 1960s—began to seek a more active role in resolving the conflict. Their actions in the years after the Madrid Agreement were, however, limited to hortatory resolutions that called for a negotiated settlement or a Sahrawi self-determination referendum. At this stage, they undertook no active mediation efforts.

Mauritania's withdrawal left two primary parties to the conflict, Morocco and the Polisario. The Polisario was then able to step up both its attacks on Moroccan forces and its international diplomatic campaign. For Morocco's part, by occupying the southern third of the territory it was able to extend its Urgency Plan to that region as well. Morocco also began constructing a "defensive berm"[7] in 1980 to counter Polisario guerrilla tactics and extend its control outside of cities and fortified areas. Meanwhile the desert war continued, and Sahrawi refugees fled to Mauritanian and Algerian border camps—the largest one in Tindouf, Algeria, the base of Polisario operations.

Two sets of negotiations took place from 1976 to 1981. First were the 1976 secret talks in which the Western Sahara was partitioned. In these talks, the two parties, hostile to "outside" interference, agreed to partition the territory. This partition was then presented as an accomplished fact, damaging the overall prospect for a negotiated peace in the territory but advancing the pursuit of Morocco's and Mauritania's own national objectives. The second set of negotiations consisted of the 1979 Mauritania-Polisario talks that brought a peace agreement between the two parties. Mauritania's internal turmoil and military setbacks at Polisario hands drained its will and capacity to continue the war. Mauritania basically used the negotiations to sue for peace and extricate itself from a losing situation.

1981-1988: A Peace Plan Develops

Though prospects for a negotiated settlement were virtually nonexistent in early 1981, by August 1988 a peace plan for the territory was in place. This plan was realized despite the absence of direct negotiations between the warring parties and despite the fact that the two parties actively continued to pursue their incompatible goals in the Sahara—Moroccan "integration" vs. Polisario "independence." For these reasons, what happened in the course of these seven years can be seen as a lesson in "improvised" negotiation, largely because of third-party involvement.

The key issue during this stage remained the question of sovereignty over the Western Sahara: Would the territory become an independent state or an integral part of the Moroccan kingdom? Primary parties to the conflict were now Morocco and the Polisario. Major secondary parties included Algeria, the OAU, and the UN.

In June 1981, King Hassan announced his acceptance of the principle of a self-determination referendum in the Sahara—something long sought by the UN and the OAU—that renewed hope for an end to the fighting and a resolution of the conflict. Although it may seem that this decision was a softening of Morocco's position and a bowing to international pressure, it was simply a shift in Moroccan strategy. Having made major strides toward raising the living standards of Sahrawis under the Urgency Plan, King Hassan was certain that Morocco had won their loyalty—and therefore their votes. He thus accepted the principle of a referendum because he thought Morocco could win at the ballot box as well as on the battlefield. He additionally thought that a referendum would resolve the conflict to Morocco's liking without direct negotiations with the Polisario, and he believed that it would be well-received internationally and allow Morocco to counter the Polisario's diplomatic gains.

The possibility that this referendum would occur was diminished the following year, however, when the OAU—the international organization that had taken the lead in organizing a Saharan referendum—voted to admit the SADR.[8] When the SADR's delegation was seated as the legitimate Saharan government two years later, Morocco withdrew from the organization. While remaining committed to the principle of a referendum, Morocco placed itself outside the sphere of African diplomacy and rejected any OAU-sponsored solution.

Isolated in Africa and growing increasingly so internationally, Morocco would begin to emphasize diplomacy for restoring its image. As part of this campaign, Morocco turned to the area by which it could benefit most through closer ties—the Maghreb. Morocco began to champion "Maghreb unity" and regional cooperation, partly as a diplomatic ploy but also in an attempt to bolster its own economy, strained by the $1 million-a-day war. Morocco focused particularly on the Maghreb countries that backed the Polisario—Libya and Algeria—hoping to counterbalance their influence and slow the flow of weapons to the Polisario. Its efforts were successful, resulting in the 1984 Arab-African Union with Libya, which dissolved in 1986, and the May 1988 restoration of relations with Algeria. The latter was especially important: It was a development that certainly would lead the Polisario to doubt Algeria's loyalty, and it provided Morocco more leverage to settle the Saharan conflict on its own terms. The Moroccan-Algerian détente also formed the cornerstone of the five-nation Arab Maghreb Union (AMU), established in 1989.

The Polisario's principal goal in this period remained an independent Western Sahara and the establishment of the SADR. It continued its dual strategy of desert war and diplomacy, although with overwhelming Moroccan military superiority—and the defensive berm—the Polisario found more success in the diplomatic realm.[9] Numerous UN and OAU resolutions coupled with Morocco's withdrawal from the OAU indicated that the Polisario's desire to isolate Morocco was working. It also seemed to indicate that the weight of world moral opinion was on its side.

Morocco's acceptance of the principle of a referendum precipitated Polisario action in another area: refugee camps. The Polisario wanted to guarantee that a referendum would result in a victory for the independence option; but in the face of the Moroccan Urgency Plan, this was by no means guaranteed. Under Polisario control, however, were thousands of refugees[10] at various camps, especially the camp in Tindouf, and the Polisario began pushing for as wide a participation as possible for these refugees in the referendum. Morocco has consistently rejected such Polisario demands, for it has maintained that many non-Sahrawis—mainly Algerians and Mauritanians that had fled Sahelian drought—are settled in the camps, inflating their population and giving the Polisario a higher bargaining number in discussions about the referendum voting lists.[11]

The reestablishing of diplomatic relations with Algeria damaged Polisario efforts to isolate Morocco. But it also opened the possibility that Algeria could be used as an indirect contact channel with Morocco. The Polisario was wary, though, of any rapprochement between its main supporter and its main enemy.

The rejection of the OAU as a potential mediator opened the door for the UN, the other international organization for which the conflict was a matter of active concern. The UN undertook the role of seeking a solution to the conflict by default. Under Javier Pérez de Cuéllar's leadership, however, the organization shifted its gears from exhortatory resolutions to shuttle diplomacy and proximity talks. Although accepting the OAU's broad framework for settling the conflict—involving direct Morocco-Polisario negotiations on a cease-fire and an eventual self-determination referendum—the UN went further. In Resolution 40/50 of December 1985, the General Assembly gave the secretary-general a mandate for intervention in the conflict to bring about a settlement. Pérez de Cuéllar has since made annual visits to North Africa to talk with regional leaders and to confer with the OAU, which the UN still hopes to incorporate in any final solution. He has also used his good offices to meet separately with Moroccan and Polisario representatives and to act as an indirect conduit between them. The secretary-general has additionally sent technical missions to the Sahara to gather data and to monitor the refugee situation. By persisting in his mission, creating an atmosphere of trust, and avoiding alienation of either party—the "cardinal sin" of mediation committed by the OAU—Pérez de Cuéllar concluded a peace proposal on August 11, 1988. Though Morocco and the Polisario both expressed reservations, they formally agreed to the proposal by month's end. For the first time in thirteen years the foundation for a nonmilitary settlement to the conflict was in place.

The UN's success in bringing agreement to its peace plan was remarkable. But this success was possible only because King Hassan, the conflict's true power broker, decided that Moroccan objectives could be obtained by means other than an increasingly expensive military conflict. His decision to accept the principle of a referendum came six years after the Urgency Plan's enactment, during which time Morocco had made massive investment in the "southern provinces."[12] Only when he felt confident that the Sahrawis would appreciate these efforts did the king accept the referendum principle.

The question of legitimacy also prompted the king's decision. In Morocco, the king's divine right and his dynasty's historical links with the territory accorded him more than enough legitimacy to rule over the Sahara. But the international community believed Moroccan legitimacy in the Sahara could only be confirmed by a Sahrawi self-determination vote—not simply by Moroccan military superiority. Solely by announcing his acceptance of the principle of a referendum, the king was able to score points in international opinion. Meanwhile, Morocco could consolidate its grip on the territory as preparations for such a referendum were made.

Another consideration surrounding UN success in formulating the peace plan is the OAU's failure in the same area. The UN, thrust into its mediation role after Moroccan withdrawal from the OAU, was quick to learn from the other organization's mistakes. While adhering to its charter, which maintains the right of self-determination, the UN General Assembly did not recognize the SADR as the legitimate Saharan government. It therefore did not alienate Morocco, whose cooperation was necessary for any peace agreement. Instead, the SADR was accorded semiofficial UN observer status, under which it opened an office in New York but did not hold a seat in the organization. The SADR's UN presence had a moral importance for the Polisario and its supporters, and it facilitated the secretary-general's work in maintaining contact with both parties to the conflict.

Morocco's Maghrebi diplomacy was also necessary for UN success in the Sahara. Renewed relations with Algeria led to Moroccan-Algerian détente, which in turn gave Morocco the opportunity to ease Algeria's ideological commitment—and supply of arms—to the Polisario. This development created a more propitious environment for a peaceful settlement to the conflict, and only three months after the renewal of Moroccan-Algerian relations, the UN peace plan was proposed and accepted.

1988-1991: Making the Peace Plan Work

The 1988 peace plan called for a UN-monitored cease-fire followed by a UN-organized referendum to allow Sahrawis the choice between the options of independence and integration with Morocco. The plan did not include provisions for bilateral talks, although other UN and OAU resolutions continued to call for such negotiations. But this peace plan was just that—a plan—and much remained to be done before its implementation.

After August 1988 the UN mediated heavily in efforts to reconcile divergent positions on the referendum-centered plan. But, as Morocco remained the conflict's true powerbroker and as UN conditions for a free and fair referendum were similar to several long-standing Polisario demands, these mediation efforts were largely bilateral Morocco-UN talks.

Although the conflict continued to center on Morocco and the Polisario over sovereignty in the Sahara, negotiations undertaken after August 1988 centered on Morocco and the UN over implementation of the peace plan. These issues included the number and location of Moroccan troops in the territory after the cease-fire; the role of Moroccan administrators in the territory after the cease-fire; the role of the UN contingent in the territory; and the voter lists, verification of voters, and voting sites. All of these issues caused sharp differences, especially the first two.

After August 1988 Morocco and the Polisario remained primary parties to the conflict; the UN remained the primary mediator. Algeria continued to be a key secondary party, as did the OAU.[13] The Arab Maghreb Union (AMU)—created in February 1989 and comprising the Maghreb states of Morocco, Mauritania, Algeria, Tunisia, and Libya—has also emerged as an important secondary party.

Rabat's ultimate objective has remained the reintegration of the "Saharan provinces" with Morocco. This objective was and is shared by the king and most Moroccans, from nationalists to communists. Accepting the UN plan was not a deviation from this objective, for King Hassan was certain that the referendum's outcome would be favorable to Morocco and that Morocco's long-standing territorial claims would therefore be legitimized. To ensure the territory's "Moroccanity"[14] and to guarantee that it would remain the arbiter over the Sahara's future, however, Morocco insisted on maintaining its military and administrative presence in the territory after the cease-fire. It also insisted that the 1974 Spanish-administered census be used as the basic list for eligible voters and that the UN update this list. Morocco wanted to avoid possible "ballot-box stuffing" by inflated numbers of refugees in the Polisario-controlled camps.

Another, more unusual, Moroccan move came in February 1989, when King Hassan—in response to a unilateral Polisario cease-fire—decided to hold talks in Marrakech with Polisario officials. Morocco emphatically described these talks as "contact" and not "negotiation," and the king justified this contact as simply part of his royal duty of maintaining dialogue with his subjects. Though no details were reported, the talks likely centered on referendum-related topics. After this initial meeting, however, the king refused further contacts, and the Polisario soon ended its unilateral truce.

Domestic and regional events have also played a role in Morocco's position on the peace plan. Domestically, in November 1989 King Hassan sought postponement of the 1990 parliamentary elections—the first since

1984—arguing that they should be held only after the Saharan self-determination referendum. He said two years should give the UN ample time to prepare and hold its vote and that after this time Morocco would "draw its own conclusions" about the delay and organize national elections in Morocco proper and the "Saharan provinces."[15] A referendum was held in December 1989 to determine the public's views on this proposal, and an overwhelming majority—more than 99 percent by official estimates—approved it.[16] The king regarded this outcome as a strong mandate for continuing his overall Saharan policy.

Regionally, events in neighboring Algeria have played to Morocco's advantage and to the Polisario's disadvantage. Massive protests for democratic and economic reform in late 1988 prompted the Algerian government to lessen its support to the Polisario—though Algeria remained its principal backer. The February 1989 formation of the Arab Maghreb Union by the five Maghreb countries represented another important regional development. Citing their common language, religion, and history, the union treaty calls for these states to formulate common economic, defense, international, and cultural policies. Like the European Community, the AMU's principal functions are in economic and trade matters, but a regional political and security consultative machinery was also created. Though Morocco would not allow the AMU jurisdiction in the Saharan issue, it has shown a willingness to discuss an eventual settlement with fellow members—mainly in the interest of "unity" for the organization Morocco was instrumental in creating.

The Polisario's ultimate objective has remained an independent Saharan state. On the referendum question, it wants complete withdrawal of Moroccan troops and administrators from the territory to assure a free and fair referendum. It also wants assurances that the estimated 100,000 Moroccan settlers in the Sahara not be eligible to vote. Its positions on various referendum-related issues have been similar to the UN's, though the latter has only called for a substantial reduction in Moroccan forces, not complete withdrawal.

The Polisario has also continued to call for negotiations with Morocco. It even declared a unilateral cease-fire shortly after accepting the UN plan to facilitate the possibility of direct talks. This tactic worked, and the king did meet with Polisario officials in February 1989—only to refuse any further talks. Attempting to pressure Morocco back into talks, the Polisario launched a major military offensive in September 1989, with significant losses for both sides.

Recent internal politics have damaged Polisario leverage in its standing in the conflict and in negotiations on the referendum's implementation. After King Hassan announced amnesty for Polisario members who joined the Moroccan cause, several prominent members did indeed defect. Once in Morocco, they provided information about internal Polisario turmoil, including severe divisions within its leadership[17] and the siphoning of refugee-destined aid. Official Moroccan accounts of the information conveyed by the defectors also indicates that the Polisario-controlled refugee camps are pro-socialist, anti-Moroccan, and anti-Western indoctrination centers where protests about living conditions have been met with repression and where many refugees are indeed non-Sahrawis who fled Sahelian drought or who support the Polisario cause.[18]

Recent regional and international events have been negative for the Polisario. The 1988 Algerian turmoil coupled with Moroccan-Algerian rapprochement has meant a decline in Algerian support. Though Algeria continues to base Polisario guerrillas and allow supplies to reach them, it no longer arms them, and its political commitment to their cause has weakened. Internationally, the 1989 East European revolutions have caused a virtual halt in military and political support from that region. Other than diplomatic recognition, the Polisario now receives little open international support.[19]

Since August 1988 the UN has been active in reconciling contending positions on the referendum's implementation and in "selling" the fairest, most practical solution to the conflict. It has also seen its prestige and leverage as a mediator bolstered by its successes in Namibia, Nicaragua, and the Persian Gulf.[20] Soon after receiving agreement on the 1988 proposal, the secretary-general named a special representative for the Western Sahara to be the UN's chief negotiator in settling the referendum's details—though Pérez de Cuéllar has also continued to play an active role.[21] The active efforts of these two UN officials resulted in the June 1990 implementation plan, which the UN Security Council unanimously adopted with the condition that the secretary-general refine the details of the plan and propose a budget. Though the Iraq-Kuwait crisis delayed the secretary-general's work in this area, it was resumed soon after the end of the Gulf War in March 1991. The new plan that was submitted and approved on April 29, 1991, had the following provisions:

- The special representative of the UN secretary-general will lead an integrated support group of military, civilian, and security personnel—the UN Mission for the Referendum in the Western Sahara, or MINURSO.

- MINURSO military personnel (approximately 1,700) will monitor the cease-fire, the exchange of prisoners of war, the reduction of Moroccan troops from the current 150,000 to 65,000, and the confinement of combatants. It will also monitor the withdrawal of Moroccan troops or the demobilization of Polisario troops, depending on the referendum's outcome.
- MINURSO civilian personnel (approximately 900) will identify eligible voters, oversee the referendum campaign, and organize and conduct the vote. They will also monitor the territory's administration and oversee the release of political prisoners.
- MINURSO security personnel (approximately 300) will be civil police who will monitor the existing police forces. They will also be charged with maintaining order in and around referendum-related facilities.
- As for a timetable, the cease-fire will begin on a date specified by the secretary-general, who will inform the two parties of this date fourteen weeks in advance. The date will be decided after the UN General Assembly approves the mission's budget, a proposed $200 million—one of the most ambitious UN undertakings ever. After the cease-fire's implementation, the referendum process will require approximately thirty-six weeks, twenty-seven of which will be dedicated to voter certification, the final nine to campaigning. After the referendum, withdrawal/demobilization of appropriate troops will require another four weeks, and the removal of UN personnel will require four more.

Several questions have emerged since August 1988. Two concern the January 1989 Morocco-Polisario talks: First, why did the king agree to them after consistently refusing talks? Second, why did he hold only one set of talks and refuse any more? A probable answer to the first is that King Hassan, although refusing any negotiated settlement to the conflict, was willing to "go through the motions" and give the impression of seeking a peaceful settlement, thereby scoring propaganda points. As for the second, by refusing further talks the king might have expected that this would lead the Polisario to break its unilateral cease-fire and resume fighting, thus providing Morocco with more propaganda ammunition. Of course there could have been much less calculation in his motives: He may simply have had referendum-related topics to discuss, with all his questions being answered in one meeting. But this is uncertain, for no details of this meeting have been disclosed.

Another question concerns the resumed fighting in late 1989: Why did the Polisario, outnumbered almost twenty to one[22] and hampered by the defensive berm, launch one of its biggest offensives since the war began? One probable motive was to pressure Morocco back into talks. Additionally, it may have wanted to demonstrate that even with dwindling Algerian and international assistance it remained determined in its quest for an independent state. Internal Polisario politics may have also been a factor, with the "hardliners" commanding the action to bolster their position in the leadership.

A simpler answer can be found to the question of the extent of the role the AMU would play in resolving the conflict—small. It is simply too young and too tenuous a union[23] to resolve major regional political and economic problems. Morocco may be committed to building a stronger, more integrated AMU, but its Saharan ambitions will certainly continue to take precedence.

There is also a simple answer to why King Hassan decided to delay national elections for two years. As stated earlier, he argued that they should be held only after the referendum in the disputed territory, for this vote would confirm Morocco's legitimate claims to the Sahara and ensure smooth, all-Moroccan elections. But, this two-year delay was also designed to pressure the UN to hold the referendum within that time frame and to give notice that Morocco could not wait indefinitely for "outside assistance" in resolving the conflict.

Questions about the UN plan and its final implementation proposal are also of interest. First, did Morocco's military advantage combined with the Polisario's internal and international weakening translate into Moroccan leverage in the implementation plan? Second, if implemented with its current provisions, would the referendum be free and fair? To answer these, one can look at how the major referendum-related issues were settled:

- On voter eligibility, it was decided that all Sahrawis counted in the 1974 census and above the age of eighteen would be permitted to vote, with the UN responsible for updating the list. This satisfied both the Moroccan demands that non-Sahrawis in the Polisario-controlled refugee camps be ineligible and the Polisario demands that Moroccan settlers in the Sahara be ineligible.

- On Moroccan troops, the plan calls only for their reduction from 150,000 to 65,000. A significant number of troops will therefore remain, and Moroccan numbers will still be several times larger than Polisario numbers. Those remaining Moroccan troops will be confined to specific locations, however, as will Polisario forces; they will all be monitored by UN personnel.
- On Moroccan administrators and police, it was decided that they would largely remain in place. But the special representative would wield significant administrative powers, and his referendum-related regulations would prevail over existing territorial laws should there be incompatibility. MINURSO's civil police would also have significant monitoring authority over the remaining territorial police and sole responsibility for UN facilities.

To answer the first question, Morocco did indeed have leverage that translated into advantages in the referendum's implementation: It would keep troops and much of its administration and police on the ground. However, Polisario demands that Morocco remove all personnel during the referendum process were both unrealistic and undesirable. Civil order must be maintained throughout the process, and possible Polisario sabotage cannot be discounted. UN forces would be incapable of patrolling and administering the entire territory, and certain "local" forces would therefore be necessary.[24] And to answer the second question, the UN has implemented numerous safeguards to ensure that, on paper, the referendum will be free and fair—or at least the freest and fairest possible.

Next Steps

Although the UN Security Council has approved the creation of MINURSO, the mission's work cannot begin until the General Assembly approves the $200 million budget, which was still under consideration at the time of publication. If approved in the early summer of 1991, the cease-fire should come into effect in October or November 1991, with the referendum scheduled for July or August 1992. Because Secretary-General Pérez de Cuéllar's term expires at the end of 1991, he will at least have the opportunity of overseeing the beginning of the Western Sahara peace process that he was so instrumental in creating.

For King Hassan, "winning" the referendum is a major political goal, yet Moroccans are concerned that such a victory may not be certain. This stems from the fact that the referendum preparation and campaigning period will last nearly nine months, during which time Polisario exiles and leaders will return to the territory and actively promote independence. Also, in other recent UN referendums—in Namibia and Nicaragua—the incumbent powers "lost" the vote (South Africa and the Sandinistas, respectively).

Moroccan anxiety has in turn caused UN concern that Morocco may derail the referendum or refuse to accept its results should the vote be for independence. Because MINURSO is a peacekeeping force—not a peace-enforcing one—it will be confined to monitoring and reporting in military matters. Should Morocco choose to scuttle the process and hold on to the territory by force, MINURSO can only condemn the action and return to New York.

But circumstances dictate that this will probably not happen. King Hassan has remained committed—by word, at least—to a Saharan referendum since 1981 and is under international pressure to hold it and accept its results. He himself has stated that should the Sahrawis vote for independence, Morocco will be first to recognize the SADR and establish an embassy in its capital—though this was said when a vote for integration was more certain. In addition, Iraq's invasion of Kuwait, while bringing Morocco "breathing space" through its participation in the anti-Iraq coalition and the UN's preoccupation with this crisis, has brought international attention to other territorial disputes that have been dealt with by force.

Because Morocco is under pressure to hold the referendum and abide by its results, it will want assurance that the result will be a vote for integration. Morocco's best means of accomplishing this is to continue its Urgency Plan and to highlight the development progress made there since 1976. It should additionally stress significant Sahrawi autonomy should the vote be for integration, as the king has occasionally hinted. Rabat may also have other ploys, however. It may try to convey to Sahrawis that if they vote for independence and if that option loses or is ignored by Morocco, they might then risk paying consequences later. This impression could come from nationalist rumblings in the Moroccan press, from "popular" demonstrations in favor of noncompromise in the Sahara, or from emotional statements by Moroccan opposition parties like the nationalist party Istiqlal. Morocco's recent sending of several dozen chaperones to accompany nineteen Sahrawi leaders to a 1990 UN identification commission meeting in Geneva could definitely be a sign of this not-so-subtle intimidation.

The Polisario, too, may attempt such intimidation, especially in the face of the economic opportunity for Sahrawis accorded by Morocco's substantial development efforts. It, too, sent many chaperones with its nineteen Sahrawi delegates to the Geneva meeting. The Polisario also faces other obstacles. Defectors have damaged its credibility, which may hurt it financially in the referendum campaign. And if information about refugee mistreatment is true, then the Polisario will be further hurt at the ballot box. The Polisario faces a still deeper problem: the lack of any real "Sahrawi nationalism" to capture, mold, and utilize in its struggle against Morocco. Although the Polisario has had success in publicizing its cause and establishing a degree of international legitimacy, Sahrawi loyalties remain tribal, not national.

The lack of Sahrawi nationalism prompts another question: Would an independent Western Sahara be a viable state? Probably not. It would be extremely underpopulated, and even with its phosphate and iron ore potential there would be few workers and expertise for full exploitation. Its cultivable land is minimal and is disappearing under the desert. An independent Sahara would be dependent on outside aid just to maintain the Moroccan-built infrastructure, a prospect that developed states would hardly welcome.[25] Though there is certainly a strong emotional appeal to the concept of independence—and the Polisario certainly recognizes and hopes to exploit this fact—logic dictates that the Sahrawis should vote for integration with Morocco. But logic often counts for little in African politics, especially where the passions of war, ideology, and nationalism are concerned.

Notes

1. Saguia al-Hamra and Rio de Oro are the two regions that form the Western Sahara.

2. A 1974 census undertaken by the Spanish put the population at about 74,000. This figure is generally believed to be far too low. Obtaining an accurate figure is difficult given the nomadic nature of the Sahrawis and the large number of Sahrawis outside the territory as refugees or exiles. Population estimates used by international organizations generally run between 120,000 and 180,000.

3. Giving up the Sahara was not a major sacrifice for the Spanish. Though there was economic potential for the territory, Spain had made relatively little investment

there, had built little infrastructure, and had made no major attempts at political and economic modernization for the Sahrawis.

4. David Lynn Price, the *Washington Papers #63: The Western Sahara* (Washington, DC: Center for Strategic and International Studies, 1979), p. 16. It should be noted that Morocco had also laid claims to all of Mauritania and parts of Algeria and Mali as domains of its former empire, but these claims all were dropped by the mid-1960s.

5. Price, *The Western Sahara*, p. 39.

6. From various Moroccan embassy press releases.

7. This berm—called the Hassan Wall by the Moroccans—is a twelve-foot tall earthen mound covered with mines and barbed wire and guarded by numerous observation posts. At the time of its completion in 1987, it was more than 1,500 miles long and encompassed practically the entire Western Sahara.

8. The vote to admit the SADR was 26 to 24, which indicates the deep division within the OAU.

9. Besides being recognized by the OAU as the legitimate Saharan government, SADR's president, Muhammad Abdelaziz, was elected one of the organization's vice presidents.

10. The Polisario puts the number of refugees at above 150,000. More reliable estimates by international organizations put the figure at around 50,000.

11. The Moroccan government also maintains that the Polisario conducts systematic "reeducation," propaganda and intimidation campaigns in the camps. It furthermore claims that imprisonment and torture are a common fate of the refugees (From various Moroccan embassy press releases).

12. In official pronouncements, Morocco refers to the Western Sahara as the "Saharan provinces" or the "southern provinces."

13. The UN still hopes to incorporate the OAU's help in any final settlement of the conflict, and it has stated this in various resolutions.

14. A term often used by Moroccan officialdom.

15. From The Economist Intelligence Unit country report for Morocco, No. 1, 1990, p. 9.

16. Although the actual numbers were probably not that high, one can assume that the king won a very comfortable majority. The Saharan question is an emotional issue in which the king can be assured a wide degree of national unity.

17. According to a February 1990 Moroccan embassy press release, one faction favors integration with Morocco; another wants to pursue the military conflict; and a third believes confederation with Morocco (with significant Sahrawi autonomy) is the best option.

18. From various Moroccan embassy press releases.

19. An exception to this is the continued support from Cuba and, more recently, Iran.

20. In Namibia, the UN was instrumental in gaining independence for the former South-West Africa and in a region-wide peace agreement. In Nicaragua, it supervised the 1990 national elections. And in the Persian Gulf, it brokered the 1988 cease-fire in the Iran-Iraq war.

21. The first special representative was Hector Gros-Espiell of Uruguay. Since January 1990 it has been Johannes Manz of Austria.

22. By the late 1980s there were an estimated 150,000 Moroccan troops in the Sahara. The Polisario claimed 8,000-9,000 guerrillas, which has been a generally accepted figure. Military historian John Laffin's *The World in Conflict 1990* (London: Brassey's, 1990), however, puts the Polisario's numbers at no more than 3,000 (p. 132).

23. "Maghreb unity," like "Arab unity," has emotional appeal but little staying power.

24. This was also the case, for example, with South African troops and administrators in Namibia.

25. US Senator Daniel P. Moynihan, in a March 1990 report to the Senate, said: "The last thing we need—the last thing Africa needs—is another impoverished microstate of 180,000." *Congressional Record*, Vol. 136, No. 12 (Washington, DC: Government Printing Office, 1990), p. S1236.

DEPARTMENTS

Looking Ahead: Diplomatic Challenges of 1992

THE YEAR AHEAD COULD BE ONE of unprecedented diplomatic activity. In every continent significant negotiations are in progress or anticipated; the list of unresolved international problems remains long. With improved relations between the United States and the Soviet Union and a general climate favoring efforts at diplomatic solutions, strong incentives exist in many regions to examine possibilities for resolving age-old issues. In addition, those chronicling diplomatic events will see, as never before, a fading of the line between internal and external issues.

Africa

Angola. With the signing of a cease-fire agreement on May 31, the efforts of Portugal, the United States, and the Soviet Union will concentrate in the ensuing months on bringing about an internal political compact and elections in the former Portuguese colony.

Ethiopia. Following the collapse of the Mengistu government in late May, a transitional government was established in July in Addis Ababa. The Eritrean demands for independence were left unresolved and were likely to dominate the politics of the country in the months ahead.

Liberia. Without a clear resolution of the internal divisions within Liberia, efforts by the West African states and the Organization of African Unity to restore the country to political health seem likely to continue into 1992.

South Africa. With the repeal of anti-apartheid legislation and the release of at least some political prisoners, South Africa's ties to the international

---

Professors Matthew Gardner and Peter Dunkley and Hans Binnendijk, director of the Institute for the Study of Diplomacy, all of Georgetown University, contributed to Looking Ahead.

community, including black African states, improved substantially. Further dramatic progress including the lifting of the UN arms embargo seems unlikely until South African blacks are brought more clearly into the political process.

Western Sahara. A UN-sponsored referendum on the future of this former Spanish colony is expected in 1992. The choices will be between independence and a union with Morocco.

Asia

Afghanistan. Future negotiations of an internal settlement in Afghanistan will be guided by a statement of principles issued by UN Secretary-General Pérez de Cuéllar on May 21. The statement has the support of Pakistan, the Soviet Union, the United States, the government in Kabul, and some, but not all, of the resistance groups.

Cambodia. The months ahead may see greater progress toward peace in Cambodia as the result of agreements reached at a meeting of the UN-created Supreme National Council in Pattaya, Thailand, in June. Although advances have been made, genuine progress toward peace will still depend in large measure on continued Chinese restraint in the supply of arms to the Khmer Rouge.

China. The Beijing government is likely to continue diplomatic policies that will preserve tight Communist party control internally while opening opportunities for profitable economic relations with the Western world, especially the United States and the European Community. Such policies may even include restraint in the supply of arms, especially missiles, to the countries of the Middle East.

India-China. Despite talks between the two nations in mid-1991, border issues remain unresolved. Further diplomatic efforts seem likely, but a general lessening of tension removes a sense of urgency on the issue. India's sanctuary for Tibet's Dalai Lama remains a continuing thorn in the relationship.

India-Pakistan. The unsettled state of Indian politics following the assassination of Rajiv Gandhi on May 21 could affect relations between India and Pakistan, especially if further violence develops in Kashmir. Following the assassination, however, the two governments were making efforts to prevent a crisis, and a renewed conflict between the two countries does not seem likely.

Japan-Soviet Union. Despite efforts made during the April 1991 visit of President Mikhail Gorbachev to Japan to develop a "land for trade and investment" deal, the dispute between the two countries over the restoration to Japan of four northern islands seized by the Soviet Union after World War II seems likely to continue.

Korea. The normalization of relations between South Korea and the Soviet Union, moves by each Korean state toward membership in the UN, and the continuing evolution of relations between Seoul and Beijing have increasingly isolated North Korea. The division between the two Koreas remains deep, and progress toward reunification is likely to be confined to modest steps.

South China Sea. Negotiations over maritime boundaries in the South China Sea between China, Indonesia, Malaysia, and Vietnam are due to conclude in 1992.

Europe

CSCE. Members of the Conference on Security and Cooperation in Europe will be preoccupied in the ensuing months with the organization and staffing arrangements for the institutions created at the Paris summit in November 1990. These will include the Secretariat in Prague, the Conflict Prevention Center in Vienna, and the Office for Free Elections in Warsaw. The first test of the new structure came in efforts to resolve the internal situation in Yugoslavia.

Yugoslavia. The possibility of a breakup of Yugoslavia into separate national states and bitter conflict between states remains high. A peace agreement negotiated by EC representatives in July called for a three-month truce between Slovenia and the Federal Yugoslav government; few predicted that this would provide sufficient time to resolve the basic issues.

European Community. Although questions relating to the unification of Germany for a time sidetracked the momentum toward a lowering of trade barriers among the members of the EC, the goal of an economically united community in 1992 seems attainable. Debate on the future of the EC over the next year will center on three other issues: the possibility of enlargement; monetary union; and political union, including the role of the community in future security arrangements.

Union of Socialist Soviet Republics. If the internal situation in the Soviet Union is to develop along positive lines, it will be based on the agreement of nine republics plus the center to negotiate a new political structure by the end of 1991. The agreement calls for a devolution of the power from the center to the republics and the negotiation of a union treaty leading to free elections. The election of Boris Yeltsin as president of the Russian Republic will spur this process. The attempted coup on August 19 momentarily derailed but did not end this process.

Latin America

El Salvador. Despite negotiations under Mexican and UN auspices between the government of El Salvador and the Farabundo Marti National Liberation Movement, unresolved issues about the future of the military, constitutional change, and electoral reform and the continuation of violent acts by extremists on both sides are likely to stand in the way of a ceasefire and peace.

Mexico-United States. With the approval on May 25 by the US Congress of "fast track" legislation, the way has been opened for negotiations on a free trade agreement. Intensive negotiations are likely to preoccupy officials of the two countries over the next two years.

Middle East

Israeli-Arab Conflicts. The United States continues efforts to find a solution for the long-standing issues involving the Palestinians and Israel's relations with its Arab neighbors. Despite acceptance in principle of the concept of an international conference of all governments concerned, questions of a UN role, Palestinian representation, and the nature of a conference continue to delay progress toward direct discussions among the parties.

Lebanon. The extension of control over the country by the Syrian-backed Lebanese Army continued through 1991, but full control appears unlikely given Israel's reluctance to leave the security zone in southern Lebanon.

Regional Security. Diplomatic efforts in the Gulf region following the war centered and will probably continue to center on how future security of the region can be assured. Agreement among the Arab nations involved seems remote, given reservations about the presence of US and other non-Arab forces in the region, Gulf countries' suspicions of Syrian and Egyptian motives, and the interests of Iran.

Western Hostages. Although two Western hostages in Lebanon were released, full resolution of the issue remained stalemated by politics within Iran and by demands of the captors for the release of Arab prisoners in Israel. Release of the Western hostages continues to be an impediment to any normalization of relations between Tehran and Washington.

Multinational

Antarctica. After June 23, 1991, any consultative member of the Antarctic Treaty may request a special review conference to amend the treaty. No such requests were forthcoming. With the resolution of the issue of mining at a meeting in Madrid in June, the probability that the treaty would continue in its current form was enhanced.[1]

Arms Control. With the signing of two major agreements between the United States and the Soviet Union on Conventional Forces in Europe and Strategic Arms Reduction, attention will turn to ratification action in the US Senate, especially on the latter START Treaty.

Chemical Weapons. Spurred by the threat of the use of chemical weapons in the Gulf War, efforts are likely to accelerate to negotiate an international ban on such weapons. The US announcement in May that it had given up its intention to retain 2 percent of its existing arsenal will provide further impetus to such negotiations.

Election of a New UN Secretary-General. Intensive negotiations between the regional blocs in the United Nations is expected late in 1991 as the process to select a successor to Pérez de Cuéllar proceeds. The General Assembly must make a choice before the end of 1991.

Environment. Multinational diplomatic activities in the environmental area will concentrate on preparations for the United Nations Conference on Environment and Development in Rio de Janeiro, June 1-12, 1992. Issues to be addressed include climate change, transboundary air pollution, the ozone layer, forests, desertification, biological diversity, biotechnology, ocean use and management, the disposition of hazardous waste, and the preservation of fresh water.[2]

Multilateral Trade Negotiations. Resumption of the Uruguay Round of Multilateral Trade Negotiations remains dependent on a resolution of issues between Europe and Latin America. The prospect of renewed negotiations was heightened but by no means assured by the extension of "fast track" authority by the US Congress in May.

Notes

1. See Christopher C. Joyner, "Antarctic Treaty Diplomacy: Problems, Prospects, and Policy Implications," *The Diplomatic Record 1989-1990* (Boulder, CO: Westview Press, 1990), pp. 155-180.

2. For further information on sessions preparatory to the United Nations Conference on Environment and Development, see Pamela Chasek, "The System of International Environmental Negotiations," Background Paper Series BP-1, April 19, 1991, The Project on Multilateral Negotiation of The American Academy of Diplomacy and the Paul H. Nitze School of Advanced International Studies of Johns Hopkins University, Washington, DC. This is also the principal source for the Environmental Diplomacy section of the chronology.

Recent Developments in Diplomatic Practice

Harold E. Horan

In its inaugural issue (*The Diplomatic Record: 1989-1990*), the *Record* indicated its intention to monitor annual developments in diplomatic governance. These developments relate to the regulation of privileges, immunities, and responsibilities concerning personnel and communications of diplomatic and consular missions, states, and international organizations. What follows are selected highlights from 1990-1991.

US Diplomatic Practice

"Diplomatic Immunity" Addressed. A key element of the Department of State's public dialogue is its serial publication entitled *gist*, a quick reference aid on US foreign policy. For the first time in this series, on October 4, 1990, the Department of State issued a *gist* on diplomatic immunity.

In this statement, the State Department confirms the US government's commitment to the Vienna Conventions on Diplomatic and Consular Relations. But the majority of the text addresses issues of abuses of diplomacy reflecting congressional and public perceptions, increasing over the past few years, that immunity has been used to license the commissions of crimes and violations of laws. The publication takes care to underscore that the Department of State enforces the view that persons entitled to immunity have the obligation and duty to respect the laws and regulations of the host country and offers examples of the steps the department takes to protect the American public from diplomatic abuses.

A quick reference aid on US foreign policy

Diplomatic Immunity

Background

Diplomatic immunity is a principle of international law by which certain foreign government officials are not subject to the jurisdiction of local courts and other authorities. The concept of immunity began with ancient tribes. In order to exchange information, messengers were allowed to travel from tribe to tribe without fear of harm. They were protected even when they brought bad news. Today, immunity protects the channels of diplomatic communication by exempting diplomats from local jurisdiction so that they can perform their duties with freedom, independence, and security. Diplomatic immunity is not meant to benefit individuals personally; it is meant to ensure that foreign officials can do their jobs. Under the concept of reciprocity, diplomats assigned to any country in the world benefit equally from diplomatic immunity.

Legal Framework

The Vienna Convention on Diplomatic Relations of 1961 and the Vienna Convention on Consular Relations of 1963 codified most modern diplomatic and consular practices, including diplomatic immunity. More than 140 nations, including the United States, are parties to these treaties. The conventions provide immunity to persons according to their rank in a diplomatic mission or consular post and according to the need for immunity in performing their duties. For example, diplomatic agents and members of their immediate families are immune from all criminal prosecution and most civil law suits. Administrative and technical staff members of embassies have a lower level of immunity. Consular officers serving in consulates throughout the country have an even lower level of immunity. Members of an embassy's service staff and consular employees are immune only for acts performed as part of their official duties.

The United States considers the Vienna conventions particularly important because of the large number of American diplomatic and consular personnel stationed in countries where judicial systems are very different and less protective of individual rights than our own or where unfriendly governments might use their police authorities to harass American diplomats and their families. Failure by US authorities to uphold the Vienna conventions would complicate US diplomatic relations and could lead to harsher treatment in foreign courts of US personnel abroad.

Abuses of Diplomatic Immunity

Under the Vienna conventions, all persons entitled to immunity have the obligation and duty to respect the laws and regulations of the host country. Immunity is not a license to commit a crime, and violations of the law are not condoned. In the United States, any time a person with immunity is alleged to have committed a crime, the Department of State advises his or her government of the incident and, where prosecution would be the normal procedure, requests a waiver of the alleged offender's immunity so that the case may be heard in the appropriate US court. If immunity is not waived, the Department of State may, in serious cases, order the withdrawal of the offender from the United States. In the case of an offense committed by a member of a diplomat's family, the diplomat and his or her entire family may be expelled. Diplomatic visas of serious offenders are cancelled, and their names are entered into a worldwide lookout system to keep them from returning to the United States.

The Department of State's Office of Protocol works with the injured parties and the foreign government to secure restitution in those cases where criminal incidents have resulted in injuries to individuals. The Diplomatic Relations Act of 1978 and related regulations require that before a person with immunity can obtain license plates for a vehicle, he or she must have liability insurance. Anyone injured in an automobile accident by a person with immunity may bring direct action against the vehicle's insurer in US District Court. In addition, diplomats do not have a right to endanger public safety by driving a vehicle while under the influence of alcohol or by disregarding the rules of the road. Police stop them and, if they are intoxicated, prevent them from driving. Police issue citations for driving offenses and the Department of State revokes drivers' permits for any persons found to be unsafe drivers or who continually abuse driving regulations. Furthermore, some countries follow the practice of investigating, and, if appropriate, taking legal action against their own diplomats who are accused of breaking a host country's laws.

In those cases where immunity prevents civil suits, the Department of State works to settle the matter and mediates disputes in an effort to find a mutually satisfactory solution. The vast majority of persons entitled to some form of diplomatic immunity are law-abiding people. Only a few ever run afoul of the law. Unfortunately, those few who do exhibit egregious behavior draw the attention of the public and the media and damage the reputation of the entire group. ■

US Department of State
Bureau of Public Affairs
Office of Public Communication

October 4, 1990

Honorary Consuls. In a circular diplomatic note[1] dated May 17, 1990, the US Department of State addressed policies relating to the establishment of honorary consuls in the United States.[2] The note culminated a three-year study of the governance of honorary consuls accredited to the United States. The study was instituted by a circular note in October 5, 1987, establishing a one-year moratorium on the opening of all new honorary consulates. The note referred to an increase in the number of requests for the establishment of consular posts headed by honorary consuls and announced that during the moratorium the department would conduct a detailed review of consular representation and, on a case-by-case basis, would contact embassies of those governments with large numbers of honorary consular offices to discuss possible adjustments.[3]

The department's review appeared to be motivated by several considerations—the growth in the number of honorary consuls, additional demands that continued to be made upon law enforcement authorities worldwide to protect diplomatic and consular premises, and a congressional desire to limit the number of persons entitled to privileges and immunities in the United States.

Against this background, the 1990 note on honorary consulates stated:

- Establishment of consular posts headed by honorary consular officers must be supported by documentation making it possible for the department to be assured meaningful consular functions will be exercised;
- The department will continue to contact individual diplomatic missions to discuss possible adjustments to their consular establishments and in particular where governments maintain large numbers of posts, there are career and honorary posts in the same city or in close proximity, honorary consuls are in charge of career posts, or offices appear to be located in remote areas;
- Finally, the note provides new guidelines as to the information required when missions request the establishment of posts headed by honorary consular officers. These guidelines require detailed information to support the need of a consular post in terms of consular workload, economic, commercial and other ties, and the expatriate community to be served.[4]

One final note on US practice with regard to honorary consular officers should be added. Such personnel must possess a consular title recognized by the US government, be a citizen or legal permanent resident of the United States, not hold an office with the US government or a position with a state, county, or other municipality of the United States considered by such municipality to be incompatible with the duties of a foreign consular officer. If the nominee holds a commission as a reserve officer in any branch of the US Armed Forces, permission to accept the nomination must be obtained from the secretary of the department concerned. And, nominees must reside in the area where recognition is requested and be more than twenty-one years of age.[5]

Office of Foreign Missions. In June 1990 the Department of State presented its seventh annual report to Congress on the activities of the Office of Foreign Missions (OFM) under the Foreign Missions Act, covering the calendar year 1989.[6] OFM has two major tasks, as reflected in the 1990 report to Congress: to ensure equitable and reciprocal allocation of benefits, privileges, and immunities to US personnel abroad and to provide a series of general services to foreign missions in the United States.[7]

Two items contained in the June 1989 report are particularly illustrative of accomplishments under the first of these objectives.

- During the period, OFM met with Somalia's ambassador to the United States to discuss the imposition of travel controls on Somali diplomats in the United States if Somalia did not immediately lift restrictions on US diplomatic personnel in Somalia. Within days of this meeting travel restrictions were lifted for the US diplomatic staff in Somalia.[8]
- In June 1989, the Department of State instructed the Embassy of Japan to return all sales tax exemption cards held by Japanese missions and personnel in the United States. This action was taken in response to the Japanese government's failure to offer relief from new value added taxes (VATS) and existing provincial sales taxes. By year's end, after intense bilateral negotiations, the government of Japan had designated 5,000 retail stores where foreign diplomatic and consular personnel could shop tax-free. In exchange, the Department of State issued new, restricted, sales tax exemptions to Japanese missions and personnel in the United States, valid on purchases of $100 or more.[9]

With regard to services to foreign missions in the United States, the report indicated that OFM is now offering the following programs of assistance involving (inter alia) the following: real property, construction, motor vehicle registration, insurance, licensing and violations, utility and sales tax, and travel services.[10] The report takes special note of the "tumultuous events in the world during 1989 [that] created a new dimension of involvement for the Office of Foreign Missions." Although general and tentative in nature, what the report has to say on this new issue warrants quoting here:

> As Eastern European countries moved toward more democratic forms of government, interest rose regarding the nature and basis of the controls and restrictions which had been placed upon certain of them. The Office's contribution to the deliberations was to remind those concerned with these developments that controls administered by the Office of Foreign Missions would be altered or dropped only on the basis of permanent, substantive change in these countries, in the behavior of their representatives abroad, and in the nature of the restrictions imposed on US personnel posted in such countries.

US Lifts Travel Restrictions

In 1990, travel restrictions (instituted by the United States in the mid-1980s) were lifted on Polish, Hungarian, and Czechoslovak diplomats posted in the United States and on US diplomats posted in those three countries.

- In March, during the visit of Prime Minister Tadeuz Mazowiecki to Washington, the Poles requested and received US agreement to end requirements that all diplomats in the US submit notification of travel outside a local area and make travel arrangements through the State Department's Office of Foreign Missions (OFM). The Poles lifted similar controls on US diplomats in Warsaw, Krakow, and Poznan.
- In September, during President Vaclav Havel's visit to the UN General Assembly, the United States lifted similar controls on Czechoslovak diplomatic personnel assigned to Washington, New York, and the UN in response to Czechoslovak requests. Czechoslovakia had unilaterally lifted its own restrictions on US diplomats in Prague in March.
- In October, restrictions on Hungarian UN personnel were also lifted in anticipation of Prime Minister Gozsef Antall's visit to the United States. Controls had not been in effect on Washington-based Hungarian diplomats. The Hungarians had previously lifted such controls on US personnel assigned to Budapest in 1989.

By the end of 1990, US diplomats no longer needed visas to enter Czechoslovakia and Hungary for short-term stays. It was agreed that the Poles would open a new consulate in Los Angeles in 1991 and that the United States would reopen its consulate in Bratislava, Czechoslovakia, in 1991.

Romania's status on travel restrictions remained unchanged: There are no restrictions on personnel assigned to Washington, but controls remain on UN diplomats. Bulgarian diplomats must make travel arrangements through OFM, and those assigned to the UN must ask permission to leave the New York metropolitan area. There are no restrictions on Yugoslav diplomats in the United States.

Canadian Diplomatic Practices

In a circular diplomatic note dated November 28, 1990, the Canadian government addressed the question of exemption of diplomatic and consular missions and personnel from a proposed federal goods and services tax, expected to take effect on January 1, 1991.[11]

The note indicates that diplomatic and consular entities and persons are not eligible for relief from the tax on all domestic purchases and imported articles except on the basis of reciprocity. Eligible entities and persons are instructed to pay the tax on all domestic purchases and then file rebate claims for tax paid in error. With regard to imported articles those eligible shall have all imported articles relieved of the tax at the time of entry. The note also indicates that all missions will be informed in due course whether reciprocity exists.

Developments in Hungarian Diplomatic Practice[12]

As a consequence of the developing international relations and growing activities of Hungary, more and more international organizations have established headquarters and representations in Hungary. To maintain effective functioning it is in the mutual interest of the institution and the host government to regulate the question of immunity. The scope of immunity beneficial to foreign nationals is easily agreed upon by the parties, but because of the lack of comprehensive internal relations, Hungarian nationals who have international status in Hungary may present practical problems in defining the range of their immunity.

One recent development has been the reintroduction of the institution of honorary consuls. Since 1987, Hungary has appointed honorary consuls in accordance with Article 68 of the 1963 Vienna Convention (VC). A decree by the foreign minister on honorary consuls—based on the provisions of Article 64—ensures that an honorary consul operating in Hungary receives the necessary protection that may be required to fulfill his or her tasks. Such protection includes an immunity from jurisdiction in respect of official acts performed in the exercise of consular functions.

On the road toward a market economy, a complex tax system was introduced in 1988. Relevant provisions of the act on taxation and a governmental decree of executive character made sure that entitled institutions and individuals are exempted from paying VATS on services and goods as Article 34 of the 1961 VC stipulates. Since 1988, the need to improve and rectify the tax system made it necessary to modify it several times, mainly the procedural aspects of the decree on diplomatic exemptions.

Just as in other countries, the overwhelming majority of incidents with regard to diplomatic immunity concern traffic violations and accidents caused by persons enjoying immunity. A well-established procedure and strong adherence to existing regulations by law enforcement institutions ensure that in Hungary such incidents are quickly and lawfully settled. In case information suggests that the liable person may enjoy a certain degree of immunity from local jurisdiction, the Ministry of Internal Affairs, which supervises the activities of the police in accordance with Decree No. 7 of 1973, may instruct the police authorities to halt the investigation. The Foreign Ministry, after considering the position of the Ministry of Justice when necessary, decides in every case whether the individual involved has immunity. This decision is final and has binding effect on further actions of concerned authorities. Members of administrative, technical, and service staff enjoy immunity only in relation to acts performed within their course of duties. When a member of a diplomatic mission with limited scope of immunity is involved in a traffic violation or accident, the Foreign Ministry, after consulting the mission in question, establishes whether the individual's action falls within the course of official duties. Civilian claims of material compensation against persons with immunity are settled, to some extent, because third-party compulsory vehicle insurance is included in the price of fuel and automatically covered by an insurance company.

Theoretically, uncertainties may occur when the immunity of a non-diplomatic member residing in Hungary is in question. Immigration and alien registration regulations do not set the necessary criteria for obtaining permanent resident status in Hungary, thus leaving room for disputes under Article 37 of the 1961 VC.

Another type of incident, unfortunately increasing in number, is the case of petty smuggling committed by those having immunity. Such acts constitute a clear breach of law. Under Article 36 of the 1961 VC, personal baggage of a diplomatic agent is exempted from customs inspection "unless there are serious grounds for presuming" that it may contain non-permissible articles or goods in excessive quantities. When such incidents occur, Hungarian institutions strictly follow international obligations and internal regulations concerning honoring the violator's personal immunity. Following legal review, Hungarian authorities have concluded that smuggled articles do not fall under permissible items and thus are to be confiscated. Countries may have different approaches toward this question because codified international legal norms have failed to define clearly this aspect of immunity.

Diplomats and individuals who enjoy immunity may fall victims to crime or felony committed by civilians. Hungary provides maximum protection and lawful rights to entitled institutions and individuals. The Criminal Code of Hungary contains no specific provisions relating to crimes or felonies committed against diplomats and diplomatic missions. In reaching decisions the courts may consider not only the crime itself but also, as an aggravating circumstance, the effect of the action on Hungary's international reputation.

International Organizations' Diplomatic Practice: Recent Developments

The 1990 (Forty-Fifth) United Nations General Assembly adopted a program of activities for the 1990-1992 period of the UN Decade of International Law. At the Forty-Fourth session the assembly had declared the period 1990-1999 the Decade of International Law.[13] Four broad objectives were enumerated:

1. Promote acceptance of and respect for the principles of international law.

2. Promote means and methods for the peaceful settlement of disputes between states, including resort to and full respect for the International Court of Justice.

3. Encourage the progressive development of international law and its codification.

4. Encourage the teaching, study, dissemination, and appreciation of international law.

The main thrust of the program adopted at the Forty-Fifth General Assembly (Resolution 45/40) is to encourage states, international organizations, and private organizations to consider specific projects or other steps in pursuance of each of these four proposals.

Notes

1. A circular diplomatic note is one sent to all diplomatic missions in a capital.
2. An honorary consul may "head a consular post and carry out most of the functions of career consuls. They are generally unpaid by the sending government and they can do much useful work, which in part explains their survival. The individuals who are so appointed welcome the social prestige thus acquired and may have a genuine pride in serving the interest of the sending state"—Grant V. McClanahan, *Diplomatic Immunity* (Washington, DC: Institute for the Study of Diplomacy, and New York: St. Martin's Press, 1989), p. 69.
3. In 1985, the number of consular posts headed by honorary consular offices was 1,012.
4. US Department of State, Circular Diplomatic Note, May 17, 1990, Attachment A.
5. *Ibid.*, p. 9.
6. US Department of State, Annual Report on the Implementation of the Foreign Missions Act of 1982, as Amended (PL 97-24).
7. *Ibid.*, pp. 1-2.
8. *Ibid.*, p. 9.
9. *Ibid*, p. 14.
10. *Ibid*, p. 20.
11. Department of External Affairs, Canada, Circular Note, Nr. XDC-4643, November 28, 1990, pp. 1-2. *The Diplomatic Record* is indebted to the administrative counselor of the Canadian Embassy in Washington, DC, Mr. R. P. Archambault, for providing this information.
12. This statement on Hungarian diplomatic practice was prepared by Hungarian diplomat Peter Sárközy, who was a diplomatic associate of the Institute for the Study of Diplomacy during the 1990-1991 academic year. The portion dealing with recent developments is reprinted here in view of the renewed interest in Hungary as the site for offices of foreign firms and international organizations.
13. For a more detailed report on this item see The American Society of International Law, *Newsletter*, January-February-March 1991, p. 1.

DIPLOMATIC CHRONOLOGY

(Arranged Topically)

DIPLOMATIC RELATIONS

1990

July 3: Indonesia and China agreed to reestablish diplomatic relations beginning August 8, 1990.

July 30: Albania and the Soviet Union restored diplomatic relations broken in 1961.

September 19: Vietnamese Deputy Prime Minister Vu Nguyen Giap visited China in the highest level diplomatic visit since the Sino-Vietnamese border war in 1979.

September 23-25: South African President F. W. de Klerk visited the United States, meeting with President George Bush and members of Congress. It was the highest-level South African diplomatic visit since a visit by Prime Minister Jan Christaan Smuts in 1945.

September 27: After eighteen months of hostility, the United Kingdom and Iran resumed diplomatic relations. The British government made the move, convinced threats from Iranian leaders supporting the killing of Salman Rushdie, the British author of *The Satanic Verses*, had subsided.

September 29: The United States and Vietnam held their highest-level talks in more than a decade.

September 30: South Korea and the Soviet Union established diplomatic relations.

______ Israel and the Soviet Union agreed to open consulates.

October 13: Poland signed an agreement in Kiev with the Soviet Ukranian Republic establishing diplomatic relations between sovereign states.

November 28: Great Britain and Syria reestablished relations after a four-year hiatus.

______ The United States reopened its embassy in Beirut, closed since September 1989.

December 6: The Vatican resumed diplomatic relations with Bulgaria at the ambassadorial level.

______ The United States and the Soviet Union exchanged archives from consular offices closed during and after the Russian Revolution in 1917.

December 10: The United States and the Soviet Union signed two treaties limiting the size of underground nuclear explosions: the Underground Nuclear Weapons Test Treaty and the Underground Nuclear Explosions for Peaceful Purposes Treaty.

1991

January 3: Israel opened a consulate in Moscow, the first step in restoring full diplomatic relations.

January 4: Czechoslovakia announced it would no longer represent Cuban interests at its embassy in Washington, DC.

January 11: Rebel attacks on the Italian embassy in Mogadishu, Somalia, resulted in the deaths of several Italian diplomats and a Korean envoy. Only the Italian and Egyptian embassies have remained open.

January 25: The Holy See issued a paper outlining its views on obstacles that prevent diplomatic relations with Israel.

January 30: Japan and North Korea opened formal talks in Pyongyang aimed at restoring diplomatic relations.

February 11: Switzerland agreed to sponsor a Cuban interests section in its embassy in Washington.

February 26: South Africa and the Soviet Union agreed to establish relations at the level of "interest sections."

March 15: Albania and the United States established full diplomatic relations.

March 17: Saudi Arabia and Iran established full diplomatic relations.

March 18: The Kremlin appointed Viktor G. Kompletov, a Soviet diplomat with a hard-line reputation, as the next Soviet Ambassador to the United States.

March 23: India announced it would extend its 1974 Friendship Treaty with the Soviet Union when the pact expires in August.

April 6: Bulgaria announced it would open secret files concerning the 1982 assassination attempt on Pope John Paul II.

______ In Peru, Maoist guerrillas cut power lines to half the population and attacked the embassies of Colombia, Japan, and Israel.

April 11: Hungary recalled its ambassador to the United States, Peter Zwack, for his outspoken criticism of Hungarian Foreign Minister Geza Jeszenszky.

April 20: The United States announced it would open an office in Hanoi, Vietnam, for the purpose of facilitating research on Americans missing in action. It would be the first official US government office in Vietnam since the Vietnam War.

May 25: Talks between Japan and North Korea to establish diplomatic relations stalled over the issue of international inspection of North Korean atomic power plants.

May 28: North Korea announced it would seek separate UN membership for itself, disavowing for the first time its policy of one seat for Korea.

June 8: South African President de Klerk flew to Kenya to urge a normalization of relations and admission of South Africa to the Organization of African Unity.

Environmental Diplomacy

1990

June 29: Sponsored by the UN Environment Program, ninety-three nations reached an agreement to stop production by the end of this century of chemicals that harm the ozone layer. An international fund to assist developing nations toward that end was also established.

August 12-September 4: The third session of the Preparatory Committee for the UN Conference on Environment and Development was held in Geneva.

November 2: During a five-day conference in London, member nations of the London Dumping Convention agreed to a global ban on the dumping of industrial waste at sea. The resolution was signed by forty-three of the largest industrial nations. Measures were also taken to restict pollution originating from land-dumping sites.

November 4: The second World Climate Conference met in Geneva and released a report calling for sizeable cutbacks in gaseous emissions, based on present technological capabilities.

November 13: Signatories of the Antarctic Treaty met in Santiago to discuss the exploration and extrication of natural resources from Antartica.

November 28: The Conference of the International Union for the Conservation of Nature (or the World Conservation Union) met in Perth, Australia, to coordinate global programs to save the world's flora, fauna, insects, and fish.

December 12: The UN General Assembly passed resolution 45/212 on protection of global climate, establishing a single intergovernmental negotiating process leading to a convention on climate change.

1991

February 14: An international conference at Chantilly, Virginia, set up a framework to curb global warming and established guidelines to assist less-developed nations.

February 25: Conservation International, a private US ecological group, negotiated a "debt for nature" swap with Mexico, in which the group will buy $4 million of Mexican discounted debt and forgive it in return for Mexican commitments to preserve the Lacandona rain forest.

March 6: The concluding session of a working group of legal experts on biological diversity was held in Nairobi.

March 9: The Fourth Session of the Preparatory Committee for the UN Conference on Environment and Development was held in New York.

April 30: At a Madrid meeting on the Antarctic, delegates reached agreement on a resolution banning mining for a period of at least fifty years. The resolution must be considered by the signatories of the Antarctic Treaty.

May 6-10: The Intergovernmental Meeting of Experts on Land-Based Sources of Marine Pollution was held in Halifax, Nova Scotia.

May 21: The UN International Atomic Energy Agency (IAEA) issued a report that criticized previous estimates of the long-term damage resulting from the Chernobyl nuclear power plant accident.

June 22: The United States announced it would not support a treaty banning mining in the Antarctic at a follow-up meeting in Madrid of the nations who had subscribed to the draft treaty in April. The accord would have imposed a fifty-year ban on mining in the region.

International Organizations

1990

September 12: Acknowledging that efforts to assist tens of thousands of people fleeing from Iraq and occupied Kuwait were inefficient, the UN selected Sadruddin Aga Khan as the new coordinator for relief efforts.

September 18: The forty-fifth UN General Assembly unanimously selected Guido de Marco, Malta's minister of foreign affairs and justice, as its president.

September 29: More than seventy world leaders gathered at the United Nations to open the first World Summit for Children, designed to improve the lives of poor children throughout the globe.

November 15: The IAEA was asked by Iraq to inspect its stockpile of highly enriched uranium and verify that it had not been used to construct nuclear weapons.

November 20: The Arab bloc in the UN General Assembly revised its strategy with respect to Israeli participation in the United Nations. Rather than attempt to expel Israel, the Arab representatives stated they would seek to lessen support for Israel by focusing on its noncompliance with UN resolutions.

November 22-24: The South Asian Association for Regional Cooperation met in the Maldives to discuss growing political turbulence as well as economic and social problems caused by rapid population growth.

December 4: The UN Committee for Social, Humanitarian, and Cultural Affairs voted overwhelmingly to condemn Iraq for human rights violations in occupied Kuwait.

December 18: The UN International Children's Education Fund (UNICEF) reported that investments in health care have helped to lower infant mortality rates throughout the developing world, also lowering birth rates as a consequence.

December 22: The UN Security Council voted to end the US strategic trusteeship over several Pacific island chains. The island chain of Palau remains the sole trusteeship in the series granted in 1948.

______ The six-nation Gulf Cooperation Council opened its eleventh annual summit meeting in Qatar. On the agenda were the Gulf crisis and strategic stability questions.

December 26: Sadoka Ogata, dean of foreign studies at Sophia University in Tokyo, was selected as UN High Commissioner for Refugees.

1991

January 16: The UN suspended food relief to the Sudan in reaction to Sudanese support for Iraq in the Gulf crisis.

March 6: The UN Human Rights Commission voted unanimously to condemn Myanmar for its human rights abuses.

March 10: The UN Human Rights Commission began an inquiry into alleged human rights abuses in Iraq and occupied Kuwait.

April 29: The UN Security Council voted to construct a referendum in the Western Sahara and install a peacekeeping force to oversee the vote.

May 21: North Korea announced that it would seek a separate UN seat rather than continue its support for a unified Korean seat.

International Trade and Economics

1990

July 9-11: Leaders of the Group of Seven (G-7) held their sixteenth summit meeting in Houston, Texas; they signed agreements on Soviet aid, agriculture, trade, and the environment.

July 13: Australia and New Zealand implemented a free-trade agreement.

October 5: Prime Minister Margaret Thatcher, after years of reticence, announced the linkage of the British pound to major European currencies.

November 1: The International Monetary Fund (IMF) announced that it is working to speed up the processing of loans to countries whose economies have suffered from events in the Gulf, including Egypt, Jordan, and Turkey, as well as the Eastern European countries.

November 3: The Soviet Union agreed to pay an unspecified sum toward bonds issued by the prerevolutionary czarist government, a debt that historically the Soviet government has disclaimed.

November 12: The Uruguay Round meeting adjourned, deadlocked by the impasse over European Community (EC) subsidies to farmers.

November 17: The United States lodged an official complaint with France that French intelligence agents attempted to collect industrial secrets at two American computer companies—International Business Machines (IBM) and Texas Instruments Corporation.

November 18: Mrs. Thatcher renewed her disavowal of a European Central Bank, but indicated she would consider a referendum vote on the issue in Great Britain.

December 3: The American National Conference on Soviet Jewry announced its support for relaxed trade restrictions on the Soviet Union.

December 4: The World Bank extended a $114.3 million loan to the People's Republic of China, the first since the student uprising in June 1989.

December 12: President George Bush lifted a fifteen-year ban on loans to the Soviet Union, simultaneously approving $1 billion in federally guaranteed loans and proposing a special relationship for the Soviet Union in the IMF and World Bank.

______ The Swedish parliament voted to seek membership in the EC in 1991.

December 14: Members of the EC agreed in principle to give $2.4 billion in emergency aid and technical assistance to the Soviet Union.

December 15: Twelve European nations formally opened negotiations aimed at achieving closer political and monetary union.

______ In Rome, EC members lifted a ban on new investments in South Africa, largely because of recent liberalizations taken by President F. W. de Klerk.

December 18: Japan extended $100 million in loans to the Soviet Union to help curb growing food shortages.

December 19: The IMF, World Bank, Organization for Economic Cooperation and Development (OECD), and the new European Bank for Reconstruction and Development jointly drafted a report stressing the innumerable obstacles the Soviet Union faces in its economic reform. An infusion of technical assistance was recommended; direct financial aid was discouraged.

December 22: US economic sanctions against Iran were relaxed as President Bush authorized limited purchases of Iranian crude oil.

1991

January 6: The United States announced it will purchase an atomic reactor from the Soviet Union.

January 7: The Council for Mutual Economic Assistance (COMECON) announced it would officially disband in February 1991. The organization will be replaced by the Organization for International Cooperation, which will seek to preserve the trade ties in existence but will allow its members to establish bilateral trade ties.

______ Czechoslovakia received approval of a $1.8 billion loan from the IMF to finance economic restructuring to a market economy.

January 9: Hungary became the first of the Eastern European countries to receive an aid/loan package from Kuwait.

January 10: Saudi Arabia confirmed it has made more than $30 billion in Gulf-related commitments.

January 23: President Bush met with Mongolian President Punsalmaagiyn Ochirbat to promote trade, particularly in development of the rich Mongolian oilfields.

January 30: Officials of the Western industrialized nations agreed to extend the Eastern European aid coverage to Romania.

February 16: Namibian Finance Minister Otto Herrigel announced the country's new foreign investment law.

______ The United States dropped its objections to the sale of a Cray "super computer" to India.

March 15: At a meeting of the informal Paris Club, Western governments agreed to forgive half of Poland's $33 billion foreign debt.

______ China extended a $730 million commodity loan to the Soviet Union.

April 9: American and international economic officials announced that Egypt would receive a package of debt forgiveness and other international assistance worth billions of dollars.

April 13: The Japanese Finance Ministry and its Export-Import Bank criticized US plans to forgive debt in Poland and Egypt, announcing they would not support Prime Minister Toshiki Kaifu's pledges of aid to Poland or any other nation that sought debt forgiveness.

May 21: The Japanese agreed to fund the exchange rate differential between the yen and dollar equivalent of Gulf War aid promised during the early days of the conflict.

May 24: The Coordinating Committee on Export Controls (COCOM) reduced by half the list of high-tech items covered by export restrictions to the Soviet Union.

______ COCOM agreed at a meeting in Paris to an extensive liberalization of rules prohibiting the export of high technology goods to the former communist countries.

May 25: The US Congress voted "fast track" authority to the president, clearing the way for Mexican trade negotiations and the resumption of the Uruguay Round of Multilateral Trade Negotiations.

______ The Paris Club agreed to relieve $10 billion of Egyptian debt.

June 4: United States and Japanese negotiators reached an agreement on market share of semiconductor sales in Japan that would attempt to allocate American manufacturers a set 20 percent of the Japanese market.

June 5: At a ministerial meeting of the OECD nations in Paris, a consensus was reached that Western aid to the Soviet Union must be preceeded by demonstrations of Moscow's commitment to economic reform.

June 12: The World Bank announced a large increase in funding to the Eastern European countries, including $2.9 billion in loans by the end of June.

June 23: At a meeting of the G-7 finance ministers and central bankers in London, US Treasury Secretary Nicholas F. Brady formally proposed that the Soviet Union be given an associate member status in the IMF.

June 24: Bonn announced that Chancellor Kohl would meet with President Gorbachev in advance of the July summit of the G-7 nations in order to help fashion a Soviet economic reform package that might be endorsed by the member nations.

REGIONAL DIPLOMACY

AFRICA

1990

August 5: US Marines landed in Monrovia, Liberia, to rescue foreigners endangered by civil war.

August 7: The African National Congress (ANC), in a cease-fire agreement with the government of South Africa, proclaimed the cessation of its thirty-year armed struggle.

August 6-7: Leaders of the Economic Community of West African States (ECOWAS) meeting in the Gambia decided to deploy a multinational peacekeeping force to intervene in the civil war in Liberia.

August 24: ECOWAS forces arrived in Liberia.

September 2: The multinational West African peacekeeping force reportedly captured the Liberian capital of Monrovia.

September 9: Liberian President Samuel K. Doe was killed by rebels.

September 16: In talks in Washington the United States and the Soviet Union agreed to work together to restart Angola's stalled peace talks.

September 19: The government of Angola reportedly agreed to allow "the prompt and efficient delivery" of food supplies to tens of thousands of Angolans in danger of starvation because of drought.

September 30: Rwanda was invaded from Uganda by a rebel force.

October 2: Uganda condemned the invasion of Rwanda.

October 5: Foreign forces from Belgium, France, and Zaire entered Rwanda, coming to the assistance of the government.

October 18: Rwandan President Juvenal Habyarimana met with French President François Mitterrand in Paris, announcing an agreement to allow neutral troops to monitor a cease-fire.

October 25: Liberian guerrilla leaders refused to sign a cease-fire agreement at peace talks in Banjul, Gambia.

October 27: The leaders of Burundi, Rwanda, Uganda, and Zaire agreed on a formula for a multinational peacekeeping force to be inserted between Rwandan government troops and rebel forces. Belgium announced it would withdraw the paratroopers it sent to protect its citizens.

October 31: The British government advised its citizens to leave the Sudan, citing food shortages and potential civil unrest.

November 1: Rwanda claimed victory over rebel forces that had invaded from Uganda. Belgium attempted to organize peace talks.

November 2: Pretoria reached agreement with ANC officials for the phased release of political prisoners and the return of political exiles.

November 3: Washington announced restrictions on economic and military aid to Zaire because of alleged human rights violations.

November 21: Ethiopia urgently called for 800,000 tons of relief food for the estimated 4.3 million people threatened by famine.

November 25: Agreement between Ethiopia and the Eritrean rebels allowed relief vessels to dock in rebel-held territory and distribute aid.

November 27: ANC leader Nelson Mandela met with President de Klerk in an attempt to rekindle the impetus for direct negotiations between the two parties.

November 28: The five-nation West African peacekeeping forces successfully brokered a cease-fire between the Liberian government and rebel forces at a meeting in Bamako, Mali.

December 8: Food and water relief supplies arrived in Monrovia, Liberia, where UN Children's Fund officials estimated 80 percent of the children were severely malnourished. Violent conflict, however, prevented rapid distribution of the supplies.

______ The United States airlifted a number of Libyan dissidents from Chad despite protests from Libyan leader Colonel Muammar Qaddafi, who had hoped to repatriate and punish the dissidents.

December 11: The United Nations ordered the evacuation of its personnel from Mogadishu, Somalia, as rebel troops pressed on the capital.

December 13: Oliver Tambo, exiled leader of the ANC, returned to South Africa after thirty-seven years.

December 14: US Secretary of State James A. Baker III and Soviet Foreign Minister Eduard Shevardnadze met in Washington with top officials of the Angolan government and Angolan guerrilla leader Jonas Savimbi. Savimbi reached tentative agreement with the Soviet-backed Angolan government that would include free elections and a cease-fire.

December 16: The ANC warned it would consider suspending talks with the government unless certain obstacles to official negotiations were eliminated by May 1—the unconditional release of all political prisoners, return of political exiles, end to political trials, and the repeal of the repressive security laws.

December 22: Nigerian President Ibrahim Babangida called for reparation payments from Western nations for damage done to Africa during the slave trade.

1991

January 5: After Western governments failed in their attempt to arrange a cease-fire in Mogadishu, Somalia, US and Italian forces began an evacuation of foreigners.

January 23: An Angolan peace plan sponsored by Portugal, the Soviet Union, and the United States was acccepted almost in its entirety by both the National Union for the Total Independence of Angola (UNITA) and the Angolan government.

January 28: Somali President Siad Barre fled from Mogadishu; the United Somali Congress formed an interim government.

January 29: Ethopian government representatives and Eritrean rebels agreed to meet in London under US mediation in February to end thirty years of civil conflict.

February 1: In a speech before parliament, South African President de Klerk called for the repeal of the Land Act, Group Areas Act, Black Communities, and eventually the Population Registration Act—all major foundations of apartheid.

February 2: de Klerk annnounced that a legal way has been found around the 1983 Population Act to make changes in the apartheid law.

______ Though welcoming de Klerk's news of reform, Nelson Mandela asserted that many obstacles must be addressed before the situation would warrant reconsideration of sanctions.

February 4: In response to de Klerk's speech of February 1, the United States praised reform in South Africa, and EC officials pledged to lift economic sanctions when the legislation dismantling apartheid is introduced in the legislature.

February 12: In talks between Mandela and de K-lerk, substantive agreement was reached, including an ANC renunciation of the use of force for armed struggle.

February 16: Peace talks in Rome between Renamo rebels and the Mozambican government broke down.

March 12: South African President de Klerk introduced legislation that would abolish discrimination in land ownership, allowing South Africans to live where they choose.

March 14: The first talks between Namibia and South Africa over the future of Walvis Bay, a strategic port in Namibia that South Africa continues to occupy, broke off after only a few hours when representatives declared they needed to consult with their governments.

March 18: Sudan agreed to a major UN relief effort to stem drought-induced famine facing eight million people.

March 21: South Africa agreed to UN assistance in aiding political exiles to return to the country.

April 5: The ANC demanded in an open letter that the government move to stop violence in the black townships by May 9 or face the prospect of ANC withdrawal from the political dialogue.

April 10: Nelson Mandela told Western diplomats that the ANC's open letter to the government should be interpreted more as a plea than as an ultimatum and that the ANC had no intention of quitting the dialogue.

April 15: The EC voted to lift economic sanctions against South Africa. The US State Department reiterated its position that South Africa would have to free all political prisoners and abolish discriminatory laws before Washington would lift sanctions.

______ Nigeria and Guinea sent troops into Sierra Leone to repel an invasion of rebels launched from Liberian territory.

April 23: President de Klerk met with Prime Minister John Major in London. deKlerk announced that he extended an open-ended invitation to

Major to visit South Africa and that British Foreign Sercretary Douglas Hurd would visit in the summer.

April 24: Angolan President José Eduardo dos Santos accepted a proposal by the Portuguese to hold the country's first multiparty elections in eighteen months.

April 27: Referring to the EC's lifting of economic sanctions against South Africa, Mandela accused the European nations of racism in subverting the policies of the ANC.

May 1: Angola and UNITA forces initialed a ceasefire agreement to be formally signed on May 31.

May 2: President de Klerk announced plans to abolish security mechanisms, such as preventative detention, which come from the Internal Security Act of 1982.

May 17: The UN General Assembly voted funding for an observer force to oversee the plebiscite in the Western Sahara scheduled in approximately thrity-six weeks.

May 18: The ANC announced its refusal to participate in constitutional talks with the government until the black factional violence that has marred South Africa in recent weeks has ended.

May 21: President Mengistu Haile Mariam of Ethiopia fled the country, taking refuge in Zimbabwe.

May 24: The last Cuban troops left Angola.

May 25: As Ethiopian separatist guerrillas captured the last port held by government forces, thus cutting off fuel and food supplies to the capital, Israel completed the evacuation of 14,500 Ethiopian Jews.

May 28: Ethiopian rebel groups took full control of Addis Ababa after brief fighting in the capital city.

May 29: The Ethiopian People's Revolutionary Democratic Front forces took control of Addis Ababa.

May 31: Angola and UNITA leaders signed a pact that ended the sixteen-year civil war.

June 5: The South African parliament repealed the Land Acts of 1913 and 1936 and the Group Areas Act, which worked to justify discrimination in property ownership.

June 17: The South African parliament formally repealed the Population Registration Act, which had set the legal foundation for the policy of apartheid.

______ The Angolan Joint Political-Military Commission, charged with implementing the peace accords signed May 31, was officially initiated by government and UNITA rebel leaders.

June 21: The South African parliament approved a major reform of the nation's Internal Security Act, including provisions for detention without trial and interrogation.

July 3: A conference of Ethiopian political factions adopted a charter establishing a transitional government and endorsing the right of self-determination.

July 5: Nelson Mandela was elected to be ANC president at the first ANC conference in South Africa.

July 9: The International Olympic Committee, meeting in Lausanne, lifted its ban on South African participation.

ASIA AND THE PACIFIC

1990

July 18: Secretary of State Baker, reflecting strong US opposition to the participation of the Khmer Rouge in the peace talks, said the United States would no longer recognize the rebel coalition in Cambodia, opting instead to begin negotiations with Vietnam in order to end the strife in Cambodia.

July 24-29: At its annual meeting in Jakarta, Indonesia, the Association of Southeast Asian Nations (ASEAN) disapproved of the US decision to withdraw recognition of the rebel coalition in Cambodia.

August 31: The UN peace plan under which power would be shared by the four factions in Cambodia was endorsed by the Cambodian government of Prime Minister Hun Sen.

September 4-6: The prime ministers of the two Koreas met for the first time since separation in 1948. The meeting in Pyongyang brought little in the way of resolution but helped to foster an atmosphere of tolerance. The two heads of state agreed to consider sharing a joint UN seat.

September 10: At a meeting in Indonesia, the four factions in Cambodia formally backed a UN framework for peace, agreeing on the formation and composition of an all-party national leadership.

September 21: Discussions on US military bases in the Philippines, which began September 18, ended without agreement on a reduced American military presence at Clark Air Force Base and Subic Bay Naval Base.

October 30: A territorial dispute among China, Formosa, and Japan concerning the Senkaku island chain (Diaoyu Islands, in Chinese) flared as

Japanese coastguard ships interdicted a Formosan flotilla attempting to plant a flag on an island.

November 7: Pakistani Prime Minister Nawaz Sharif said Pakistan will accelerate its nuclear energy program to lessen dependence on foreign oil. Reports that Pakistan is developing a nuclear device for military use have been a source of contention in US-Pakistani relations.

November 9: US and Philippine officials announced in Manila that in negotiations over the future of US military bases in the Philippines the existing security treaty would be set aside and a new agreement devised.

November 13: Singapore signed an agreement with the United States to allow use of a military base for training and as a port of call.

November 25: In a final draft of a Cambodian peace settlement approved by the five permanent members of the Security Council, the four Cambodian factions would jointly comprise a Supreme National Council to rule Cambodia until elections could be held.

November 30: Following an invitation extended in recognition of Chinese support for UN action in the Gulf, Chinese Foreign Minister Qian Qichen visited Washington for talks.

December 13: The third round of talks aimed at reducing tensions in North and South Korea's relationship ended without dispelling mistrust and suspicion. The only agreement reached was to meet again in February.

______ South Korean President Roh Tae Woo met with Soviet President Mikhail Gorbachev.

December 20: Japan announced an increased share of the costs of maintaining US troops on its soil from 40 percent to 50 percent.

December 23: At the end of a two-day meeting to discuss a UN plan providing for a cease-fire and free elections in Cambodia, the major point preventing an agreement appeared to be the time frame under which disarmament of the respective groups would occur.

1991

January 1: Tamil separatist leaders declared a cease-fire in Sri Lanka.

January 10: Japan agreed to halt the fingerprinting of Japanese of South Korean heritage who are considered resident aliens.

January 28: The United States expressed dismay over the sentencing of five participants of China's democracy movement to prison sentences.

February 6: By persuading Vietnamese refugees to stay in or near Vietnam, UN officials successfully slowed the exodus of boat people to Hong Kong.

February 12: The two Koreas announced they would field joint sports teams in soccer and table tennis.

February 18: In response to alleged provocative military exercises by US and South Korean troops, the North Korean government called off the scheduled round of peace talks between the two Koreas.

March 16: Foreign ministry officials of the new Thai military government, which took power in a coup February 23, moved to sever links with the Cambodian government until the UN peace initiative created a representative government in Cambodia.

April 15: The Dalai Lama met with President Bush and pushed for linkage between Most Favored Nation (MFN) status and human rights abuses in China.

April 16-18: President Gorbachev and Prime Minister Kaifu finished their meetings in Tokyo with a number of agreements on a broad range of issues, but without agreement on the Kurile Islands.

______ China lodged an offical protest in the United States following a reception for the Dalai Lama in the Capitol Rotunda in Washington.

April 19-20: President Gorbachev met with President Roh Tae Woo in South Korea. President Roh agreed to provide economic aid to the Soviet Union, negotiate a mutual cooperation treaty, and expand trade. Gorbachev agreed to support the South Korean bid for UN membership and to call for North Korea to open its nuclear facilities to international inspection.

April 25: The United States announced $1 million in humanitarian assistance to Vietnam.

April 26: The Cambodian government in Phnom Penh provided numerous amendments to the UN-sponsored peace treaty, effectively blocking a rapid conclusion of the process.

April 30: President Lee Teng-Hui of Taiwan ended the nation's forty-three-year-old emergency decree, opening the way for a representative vote.

May 4: Philippine Foreign Secretary Raul Manglapus announced that negotiations over US bases had stalled because of differences concerning the length of new leases.

May 7: US Under Secretary of State for Political Affairs Robert Kimmitt held talks with Chinese Foreign Minister Qian Qichen in Beijing concerning human rights, trade, and weapon sales.

May 11: Hong Kong refugee officials reported a large upsurge in the number of Vietnamese fleeing to Hong Kong by boat.

May 15: China's Communist party leader, Jiang Zenmin, arrived in Moscow for the highest level of talks since 1957.

______ President Bush announced he wanted to extend MFN status to China for another year.

______ Jiang Zenmin announced in Moscow that the long-standing border dispute between China and the Soviet Union had been settled on the basis of mutual concessions.

______ US military troops began assisting in relief efforts following the cyclone disaster in Bangladesh. The movement of US forces into the area raised concern in India.

May 21: Rajiv Gandhi, leader of India's Congress party, was assassinated. Suspicion centered on a radical Tamil group from Sri Lanka.

May 27: President Bush announced he would renew MFN status for China but imposed new restrictions on the export of missile technology to the country.

June 7: Pakistan's request for international talks for the creation of a nuclear weapons–free zone in South Asia was rejected by India.

June 8: North Korea announced it would allow the IAEA to inspect its nuclear facilities.

June 12: Secretary Baker warned China of the "profound consequences" of missile sales to Syria and Pakistan.

June 20: P. V. Narasimha Rao was chosen by the Congress party to be India's next prime minister.

______ The United States evacuated more than half of its military personnel in the Philippines following the eruption of the Mount Pinatubo volcano.

June 24: The twelve-member Supreme National Council of Cambodia, set up by the UN Security Council to carry out the Cambodia Peace Plan, formally accepted the indefinite truce negotiated in Bangkok and voted favorably to a ban on the import of arms.

______ North Korea returned the remains of eleven fallen US servicemen from the Korean War, and US Senator Robert C. Smith announced that the US and Korea had reached tentative agreement to set up a joint committee that would supervise the return of remaining MIAs.

July 17: In an agreement announced by the United States and the Philippines, the United States will give up Clark Air Base but retain access to Subic Bay Naval Base for ten years. The agreement is subject to ratification by the Philippine Senate.

EUROPE

1990

July 1: A treaty between the two German nations on economic and monetary unification entered into force.

July 2: Responding to the Lithuanian Supreme Council's decision to suspend Lithuania's declaration of independence, the Soviet Union said it would lift the economic embargo on the republic, which had begun in April.

July 6: At a summit in London, the North Atlantic Treaty Organization (NATO) agreed to alter military strategy and make overtures to the nations of the Warsaw Treaty Organization (WTO, or Warsaw Pact) in order to operate within a more peaceful framework.

July 10-27: The Preparatory Committee for the CSCE summit met in Vienna.

July 16: President Gorbachev and West German Chancellor Helmut Kohl worked out an agreement permitting unified Germany to become part of NATO.

August 1: US Secretary of State Baker met with Soviet Foreign Minister Shevardnadze in Irkutsk for arms control talks. Shevardnadze announced that the Soviet Union would end production of SS-24 missiles.

August 31: Representatives of the two German nations signed a treaty on the details of unification.

September 4 - November 17: The second session of the Preparatory Committee for the CSCE summit met in Vienna.

September 12: The Four Powers—Britain, France, the Soviet Union, and the United States—signed a treaty relinquishing their occupation rights in Germany as of October 1.

September 13: The Soviet Union and the Federal Republic signed a broad "treaty on good-neighborliness, partnership and cooperation."

September 20: Legislators of both German nations ratified a treaty to serve as the formal unification document.

September 24: East Germany withdrew from the Warsaw Pact.

September 25: Lithuanian Prime Minister Kazimiera Prunskiene met with President Gorbachev and reasserted Lithuania's right to secede from the union and become fully independent.

October 1-2: CSCE foreign ministers met in New York, the first CSCE meeting in the United States.

October 3: East and West Germany unite.

______ Shevardnadze and Baker, meeting in New York, announced agreement on the main points of a conventional arms treaty for Europe.

October 24: In a joint communiqué, leaders of the Balkan nations—Albania, Bulgaria, Greece, Romania, Turkey, and Yugoslavia—stressed the principle of noninterference and the protection of human rights.

October 26: Gorbachev arrived in Spain, his first stop on a European tour to garner support for his economic reforms.

October 29: The Norwegian coalition government dissolved over the issue of membership in the EC.

November 4: The Council of Europe marked the fortieth anniversary of its human rights charter as it prepared to admit Hungary to its ranks. Hungary was the first of the Eastern European nations to join. The council also extended an offer to Canada, the Soviet Union, and the United States to participate in some of its functions, including participation in a quasi-legislature with the nations of Eastern Europe included.

November 8: Germany agreed to a guarantee of the Oder-Neisse rivers as Poland's western border. The accord relieved tension in Polish-German relations and also met the demands of the "Two plus Four" talks leading to the restoration of German unity.

November 9: Gorbachev became the first foreign leader to visit the unified Germany and signed a Treaty of Good-Neighborliness, Partnership and Cooperation.

November 10: Voters in Macedonia, Yugoslavia, voted in the first free multiparty election in the republic's forty-five-year history; the election was the first of six national elections to determine the future of the Yugoslav federation.

November 17: President Bush, on a visit to Prague, presented Czechoslovakia with a commemorative replica of the Liberty Bell in honor of the first anniversary of its democratic revolution.

November 19: A three-day summit session of the Conference on Security and Cooperation in Europe began in Paris with twenty-two nations, comprising both NATO and the Warsaw Treaty Organization, signing the most ambitious arms control agreement in history.

November 21: Thirty-four nations signed the Charter of Paris for a New Europe, the concluding document of the meeting of the Conference on Security and Cooperation in Europe. The Charter was seen as marking a definite end to the Cold War in Europe and raised issues of human rights, economic and social justice, and equal security as the main pillars of a new Europe.

December 1: British and French transportation secretaries celebrated the Channel Tunnel's first symbolic breakthrough; the tunnel was planned to open to train traffic in two-and-a-half years.

December 7: France and Germany proposed the creation of a twelve-nation European Group to develop regional and security policy to serve as the "European Pillar" within the greater NATO alliance.

December 10: Separatists won in an important Serbian election, increasing divisive pressures in the Yugoslav federation.

______ Gorbachev accepted the Nobel Peace Prize in absentia, warning of the great potential for aggression and totalitarianism that continued to threaten the world.

December 13: Shevardnadze arrived in Ankara for two days of talks aimed at improving relations with Turkey.

______ South Korean President Roh Tae Woo met with President Gorbachev in Moscow.

December 15: The Czechoslovak parliament approved a power-sharing arrangement between the Czeck and Slovak republics that reduces the authority of the federal government.

December 20: Shevardnadze resigned his post, voicing criticism of conservative intransigence and the Soviet Union's precipitous slide toward dictatorship.

______ The newly elected German parliament met in the Reichstag building in Berlin. A vote on whether to move the parliament permanently to Berlin was postponed.

December 23: The Irish Republican Army announced a three-day cease-fire in its war against British rule in Northern Ireland.

______ Citizens of the Yugoslav republic Slovenia voted overwhelming for independence.

______ Ground-breaking began for a new NATO air base near Crotone, Italy.

1991

January 2: Greek Prime Minister Constantine Mitsotakis declared a state of emergency for the region bordering Albania as thousands of Albanian refugees crossed into Greece.

January - February: The first CSCE meeting of experts on the Peaceful Settlement of Disputes was held in Valletta, Malta.

January 11: Soviet troops occupied various government buildings in Lithuania. Pronationalist forces erected a guard around the parliament building.

January 13: Soviet army forces killed thirteen and injured more than one hundred Lithuanians while taking control of local press and government buildings in Vilnius.

______ The EC condemned the Soviet actions, linking future economic aid to the cessation of overt force.

______ Talks between Albania and Greece concerning the issue of minorities fleeing Albania stalled amid deep hostility and suspicion.

January 14: Gorbachev blamed Lithuanian nationalists for sparking the clash in Vilnius.

January 16: Latvian leaders sought to dissuade Soviet use of force in Riga by using conciliatory tones in messages addressed to Moscow.

______ Poland sought assurances that the Soviet army would be leaving Poland at a future unspecified date.

January 21: Latvia created a self-defense force composed of young Latvians who refused to join the Soviet army. Moscow threatened to extend direct presidential rule to the country.

______ The EC prepared to halt economic aid to the Soviet Union and impose sanctions as a result of Soviet repression in the Baltic nations. President Bush also appealed to President Gorbachev to end the violence.

January 22: The EC suspended a $1 billion aid package to the Soviet Union in protest over events in the Baltic states.

January 26: Soviet Foreign Minister Aleksandr Bessmertnykh met with Secretary of State Baker to repair relations damaged by the Gulf conflict and events in the Baltics.

January 28 : Baker and Bessmertnykh announced the United States and Soviet Union had postponed indefinitely the planned summit meeting originally scheduled for February.

February 1: Gorbachev offered a more conciliatory approach toward the Baltics as he appointed delegations to begin "a discussion of issues" with the secessionist republics.

February 5: Gorbachev declared the upcoming Lithuanian plebiscite on independence illegal.

______ Lech Walesa, in his new capacity as Poland's president, was received warmly by Pope John Paul II.

February 9: In a nationwide plebiscite, Lithuania voted overwhelmingly to support independence.

February 11: President Gorbachev called for the official disbandment of the Warsaw Pact Treaty Organization by April 1.

February 13: France toughened its political refugee policy to stem the flows of refugees from the Third World and Eastern Europe.

February 14: The second round of talks to reduce conventional forces in Europe opened in Vienna.

______ Poland called for an increased pace in Soviet military withdrawal from Polish territory.

February 16: Leaders of Czechoslovakia, Hungary, and Poland, met in Visegrad, Hungary, to pledge cooperation while assuring the Soviet Union that cooperation would not be a weapon used against their larger neighbor.

February 24: Polish Prime Minister Jan Krystof announced a three-year accord with the IMF to provide $2 billion in loans.

February 25: Meeting in Budapest, members of the Warsaw Treaty Organization agreed to dissolve the pact by March 31.

March 3: Latvia and Estonia held plebiscites voting favorably for independence.

March 6: A mass exodus of Albanians fleeing to Italy began for the third time in seven months.

March 14: Former East German leader Erich Honecker was secretly moved to a Soviet hospital; Bonn lodged an official protest with the Soviet Union.

March 15: Secretary Baker met with President Gorbachev in Moscow to discuss disagreements on two arms control treaties being discussed in Vienna—a long-range strategic arms treaty and a conventional forces in Europe treaty.

March 16: Secretary Baker in Moscow met with officials from the Baltic republics to discuss Soviet policy toward secession.

March 17: In a nationwide referendum Soviet citizens voted with mixed results on whether to preserve the unity of the Soviet Union.

March 20: Polish President Lech Walesa met with President Bush in Washington and received a pledge that the United States would forgive $800 million of Polish debt.

March 29: Belgium, France, Germany, Italy, Luxembourg, and the Netherlands agreed to allow Polish citizens to travel in their country without visas, provided they respect the three-month travel limit and labor laws.

April 9: Soviet Georgia proclaimed its independence from the Soviet Union.

______ The Soviet Union began withdrawing 10,000 of its 50,000 troops from Poland.

April 13: Chiefs of Staff of the sixteen NATO member nations agreed to enlarge the rapid reaction forces to enhance response capability in times of changing security needs.

______ Pope John Paul II appointed an archbishop to Moscow and named several other bishops in Siberia and Kazakhistan, a first step in laying the foundation of a future papal visit to the Soviet Union.

April 22: In Washington, administration officials and congressional leaders met with the prime ministers of the Baltic republics.

April 25: The Soviet Union dropped its insistence that coastal troops were not covered by the November 1990 arms agreement, opening the way for US ratification of the treaty and further progess on the two treaties under negotiation.

April 26: Great Britain and Ireland agreed to hold a new phase of talks on Irish unity.

May 8: President Bush met with leaders of the Baltic

republics in Washington.

May 15: Ulster Unionists and British Prime Minister John Major reached agreement that would allow the current peace process to continue while the groups negotiate their positions.

May 19: Croatian voters passed a proposition advocating sovereignty for the republic with limited confederation to the other Yugoslav republics.

May 20: The Congress of the People's Deputies of the Soviet Union enacted legislation permitting the free travel and emigration of its citizens.

May 24: Latvia and Lithuania reported that Soviet commandos had attacked and destroyed various border posts contiguous with the other Soviet republics.

May 26: President Gorbachev of the Soviet Union, after meeting with the presidents of nine republics, announced the "near" completion of a new union treaty.

May 28: NATO defense ministers meeting in Brussels approved a major restructuring of the alliance military posture.

______ NATO agreed to restructure its forces into smaller, more mobile units and to the withdrawal of nearly 160,000 US troops from Europe.

June 1: Secretary Baker reached an agreement with Soviet Foreign Minister Bessmertnykh in Lisbon concerning the Soviet interpretation of the Treaty on Conventional Forces in Europe.

______ Pope John Paul II began an eight-day visit to Poland in which he praised the democratic process under way, but offered significant criticism of the government's stance on abortion.

June 3: France announced its readiness to sign the Nuclear Non-Proliferation Treaty as part of a newly unveiled global arms control and disarmament program that would include a ban on chemical and biological weapons, reductions in nuclear arsenals, tightening of controls on technology transfers, and exports of conventional weapons.

June 6: British Prime Minister Major proposed that President Gorbachev be invited to July's summit meeting of the G-7 nations in London.

June 7: Secretary Baker met with Foreign Minister Bessmertnykh in Geneva to discuss disputes in the nuclear arms treaty being negotiated; no progress was reported.

June 11: The United States extended $1.5 billion in agricultural credits to the Soviet Union.

June 13: Boris Yeltsin easily won the presidency of the Russian Republic in the first popular election in Russian history.

______ Italy announced $50 million in aid to help Albania overcome its economic collapse.

June 14: NATO allies and five East European countries formally approved the compromise reached by Soviet and American negotiators concerning the disputed interpretation of the conventional forces in Europe treaty.

______ Sweden announced it would formally apply for membership in the European Community on July 1.

June 17: Germany and Poland signed a treaty in Bonn that mutually recognizes the current borders, guarantees minority rights, and pledges future cooperation. Germany additionally pledged to support Poland's bid to accede to the European Community as well as obtain debt relief from Western nations.

______ An operational meeting of the foreign ministers of the CSCE member nations opened in Berlin. The agenda included Western participation in the reform process in East European countries and ethnic instability in Yugoslavia.

June 19: The foreign ministers of the CSCE-member nations commenced the first post–Cold War meeting in Berlin, discussing the topic of aid to the former East Bloc countries.

June 21: The Bundestag narrowly voted to return the capital of Germany to Berlin.

June 25: The Slovene and Croatian parliaments voted for declarations of independence. If their demands for greater autonomy remain unmet, the declarations provide for full secession from the Yugoslav Republic.

______ The European Community, the CSCE administration, and the US government all released statements critical of the Slovene and Croatian moves toward secession.

______ The Soviet Union and Czechoslovakia signed a protocol that signaled an end to the Soviet occupation since 1968.

July 1: The Soviet Union and five East European nations meeting in Prague formally dissolved the Warsaw Pact.

July 3: Northern Ireland talks collapsed.

MIDDLE EAST

1990

July 3: For the first time since the end of the Iran-Iraq War in August 1988, the foreign ministers of Iran and Iraq held direct talks in Geneva.

July 9-10: Iranian Foreign Minister Ali Akbar Velayati visited Kuwait, reducing hostility between the two nations after the war in which Kuwait supported Iraq.

July 14-16: Syrian President Hafiz al-Asad visited

Egypt for the first time in the more than thirteen years since Egypt and Israel signed a peace treaty.

September 14: Iran released a US citizen held in Iranian prison since October 1984. The American had been charged with violating foreign currency regulations.

October 8: In a battle between Israeli policemen and thousands of Arabs outside Al Aksa Mosque (Temple Mount) in Jerusalem, nineteen Palestinians were killed.

October 9: The Lebanese government of President Elias Hrawi requested Syrian assistance to remove General Michel Aoun, commander of the Christian militia.

October 13: Pressured by Syrian forces, Aoun surrendered after opposing the government for two years.

October 13: The UN Security Council passed a resolution condemning the Palestinian killings at the mosque in Jerusalem and calling for a delegation to investigate.

October 25: Israel rejected the latest UN resolution calling for compliance with previous UN resolution 672, which attempted to set up a commission to investigate killings at the Al Aksa Mosque.

October 30: Rival Shiite Muslim groups in Lebanon agreed to a cease-fire.

______ Israel restricted the entry of Palestinians from Gaza and the West Bank from entering Israel proper following the latest violence.

November 4: Israel rejected a UN call for signatories of the Geneva Convention to meet to discuss protection for Palestinians in the occupied territories.

November 6: Under Iranian and Syrian supervision, Lebanon's two main Shiite Muslim militias signed a peace agreement that called for a cease-fire and a release of hostages.

November 8: Israel stated it would not allow the Syrian-backed Lebanese government to gain control of the "security zone" in southern Lebanon.

November 14: Israel announced it will allow a UN representative to investigate recent violence in the occupied territories and proposed solutions to avoid further bloodshed.

November 16: Iran and Iraq reached agreement on a series of steps to end major disputes lingering from their eight-year war.

November 21: Talks between Afghan rebel leaders and Afghan President Muhammad Najibullah opened in Geneva.

December 1: The Lebanese Christian militia—the Lebanese Forces—completed its evacuation of Beirut under the terms laid down in a cease-fire agreement.

December 9: European countries, including Great Britain, withdrew sanctions against Iran and began to normalize relations. Iranian President Ali Akbar Hashemi Rafsanjani also made overtures to the Gulf states.

December 11: President Bush and Israeli Prime Minister Yitzhak Shamir met to smooth the increasingly tense relations between the two countries.

December 16: Israeli Defense Minister Moshe Arens stated that Israel will deport more Palestinians from the occupied territories in order to deter further terrorism.

December 20: The UN Security Council voted to criticize Israel for deportation of Arabs; the United States cosponsored the resolution in a move designed to preserve Arab participation in the Gulf coalition.

1991

January 4: The UN Security Council passed a resolution deploring Israeli use of force in the occupied territories; the United States supported the resolution.

______ Israel reported that nearly 200,000 Soviet Jews immigrated since the beginning of 1990 and another 40,000 are expected to arrive in the first few months of 1991.

______ The United States postponed a $13 billion arms deal with Saudi Arabia pending resolution of the Gulf crisis.

February 15: Washington lodged official complaints to Israel concerning the outspoken criticisms of the United States by Israeli Ambassador Zalman Shoval.

February 19: US State Department officials criticized Israel for its policy of detaining Palestinian suspects without trial.

March 13: A PLO spokesman noted a warming of relations between the PLO and Syria following Syria's release of hundreds of PLO supporters.

March 24: Bahrain and the United States reached an agreement to establish a forward military headquarters for the US Central Command.

April 1: Mujahidin rebels in Afghanistan took the garrison town of Khost in the beginning of their spring offensive.

______ The PLO rejected a Lebanese government order for all private armed groups to disband, stating they would continue attacks on Israel from bases in southern Lebanon.

April 16: A new Jewish settlement in the occupied West Bank opened days before a visit by US Secretary Baker, drawing severe criticism from Washington as an obstacle to the Arab-Israeli peace process.

April 20: Iran offered to use its influence to gain the release of Western hostages in Lebanon. The announcement followed the visit of a British official who indicated that British influence in Israel might be used to secure the release of Shiite prisoners.

April 29: President al-Asad and Prime Minister Rafsanjani reached agreement that Iranian-backed Party of God troops in Lebanon could remain in the south and deep in the Bekka valley.

May 10: Soviet Foreign Minister Bessmertnykh visited Israel. Although no agreement was reached on the establishment of diplomatic relations or on the regional crisis, the visit was marked by the absence of deep disagreements.

May 20: On a visit to Israel, Polish President Lech Walesa apologized for Poland's anti-semitist history.

May 22: The leaders of Syria and Lebanon signed a cooperative pact, entitled the Treaty of Brotherhood, Cooperation, and Coordination, that works to secure relations between the two nations.

______ The IAEA completed its first post-war inspection of Iraqi nuclear facilities, placing most of its enriched uranium under seals that would make it easy to track.

May 23: Israeli officials reacted angrily to Secretary Baker's allegations that the Jewish settlements in the occupied territories are the greatest obstacle to the Middle East peace conference.

______ Several hundred UN security guards will move into northern Iraq under an agreement reached between the UN and Iraq.

May 24: The UN Security Council voted unanimously to call on Israel to halt the deportation of Palestinians from the occupied territories.

May 26: Israel completed the evacuation of 14,000 Ethiopian Jews.

May 31: The United States announced it would stockpile military equipment in Israel for use in any future regional conflict.

June 9: British Minister Douglas Hogg arrived in Beirut on a diplomatic mission to secure the release of Western hostages.

June 10: Israeli Prime Minister Shamir added a new condition for participation in a Middle East peace conference: Israel must have the right to approve any potential Palestinians named to the joint Jordanian-Palestinian delegation.

June 12: British Minister Hogg met with Syrian officials in Damascus concerning the release of Western hostages in Lebanon.

June 17: The UN Security Council passed a resolution requiring Iraq to bear the financial cost of destroying its chemcial and biological weapons and nuclear materials.

June 21: European and US officials announced that a 5,000-member force would remain in Turkey to protect the Kurds once coalition forces had left Iraq.

June 25: Martial law was suspended in Kuwait as the crown prince reassumed his position as prime minister.

______ UN officials reported that Iraq twice blocked attempts to inspect a military site north of Baghdad.

June 26: The United States showed secret reconnaissance photographs to the Security Council that reveal Iraqi attempts to hide equipment capable of making nuclear bombs from areas to be inspected by UN officials.

______ Kuwait commuted the death sentences of convicted collaborators to life in prison.

July 4: The PLO agreed to turn over heavy weapons to the Lebanese Army in a move that enhanced Lebanese government control over the south.

July 9: The five permanent members of the UN Security Council meeting in Paris committed themselves to the elimination of weapons of mass destruction from the Middle East and to restrain the supply of conventional weapons.

July 17: The United States and the Soviet Union announced agreement on the Strategic Arms Reduction Treaty (START).

WESTERN HEMISPHERE

1990

June 27: President George Bush proposed forgiveness of Latin American debt and a free-trade zone for North, Central, and South America supporting free-market economies in Latin America.

August 20: President Bush signed the Customs and Trade Act of 1990 making permanent the duty-free status of most Caribbean exports to the United States.

September 4: After assurances that Cuban dissidents seeking asylum would not be prosecuted, approximately sixty dissidents left the foreign embassies in Havana in which they had sought refuge.

September 18: Talks in San José, Costa Rica, between the El Salvadoran government and

Farabundo Marti National Liberation Front (FMLN) rebels broke down without an agreement on a cease-fire.

Septemer 24: El Salvadoran President Alfredo Cristiani visited Washington to discuss human rights abuses and the civil war.

October 29: The United States ended its intervention in Panama as it phased out joint police patrols with the Panamanian police.

November 26: President Bush met with Mexican President Carlos Salinas de Gortari in Monterrey, Mexico, for discussions concerning a free-trade pact.

November 28: Brazil and Argentina formally renounced the manufacture of nuclear weapons, declaring that their nuclear potential would be utilized solely for peaceful purposes. Neither party is a signatory to the Nuclear Non-Proliferation Treaty, but they agreed to allow the International Atomic Energy Agency to inspect their nuclear facilities.

December 2: President Bush began a tour of five South American nations (Argentina, Brazil, Chile, Uruguay, and Venezuela). He stated his intention to focus on the democratization process under way in South America as well as the need for further economic liberalization.

December 5: President Bush visited Argentina, praising its democratic victory over the recent military coup attempt.

December 6: Former Chilean dictator General August Pinochet greeted United States President Bush on his arrival in Santiago.

December 7: The United States increased military aid to El Salvador as a result of a strong offensive from guerrilla forces.

December 21: The United States suspended military aid to Guatemala, citing continued human rights abuses and lack of Guatemalan diligence in solving the murder of a US citizen.

1991

January 15: Two grenades were thrown at the US embassy in Panama.

January 16: President George Bush authorized a $42.5 million aid package for El Salvador but delayed its release for sixty days to give negotiations with rebel forces a better chance for success.

February 1: Peace talks between El Salvador guerrillas and government negotiatiors opened in Mexico City.

February 2: Fighting between Honduran and Nicaraguan naval vessels broke out in the disputed Gulf of Fonseca.

February 11: US aid officials announced an increase in financial assistance to Haiti by 50 percent to help the fledgling democracy.

February 21: President Violeta Barrias de Chamorro of Nicaragua received pledges of $65 million in new aid from Germany while visiting Bonn.

February 26: President Bush praised the antidrug policies of Colombian President César Gaviria Trujillo, who met with Bush in Washington.

March 1: Nicaragua criticized US attempts to have the Soviet Union halt its military aid to the Nicaraguan army.

March 9: The United States sent medical aid to Peru to combat a cholera epidemic.

March 16: Leaders of Dominica, St. Lucia, and St. Vincent and the Grenadines began a series of meetings that potentially could lead to a union.

April 16: Nicaraguan President Chamorro pleaded for sustained economic aid in a speech before the US Congress.

April 17: President Bush agreed to help forgive $360 million in overdue Nicaraguan debt payments.

May 28: Argentina announced it was dismantling the Condor-II ballistic missile project.

June 12: In a meeting with President Cristiani in Washington, President Bush praised the El Salvador government's sincerity in attempting to end the civil war and confirmed that the US would soon distribute aid that had been withheld. The FMLN rebel forces had recently stepped up their attacks on government posts.

The Gulf Crisis

1990

July 17: Iraqi President Saddam Hussein criticized Kuwait and the United Arab Emirates (UAE) for overshooting their quotas for oil production, thereby keeping the price of oil down.

July 27: Nearly 100,000 Iraqi troops amassed on the border between Iraq and Kuwait. Iraq asked Kuwait to slow oil production, compensate for $2.5 billion worth of oil, and forgive approximately $20 billion worth of debt acquired in Iraq's war with Iran. Iraq also requested control over the islands of Bubiyan and Warba in order to acquire access to the sea.

______ The Oil Producing and Exporting Countries (OPEC) lifted the price of oil to $21 per barrel.

______ US Ambassador to Iraq, April Glaspie, met with Saddam Hussein.

August 2: Iraq invaded Kuwait. President Bush, calling the invasion "naked aggression," froze Iraqi and Kuwaiti assets. The UN Security Council issued resolution 660 condemning the invasion and calling for immediate, complete, and unconditional withdrawal. (See Appendix A for text of this and subsequent resolutions.)

August 3: Bush, concerned with Iraqi troop movement to the Saudi Arabian border, reiterated US interest in the "integrity of Saudi Arabia."

______ The United States and the Soviet Union jointly condemned Iraq and called for an international arms embargo against Iraq.

______ The Arab League foreign ministers issued a resolution condemning "Iraqi aggression against Kuwait."

August 4: The EC, joining the United States, imposed an embargo on the importation of oil from Iraq and Kuwait.

August 5: Japan and China joined the embargo against Iraq.

August 6: The UN Security Council issued resolution 661, prescribing a widespread trade and financial boycott against Iraq and occupied Kuwait.

August 7: Bush ordered military forces be sent to the Gulf area.

August 8: Baghdad proclaimed Kuwait annexed.

August 9: The UN Security Council issued resolution 662 proclaiming the illegality of Iraq's annexation of Kuwait.

______ Jordan's King Hussein announced that Jordan would enforce UN economic sanctions against Iraq.

August 10: The Arab League agreed to condemn Iraq's invasion of Kuwait and to send troops to Saudi Arabia. Libya, Iraq, and the Palestine Liberation Organization (PLO) opposed the resolution, Algeria and Yemen abstained, and Mauritania, Jordan, and the Sudan expressed reservations.

August 11: Troops from Egypt and Morocco arrived in Saudi Arabia.

August 12: Bush supplemented the embargo by ordering US troops to stop oil exports from Iraq and all imports to Iraq, except for humanitarian necessities.

August 14: Syrian troops landed in Saudi Arabia.

August 15: To prevent the complete isolation of Iraq, President Saddam Hussein offered to accept virtually all of Iran's postwar claims as a way of resolving outstanding issues.

August 16: A meeting in Kennebunkport, Maine, between President Bush and King Hussein of Jordan resulted in little progress toward resolving the Middle East crisis.

August. 17: Iraqi officials said that as many as 10,000 American, British, and other foreign citizens in Iraq and Kuwait would be scattered among sensitive Iraqi installations to serve as virtual human shields.

August 18: Saudi Arabia announced it would exceed its current production by two million barrels per day.

______ Saddam Hussein proclaimed the blockade "an act of war."

September 1: Talks between Secretary-General Pérez de Cuéllar and Foreign Minister Tariq Aziz of Iraq ended without reconciliation.

September 17: The twelve nations of the European Community expelled Iraq's military attachés, responding to Iraqi raids on four Western embassies in Kuwait.

October 25: President Ali Abdullah Saleh of Yemen criticized Saudi Arabia for bringing foreign forces into the Middle East and revoking the residence permits of 500,000 Yemeni workers.

______ Washington announced an increase in its forces in the Gulf of 100,000, bringing their total to 340,000.

______ Iraq freed 700 Bulgarian workers.

October 26: Colombia, Cuba, Malaysia, and Yemen criticized a Security Council resolution to strengthen pressure on Iraq and sought a more moderate resolution.

October 27: The Soviet Union asked the Security Council to delay action on a resolution concerning the Gulf crisis until after the visit of a Soviet envoy to Baghdad.

October 28: EC leaders pledged not to negotiate the separate release of hostages in Iraq.

______ Gorbachev met with French President François Mitterrand to discuss French ideas for reducing tensions in the Gulf.

October 30: The visit to Baghdad of Soviet envoy Yevgeniy Primakov ended inconclusively.

Novermber 1: The UN Security Council approved a resolution holding Iraq liable for damage done to Kuwait and asking nations to prepare claims for financial compensation.

November 2: Iraqi forces captured three French soldiers and returned them to the French embassy in Baghdad.

November 3: Iraqi President Saddam Hussein offered to free the foreign hostages if two of five major countries (China, France, Germany, Japan, and the Soviet Union) would guarantee Iraq against military attack. He vowed that any military conflict would lead to a protracted war.

November 4: Syria sent an armored division to Saudi Arabia.

November 5: After meeting with US officials, Saudi Arabia agreed to place its forces under US command in the event of military action in the Gulf, but the initiation of hostilities would require joint sanction.

_____ Former German Chancellor Willy Brandt flew to Baghdad on a mission to secure the release of hostages.

_____ The Gulf Crisis Financial Coordination Group announced that $13 billion in special aid would be available for countries suffering economic hardships related to the Gulf crisis. Egypt, Jordan, and Turkey were expected to receive the majority of funds being made available by the European Community, Japan, and the United States.

November 8: President Bush ordered 150,000 more troops to the Gulf to provide an offensive option and repeated his "no troop rotation" policy. Both Syria and Egypt expressed their willingness to consider an offensive option, although Egyptian President Hosni Mubarak stressed that sanctions should be given another few months. Foreign Minister Shevardnadze refused to rule out the use of force, providing the action had Security Council authority.

_____ Former Japanese Prime Minister Yasuhiro Nakasone returned from a diplomatic mission to Baghdad, in which he won the release of seventy-four captives.

November 10: Secretary Baker concluded his week-long shuttle diplomacy to America's main partners in the UN coalition; although the coalition remained solid, differences existed over when and if to use force.

November 11: King Hassan II of Morocco called for an emergency Arab summit but received little response.

_____ Chinese Foreign Minister Qian Qichen met with Foreign Minister Aziz in Baghdad.

November 12: EC ministers consulted with North African foreign ministers in an attempt to gain help in freeing hostages in Iraq.

November 15: Saddam announced he would welcome negotiations with the United States if they were to begin without preconditions.

November 16: The Kuwait government-in-exile asked the UN for its help in preserving population lists that existed before the Iraqi invasion.

November 17: The IMF extended $400-$450 million in relief funds to India in compensation for shortages and rising costs due to the Gulf crisis.

_____ Secretary Baker visited the delegations of a number of Security Council nations in the hope of securing support for a resolution authorizing the use of force in the Gulf. The foreign ministers of Ethiopia, the Ivory Coast, and Zaire indicated their support.

November 18: German Chancellor Helmut Kohl, meeting with Bush, stressed negotiation with Iraq as a means to solving the Gulf crisis.

November 19: Bush met with Gorbachev in Paris for two hours in an attempt to win support for the use of force in the Gulf. Gorbachev gave no indication he would support a UN resolution authorizing the use of force.

November 24: Colombia expressed qualified support for a UN Security Council resolution that would authorize the use of force in the Gulf crisis.

_____ Yemeni President Ali Abdullah Saleh told Secretary Baker that the presence of foreign troops complicated the issue of using force in the Gulf area.

November 28: Japan announced a plan to send troops to the multinational effort in the Gulf provided that their troops fulfilled only noncombatant roles.

November 29: The Security Council passed resolution 678, which set January 15 as the deadline for Iraqi troops to evacuate occupied Kuwait. The resolution authorized the use of "all necessary measures" to expel Iraqi forces after that date.

November 30: Bush indicated interest in direct talks between the foreign ministers of the United States and Iraq and offered to send Secretary Baker to Baghdad at an agreed-upon date.

December 1: Saddam accepted Bush's offer for Baker to meet with Foreign Minister Aziz in Baghdad but stipulated that the talks must include discussion of the Palestinian issue.

December 5: Saudi Arabia announced it would compensate Egypt $1.5 billion for losses incurred during the Gulf crisis.

December 6: Saddam announced he would free all foreign hostages as a gesture to encourage diplomatic solutions to the Gulf crisis.

December 7: An international coalition of former national leaders announced their intention to mediate a peaceful solution to the Gulf crisis. These leaders included former Nicaraguan president Daniel Ortega, former German chancellor Willy Brandt, former Indian prime minister Rajiv Gandhi, and former Japanese prime minister Yasuhiro Nakasone. (For details of various peace proposals, see page 16.)

December 9: US and British embassies evacuated their nationals from Iraq and Kuwait in anticipation of the use of force in January.

December 11: France announced it will send another 4,000 men to its Gulf contingent, bringing the total of French forces to 10,000.

December 12: Iraq offered January 12 as the date for the proposed visit of Secretary Baker to Baghdad. US officials, however, rejected that date as being too close to the January 15 deadline.

December 17: President Mubarak acknowledged that no new peace initiatives resulted from the shuttle diplomacy conducted by Algerian President Chadbi Benjedid.

December 27: Iraqi ambassadors returned after consultation with the message that the Iraqi president was ready for serious dialogue with the United States. Saddam, however, continued to link withdrawal from Kuwait to an international conference on the Palestinian question.

______ Japan froze $2.6 billion in credits that had been extended to Iraq in negotiations last July.

December 29: Iraqi and Soviet negotiators agreed to conditions under which 2,500 Soviet workers could leave Iraq. Diplomats speculated Iraq had delayed their departure partly because of the insufficient training of workers to run Soviet-built factories and partly to inhibit Soviet cooperation with the UN forces.

1991

January 1: NATO deployed three squadrons of jet fighters from Belgium, Germany, and Italy to provide for the defense of Turkey.

January 3: Great Britain expelled seventy-five Iraqi diplomats and residents, citing security concerns.

January 4: Iraq accepted an American offer for talks at the foreign minister level in Geneva.

______ The EC pledged to work toward resolution of Middle East problems if Iraq pulled out of Kuwait before the deadline and urged Iraq to conduct further negotiations.

January 6: The United States rejected a French peace plan that linked Iraqi withdrawal to settlement of Arab-Israeli problems.

January 7: UN nonessential personnel were advised to evacuate Israel.

January 8: Foreign Minister Aziz arrived in Geneva for talks with his American counterpart.

January 9: Talks between American and Iraqi foreign ministers ended with no progress toward a peaceful solution in the Gulf crisis.

______ Egypt warned Israel not to participate in military actions against Iraq that might necessitate a revision of Egyptian policy in the coalition forces.

______ US embassy personnel in Iraq were told to evacuate Baghdad.

January 10: EC foreign ministers pursued contacts with Arab diplomats in an effort to create a new initiative in the Gulf crisis.

______ Secretary Baker met with King Fahd of Saudi Arabia to discuss plans for the use of force.

______ Great Britain closed its embassy in Baghdad but did not break relations. The United States also reduced embassy staff in Yemen and asked nonessential personnel in Algeria, Morocco, and Tunisia to evacuate.

January 11: Secretary Baker warned Iraq that coalition forces would not delay long after the January 15 deadline before utilizing military force.

______ President Bush sent Deputy Secretary of State Lawrence Eagleburger to Israel to solidify confidence in US protection in the event of hostilities in the Gulf.

January 12: The US Congress approved the use of American military power to uphold UN resolutions in the Iraq-Kuwait conflict.

______ The United States closed its embassy in Baghdad.

______ Pérez de Cuéllar arrived in Baghdad to discuss substantive proposals to avert military conflict.

______ After meeting with Secretary Baker, Syrian President al-Asad urged Iraq to quit Kuwait and guaranteed Iraq's territorial integrity if it adhered to the UN resolutions.

January 13: Pérez de Cuéllar reported no significant progress after talks with Iraqi leaders in Baghdad.

______ Turkey agreed to allow coalition forces to use its airfields for humanitarian and logistical operations.

______ Jordan reinforced its border with Israel in preparation for the outbreak of hostilities and possible Iraqi attack on Israel. Israeli Defense Minister Moshe Arens declared that the country would respond to an attack by hostile forces.

______ Great Britain expelled all but four Iraqi diplomats after recalling all of its foreign service officers from Baghdad.

January 14: The Iraqi parliament voted to wage war against coalition forces.

January 15: After a last-minute effort, France announced it would no longer seek to mediate a diplomatic peace in the Gulf conflict.

______ Pérez de Cuéllar issued a last appeal for an Iraqi withdrawal. Security Council members failed to agree on the text of their own appeal.

January 16: UN coalition forces launched an air attack on Iraq with numerous strikes at military targets throughout Iraq and Kuwait. Israel declared emergency status. France chose to participate in the conflict under US command.

January 17: When eight Iraqi Scud missiles hit Israel, US officials urged Israel not to retaliate. An earlier US-Israeli agreement specified the two nations would consult in the event of a successful Iraqi attack.

January 18: Palestinians in Jordan rejoiced at the news of Scud missile attacks on Israel. Western nations joined in the pressure for Israel not to retaliate. The Soviet Union called for Arab nations to show caution and restraint in avoiding another Arab-Israeli war.

_____ Coalition forces began air attacks on Iraq from air bases in Turkey despite opposition from several domestic political parties in Turkey.

January 19: Israel asserted its right to self-defense and retaliation but accepted US-manned Patriot missile batteries to help defend against Scud missile attacks.

January 21: Iraq placed prisoners of war near probable bombing targets to act as "human shields."

January 22: Iraq set fire to several Kuwaiti oil refineries and oilfields.

_____ A Scud missile landed in Tel Aviv despite the Patriot missile defense. Nations again called for Israel not to retalitate.

January 23: Israel declared it would not retaliate immediately to Scud missile attacks but reasserted its right to do so.

_____ Germany announced a $165 million humanitarian aid package for Israel following repeated Iraqi attacks.

January 24: Iraq closed its border with Jordan to halt the flow of refugees leaving the war-torn country.

_____ Germany ordered twenty-eight Iraqi diplomats to leave the country.

January 25: Anti-US sentiment in North Africa rose dramatically, as evidenced by a series of public protests and food and blood drives in support of Iraq.

_____ Iran formally asserted its neutrality in the Gulf War.

January 28: More than one hundred Iraqi warplanes flew to Iran.

January 29: Germany announced it would increase its financial support for the coalition forces by $5.5 billion, bringing its total to $9 billion.

_____ Indian provisions for refueling of US aircraft en route to the Gulf created domestic opposition.

January 30: Egypt conducted military manuevers aimed at deterring neighboring Sudan from military action in support of Iraq in the Gulf conflict.

_____ Sri Lanka denied port access to two US naval vessels en route to the Persian Gulf.

January 31: Iraqi Deputy Prime Minister Saddoun Hammadi was told during a mission to Iran that Iraqi warplanes would be held until the war's end.

_____ Spain agreed to the use of its airfields to launch bombing missions of Iraq by American B-52s.

_____ Germany agreed to compensate Great Britain $535 million to help with Gulf war expenses, bringing the total German commitment to nearly $10 billion.

February 1: France agreed to the use of its airspace for American B-52s flying bombing missions to Iraq from British airfields.

February 4: President Carlos Menem announced that Argentina would join the coalition forces fighting Iraq and sent two battleships to the Gulf.

February 6: Iraqi radio announced the severance of diplomatic ties with Egypt, France, Great Britain, Italy, Saudi Arabia, and the United States.

_____ Jordan's King Hussein officially aligned his country with Iraq, eschewing his earlier policy of neutrality.

February 7: Romania sent a field hospital and an antichemical decontamination unit to join coalition forces in the Gulf.

_____ The United States closed its embassy in the Sudan, cut its diplomatic presence in Tanzania, and put embassies in Uganda and Kenya on alert status as fear of terrorist attacks grew as a result of the Gulf War.

February 9: President Gorbachev expressed concern that, by their attacks in Iraq, coalition forces were exceeding the UN mandate.

February 10: The United States announced it had received more than $50 billion in pledges for financial assistance in conducting the Gulf War from Germany, Japan, Korea, Kuwait, Saudi Arabia, and the United Arab Emirates.

February 11: Israel's Defense Minister Arens met with President Bush to discuss damage from Scud missile attacks.

February 12: Saddam met with Soviet Envoy Yevgeniy Primakov, giving assurances of his desire to cooperate with Soviet peace initiatives but pledging to keep fighting allied aggression.

February 13: US and Iraqi officials exchanged bitter polemics following the bombing of a reinforced concrete building that allies believed housed a command and control facility but that housed a large number of civilians at the time of the explosion.

February 15: Iraq announced its readiness to discuss compliance with UN resolutions if its own ten demands were met. Coalition leaders denounced the demands as inappropriate, demanding Iraqi withdrawal from Kuwait before a cease-fire. The Soviet Union praised Iraqi moves toward peace.

February 16: Gorbachev sent Special Envoy Primakov back to Iraq in further attempts to negotiate an end to the crisis.

_____ Bush called Saddam's offer to withdraw in compliance with UN resolutions a "cruel hoax" and suggested that the Iraqi people should overthrow their leader.

_____ Yasir Arafat, returning from a meeting with Saddam, reported to King Hussein of Jordan that

Iraq was confident and prepared for war.

______ Arab members of the coalition forces ended a meeting in Cairo by reaffirming their united stand and commitment to Iraqi withdrawal.

February 17: Iraqi Foreign Minister Aziz flew to the Soviet Union for talks.

February 18: President Gorbachev presented Aziz with another peace proposal, the details of which were not announced.

February 19: President Bush rejected the terms of the Soviet peace proposal without disclosing the details, saying they fell "well short of what would be required to stop the war with Iraq."

______ Soviet officials stated their desire to delay a ground offensive until further exploration of peace initiatives had occurred.

______ The United States halted its refueling of jet planes in India after significant domestic opposition was raised in the Indian parliament.

February 20: United States and Great Britain demanded a specific timetable for Iraqi withdrawal and acceptance of all UN resolutions as part of any peace initiative.

February 21: Moscow reported that Saddam Hussein gave a positive response to the Soviet peace proposal that called for unconditional withdrawal in an unspecified time period, exchange of prisoners, lapse of UN resolutions after completion of the withdrawal, and made no mention of a Middle East peace conference.

______ President Bush called the Iraqi response a positive step but withheld comment pending further study.

February 22: Responding to Iraq's acceptance of the Soviet peace initiative, Bush demanded that Iraq begin its withdrawal in one day and abandon Kuwait within a week.

______ The Soviet Union sent a last-minute peace proposal to Iraq in an attempt to bridge the gap between the American ultimatum and the Iraqi position.

______ The Western European Union issued a statement giving full support to Bush's ultimatum.

February 24: US-led coalition forces invaded Iraq and Kuwait.

February 25: Saddam Hussein ordered Iraqi troops to evacuate Kuwait.

______ UN Security Council President Simbarashe Simbanenduku of Zimbabwe called for a formal Iraqi offer for peace.

February 26: The UN Security Council reached a general agreement that Iraq would have to formally accept all demands called for in the twelve Security Council resolutions before a cease-fire would go into effect.

______ Saddam publicly announced his orders for withdrawal from Kuwait, and Bush called for Iraqi surrender.

February 27: President Bush declared that Kuwait was liberated and Iraq defeated. He followed by declaring an end to offensive military action pending a formal cease-fire.

February 28: The Bush administration stated that US forces would remain in Iraq until the administration was sufficiently satisfied of Iraqi compliance with UN terms for a permanent cease-fire being formulated in the Security Council.

______ Iraq sent a letter to the Security Council stating its intent to comply with all UN resolutions.

March 1: The United States raised its flag over its Kuwaiti embassy.

______ King Hussein publicly sought forgiveness from fellow Arab states, while seeking to be included in the development of a new regional order based on forgiveness, democracy, and a resolution of the Palestinian issue.

March 3: Iraqi generals agreed to all allied terms of peace forwarded by US General Norman Schwarzkopf and Saudi General Khalid bin Sultan at a meeting between the two military leaderships.

______ Member nations of the coalition forces offered to speed relief supplies to Iraq in return for the withdrawal of a proposed UN resolution (sponsored by Cuba, Ecuador, India, and Yemen) that would lift the UN embargo on trade with Iraq.

______ President Mubarak called for an all-Arab security order in the region.

March 4: The crown prince of Kuwait, Sheikh Saad al-Abdullah al-Sabah, returned to Kuwait from exile, the first member of the royal family to do so.

March 5: Saddam voided annexation of Kuwait and agreed to return Kuwaiti assets.

______ Israel and the United States reached agreement on an aid package of $640 million to help cover expenses in Israel related to the Gulf War.

March 6: British Prime Minister John Major visited his troops in the Gulf.

March 8: Iranian President Rafsanjani called for Saddam's resignation.

______ Secretary Baker met with Saudi King Fahd in Riyadh to share ideas on regional issues and received Fahd's pledges of Saudi active support in setting up a new framework for Middle East peace.

March 10: Bahrain, Egypt, Kuwait, Oman, Qatar, Saudi Arabia, Syria, and the United Arab Emirates met in Riyadh and indicated support for

Bush's broad framework for Middle East peace, including a continued US military presence.

March 11: While meeting with Israeli officials in Jerusalem, Secretary Baker called for Israeli reciprocity of Arab "new thinking" on Middle East peace.

March 12: Baker reported from Jerusalem that neither Israel nor the Palestinians indicated any fundamental change in their views.

______ King Hussein of Jordan announced he would represent Palestinians at a Middle East peace conference only if a clear mandate had been given to do so; he also acknowledged that Jordan could never be a substitute for the PLO.

March 14: Emir Sheikh Jaber al-Ahmed al-Sabah returned to Kuwait from exile.

______ President Hafiz al-Asad of Syria met with Secretary Baker and concluded the talks with an announcement that the time was ripe for a settlement of the Palestinian issue; however, no conclusive steps were taken toward an accomodation with Israel.

______ President Bush met with French President Mitterrand in Martinique to discuss a Middle East peace initiative but later announced that a common approach was not forthcoming.

March 15: The United States announced it had found no conclusive evidence that Jordan had shipped arms to Iraq either before or during the UN embargo.

March 16: President Bush and Prime Minister Major met in Bermuda and agreed to call for the elimination of Iraqi chemical and biological weapons as part of a permanent cease-fire agreement.

March 17: Allied commanders denied an Iraqi request to move its air force.

March 21: A UN survey of the war damage done to Iraq described it as near-apocalyptic and called for an end to the UN embargo on imports of essential goods.

March 25: Syrian Foreign Minister Farouk al-Sharaa voiced his doubts that Saddam could remain in power and stated his confidence in the ability of the opposition groups to form a government.

March 26: The Bush administration announced it would not intervene in Iraq's civil conflict to aid rebel forces.

______ The UN Security Council draft resolution for a permanent cease-fire called for the destruction of Iraq's most potent military weapons, a halt in arms sales, a designated percentage of Iraq's oil revenues to be used to pay for damage caused by the war, and acceptance of the 1963 negotiated boundary between Iraq and Kuwait.

______ Syria announced plans to double the size of its Gulf contingent to strengthen security in the region.

March 27: The Bush administration forwarded a peace plan that calls for a Middle East peace conference cosponsored by the United States and Soviet Union, providing an opportunity for direct negotiations between Israel and its Arab neighbors.

March 28: The Iraqi military launched an offensive against Kurdish rebels in the north.

March 30: At a meeting of the Arab League, pro-Western Arab nations (Egypt, Saudi Arabia, and Syria) forwarded a framework for a new Arab order, which would no longer recognize the PLO as the sole legitimate spokesman for the Palestinians, and called for the renunciation of the use of force by Arab nations against Arab nations.

March 31: US troops began to withdraw from southern Iraq.

April 1: Presidents Mubarak and al-Asad met in Cairo and called for an international peace conference to discuss resolution of the Arab-Israeli conflict. They also stated their opposition to the break-up of Iraq.

April 2: Iraqi rebellions ebbed as Kurds fled north into Iranian and Turkish territory and Shiites fled east into Iran.

April 3: The UN Security Council approved resolution 687 that set terms for the end of the Gulf War, including Iraqi renunciation of terrorism, billions of dollars in reparations, acceptance of the 1963 boundaries, and the destruction of all chemical and biological weapons. Great Britain and Belgium also sought greater help for the Kurdish refugees.

April 4: The United States called on Turkey to open its borders to the fleeing Kurds, but the Turkish government refused on the grounds that it could not facilitate the large numbers of refugees.

______ The permanent members of the Security Council agreed to contribute to a UN observer force along the Iraq-Kuwait border.

______ President Bush met Japanese Prime Minister Kaifu in California to reduce US-Japan friction caused by perceptions of cool Japanese response to the Gulf War.

April 5: President Bush approved air drops of relief supplies to Kurdish refugees camped in the mountains of northern Iraq.

______ The UN Security Council voted to condemn Iraq for actions that contributed to the Kurdish and Shiite refugee problem that "threatens international peace and security."

April 6: Iraq formally accepted the terms of UN resolution 687 for a permanent cease-fire, but Iraqi

Ambassador to the UN Abdul Amir al-Anball termed the conditions "one-sided and unfair."

April 7: Secretary Baker began a new shuttle trip to the Middle East to continue exploratory efforts for an Arab-Israeli peace settlement.

April 8: Baker visited Kurdish refugees and declared that "it was up to the international community as a whole to do something about this tragic crime."

April 9: Visiting Israel, Secretary Baker was informed that Israel was willing in principle to attend a regional peace conference cosponsored by the United States and the Soviet Union.

______ Iraq rejected the EC plan for safe havens in northern Iraq.

April 10: At a meeting in Cairo, Secretary Baker obtained Egyptian backing for his peace conference proposal.

April 11: President Bush and EC leaders agreed to the establishment of informal safe camps in northern Iraq. Concern was expressed that a Kurdish enclave might pose a challenge to Iraqi statehood.

______ Secretary Baker's talks with President al-Asad produced inconclusive results concerning the US-Arab-Israeli peace proposal.

April 12: Iranian President Rafsanjani criticized Iraq and Western nations for creating a regional disaster and identified the United States in particular as responsible for the plight of the Kurds.

______ Secretary Baker concluded his Middle East trip with assurances from both Jordan and Syria that they would attend an international peace conference.

April 13: Major General Gunther Greindl, head of the UN peacekeeping forces, arrived in Kuwait to begin implementation of a UN-monitored buffer zone along the Iraq-Kuwait border.

April 14: US forces in southern Iraq began pulling back to a small buffer zone.

______ Turkey agreed to allow between 20,000 and 40,000 Kurdish refugees to enter Turkey.

April 16: US and French forces began to construct secure camps in northern Iraq for the Kurdish refugees.

April 17: Iraq announced it had reached agreement with the UN for humanitarian centers in northern and southern Iraq to provide for the refugees. They called a US plan for safe havens an illegal invasion of their sovereignty.

April 19: Secretary Baker met with Prime Minister Shamir and stressed the need for compromise if peace is to be attained in the Middle East. Israel rejected a European role in an international peace conference.

April 21: Iraqi forces began to pull back from the Kurdish refugee camps in northern Iraq in compliance with allied demands.

______ While in Saudi Arabia, Secretary Baker announced his plan to build a two-phased peace process: in the first phase, there would be an Arab-Israeli discussion to be followed by a discussion of general regional issues in a second phase.

April 23: Iraq asked the UN to take over administration of the refugee camps built by France, Great Britain, and the United States.

______ Secretary Baker held inconclusive talks with President al-Asad in Damascus.

April 24: Japan sent a small flotilla of mine-sweepers to the Gulf region, in what was seen as a major change in defense policy.

April 25: US military commanders ordered Iraq to pull its police forces out of the refugee camp areas.

______ The Soviet Union announced its willingness to cosponsor a Middle East peace conference.

______ The new Iraqi prime minister, Saddoun Hammadi, announced Iraq's desire for reconciliation and acceptance of the UN terms for lifting sanctions.

April 27: President al-Asad met with Prime Minister Rafsanjani in Damascus to discuss Iraq and regional development issues.

May 8: Soviet Foreign Minister Bessmertnykh met with President al-Asad, and reiterated Soviet support for Arab positions.

May 9 : US Secretary of Defense Dick Cheney announced that agreement was reached among the United States and several Persian Gulf countries for the storage of US military equipment on a long-term basis in the region.

May 11: Saudi Foreign Minister Saud al-Faisal announced at a meeting with EC officials in Luxembourg that nations of the Gulf Cooperation Council would send an observer to a Middle East peace conference. EC officials endorsed the statement, declaring that they have an important role to play in Middle East diplomacy.

May 12: During Secretary Baker's visit to Damascus, President al-Asad rejected the US compromise proposals for a peace conference. Baker then flew to Cairo to meet with the Soviet foreign minister

May 13: UN officials took over the administration of the Zhako Kurdish refugee camp.

May 14: The permanent members of the UN Security Council reached consensus on a plan that would designate 25 percent of Iraqi oil revenues as reparations for damage done to other countries in the Gulf War.

______ Secretary Baker drove from Amman, Jordan, to Jerusalem after talks with King Hussein, who indicated Jordan was not ready for a peace conference until certain requirements were met, including Syrian participation.

May 15: UN nuclear energy experts began inspection of Iraqi power plants to check compliance with UN resolutions.

______ Israel formally rejected Secretary Baker's latest peace proposals

May 17: Iraq agreed to UN inspection of its military and scientific installations.

SOURCES

Christian Science World Monitor
The Economist
Europe
Facts on File
Foreign Broadcast Information Service news summaries
Keesing's Record of World Events
New York Times
Washington Post
Wall Street Journal

APPENDIX A: Letter of January 5, 1991, from US President George Bush to Iraqi President Saddam Hussein

Mr. President:

We stand today at the brink of war between Iraq and the world. This is a war that began with your invasion of Kuwait; this is a war that can be ended only Iraq's full and unconditional compliance with U.N. Security Council Resolution 678.

I am writing you now, directly, because what is at stake demands that no opportunity be lost to avoid what would be a certain calamity for the people of Iraq. I am writing, as well, because it is said by some that you do not understand just how isolated Iraq is and what Iraq faces as a result.

I am not in a position to judge whether this impression is correct; what I can do, though, is try in this letter to reinforce what Secretary of State [James A.] Baker [III] told your Foreign Minister and eliminate any uncertainty or ambiguity that might exist in your mind about where we stand and what we are prepared to do.

The international community is united in its call for Iraq to leave all of Kuwait without condition and without further delay. This is not simply the policy of the United States; it is the position of the world community as expressed in no less than 12 Security Council resolutions.

We prefer a peaceful outcome. However, anything less than full compliance with U.N. Security Resolution 678 and its predecessors is unacceptable.

There can be no reward for aggression. Nor will there e any negotiation. Principle cannot be compromised. However, by its full compliance, Iraq will gain the opportunity to rejoin the international community.

More immediately, the Iraqi military establishment will escape destruction. But unless you withdraw fro Kuwait completely and without condition, you will lose more than Kuwait.

What is at issue here is not the future of Kuwait—it will be free, its government will be restored—but rather the future of Iraq. This choice is yours to make.

The United States will not be separated from its coalition partners. Twelve Security Council resolutions, 28 countries providing military units to enforce them, more than 100 governments complying with sanctions—all highlight the fact that it is not Iraq against the United States, but Iraq against the world.

That most Arab and Muslim countries are arrayed against you as well should reinforce what I am saying. Iraq cannot and will not be able to hold on to Kuwait or exact a price for leaving.

You may be tempted to find solace in the diversity of opinion that is American democracy. You should resist any such temptation. Diversity ought not to be confused with division. Nor should you underestimate, as others have before you, America's will.

Iraq is already feeling the effects of the sanctions mandated by the United Nations. Should war come, it will be a far greater tragedy for you and your country.

Let me state, too, that the United States will not tolerate the use of chemical or biological weapons or the destruction of Kuwait's oil fields and installations. Further, you will be held directly responsible for terrorist actions against any member of the coalition.

The American people would demand the strongest possible response. You and your country will pay a terrible price if you order unconsionable acts of this sort.

I write this letter not to threaten, but to inform. I do so with no sense of satisfaction, for the people of the United States have no quarrel with the people of Iraq.

Mr. President, U.N. Security Council Resolution 678 establishes the period before Jan. 15 of this year as a 'pause of good will' so that this crisis may end without further violence.

Whether this pause is used as intended, or merely becomes a prelude to further violence, is in your hands, and yours alone. I hope you weigh your choice carefully and choose wisely, for much will depend upon it.

George Bush

APPENDIX B: United Nations Security Council Resolutions Relating to the Crisis in the Gulf

The Resolutions

Between 2 August 1990, the date of the invasion of Kuwait by Iraq, and 29 November 1990, the Security Council adopted twelve resolutions relating to the crisis in the Gulf, beginning with resolution 660. The full text of selected resolutions is reproduced on the following pages.

On 28 November 1990, at its 2962nd meeting, the Security Council adopted resolution 677, relating, *inter alia*, to attempts by Iraq to alter the demographic composition of the population of Kuwait. On 29 November 1990, at its 2963rd meeting, the Security Council adopted resolution 678, which, *inter alia*, authorized Member States "to use all necessary means to uphold and implement resolution 660 (1990) and all subsequent relevant resolutions and to restore international peace and security in the area." Thirteen of the fifteen members of the Council were represented at this meeting by their Foreign Ministers. Thirteen Foreign Ministers had also represented their countries at the 2943rd meeting on 25 September, when the Council adopted resolution 670.

The Council

The United Nations Security Council is composed of 15 members. Five are permanent: China, France, Soviet Union, United Kingdom, United States. The ten non-permanent members are elected by the General Assembly to serve two-year terms. At the time these resolutions were adopted, the non-permanent members of the Security Council were: Canada, Colombia, Côte d'Ivoire, Cuba, Ethiopia, Finland, Malaysia, Romania, Yemen, Zaire.

Resolution 660
2 August 1990

Relating, *inter alia*, to the Council's condemnation of the Iraqi invasion of Kuwait.

Adopted by a vote of 14 in favour and 0 against. One member, Yemen, did not participate in the vote.

Sponsors: Canada, Colombia, Côte d'Ivoire, Ethiopia, Finland, France, Malaysia, United Kingdom, United States.

Resolution 661
6 August 1990

Relating, *inter alia*, to the imposition of mandatory sanctions and to the establishment of a Committee to undertake certain tasks regarding the implementation of the resolution.

Adopted by a vote of 13 in favour, 0 against and 2 abstentions (Cuba and Yemen).

Sponsors: Canada, Colombia, Côte d'Ivoire, Ethiopia, Finland, France, Malaysia, United Kingdom, United States, Zaire.

Resolution 662
9 August 1990

Relating, *inter alia*, to the non-validity of the Iraqi annexation of Kuwait.

Adopted by unanimous vote.

Prepared in the course of the Council's consultations.

Resolution 664
18 August 1990

Relating, *inter alia*, to the nationals of third countries in Iraq and Kuwait and to diplomatic and consular missions in Kuwait.

Adopted by unanimous vote.

Prepared in the course of the Council's consultations.

Resolution 665
25 August 1990

Relating, *inter alia*, to measures to ensure implementation of resolution 661.

Adopted by a vote of 13 in favour, 0 against and 2 abstentions (Cuba and Yemen).

Sponsors: Canada, Côte d'Ivoire, Finland, France, United Kingdom, United States, Zaire.

Resolution 666
13 September 1990

Relating, *inter alia*, to the determination of humanitarian circumstances.

Adopted by a vote of 13 in favour and 2 against (Cuba and Yemen).

Sponsors: Canada, Finland, France, Soviet Union, United Kingdom, United States.

Resolution 667
16 September 1990

Relating, *inter alia*, to diplomatic and consular personnel and premises.

Adopted by unanimous vote.

Sponsors: Canada, Côte d'Ivoire, Finland, France, United Kingdom, Zaire.

Resolution 669
24 September 1990

Relating, *inter alia*, to requests for assistance under the provisions of Article 50.*

Adopted by unanimous vote.

Prepared in the course of the Council's consultations.

Resolution 670
25 September 1990

Relating, *inter alia*, to the applicability of sanctions to all means of transport, including aircraft.

Adopted by a vote of 14 in favour and 1 against (Cuba).

Sponsors: Canada, Côte d'Ivoire, Finland, France, Romania, Soviet Union, United Kingdom, United States, Zaire.

Resolution 674
29 October 1990

Relating, *inter alia*, to the situation of Kuwaiti and third-State nationals in Kuwait and Iraq, to further measures in the event of non-compliance by Iraq with Security Council resolutions and to the good offices of the Secretary-General.

Adopted by a vote of 13 in favour, 0 against and 2 abstentions (Cuba and Yemen).

Sponsors: Canada, Finland, France, Romania, Soviet Union, United Kingdom, United States, Zaire.

Resolution 660
2 August 1990

The Security Council,

Alarmed by the invasion of Kuwait on 2 August

---

*As of 8 November 1990, 19 States had invoked the provisions of Article 50: Bangladesh, Bulgaria, Czechoslovakia, India, Jordan, Lebanon, Mauritania, Pakistan, Philippines, Poland, Romania, Seychelles, Sri Lanka, Sudan, Tunisia, Uruguay, Viet Nam, Yemen, Yugoslavia. Botswana had given notice of its intention to do so.

1990 by the military forces of Iraq,

Determining that there exists a breach of international peace and security as regards the Iraqi invasion of Kuwait,

Acting under Articles 39 and 40 of the Charter of the United Nations,

1. **Condemns** the Iraqi invasion of Kuwait;

2. **Demands** that Iraq withdraw immediately and unconditionally all its forces to the positions in which they were located on 1 August 1990;

3. **Calls upon** Iraq and Kuwait to begin immediately intensive negotiations for the resolution of their differences and supports all efforts in this regard, and especially those of the League of Arab States;

4. **Decides** to meet again as necessary to consider further steps to ensure compliance with the present resolution.

Resolution 661
6 August 1990

The Security Council,

Reaffirming its resolution 660 (1990) of 2 August 1990,

Deeply concerned that that resolution has not been implemented and that the invasion by Iraq of Kuwait continues with further loss of human life and material destruction,

Determined to bring the invasion and occupation of Kuwait by Iraq to an end and to restore the sovereignty, independence and territorial integrity of Kuwait,

Noting that the legitimate Government of Kuwait has expressed its readiness to comply with Resolution 660 (1990),

Mindful of its responsibilities under the Charter of the United Nations for the maintenance of international peace and security,

Affirming the inherent right of individual or collective self-defence, in response to the armed attack by Iraq against Kuwait, in accordance with Article 51 of the Charter,

Acting under Chapter VII of the Charter of the United Nations,

1. **Determines** that Iraq so far has failed to comply with paragraph 2 of resolution 660 (1990) and has usurped the authority of the legitimate Government of Kuwait;

2. **Decides,** as a consequence, to take the following measures to secure compliance of Iraq with paragraph 2 of resolution 660 (1990) and to restore the authority of the legitimate Government of Kuwait;

3. **Decides** that all States shall prevent:

(a) The import into their territories of all commodities and products originating in Iraq or Kuwait exported therefrom after the date of the present resolution;

(b) Any activities by their nationals or in their territories which would promote or are calculated to promote the export or transshipment of any commodities or products from Iraq or Kuwait; and any dealings by their nationals or their flag vessels or in their territories in any commodities or products originating in Iraq or Kuwait and exported therefrom after the date of the present resolution, including in particular any transfer of funds to Iraq or Kuwait for the purposes of such activities or dealings;

(c) The sale or supply by their nationals or from their territories or using their flag vessels of any commodities or products, including weapons or any other military equipment, whether or not originating in their territories but not including supplies intended strictly for medical purposes, and, in humanitarian circumstances, foodstuffs, to any person or body in Iraq or Kuwait or to any person or body for the purposes of any business carried on in or operated from Iraq or Kuwait, and any activities by their nationals or in their territories which promote or are calculated to promote such sale or supply of such commodities or products;

4. **Decides** that all States shall not make available to the Government of Iraq or to any commercial, industrial or public utility undertaking in Iraq or Kuwait, any funds or any other financial or economic resources and shall prevent their nationals and any persons within their territories from removing from their territories or otherwise making available to that Government or to any such undertaking any such funds or resources and from remitting any other funds to persons or bodies within Iraq or Kuwait, except payments exclusively for strictly medical or humanitarian purposes and, in humanitarian circumstances, foodstuffs;

5. **Calls upon** all States, including States non-members of the United Nations, to act strictly in accordance with the provisions of the present resolution notwithstanding any contract entered into or license granted before the date of the present resolution;

6. **Decides** to establish, in accordance with rule 28 of the provisional rules of procedure of the Security Council, a Committee of the Security Council consisting of all the members of the Council, to undertake the following tasks and to report on its work to the Council with its observations and recommendations:

(a) To examine the reports on the progress of the implementation of the present resolution which will be submitted by the Secretary-General;

(b) To seek from all States further information regarding the action taken by them concerning the effective implementation of the provisions laid down in the present resolution;

7. Calls upon all States to co-operate fully with the Committee in the fulfillment of its task, including supplying such information as may be sought by the Committee in pursuance of the present resolution;

8. Requests the Secretary-General to provide all necessary assistance to the Committee and to make the necessary arrangements in the Secretariat for the purpose;

9. Decides that, notwithstanding paragraphs 4 through 8 above, nothing in the present resolution shall prohibit assistance to the legitimate Government of Kuwait, and calls upon all States:

(a) To take appropriate measures to protect assets of the legitimate Government of Kuwait and its agencies;

(b) Not to recognize any regime set up by the occupying Power;

10. Requests the Secretary-General to report to the Council on the progress of the implementation of the present resolution, the first report to be submitted within thirty days;

11. Decides to keep this item on its agenda and to continue its efforts to put an early end to the invasion by Iraq.

Resolution 666

13 September 1990

The Security Council,

Recalling its resolution 661 (1990), paragraphs 3(c) and 4 of which apply, except in humanitarian circumstances, to foodstuffs,

Recognizing that circumstances may arise in which it will be necessary for foodstuffs to be supplied to the civilian population in Iraq or Kuwait in order to relieve human suffering,

Noting that in this respect the Committee established under paragraph 6 of that resolution has received communications from several Member States,

Emphasizing that it is for the Security Council, alone or acting through the Committee, to determine whether humanitarian circumstances have arisen,

Deeply concerned that Iraq has failed to comply with its obligations under Security Council resolution 664 (1990) in respect of the safety and well-being of third State nationals, and reaffirming that Iraq retains full responsibility in this regard under international humanitarian law including, where applicable, the Fourth Geneva Convention,

Acting under Chapter VII of the Charter of the United Nations,

1. Decides that in order to make the necessary determination whether or not for the purposes of paragraph 3 (c) and paragraph 4 of resolution 661 (1990) humanitarian circumstances have arisen, the Committee shall keep the situation regarding foodstuffs in Iraq and Kuwait under constant review;

2. Expects Iraq to comply with its obligations under Security Council resolution 664 (1990) in respect of third State nationals and reaffirms that Iraq remains fully responsible for their safety and well-being in accordance with international humanitarian law including, where applicable, the Fourth Geneva Convention;

3. Requests, for the purposes of paragraphs 1 and 2 of this resolution, that the Secretary-General seek urgently, and on a continuing basis, information form relevant United Nations and other appropriate humanitarian agencies and all other sources on the availability of food in Iraq and Kuwait, such information to be communicated by the Secretary-General to the Committee regularly;

4. Requests further that in seeking and supplying such information particular attention will be paid to such categories of persons who might suffer specially, such as children under 15 years of age, expectant mothers, maternity cases, the sick and the elderly;

5. Decides that if the Committee, after receiving the reports from the Secretary-General, determines that circumstances have arisen in which there is an urgent humanitarian need to supply foodstuffs to Iraq or Kuwait in order to relieve human suffering, it will report promptly to the Council its decision as to how such need should be met;

6. Directs the Committee that in formulating its decisions it should bear in mind that foodstuffs should be provided through the United Nations in co-operation with the International Committee of the Red Cross or other appropriate humanitarian agencies and distributed by them or under their supervision in order to ensure that they reach the intended beneficiaries;

7. Requests the Secretary-General to use his good offices to facilitate the delivery and distribution of foodstuffs to Kuwait and Iraq in accordance with the provisions of this and other relevant resolutions;

8. Recalls that resolution 661 (1990) does not apply to supplies intended strictly for medical purposes, but in this connection recommends that medical supplies should be exported under the strict supervision of the Government of the exporting State or by appropriate humanitarian agencies.

Resolution 678

29 November 1990

Adopted by a vote of 12 in favour, 2 against (Cuba and Yemen) and 1 abstention (China).

Sponsors: Canada, France, Romania, Soviet Union, United Kingdom, United States.

The Security Council,

Recalling and reaffirming its resolutions 660 (1990) of 2 August 1990, 661 (1990) of 6 August 1990, 662 (1990) of 9 August 1990, 664 (1990) of 18 August 1990, 665 (1990) of 25 August 1990, 666 (1990) of 13 September 1990, 67 (1990) of 16 September 1990, 669 (1990) of 24 September 1990, 670 (1990) of 25 September 1990, 674 (1990) of 29 October 1990 and 677 (1990) of 28 November 1990,

Noting that, despite all efforts by the United Nations, Iraq refuses to comply with its obligation to implement resolution 660 (1990) and the above-mentioned subsequent relevant resolutions, in flagrant contempt of the Security Council,

Mindful of its duties and responsibilities under the Charter of the United Nations for the maintenance and preservation of international peace and security,

Determined to secure full compliance with its decisions,

Acting under Chapter VII of the Charter,

1. **Demands** that Iraq comply fully with resolution 660 (1990) and all subsequent relevant resolutions, and decides, while maintaining all its decisions, to allow Iraq one final opportunity, as a pause of goodwill, to do so;

2. **Authorizes** Member States co-operating with the Government of Kuwait, unless Iraq on or before 15 January 1991 fully implements, as set forth in paragraph 1 above, the foregoing resolutions, to use all necessary means to uphold and implement resolution 660 (1990) and all subsequent relevant resolutions and to restore international peace and security in the area;

3. **Requests** all States to provide appropriate support for the actions undertaken in pursuance of paragraph 2 of the present resolution;

4. **Requests** the States concerned to keep the Security Council regularly informed on the progress of actions undertaken pursuant to paragraphs 2 and 3 of the present resolution;

5. **Decides** to remain seized of the matter.

Issued by the United Nations Department of Public Information, DPI/1104 Add.1-December 1990

Annex
The Charter of the United Nations
Chapter VII

Action With Respect To The Threats To Peace, Breaches Of The Peace, And Acts Of Aggression

Article 39

The Security Council shall determine the existence of any threat to the peace, breach of the peace, or act of aggression and shall make recommendations, or decide what measures shall be taken in accordance with Articles 41 and 42, to maintain or restore international peace and security.

Article 40

In order to prevent an aggravation of the situation, the Security Council may, before making the recommendations or deciding upon the measures provided for in Article 39, call upon the parties concerned to comply with such provisional measures as it deems necessary or desirable. Such provisional measures shall be without prejudice to the rights, claims, or position of the parties concerned. The Security Council shall duly take account of failure to comply with such provisional measures.

Article 41

The Security Council may decide what measures not involving the use of armed force are to be employed to give effect to its decisions, and it may call upon the Members of the United Nations to apply such measures. These may include complete or partial interruption of economic relations and of rail, sea, air, postal, telegraphic, radio, and other means of communication, and the severance of diplomatic relations.

Article 42

Should the Security Council consider that measures provided for in Article 41 would be inadequate or have proved to be inadequate, it may take such action by air, sea, or land forces as may be necessary to maintain or restore international peace and security. Such action may include demonstrations, blockade, and other operations by air, sea, or land forces of Members of the United Nations.

Article 43

1. All Members of the United Nations, in order to contribute to the maintenance of international peace and security, undertake to make available to the Security Council, on its call and in accordance with a special agreement or agreements, armed forces, assistance, and facilities, including rights of passage, necessary for the purpose of maintaining international peace and security.

2. Such agreement or agreements shall govern the numbers and types of forces, their degree of readiness and general location, and the nature of the facilities and assistance to be provided.

3. The agreement or agreements shall be negotiated as soon as possible on the initiative of the Security Council. They shall be concluded between the Security Council and Members or between the

Security Council and groups of Members and shall be subject to ratification by the signatory states in accordance with their respective constitutional processes.

Article 44

When the Security Council has decided to use force it shall, before calling upon a Member not represented on it to provide armed forces in fulfillment of the obligations assumed under Article 43, invite that Member, if the member so desires, to participate in the decisions of the Security Council concerning the employment of contingents of that Member's armed forces.

Article 45

In order to enable the United Nations to take urgent military measures, Members shall hold immediately available national air-force contingents for combined international enforcement action. The strength and degree of readiness of these contingents and plans for their combined action shall be determined, within the limits laid down in the special agreement or agreements referred to in Article 43, by the Security Council with the assistance of the Military Staff Committee.

Article 46

Plans for the application of armed force shall be made by the Security Council with the assistance of the Military Staff Committee.

Article 47

1. There shall be established a Military Staff Committee to advise and assist the Security Council on all questions relating to the Security Council's military requirements for the maintenance of international peace and security, the employment and command of forces placed at its disposal, the regulation of armaments, and possible disarmament.

2. The Military Staff Committee shall consist of the Chiefs of Staff of the permanent members of the Security Council or their representatives. Any Member of the United Nations not permanently represented on the Committee shall be invited by the Committee to be associated with it when the efficient discharge of the Committee's responsibilities requires the participation of that Member in its work.

3. The Military Staff Committee shall be responsible under the Security Council for the strategic direction of any armed forces placed at the disposal of the Security Council. Questions relating to the command of such forces shall be worked out subsequently.

4. The Military Staff Committee, with the authorization of the Security Council and after consultation with appropriate regional agencies, may establish regional sub-committees.

Article 48

1. The action required to carry out the decisions of the Security Council for the maintenance of international peace and security shall be taken by all the Members of the United Nations or by some of them, as the Security Council may determine.

2. Such decisions shall be carried out by the Members of the United Nations directly and through their action in the appropriate international agencies of which they are members.

Article 49

The Members of the United Nations shall join in affording mutual assistance in carrying out the measures decided upon by the Security Council.

Article 50

If preventive or enforcement measures against any state are taken by the Security Council, any other state, whether a Member of the United Nations or not, which finds itself confronted with special economic problems arising from the carrying out of those measures shall have the right to consult the Security Council with regard to a solution of those problems.

Article 51

Nothing in the present Charter shall impair the inherent right of individual or collective self-defence if an armed attack occurs against a Member of the United Nations, until the Security Council has taken measures necessary to maintain international peace and security. Measures taken by Members in the exercise of this right of self-defence shall be immediately reported to the Security Council and shall not in any way affect the authority and responsibility of the Security Council under the present Charter to take at any time such action as it deems necessary in order to maintain or restore international peace and security.

United Nations Department of Public Information,
DPI/1104—41090—November 1990—5M

Acronyms and Abbreviations

ACC	Arab Cooperation Council
ACDA	US Arms Control and Disarmament Agency
AFL	Armed Forces of Liberia
AMU	Arab Maghreb Union
ANC	African National Congress
ASEAN	Association of Southeast Asian Nations
CFE	Conventional Forces in Europe
CHD	Conference on the Human Dimension
CIAV	International Commission of Support on Verification
CMEA	Council for Mutual Economic Assistance
CNN	Cable News Network
COCOM	Coordinating Committee on Export Controls
COMECON	Council for Mutual Economic Assistance
CPC	Conflict Prevention Center
CSBM	Confidence- and Security-Building Measures
CPSU	Communist Part of the Soviet Union
CSCE	Conference on Security and Cooperation in Europe (or the Helsinki Process)
EC	European Community
ECOMOG	ECOWAS Monitoring Group
ECOWAS	Economic Commission of West African States
FBIS	Foreign Broadcasting Information Service
FMLN	Farabundo Marti National Liberation Front
G-7	Group of Seven
GCC	Gulf Cooperation Council
GDR	German Democratic Republic
HAMAS	Islamic Resistance Movement
IAEA	International Atomic Energy Agency
IEA	International Energy Agency
IGNU	Interim Government of National Unity
IMF	International Monetary Fund
INF	Intermediate Nuclear Forces
INPFL	Independent Petroleum Association of America
IPAA	Independent National Patriotic Front of Liberia
JOMA	Movement of Justice in Africa
KPC	Kuwait Petroleum Corporation
KPI	Kuwait Petroleum International

LLP	Liberia Liberation Party
MAD	Mutually Assured Destruction
MENA	Middle East News Agency
MERIP	Middle East Research and Information Project
MFN	Most Favored Nation
MINURSO	UN Mission for the Referendum in the Western Sahara
mmbd	million barrels per day
MOJA	Movement for Justice in Africa
NAM	Non-Aligned National Movement
NDLP	National Democratic Party of Liberia
NES	Near East and South Asia
NN	Neutral and Nonaligned
NPFL	National Patriotic Front of Liberia
NPT	Non-Proliferation Treaty
NSC	National Security Council
OFM	Office of Foreign Missions (of the US State Department)
OAU	Organization of African Unity
OIC	Organization of the Islamic Conference
ONUCA	UN Observer Group in Central America
ONUVEN	UN Observer Mission to Nicaragua
OPEC	Organization of Producing and Exporting Countries
PAL	Progressive Alliance of Liberia
PFLP	Popular Front for the Liberation of Palestine
PLF	Palestine Liberation Front
PLO	Palestine Liberation Organization
PNC	Palestinian National Council
Polisario	Popular Front for the Liberation of Saguia al-Hamra and Rio de Oro
PPP	Progressive People's Party
PRC	People's Redemption Council
Prepcom	The Preparatory Committee (for the Paris summit)
PTBT	Partial Test Ban Treaty
SADR	Sahrawi Arab Democratic Republic
SADCC	Southern African Development Coordination Conference
SED	Socialist Unity Party
START	Strategic Arms Reduction Talks
UAE	United Arab Emirates
UNICEF	UN International Children's Education Fund
UNITA	National Union for the Total Independence of Angola
UNTAG	UN Transition Assistance Group
VATS	value added taxes
VC	Vienna Convention
WTO	Warsaw Treaty Organization
WEU	West European Union

Bibliography

Assiri, Abdul-Reda, *Kuwait's Foreign Policy: City-State in World Politics*. Boulder, CO: Westview Press, 1990.

Baldwin, David A., and Helen V. Milner, *East-West Trade and the Atlantic Alliance*. New York: St. Martin's Press, 1990.

Barber, John, and John Barratt, *South Africa's Foreign Policy: The Search for Status and Security 1945-1988*. Cambridge, England: Cambridge University Press, 1990.

Benedick, Richard Elliot, *Ozone Diplomacy: New Directions in Safeguarding the Planet*. Cambridge, MA, and London: Harvard University Press, 1990.

Bills, Scott L., *Empire and Cold War: The Roots of U.S.-Third World Antagonism 1945-47*. New York: St. Martin's Press, 1990.

Braun, Aurel, ed., *The Soviet-East European Relationship in the Gorbachev Era: The Prospects for Adaptation*. Boulder, CO: Westview Press, 1990.

Breslauer, George W., et al., *Soviet Strategy in the Middle East*. Boston: Unwin Hyman, 1990.

Brinton, William M. and Alan Rinzler, *Without Force or Lies: Voices from the Revolution of Central Europe in 1989-90*. San Francisco, CA: Mercury House, 1990.

Brown, Frederick Z., *Second Chance: The United States and Indochina in the 1990's*. New York: Council on Foreign Relations Press, 1989.

Brown, L. Carl, *Centerstage: American Diplomacy Since World War II*. New York: Holmes & Meier, 1990.

Burrows, Bernard, *Footnotes in the Sand: The Gulf in Transition. 1953-1958*. Wilton, UK: Michael Russell, 1990.

Castro, Luiz Augusto de Araujo, *O Brasil e o Novo Direito do Mar: Mar Territorial e Zona Economica Exclusiva*. Brasilia: Instituto de Pesquisas de Relações Internacionais, 1990.

Chang, Gordon H., *Friends and Enemies: The United States, China and the Soviet Union, 1948-1972*. Stanford, CA: Stanford University Press, 1990.

Clark, The Rt. Hon. Joe, et al., *Canada and the United States in the 1990's: An Emerging Partnership*. Cambridge, MA: Institute for Foreign Policy Analysis, 1990.

Clarkson, S., *Trudeau and Our Times*. Toronto: McClelland, 1990.

Cohen, Raymond, *Culture and Conflict in Egyptian-Israeli Relations: A Dialogue of the Deaf.* Bloomington, IN: Indiana University Press, 1990.

Cohn, Theodore H., *The International Politics of Agricultural Trade: Canadian-American Relations in a Global Context.* Vancouver: University of British Columbia Press, 1990.

Deere, Carmen, et al., *In the Shadows of the Sun: Caribbean Development Alternatives and U.S. Policy.* Boulder, CO: Westview Press, 1990.

Fonseca, Gelson, Jr., and Valdemar Carneiro Leão, eds., *Temas de Politica Externa Brasileira.* Brasilia: Instituto de Pesquisas de Relações Internacionais, 1990.

de Fonseca, Luiz Henrique Pereira, *Organização Maritima Internacional (IMO)—Visão Politica de um Organismo Especializado das Nações Unidas.* Brasilia: Instituto de Pesquisas de Relações Internacionais, 1990.

Freedman, Robert O., *Moscow and the Middle East.* New York: Cambridge University Press, 1990.

Gati, Charles, *The Bloc That Failed: Soviet-East European Relations in Transition.* Bloomington, IN: Indiana University Press, 1990.

Gill, Stephen, *American Hegemony and the Trilateral Commission.* New York: Cambridge University Press, 1990.

Globerman, Steve, ed., *Continental Accord: North American Economic Integration.* Vancouver: The Fraser Institute, 1991.

Golan, Galia, *Soviet Policies in the Middle East: From World War II to Gorbachev.* New York: Cambridge University Press, 1990.

Granatstein, J. L., and R. Bothwell, *Pirouette: Pierre Trudeau and Canadian Foreign Policy.* Toronto: University of Toronto Press, 1990.

Grieco, Joseph M., *Cooperation Among Nations: Europe, America, and Non-Tariff Barriers to Trade.* Ithaca, NY: Cornell University Press, 1990.

Gromyko, Anatoly A., and C. S. Whitaker, *Agenda for Action: African-Soviet-U.S. Cooperation.* Boulder, CO: Lynne Rienner, 1990.

Haas, Peter M., *Saving the Mediterranean: The Politics of International Environment Cooperation.* New York: Columbia University Press, 1990.

Hahn, Peter L., *The United States, Great Britain, and Egypt 1945-1956: Strategy and Diplomacy in the Early Cold War.* Chapel Hill, NC: The University of North Carolina Press, 1990.

Hart, Parker T., *Two NATO Allies at the Threshold of War: Cyprus, A Firsthand Account of Crisis Management, 1965-1968.* Durham, NC, and London: Duke University Press, 1990.

Heep, Barbara D., *Helmut Schmidt und Amerika: Eine Schwierige Partnerschaft.* Bonn: Bouvier Verlag, 1990.

Herf, Jeffrey, *War By Other Means: Soviet Power, West German Resistance, and the Battle of the Euromissiles.* New York: The Free Press, 1991.

Hufbauer, Gary Clyde, ed., *Europe 1991: An American Perspective.* Washington DC: The Brookings Institution, 1990.

Immerman, Richard H., *John Foster Dulles and the Diplomacy of the Cold War.* Princeton, NJ: Princeton University Press, 1990.

Jackson, John H., *Restructuring the GATT System.* New York: Council on Foreign Relations Press, 1990.

Johnson, John J., *A Hemisphere Apart: The Foundations of United States Policy Toward Latin America.* Baltimore, MD: Johns Hopkins Press, 1990.

Keddie, Nikki R., and Mark Gasiorowski, *Neither East Nor West: Iran, the Soviet Union, and the United States.* New Haven, CT: Yale University Press, 1990.

Khan, Riaz M., *Untying the Afghan Knot: Negotiating Soviet Withdrawal.* Durham, NC, and London: Duke University Press, 1991.

Kovrig, Bennett, *Of Walls and Bridges: The United States and Eastern Europe.* New York: New York University Press, 1990.

Kruzel, Joseph, and Michael H. Haltzel, eds., *Between the Blocs: Problems and Prospects for Europe's Neutral and Nonaligned States.* Washington DC: Woodrow Wilson International Center for Scholars; Cambridge, England: Cambridge University Press, 1989.

Labbe, Marie-Hélène, *La Politique Américaine de Commerce Avec L'est 1969-1989.* Paris: Presse Universitaires de France, 1990.

Laidi, Zaki, *The Superpowers and Africa: The Constraints of a Rivalry, 1960-1990.* Chicago: University of Chicago Press, 1990.

Laird, Robbin F., and Susan L. Clark, eds., *The USSR and the Western Alliance.* Boston: Unwin Hyman, 1990.

LaLoy, Jean, *Yalta Yesterday, Today, Tommorrow.* New York: Harper & Row, 1990.

Lamont, Lansing, and J. Duncan Edmonds, eds., *Friends So Different: Essays of Canada and the United States in the 1980's.* Ottawa: The University of Ottawa Press, 1989.

Leacock, Ruth, *Requiem for Revolution: The United States and Brazil 1961-1969.* Kent, OH: Kent State University Press, 1990.

LeBlanc, Lawrence J., *The United States and the Genocide Convention.* Durham, NC: Duke University Press, 1991.

Lisée, Jean-François, *Dans L'Oeil de L'Aigle: Washington Face Au Québec.* Montreal: Boréal, 1990.

Liska, George, *Fallen Dominions, Reviving Powers: Germany, The Slavs, and Europe's Unfinished Agenda.* Prague: Czechoslovak Institute of International Relations, 1991.

Lowenthal, Abraham F., *Partners In Conflict: The United States and Latin America in the 1990's.* Baltimore, MD: The Johns Hopkins University Press, 1990.

Luard, Evan, *The Globalization of Politics: The Changed Focus of Political Action in the Modern World.* New York: New York University Press, 1990.

Lynn-Jones, Sean M., Steven E. Miller, and Stephen Van Evera, *Nuclear Diplomacy and Crisis Management.* Cambridge, MA: The MIT Press, 1990.

Malone, Gifford, *American Diplomacy in the Information Age.* Lanham, MD: University Press of America / Dacor Bacon House Foundation, 1990.

Marks, Frederick W. III, *Wind Over Sand: The Diplomacy of Franklin Roosevelt.* Athens, GA: The University of Georgia Press, 1990.

Mathews, Jessica Tuchman, ed., *Preserving the Global Environment: The Challenge of Shared Leadership.* New York: Norton, 1990.

McCormick, Thomas J., *America's Half-Century: United States Foreign Policy in the Cold War.* Baltimore, MD: John Hopkins, 1990.

McGhee, George, *The US-Turkish-NATO Middle East Connection.* New York: St. Martin's Press, 1990.

Moreno, Dario, *U.S. Policy in Central America: The Endless Debate.* Miami, FL: International University Press, 1990.

Morici, Peter, *Making Free Trade Work: The Canada-U.S. Agreement.* New York: Council of Foreign Relations Press, 1990.

Moynihan, Daniel Patrick, *On the Law of Nations.* Cambridge, MA: Harvard University Press, 1990.

Neto, Valdemar Carneiro Leão, *A Crise da Imigração Japonesa no Brasil.* Brasilia: Instituto de Pesquisas de Relações Internacionais, 1990.

Newsom, David D., ed., *Diplomacy under a Foreign Flag: When Nations Break Relations.* Washington DC: Institute for the Study of Diplomacy, Georgetown University, 1990.

Ohmae, Kenichi, *The Borderless World: Power and Strategy in the Interlinked Economy.* New York: Harper Business, 1990.

Okawara, Yoshio, *To Avoid Isolation: An Ambassador's View of U.S.-Japanese Relations.* Columbia, SC: University of South Carolina Press, 1990.

Oudenaren, John Van, *Détente in Europe: The Soviet Union and the West since 1953.* Durham, NC: Duke University Press, 1991.

Painchaud, Paul, ed., *De Mackenzie King à Pierre Trudeau: quarante ans de diplomatie canadienne, 1945-1985.* Québec: Les Presses de l'Université Laval, 1989.

Perez, Louis A., Jr., *Cuba and the United States: Ties of Singular Intimacy.* Athens, GA: University of Georgia Press, 1990.

Pond, Elizabeth, *After the Wall: American Policy Toward Germany*. New York: Priority Press Publications, 1990.

Porto, João Gualberto Marques, *O Brasil e as Comunidades Europeias—Discussão de uma Parceria Necessaria*. Brasilia: Instituto de Pesquisas de Relações Internacionais, 1990.

Pratt, Cranford, *Middle Power Internationalism: The North-South Dimension*. Montreal: McGill-Queen's University Press, 1990.

Quandt, William B., *The United States and Egypt: An Essay on Policy for the 1990's*. Washington DC: The Brookings Institution, 1990.

Ramet, Pedro, *The Soviet-Syrian Relationship Since 1955: A Troubled Alliance*. Boulder, CO: Westview Press, 1990.

Ribeiro, Edgar Telles, *Diplomacia Cultural: Seu Papel na Politica Externa Brasileira*. Brasilia: Instituto de Pesquisas de Relações Internacionais, 1990.

Rizopoulos, Nicholas X., *Sea-Changes: American Foreign Policy in a World Transformed*. New York: Council on Foreign Relations Press, 1990.

Rollo, J. M. C., et al., *The New Eastern Europe: Western Responses*. New York: Council on Foreign Relations Press, 1990.

Sater, William F., *Chile and the United States: Empires in Conflict*. Athens, GA: The University of Georgia Press, 1990.

Schott, Jeffrey J., ed., *Completing the Uruguay Round: A Results-Oriented Approach to the GATT Trade Negotiations*. Washington DC: Institute for International Economics, 1990.

Segal, Gerald, *Rethinking the Pacific*. New York: Oxford University Press, 1990.

______, *The Soviet Union and the Pacific*. Boston: Unwin Hyman, 1990.

de la Serre, Francoise, Jacques Lereuz, and Helen Wallace, eds., *French and British Foreign Policies in Transition*. New York: Berg, 1990.

Sherwood, Elizabeth, *Allies in Crisis: Meeting Global Challenges to Western Security*. New Haven, CT: Yale University Press, 1990.

Smoke, Richard, and Andrei Kortunov, *Mutual Security: A New Approach to Soviet-American Relations*. New York: St. Martin's Press, 1991.

Smolansky, Oles M., with Bettie M. Smolansky, *The USSR and Iraq: The Soviet Quest for Influence*. Durham, NC: Duke University Press, 1991.

Smyser, W. R., *Restive Partners: Washington and Bonn Diverge*. Boulder, CO: Westview Press, 1990.

Stassen, Harold, and Marshall Houts, *Eisenhower: Turning the World Toward Peace*. St. Paul, MN: Merrill/Magnus, 1990.

Stern, Robert M., *Trade and Investment Relations Among the United States, Canada, and Japan*. Chicago: University of Chicago Press, 1990.

Stuart, Douglas, and William Tow, *The Limits of Alliance: NATO Out-of-Area Problems Since 1949*. Baltimore, MD: Johns Hopkins University Press, 1990.

Sutter, Robert G., *The Cambodian Crisis and U.S. Policy Dilemnas*. Boulder, CO: Westview Press, 1990.

Taft, John, *American Power: The Rise and Decline of U.S. Globalism, 1918-1988*. New York: Harper Collins, 1990.

ter Haar, Barend, *The Future of Biological Disarmament*. CSIS Washington Papers. New York: Praeger, 1991.

Trindade, Antonio Augusto Cancado, Hector Gross Espiell, Christophe Swnarshi, Jean-Marc Bornet, and Jose Francisco Rezek, *Direito Internacional Humanitario*. Brasilia: Instituto de Pesquisas de Relações Internacionais, 1990.

Valenta, Jiri, and Frank Cibulka, *Gorbachev's New Thinking and Third World Conflicts*. New Brunswick, NJ: Transaction Books, 1990.

Wala, Michael, *Winning the Peace: Amerikanische Aussenpolitik und der Council on Foreign Relations 1945-1950*. Stuttgart: Franz Steiner Verlag, 1990.

Weintraub, Sidney, *A Marriage of Convenience: Relations Between Mexico and the United States*. New York: Oxford University Press, 1990.

Whiting, Allen S., *China Eyes Japan*. Berkeley, CA: University of California Press, 1990.

Wollemborg, Leo J., *Stars, Stripes and Italian Tricolor: The United States and Italy, 1946-1989*. New York: Praeger, 1990.

Yergin, Daniel, *The Prize: The Epic Quest for Oil, Money and Power*. New York: Simon and Schuster, 1991.

Young, Jeh Kim, *The Political Unification of Korea in the 1990's: Key to World Peace*. Lewiston, NY: Edwin Mellen Press, 1989.

INDEX